Other Doubleday books by Bill Libby

CHARLIE O. AND THE ANGRY A'S
LIFE IN THE PIT

"King Richard"

"King Richard"

"King Richard"

THE RICHARD PETTY STORY

By Bill Libby
with Richard Petty

1977
DOUBLEDAY & COMPANY, INC.
GARDEN CITY, NEW YORK

Library of Congress Cataloging in Publication Data
Libby, Bill.
"King Richard."
1. Petty, Richard. 2. Automobile racing drivers—
United States—Biography. I. Petty, Richard, joint
author. II. Title.
GV1032.P47L52   796.7′2′0924 [B]
ISBN 0-385-11404-4
Library of Congress Catalog Card Number 76-40884

For Esther, Ross,
Becky, and Emily
Fraser

Acknowledgments

The authors wish to thank Lynda and the rest of Richard's family, Maurice and the other Pettys, Dale Inman and the crew, Bill Dredge, Jeff Cushing and others of STP, Bob Preddy of Victory Lane Enterprises, and Louise Laflin and Brenda Williams and others at the compound, and transcriber Jackie Sommers for all of their help in putting this book together.

They also wish to thank Bill France, Joe Whitlock, D. Lynn Justis, and others at NASCAR and the Daytona Speedway; Les Richter, Jack Matthews, Deke Houlgate, and others at Riverside Raceway; Hank Ives, Bob Russo, and all of those at Ontario Speedway; Jim Donoho of Nashville Speedway; and all the other officials and all the drivers and mechanics whose co-operation was so critical.

They wish to thank Rich Benyo and Neil Britt of *Stock Car Racing Magazine*; Hank Schoolfield and the staff of *Southern Mo-toRacing*; Bob Hoffman and the staff of *Southern Motor Sports*; Chris Economaki of *National Speed Sport News*; Ken Squier of the Motor Racing Network; Shav Glick, Allen Wolfe, Dorsey Patrick, Tom Shaw, Russ Elder, Dozier Mobley, Greg Fielden, Darryl Norenberg, Wen Roberts, and Johnny Johnson of Photography, Inc.; and all the other writers and photographers who have contributed so much.

Finally, they wish to thank Matt Merola of Mattgo Enterprises for putting the package together, and Harold Kuebler as well as Jim Menick, James Ricketson, and other editors of Doubleday for bringing it to reality.

Lyrics "The Grand Tour" (Algee Music Corp. and Al Gallico Music Corp., Copyright 1974) and "These Days I Barely Get By" (Altam Music Corp., Copyright 1975) reprinted courtesy of George Jones and Quinnie Acuff of George Jones Enterprises.

Contents

"King Richard"

1

JANUARY

Richard Lee Petty sat on a pile of tires outside the garage that had been assigned to his racing team at Riverside. He is tall and thin. His large, strong hands and long fingers held a small, thin, seven-cent Muriel Coronella, which he puffed periodically. He is not given much to pretensions, so he does not feel he needs to smoke more expensive or more impressive cigars. Cigars are all he smokes and he takes ten with him every day he goes to a race track. He sat on the tires outside his garage smoking his little cigar and taking in the warm winter sun of southern California.

He has a funny, floppy black hat he wears when he is relaxing around the race tracks he drives to back home in the Southeast; but he hasn't figured out how to pack it without crushing it when he flies to the Far West, so he leaves it home when he comes to California. It looks like something the Indians wore when they first started to wear white men's clothes, which some white men still wear in the hills. Now, Richard Petty was wearing a red baseball cap bearing the blue insignia of his sponsor, STP. It hid most of his mass of long, curly, brown hair. Dark, wraparound sunglasses hid his eyes. He squinted into the sun from behind his sunglasses as a visitor moved up to him.

"Pull up ah tire and sit ah spell," Petty said in soft accents. (We are not going to do more than suggest in this book the southern drawl bred into Richard and those others around him who come from his part of the country, but we will say at the start that the southern flavor of their speech rolls thick as syrup from their tongues.)

He is the king of southern stock-car drivers: King Richard the Fast, King Richard of Racing. The King was holding court, welcoming company to kill the time between his stints on the track.

As he issued his invitation, he smiled, showing a lot of bright, white teeth. He smiles a lot, and he shows his teeth a lot. Some say they are his best feature, but he has a handsome face anyway, sun-tanned and attractive. He looks a lot like the actor Robert Stack at times—in certain lights and from certain angles. Perhaps we should say Robert Stack looks like him. There are places where Robert Stack would be better known, but not around the racing circuit in general and the auto-racing arenas of the Deep South in particular.

Richard Petty is a better-known and more-admired celebrity in the South than any other athlete in this country. He is becoming known all across the country, but when Petty passes along the roads of rural North Carolina, his home state, it probably is the way it would be if Babe Ruth appeared, alive and at his peak, on the sidewalks of New York. No athlete alive today, probably no movie or television star, approaches Petty's popularity in his part of the country. His fan club has fifteen thousand paid-up members, which is more than that of any movie or television star of today. When he had an open house, at his home, hidden behind trees in the back country, some thirty-five thousand fans found their way there to be with him. On the same day, an Indianapolis-style championship race at Phoenix drew half as many fans.

His popularity in the southern United States probably approximates that of Pelé, the soccer star, in Brazil. Only the greatest of rock stars, such as an Elton John or one of the former Beatles, have a greater grip on their kingdoms; and these do not host open houses, they do not mingle with commoners or speak to the paying public. King Richard is an uncommon man with a common touch. He speaks softly and smiles brightly. He moves easily around his domain.

Excusing himself, he got up off his throne of tires to greet some fans who thrust pencil and paper at him through the wire fence which separated them from him. "Howdy," he drawled, starting to sign autographs with a flourish, with such a mass of loops and curls that it takes him two or three times as long to sign each one as it would another athlete scrawling his signature so fast it would be illegible. It doesn't bother Richard that it takes him so long. In fact, without telling anyone, he took a handwriting course back in the beginning so he could do something distinctive for his fans.

"You gonna win this one, Richard?" one of them asked.

"I'm a-gonna try," Richard said softly, smiling.

"You're gonna win," he was assured.

Possibly. More probably than anyone else on any racing circuit anywhere. While the National Association for Stock Car Auto Racing sanctions several minor leagues of stock-car racing, its major league is the Grand National tour of thirty or so races annually. It is *the* sport of the South. Richard Petty's dad, Lee, was the first three-time driving champion of this tough tour, and the first winner of its biggest race, the Daytona 500. And he won more races than anyone until his son started driving. Now Richard had won 164 Grand National races, almost twice as many as any other driver ever on this or any other tour. He had won the Daytona 500 five times, while no one else had won it more than once. He had won the driving title—the NASCAR Grand National championship—five times, while no one else had won it more than three times. This was 1975 and Petty was at his peak.

In the last eight seasons, in his prime, Petty had been winning about one of every three races he entered, and he entered more races than anyone else in the majors. In a sport of intense competition, accidents, and mechanical breakdowns, that was an awesome mark, unmatched by the A. J. Foyts of USAC's championship trail of Indianapolis cars or the Jackie Stewarts of the Grand Prix worldwide circuit of Formula One machinery. They won in more different kinds of cars, but he has won more in his kind of car.

"It's as tough to win here as it is anywhere," he said. "I do the best I can. I try to do it better than the other boys. I try to do it better than I did the last time. I jus' go out and do the best I can. Often as not, it's been good enough. But if I won more than anyone else, mebbe I also lost more. I lost twice as many as I won. Three times as many, I guess, over the years."

At the age of thirty-seven he had been driving in the big time for seventeen seasons. He said, "My daddy was a race driver, so I became a race driver. If he'd been a grocer, I might have been a grocer. If he'd been a baseball player, I'd probably have wanted to be a baseball player. But he was a race driver, so here I am. I grew up around race cars. I been working on 'em since I was twelve years old and driving 'em since I was twenty-one. It's all I know, really.

"I drive the kind of cars I grew up with. If I'd growed up in Indianapolis, I'd probably drive Indy cars. If I'd growed up in Italy or France or some such place I'd probably drive those Grand Prix cars. I grew up in Randleman, North Carolina, in the good old U.S.A., so I drive the kind of cars we race in our part of the world. I know 'em and I don't know those other cars. I guess there's a lot of money to be made in some of those other places. But I don't need a lot of money. I make enough in my own backyard."

He had won $100,000 or more in purses for six straight seasons. He was the first to win $300,000 or more in a single season and the first to win $1,000,000 in a career. Now he was close to $2,000,000 in his career. "I can't even imagine that much money," he admitted. "Of course I didn't get it all. The team gets it, and on our team it's divided between my daddy, my brother, and me, and we put a lot of it back into our racing operation, which is why we stay ahead of the others. We can have anything we want. My wife wanted a new house; she's got it now. The fact is, we don't want much. We're just country folk, really. We stay home. No need to go to the big city. You don't ever want to get above your raisin's, you know," he said with a smile.

So this, then, is the secret of his popularity. He is the best at the sport that is biggest in his part of the world. But he does not act like he is the best. When he had his open house, he met and greeted his fans personally and signed autographs for them and chatted with them for hours. He will stand and talk to and sign autographs for fans for hours at race tracks, in airline terminals, at motels, on street corners, wherever they find him. He is attractive and almost squeaky clean. He smokes a little—those little cigars— but he does not drink hard stuff. He has a wife and four children, and he is faithful to them and does not run around in a world on the run.

Sometimes it seems he is too good to be true. Is he?

"I guess you'll find out." He smiled, back at his perch on the tires, taking in the sun, while the loud roar of powerful engines pours from nearby garages and the track which surrounded us, on which other cars were practicing. "I don't never try to be nothing I'm not," he said. "I think I'm one thing. I guess my wife, Lynda, thinks I'm another thing. You might decide I'm something else by the time you finish with this here book."

"You sure you want to do this book?"

"I ain't sure," he admitted. "But my sponsor wants me to do it, so I'll do it."

"You did a book before."

"That was a long time ago. A lot's happened since. Anyway, I don't think it really got into me. It had a lot of facts in it, but it didn't have a lot of me in it. I'd like to do a different kind of book."

"What kind of book?"

"A book that tells what my life, what the life of a race-car driver, really is."

"What is it?"

"I guess you'll find out. It's not what a lot of writers and other people think it is. It's not as gol-dang glamorous as it's supposed to be. Maybe there's glamour in racing, but I don't see much of it. All I see is the inside of an airplane terminal and an airplane or a truck carting my car somewhere, the inside of a car, and the other cars and the track, a motel room somewhere with a television set playing a football game or an old movie. I hear the cheers when I win, but I'm usually too tired to enjoy them by then. I don't always win. And it's on to the next race. You just keep shovin'."

"You're not excited about it?"

"I been doin' it too long. I done too much of it to get excited about it. I like it, but I'm not excited about it."

"And you're not excited about the book."

"I want to do a good book, but I'm not excited about anything." He smiled. "The more you get to know me, the more you'll get to know that."

"I've known you a long time. My first interview with you was about ten years back."

"I reckon that's a long time," Richard said.

"I guess I'll get to know you better though, doing a book with you."

"Guess so." He grinned.

"I'll have to spend a lot of time with you."

"We'll find the time. When you movin' in?"

"Soon now. You tell your wife."

"Lynda will love that," he said, laughing.

His crew, which had been working on his car inside the garage, pushed the gaudy red-and-blue Number 43 car out into the sunshine. It is the most recognizable single race car in this country.

Picking a number off a nearby license plate while having his first car painted, Lee drove 42s. When Richard went racing, he adopted and made famous his 43. Petty-blue Plymouths were the most prominent cars on race tracks until the team switched to Dodges, accepted STP sponsorship, and reluctantly agreed to combine flamboyant STP promoter Andy Granatelli's beloved fluorescent red with their own pale blue.

Before he broke with STP, Granatelli shifted his firm's sponsorship money from the championship circuit of the Midwest and West to the stock-car circuit of the South. The feeling was that people identified with these cars, which at least looked like the cars they drove on city streets and public highways. He went for the best and got it, the Petty team. He had to go high to get it, and his successors have had to go higher to keep it. Racing is an expensive business which could not survive without sponsors in search of publicity. The Petty people will not confirm it, but since they figure it costs them on the average of $13,000 a race to run a competitive car, that's what STP pays them, plus bonuses for winning races. STP wants them to run every race on their circuit, so this is a $400,000-a-year deal, by far the best in this sport. For the Pettys, the lesser but still substantial returns from other sponsors and their large race winnings are pure profit.

The decals of a dozen other sponsors—Goodyear Tires, Union Oil, Winston Cigarettes—make a moving billboard of the Petty car, as they do of all the cars on this circuit, but by far the biggest, the brightest, and the most numerous decals on the car consist of the famous STP logo. This was sufficient by itelf to separate the car from the others that look like it that run on the streets and highways, but what really separates it is the hollowed-out interior beefed up with roll bars around the driver's seat, the meticulously balanced suspension system, the souped-up engine that spits power. It only looks like our cars. It is nothing like them at all. It is a metal monster—massive, swift and rugged.

The Winston Western 500 is a road race, in which drivers have to steer right as well as left and shift up and down over a twisting course, so this car was their road-race and short-track car. The Pettys prepare three cars a season, sister cars, but set up especially for the races they must run. Two are readied for the major races— the long races on the big superspeedways of this sport. While one is being raced, the other is being readied for the next race. Maurice Petty is the crew chief in charge of preparing these cars. He was not here now at Riverside but back in North Carolina preparing the car that Richard would run in the next race—at Daytona. His specialty is the engine, and it takes the most meticulous work. Dale Inman was here, crew chief for the Riverside race. The chassis is his particular concern. He is a cousin—part of the family, but not a part of the corporation. He is on the payroll rather than in for a share.

The Petty pa, Lee, still has a say and a share. Lee lays down the law at times but lets the boys run the races these days. He goes to some races but resents the sidelines. "Why you doin' a book on Richard?" he grumbles. "I'm the one you should be doin' the book on. If it weren't for me, Richard wouldn't be nowhere. I set it up for the boy. I ran the hard road. It's all paved over, smooth and soft now." Lee is unlike his eldest son. Lee is tough, Richard is tough too, but with a smooth exterior, while Lee is as rough outside as he is tough inside. He gave Richard his first car, raced against him for a few years, took his first win right away from him. Maurice is more like Lee than Richard. Tough, rough, gruff.

Maurice doesn't make all the races. He is busy winning them where some say they are won—back at the shop. Dale makes all the races, so he is the crew chief much of the time, making the changes in the car the track requires, running the races. But when you are at a race and you are watching Dale boss the operation and when you ask who is the real chief, Dale or Maurice, a member of the crew will smile and say, "You'll find out when the Chief gets here."

Dale says, "Maurice is the boss." (It is pronounced as Morris rather than Maurice, because that is the way it used to be pronounced and the way his mother, Elizabeth, wanted it pronounced. He is often called simply "Chief.") "Maurice is for sure the Chief." Dale grins. He is a lot like Richard. He seems easygoing and relaxed, but when he is running the show, he runs it.

"Time to go to work, Richard," he said then, that bright, sunny afternoon at Riverside. Everyone calls him Richard. That is what his mother named him and that is what he wants. About the only thing that bothers him is to be called "Dick."

"Time to go to work," Richard said, unwinding off the tires, stomping out his cigar with the high, hard heel of his cowboy boot. Going back into the garage, Richard said, "Maurice is the boss there, and Dale is the boss here; but I am the boss here and there. They can say what they want and do what they want, but I have the last say as to what they do because I am the one who has to take that thing out on the track and they wouldn't want to do that, you see?" He was smiling when he said it.

There are those drivers who think they are better than Richard. There are those who think David Pearson or Bobby Allison or Cale Yarborough is better, but the numbers are against them. They haven't won what Richard has won. Foyt has won more different kinds of races in more different kinds of cars on more different kinds of tracks than has Richard. Foyt has won the Daytona 500 and the 24-Hours of Le Mans as well as his own Indianapolis 500. He is the only one who has won more money than Richard. Maybe Foyt has been better. Maybe. But no one has been better on Richard's circuit. However, there are those who think it is Richard's team that is best more than it is Richard. Richard is one of them.

"I'm not the best driver," he said as he stripped off his sport shirt, slacks, and cowboy boots in a corner of his garage. "I may be the best racer. There is a difference between driving fast and racing to win. For sure I have the best team. The Wood Brothers are supposed to be the best, but they ain't. They ain't no better than the Pettys. They haven't won what the Pettys have won. They have David Pearson now, and most years he won't win with them what Richard Petty will win. My brother, my cousin, and me, we been together a long time, unlike most teams. They're good at what they do and I'm good at what I do. We know what we have to do. We do more than anyone else. We put the money into the car. We run a high-buck operation. We don't even have to talk. We just do what has to be done to win. We may make it look easy, but it ain't easy," he said, not smiling.

Stripped to his shorts, he looked very thin. His face was tanned, but with his clothes off you could see he was pale. He has to be strong to drive four-hour races, but he doesn't look it. It may be more a matter of being tough. He is asked about his health a lot, and he always says, "I'm healthy as a horse," but you wonder about it. His eyesight has to be good for him to survive in his sport, but he squints a lot. He is hard of hearing, so much so he can't hear you over the telephone if he is not used to your speech. They say it is an occupational hazard from being too close for too long to those too-loud engines; but he says it isn't so, that he has been hard of hearing from birth and just never has been able to adjust to wearing a hearing aid all the time.

He has not had a lot of accidents, but he has had a few bad ones and he has broken some bones. They say he inhaled flames in an early accident, but he denies it did any lasting damage. Still, he pops pills during races—aspirin and gelatin pills. He admits, "I get headaches, but I get them off the track as well as on. I take aspirin for them when I'm on the track and they upset my stomach so I take the other pills to settle my stomach. It's not my racing, it's me," he insists. "I take things as they come. I stay loose." He looks loose as he moves easily through life, on and off the track. But you wonder if he is not holding his worries in. Pressure pounds at him. Doesn't he feel it?

He pulled on a two-piece white uniform and driving shoes. "My mom made my uniform," he pointed out proudly. "Most driver's uniforms are one-piece and they look like pajamas to me. I mentioned that to her, so she made me this two-piece job."

"Petty, the style-setter!"

He laughed. "Well, I'll tell ya, Benny Parsons went right out and got hisself a yellow one just like this one. Ma is making me a red one and a blue one, and before you know it all the boys will be wearing ones like this one."

"Fireproof?"

"Yeh, but we don't worry about fire as much as the Indy guys. Our gas tanks are better protected, so our cars don't catch fire like theirs do. We don't wear all the hot stuff they do." He pulled on and laced up his heavy driving shoes and walked out into the sunshine.

Benny Parsons came up in his yellow uniform and asked Petty if he'd been out yet. Richard said he was just going. Benny said that when Richard figured out how to drive this fool place to be sure and tell him. Richard said he would, but if Benny figured out how to get through turn nine to be sure and tell him.

"I been comin' out to this fool place a few years now and I never have gotten all the way through that turn nine," Richard said, grinning as he exaggerated.

"You can't drive is your only problem," Dale said. Everyone laughed. They all thought that was funny. "Now quit talkin' and sunnin' and get in the gol-durn car and try to find the track," Dale added.

Petty pulled on his shiny hard helmet and hoisted himself through the window of the bolted-down driver's door and squeezed himself into the cramped cockpit, which had been molded to fit his frame.

Hands reached in to help him buckle into his waist and shoulder straps and to attach the wire which ran from his helmet to the roof and kept his neck and head from snapping too hard to one side when he turned the car the other way. They pulled up the screen where the window would be normally on the driver's side, a Petty invention designed to keep the driver in the car if it spins or crashes, which has been copied by all the others.

Richard fired up the 800-horsepower engine and rolled away from the garage on his way to "find" the track to practice. His crew followed, going into the pits and along the pit wall which ran alongside the frontstretch of this curving course, in front of the spectator stand and the high-up press box.

As Richard rolled onto the track and accelerated toward the first turn, Dale perched on the pit wall. "Richard's getting lazy," he said, smiling. "He used to help us work on the cars, but now all he wants to do is drive 'em. He practices less than anyone else. All he wants to work is a few hours on race day."

He stopped talking and grew intent as the red-and-blue 43 flew past, roaring as it finished its first lap. A good-looking guy, powerfully built, Dale hunched over, his eyes hard as he studied the car as it came by. Another member of the crew, holding a stop watch, punched it and called out the time.

"Too slow. Too darn slow. C'mon Richard," said Dale, who with one of the crew had hauled the car and equipment three thousand miles, stopping only for food, from North Carolina to California early in the week. Richard flew in later. It seemed like a long run for one race. "Not if we get the long end of the purse," Dale said with a laugh. The prize was $114,000, about a fourth to the winner. "Too slow, too slow," Dale muttered as the car came around again.

The next time around, Richard came in. "Put some speed into it," he said to Dale as he hauled himself out of the car. They huddled awhile, talking about the best way to do that.

"It's handling all right," Richard said.

"Did you get through turn nine?" Dale asked, smiling.

"The handling could be better," Richard decided.

They went to work.

Petty has fan-club chapters in many states, including California. The California chapter threw him a party prior to race weekend. Although located a long way from his home, close to a thousand turned out for the shindig. "Not all are members," Petty pointed out.

One fan said, "He is the greatest human being I've ever met."

"And a good driver?"

"Oh, a great driver. But an even greater human being."

Richard had to laugh, but he hugged her. "I don't really compare myself to Christ," he confessed.

Frank Hyland wrote of Richard, "Heroes are handsome and wholesome and clean-living. Heroes smile and are nice to their fans and family. Heroes visit sick children and win one for a kid who may never walk again. Heroes rarely drink and are at least mildly religious. . . ."

There is a patch on Richard's uniform which reads, "With God, you're always a winner."

Richard smiled and said, "I'm religious . . . just in case."

On Friday night Richard sat in his room in the Motelodge on University Avenue in Riverside and spoke of the course, the only road course they run. "Like the rest of the tracks we run, we run two races a year here. I like it because it's different. That makes it fun. I'm no good at it, but it's fun. Oh, I won this one and the one in June a couple times, but usually I'm lucky to stay on the course, much less win.

"It's nothing like the big, high-banked, oval superspeedways we run, or even the little tracks. It's flat and it's got all kinds of different turns and you have to turn different ways and keep shifting gears. You speed up and brake and shift gears and speed up again and turn this way and that way over and over again. You can't let your concentration slip or you'll run right off the track because it's always winding away from you. And you get blisters shifting so much for five hundred miles.

"I think Dale likes it because it's a challenge. We have to get the chassis set up to handle through all different kinds of corners.

We have to find a happy medium. You're not gonna be great in any one corner because you have to be good in all of them. It's scientific. Brute strength won't do it here. Turn nine? It's tough. It's a sweeping right-hander and it has a high, hard wall waiting for you if you make a mistake in it. You come in too hard or you don't brake fast enough and you'll whack right into the wall. I usually screw it up and run right off the course steering clear of that wall. I run through so much sand in that turn it's like going to the beach," he said, smiling.

He had crashed there once. So did Billy Foster, who died there. But it was not turn nine but turn six that turned against the drivers who drove in a late-model sportsman race on Saturday, which served as a preliminary to the Grand National race for the late-model stock cars on Sunday. It was in turn six where the popular and powerful performer Joe Weatherly lost his life in 1964. Now, eleven years later, Bill Spencer, a twenty-six-year-old youngster who was the champion of a local track, Speedway 605 in Irwindale, went into the turn too fast, banged into the barrier, was carried from his car unconscious, and died in Riverside Community Hospital.

Richard Petty sat in his garage, hunched over, an unlit cigar in his fingers. "We have the safest racing in the world," he said. "But it ain't safe."

The race went on. The race always goes on. Bobby Allison, the only Grand National driver who also drives the sportsman cars, dueled local star Jimmy Insolo most of the race and lost. As Allison walked away, someone said to him, "Allison, you'd drive a baby buggy if there was a buck in front of it."

Bobby smiled and said to himself, "That's what we're here for." The slender, thirty-seven-year-old father of four from Hueytown, Alabama, went back to his garage to watch his crew work on his Grand National car for the next day's race. He had won it last year.

"Let's keep it clean," someone hollered as Allison entered his garage.

Sunday dawned hot, and by race time temperatures of 85 degrees roasted the 53,000 fans spread around the sprawling layout in the desert in front of the smog-shrouded San Bernardino Mountains. Allison led from the first, pulling out in front as the green flag flew and snaking through the turns spectacularly at speeds of up to 130 miles per hour in places.

Not wanting to let Allison get too far in front, Petty put his foot into it, caught up on the twelfth time around the 2.62-mile course, and passed into the lead on the thirteenth lap. Three laps later a minor mishap on the course slowed the cars under yellow caution signals, sent them into the pits for fuel and tires, and scrambled the standings.

Petty came out second and it took him into the thirty-third lap before he could catch Allison again. Then, as he was passing a slower car prior to trying to pass Bobby going into turn nine, Richard got his right foot tangled in the accelerator and the brake. He went in too hard and by the time he got his foot untangled and tried to brake, he slowed too sharply and started to spin. The rear end of his car came around and carried the 4,000-pound machine up into the wall with a loud sound of rending metal.

Richard kept going and limped into the pits, where he exchanged harsh words with Dale while the crew rebuilt the right side of his smashed car with pry bars, hammer, and silver tape. He lost eight laps but, rather than quit, returned to the fray to the cheers of the crowd, who yelled loudly, laughingly, at him every time his bent and bandaged car came around from then on. He was running for a few points at that point, settling for seventh, while Bobby went on to win easily by a wide margin. Twenty-three of the thirty-five starters crashed or came apart along the way. Bobby averaged 98 miles per hour for the long, 191-lap marathon.

"Richard was the only one who could run with me, and once he ran into the wall I could outrun everyone else," Allison said in Victory Lane after climbing out of his Coca-Cola-sponsored Matador.

"I could run with him. I could outrun him. I just tried to outrun myself," Petty said as he sat in his garage afterwards, sweating and soiled, sipping a soft drink.

"I went in too hard, trying to pass two cars at once. I just got impatient, which you should never do, lose your patience. I got out of the groove trying to pass that other car, got my foot tangled up, and lost it. It was pilot error. The car was right."

"What did Dale say to you?"

"He said I should learn how to drive."

"What did you say to him?"

"I said it was easier to drive in the pits than out on the track."

"Are you angry at each other?"

"Oh, well, I was angry, but I'm not now. I was more angry at myself than I was at him. He's the one that's got the right to be angry."

"You damn right," Dale said, coming in and dropping a hammer into a toolbox with a bit of clatter.

The crew was loading the damaged machine onto its trailer. It would be repaired back in North Carolina.

"Let a couple of the boys drive it back. You fly back with me," Richard said.

"You darn right," Dale said.

Daytona lay ahead, less than a month away. Riverside is sort of a tuneup for Daytona. It's an interesting race, but it's a different race from the rest they run. They run different cars here, and many of the Daytona drivers do not even make the long trip to run Riverside. Riverside is the first race of the season for these drivers, but Daytona is the first important race of the season.

"If you win it, it's a good season. If you lose it, you spend the rest of the season catching up," commented Petty, the defending champion of Daytona as well as the Grand National tour, who had left his first race of the new season on the wall here. "We'll just keep shoving," he said as he stopped to sign autographs for fans on the way to his rented car, his motel room, the airport, and, a few hours away, his home in Randleman.

2

FEBRUARY

Daytona Beach doubles its population of 50,000 during Speed Weeks in February when every kind of car-racing fanatic comes to town to see a whole series of stock-car races leading up to the 500 in midmonth. They are all here: the Grand National group—the officials, the drivers, of course, and their crews, the sponsors, the big-money men from the big automotive concerns and advertising agencies, the press people, as well as the fans. The guys who follow the races, the gals who follow the racers, and the young people who go where the crowds gather and the action is. They pour into this place. Some may go to other races. They all go to this race.

The motels along Atlantic Avenue which runs along the Atlantic Ocean in this East Coast beach town 250 miles north of Miami, bear banners blowing in the winds which read, "Welcome Race Fans" or "Welcome NASCAR" or "Welcome ABC-TV" or "Welcome STP" or "Welcome" someone else. The bars and restaurants are mobbed. One must wait a long time to eat or drink. No one minds. Everyone is happy. The music of a hundred country bands and singers interrupts the stillness of the night.

Richard Petty walked the beach with Lynda and their four children—Kyle, Sharon, Lisa, and Rebecca.

Later, he said, "It's a family thing. A lot of us bring our families here because they want to come here. They come to the closer races, too, because they can drive there. And Lynda flies to the ones further away. But she won't fly in till the last day or two 'cause she doesn't want to leave the kids. It's nice having the whole family together on a trip. It's distractin', but it's nice. You get locked up in motel rooms with the crew, you talk racin' too much sometimes. It's nice takin' your mind off racing by talking about the kids sometimes. The pressure is so bad here, it's nice to take it off your back. I don't feel the pressure much, but more here than somewhere else."

Bill Dredge, tall, gaunt, gray, in his sixties, the public relations director for STP, said, "This is our biggest race. The Southern 500 at Darlington is the oldest and has the most tradition. The World 600 at Charlotte is the longest. The Alabama races at Talladega are the fastest. But the Daytona 500 is our biggest race. It draws the biggest crowd and pays the most money. It draws the big-money men, which is important to the teams that need sponsors. For STP and Petty it is important because of the exposure we get from it. It doesn't draw the kind of crowd or pay the kind of money Indianapolis does, but it's the Indianapolis of the South."

Petty said, "It's our prestige race, but it's not Indianapolis. Sometimes I think Indianapolis is all those guys have. They drive the rest of the races, but all year long they're aiming at Indy. They have two other five-hundred-mile races—one in Pennsylvania and one in California—but it's like they didn't matter. We run fifteen 500s and four 400s and a 600, and they all count. I'll admit the Daytona 500 comes first, but I wouldn't trade it for any three or four other 500s I might win. I think the Indy guys would trade one Indy 500 win for all the other races they might win the rest of their lives. No way I would do that for Daytona."

"Maybe because you've won it so often."

"Maybe, but I don't think so. I've won it and I've lost it. I always want to win it more than any other, but losing it never ruined the rest of the season for me. I want to win every race I run, no matter how many I win, and if you told me losing this one would set me up to win the next three or four, I guess I'd buy it. The best year I ever had, 1967, I didn't win Daytona. One of the worst years I've had, 1973, I won Daytona. I've won Daytona and I've lost Daytona, and winnin' it or losin' it didn't decide what kind of year I'd go on to have. It's important because everyone wants to win it so much. It's a pride thing. And everyone is showing off the new equipment they're going to win with that year. Every year one car or another is better than the others, and the guys drivin' that kind of car are going to go better than the other guys. Every year's going to be a big year for you until you get into it. Every year guys' dreams begin to get busted up at Daytona."

He remembers every Daytona 500 as vividly as if each happened that day; but then he remembers every race of every year almost as vividly, as do most of the top drivers. They may get mixed up on a detail here or there, but they have that sort of intense concentration on their careers that fixes each event in their minds almost as firmly as when it is set in type in the record books, and they remember what the record books do not reveal.

They used to run on the beach at Daytona. Lee Petty won there. Darlington opened in 1950, the first of the so-called superspeedways. Daytona was the second one, but the first of the Indianapolis-sized tracks and maybe the best, and when it opened in 1959, Lee Petty won the first 500 there, though it was so close it took officials three days studying still photos to decide to take the trophy away from Johnny Beauchamp and give it to Lee.

Daytona was the first of the "high-banks" for the superspeedways, banked all the way around and up to 31 degrees in the corner so a car could go full out the full distance, as they cannot on the flat Indy ovals. Cars went fast here, so fast it was scary, even for the drivers. The first year the fastest qualifier, Cotton Owens, went more than 143 miles per hour, but only one year later Fireball Roberts shoved the speed up past 151, which was faster than the lower, lighter cars were running at Indianapolis. Between the 1963 and 1964 renewals the speed shot up almost ten miles per hour from 165 to close to 175. By 1967 they had topped 180; by 1969, 190; and by 1971 they were so close to 200 that NASCAR officials pulled the wings off the cars and closed down the engines in the interest of safety.

"They had to do it or the cars would be going faster than we could drive 'em," Richard points out. "You can drive fast as long as everything's working right, but when you get to going faster than your reflexes can respond when something breaks on your car or you lose control or you come up on a spinning car or a wreck, then it's just too dang dangerous. The speeds come from stronger engines and better-handling, more aerodynamic chassis and better tire traction. But the boys driving the cars aren't being improved at the same pace. You can adjust to going faster a little bit at a time. You don't even notice a little increased speed because the car has been built for it and it runs as smooth as it did at a slower speed. But when you make a big jump like we did that one year when we went from moving up three or four miles per hour a year to ten miles an hour or so all at once, it was too much. The cars was handlin' bad and we couldn't handle 'em. Drivin' those cars that year, we felt so much on the verge of being out of control of them that we were thinking about it and worried about it all the way. We didn't want to get close to another car then, so it wasn't competitive.

"Speed is part of racing, but it's not the most important part. Without competition, speed don't mean much. Only at Indy will many people come out just to see one car run fast. A car's got to be runnin' against another car. We're racers, and we want to race. The cats in the stands want to see racin'. Our competition is so keen that the cats in the stands never noticed the cutback in our speeds. We're still pushing as hard as the cars will go. In Indy you just never see two cars coming across at the finish together. One's always way out in front. At Daytona and our other tracks one car seldom wins easy; there's almost always two or three dueling for the lead through the last laps and coming across so close you could throw a blanket over them. That's racin', and at Daytona I've run a lot of races like that."

His first race there was in 1959, the first Daytona 500, when his father won, and Richard's car quit on him early and he finished fifty-seventh in the fat field of cars they started there in those days. That was his second year in Grand National competition.

The next year Richard ran with the leaders, but settled for third place, while Junior Johnson won. "Inexperience beat me," Richard recalled. "We didn't have two-way radios then and the drivers relied on signs from his crew in the pits to know what was going on, and there was no way for him to tell them anything except in pit stops. It was up to the driver to pit when he thought it was time and I pitted at a bad time. I pitted under the green, when everyone was runnin' fast, instead of under a yellow, when everyone was runnin' slow, and I pitted when my crew wasn't expecting me. Daddy was out on the track with me and Dale wasn't in the pits that year, though Maurice was. Our pit crew wasn't coordinated then the way it is now. Daddy's car wasn't a winner that race, and while mine might have been, I lost time in the pits I never could make up on the track."

In 1961 both Richard and Lee crashed in the qualifying races that follow the time trials and precede the big race, and neither ran the big race. Lee never ran it again, and after that it was up to Richard to put the Petty team on top. He was finding his way fast, piling up enough points with victories on the short tracks and high places in races on all the tracks, short and long, to finish second in the driver standings in 1960, 1962, and 1963, but he wasn't yet winning on the Daytona or other long tracks.

In 1962 he was satisfied to finish second to Fireball Roberts because the Petty car did not appear to be competitive. "I really think that was the best race I ever drove," he said. "At least it was the best race I drove up to that time, and I don't know of any I drove better since, though I'm a better driver now by far. The thing was the car wasn't working right, but I got everything out of it I could and I kept shovin' while others was droppin' out. I was really proud of my second place, though I wasn't going to admit it to no one, and if Fireball had of broke, we'd have won her when we had no business even being close. That was the race that really made me realize I could run with any of 'em, even though the next year nothing worked right and we settled for sixth, a couple laps back of Tiny Lund. Then in '64 we finally won 'er."

It was a memorable moment for him because it was his first superspeedway victory and sent him on his way to his first Grand National driving title. The car companies were competing for prominence on the race courses then as they are not now. They were spending fortunes in quest of victories before economic conditions caused a cutback. What happened at Daytona on Sunday hit hard in Detroit on Monday. Ford had dominated recent stock-car racing with its Fords and Mercuries and Fireball Roberts as its star. Determined to outdo his rival, Ronnie Householder of Chrysler had invested heavily in streamlined Plymouths and Dodges with dynamic new engines and put its sponsorship push to the Petty team Plymouth and other entries. The push paid off spectacularly, with Plymouths finishing first, second, and third, and Petty finishing one lap in front of the second-place car and two laps in front of the third-place car.

Richard recalls, "Fireball's engine failed fast, and he fell out early. Foyt in another Ford pressed me awhile, but I felt I could pull away any time I wanted. Then his engine failed and he fell out a little past the midway mark. It was smooth sailing from then on. It's funny, even though I'd never won a big one up to then, I felt I'd win that one going in. I really liked our new setup. We did have tire trouble at the start, but so did everyone else. Maurice and Dale saw it before anyone else and they put on harder tires a couple of laps before anyone else, and while those soft tires was throwin' rubber and losin' laps for the other guys, we were running away from them. The funny thing was the Fords was cheatin' with laid-down windshields to streamline their cars, and the way they was set up, the chunks of rubber just knocked a couple of them right out of the cars.

"We win easy and the only thing I didn't like about it was Lynda didn't get to see it. We had two kids then and they came down with the measles. She was pregnant with our third and stuck back at the motel listening to me win and nursin' the kids. It's funny how the things in your private and professional lives get mixed up."

Well, he won, anyway, and he was no longer Lee Petty's kid but Richard Petty, the champion-to-be. He earned around $35,000 for his success, which was about $15,000 more than Lee had landed in his victory five years earlier. Richard's prizes included $1,000 an eccentric restaurateur had posted for the leader of lap 107, and later Richard admitted, "I kept looking at the board for the lap number and made sure I led 'er." He was then yet young and hungry. Later on, he would take such extras in stride.

John Holman of Holman & Moody, Ford's top team, had looked defeat in the face and refused to accept it. NASCAR's rules specify any racing engine has to be available to all, so Holman, sure this new one was not, went to the Plymouth dealer and demanded one. To his surprise, he was sold one. Jacque Passino, the Ford factory chief, shrugged and said, "Stock-car racing is just a carnival. To get people out, you have to throw some Christians to the lions. This year it seems to be our turn to be thrown."

Ford fought back and for some years yet finished in front of the other makes, but the Chrysler cars continued to cut into their lead and by the 1970s took over as Ford faded and fell out. A Ford won for Freddie Lorenzen at Daytona in 1965 when the Chrysler engine was declared ineligible and the company pulled out of the event, but Petty put Chrysler back in Daytona's Victory Circle in 1966.

Petty set a qualifying time-trial record of better than 175 miles per hour. He had the fastest car. Still, he had to drive it the hardest to win the race. He had a car that didn't handle right. It tore his tires to pieces. He flew away from the field at the start but had to pit at twenty laps to replace his tires and fell behind. The lead seesawed among several drivers, changing every time the leader had to pit. But Petty had to pit more than anyone else. He'd roar out, make up a lot of ground, then lose some of it back when he had to stop to take on new tires.

The crew tried harder tires. They tried to jack the car's weight around as much as they could on pit stops. But it was the driver who discovered how to handle this ill-handling car who made the difference. He had fallen two laps back, but he drove so much faster than the rest that he passed every other car twice and, just past the 280-mile mark, retook the lead. The crowd, who had welcomed him back to Daytona with "Go, Petty, Go" banners, had come to its feet and started to wave white handkerchiefs at him as he sped past on his relentless pursuit of first place, and he said later that this inspired him.

Dark clouds blew over the awesome arena. The fans shivered as a moist breeze blew across the course. Petty led with fifty miles to go, forty, thirty, twenty. It started to rain. The track got wet. The cars started to slide on the slick pavement. The officials huddled to discuss the dangers. Ten miles to go, then five. The rain was pounding down then and the officials put out the checkered flag. It flew in front of the Petty Plymouth as it splashed across the finish line two laps short of the scheduled distance.

He had made seven pit stops, changed eight tires and come from two laps down to win by one lap the fastest stock-car race ever run. He had averaged more than 160 miles per hour for more than three hours to become the first man to capture this coveted classic a second time.

He says, "I had fallen so far back, I never thought I had a chance to catch up until those fans started waving those white hankies at me. I figured if they thought I could make it, maybe I could. I was going to go for it anyway, and I got it. We were a lot quicker than anyone else, but we were clumsier too. As usual, it was a combination. The crew put a fast car on the track, but I had to overcome a clumsy one. One good thing, Lynda saw this one. And she still wasn't entirely happy. She complained something awful about gettin' soaked in that rain. As far as I was concerned, the sun was shinin' nice and bright. But I was glad they stopped the thing before I slid right out of the lead. I got a little nervous runnin' on rain."

In 1967, 1968, and 1969 the Petty team placed eighth each year.

"We were consistent, we just weren't too good," Richard said, grinning. "A couple of Fords won those years and one Merc. Mario Andretti won one. Cale Yarborough won one. LeeRoy Yarbrough won one. Actually, we could have won in '68, the year Cale caught 'er. We run 189 and the rest of the Chryslers was running 182s—that's how much faster we was than them. The Fords was running 182s, too, but they took 'em away and chopped 'em up and brought 'em back about four miles faster and Cale got a combination that could cut 190. It would just flat fly, I mean it would fly! We got in the race and we couldn't keep up with that cat, though we could outrun the rest.

"Then the top pulled up. I mean the top just pulled off the front. We were running a vinyl roof for some fool reason I forget, maybe to sell cars with vinyl roofs. I was just movin', mindin' my own business, when somebody blew an engine in front of me and a piece came out of the engine and caught the windshield where it joined the roof and opened it up a little. The air rushed in and blew the roof right up. When it first happened, I didn't know what was happening. All at once a lot of air was blowin' in my face and I was looking everywhere to see where it was coming from. Then, voom! the top pulled off and the sides caved in and I slowed right down.

"I was out of sight of my crew, and when I slowed down, the roof closed back down; so when I went into the pits, they didn't know I was in trouble. They started to jack up the car to change tires and put fuel in her, while I was trying to tell them what was wrong. I started beating on the top of the car and they thought I'd gone berserk. They thought, 'Man, that cat's done flipped his lid.' Finally, I got my message to them, and they jumped on top and knocked some holes in the roof and ran some tape through it and strapped it down. By the time I went back out, I was bandaged and beaten.

"The craziest things happen to you when you're driving a car around 200 miles per hour and other cars are machine-gunnin' spare parts at you," he said, smiling.

In 1970 his car came apart completely shortly after the start, but the Petty team was running two Plymouths in the major races at that time and teammate Pete Hamilton in a sister car surprised by winning. "That was some consolation and a tribute to our team," Richard remarked.

In 1972 Buddy Baker drove the second car and gave Richard and the first car considerable competition before Petty won by ten seconds. Richard remembers, "I could beat Buddy, but I had my hands full with Foyt in a Ford. He led five or six times, so he gave me all I could handle, but he ran out of gas. He got to the pit, but when he got out, a caution flag came out and he lost a lap and couldn't get it back. The next year, though, he got me when I got a broken valve spring. I could outrun him that day but the dang thing blowed up." That was a Dodge, then.

In 1973 Richard arrived at Daytona with a Fu Manchu mustache, surprising everyone and startling his new sponsor, STP. "The boys like to blowed their minds. They thought they was hirin' this clean-cut chap. I guess that's why I grew it, but I shaved it off before long. The guy in the mirror didn't look like me," he said, grinning.

"Buddy Baker might have had a better car that year, but we outraced him. The car wasn't handling good at all going into the race and we kept changing it right up to the race. The boys finally got it right, but we didn't know that going into the race. The strategy was for me to take it easy at first and get the feel of it before I pushed it. So I fell behind at first, but the boys had worked their head off and got something that worked.

"Buddy led most of the way, but I never let him get away from me. I was lucky. A tire let go, but it was in the fourth turn and I could just turn right into the pits and get it replaced. He was drivin' for someone else, and his pit crew couldn't compete with mine. I caught up, and when we made our last pit stops I made a fast one and he made a slow one and that put me ahead. Running hard, trying to catch up, his engine blew up. That was it and I won. I couldn't put the pressure on him, but my pit crew could and that's what won us our fourth at Daytona. It cost me, though. Big Granatelli ran into Victory Lane and kissed me before I could duck," he said with a grin.

In 1974 Richard not only captured the Daytona 500 for the fifth time but set a mark of two straight. It was a wild one. Fortunately he ran second fastest in time trials to secure a front-row start regardless of the results of the qualifying races. Beyond the first two, starting spots hinge on the qualifying races. Richard's Dodge blew its engine in its qualifying race on Friday, but his crew had plenty of time to put in a new one before Sunday. Maurice had one ready, of course.

Bobby Allison's car blew its engine just past the midway point in the 500, and the way things were that year in this race that left it to Bobby's brother Donnie in a Chevy or Richard in his Dodge. The two drove in front in a duel that dazzled the 90,000 screaming fans on a windy, wet afternoon. Petty appeared beaten when a tire blew with less than fifty miles to go and he fell behind replacing it, but again Petty luck let it happen in the fourth turn and he didn't lose a lot.

A few laps later Allison's luck was that a car blew its engine in front of him on the first turn, he ran over some debris, and his tire banged apart as loudly as if a cannon had been fired, flinging a hunk of rubber high in the air, and he spun through the short chute before wrestling his car under control. He had to limp all the way around before replacing the tire, and by then he was beaten. Petty flew home far in front—grateful that, since Granatelli had separated from STP, at least he would not have to endure another kiss from the big guy.

The fuel crisis had caused the race to be cut to 450 miles, and in his garage a dejected Donnie Allison cursed the fates. "We just got bad breaks. If we'd had a little more time, maybe we could have caught up."

In Victory Lane, Richard Petty pointed out, "We got good breaks, but you have to be good to get yourself to where you can take advantage of them. This is a hard race and you have to be both good *and* lucky to win 'er. We been both, which is the only way I can explain why we've won five and no one else has won more than one."

And, he was asked, now that he had won his fifth, what were his plans for the future? "Go for a sixth," he answered, grinning.

He was going for just that in 1975 at Daytona.

He knew the layout as well as he knew any on his circuit. It was an irregular oval, 2½ miles around with a 3,000-foot straightaway through the backstretch, the fastest part of the course. "We been runnin' here fifteen-some years now and it's become a bit bumpy," Petty pointed out. "There's a little bitty bump in the second turn and bigger bumps in the first and fourth corners. Bumps don't bother you on the straights, but they do in the corners, when you're turning. A bump can bounce you right out of control. You have to know it's there and look out for it and take it just right.

"It's a good-sized track, but there's still not much room for error. It's so steeply banked that if you get sideways you're gonna slide right off the track, even if the speed of the thing throws you up against the wall first. That's the thing to look for if there's accidents in front of you. You go high because you know those cars are going to slide down sooner or later. I like the high groove at Daytona anyway and run a lot higher all the way around than a lot of those other cats.

"It's not the fastest track we run anymore, but there's still a bunch of speed here. You got to go, but it's not as tough as some smaller tracks because you don't have to work as hard. You have to really drive the smaller tracks. The bigger the track the more important the car, because there's more room for the faster car to stretch out. It's a crew's race and I figure my crew has given me one of the strongest cars and one of the fastest cars, so I have a real good chance to win her," he said about a week before the race.

He spent that week taking the car out to practice it, then bringing it in so Maurice, Dale, and the rest could work on it. Maurice was here early, of course. This was Daytona. The rest could wait. Richard would come in and tell Maurice the engine was missing or he'd tell Dale the chassis was too loose or was pushing too much, and Maurice would dig down into the guts of the power plant and poke around and change this or change that, while Dale would jack the chassis up and put a little wedge in here or there or put in stiffer shocks or softer ones or change this or that.

Conferring concernedly, they would use the words only others of their secret society really understand and do the things only they know how to do. They brought the car to Daytona set up for Daytona, knowing how Daytona was, and then Daytona was a little different in one way or another than they expected it to be—a track is always a little different than you expect it to be—and the car was working a little different than they expected—cars are unpredictable, like people—and so they went to work.

They had worked hard for a long time to get the car ready, and now they would work harder for a shorter time to get it as right as they could get it. And while they did this or that in the guts of that mighty machine, they worked greasy and sweating in the garage, Richard sat outside and held court or walked around and visited. And when they were ready, they called him and he took it out and tried it, and then he came back in and told them if what they had done had worked or not. It never really worked as well as they wanted it to work. Whatever they tried, there was always something else to try.

"What you tryin' now?" Benny Parsons asked Richard as he came up and sat down alongside the King on another throne of tires.

"They're puttin' a jet in it, I think." Richard smiled, whittling on some wood with a sharp paring knife.

"Gonna need a jet to catch me," Benny said, smiling too.

Richard, his eyes hidden behind his sunglasses, tilted his head at Benny and said, "This your year, Ben?"

"Mebbe," Benny said.

Richard shrugged and said, "If not me, why not you?"

"Why not?" Benny answered.

Because he had won only two races in his entire career, both small ones—a 100-miler at South Boston, Virginia, in 1971 and a 250-miler at Bristol, Tennessee, in 1973. He had won the driving title in 1973 because he was one of the few who drove the entire circuit. The others did not do well that year and he piled up points with a second here, a third there, a fourth or fifth or sixth here or there, but no one compared him to Petty or even Pearson or Yarborough or one of the Allisons. He was a good driver, but how good? He had a good car, but good enough?

"No one knows, not even me," Benny Parsons agreed.

Growing up, Parsons spent summers with his mother and father in Detroit and winters with his grandmother in North Carolina. His parents worked and felt they couldn't keep him properly. His grandmother, "Mama Julie," who was eighty when Ben was born, did her best. Their home was an old farmhouse, without electricity or hot water. The only heat was from a fireplace and the only toilet was an outhouse out back. They kept a cow and some chickens and raised and sold a hog every year, and otherwise got by on her $27-a-month pension.

As a boy he got hooked on stock-car racing when his father took him to see a race. When he left school, he went to Detroit and found work on an assembly line at the Chevrolet plant. After a while he went to work in his father's small cab business, working on and driving taxis. He met a man who raced stock cars and talked his way into a spot on the crew in 1960. He started to drive with a fifty-dollar car in 1963. He hustled through the small time, winning a couple of titles and bending a lot of cars. "I knocked down every wall in Michigan, Ohio, and Indiana," he says.

Settling in little Ellerbe, North Carolina, Parsons started to drive on the Grand National circuit in 1970 but in his first year failed to win in forty-five starts, and now after five years he had won only twice in 174 starts. He drove as an independent most of those years, picking up sponsorship support here and there, which is no way to compete with the well-financed and fully sponsored top teams. He won the title with one victory in twenty-eight starts in 1973 but, after being shut out in thirty starts in 1974, decided to call it quits.

"I had a wife and two kids and poor prospects in this sport," sighed the chunky, balding ex-cabbie, "but after deciding to give it up, I decided to give it one more year. I'm about broke, but I've got me a good sponsor and a good car now, and I think mebbe my luck is about to turn."

Perhaps partly because they are North Carolina neighbors, Petty and Parsons are pals. Petty said, "I try not to get too close to anyone I drive against, but Ben is a good ol' boy." Parsons said, "Petty treats the other drivers just the way he does the fans—as though he and they was equals."

Clad in a crimson uniform, Parsons got up and walked down the row to his copper-and-white Kings Row Fireplace Chevy, climbed in, and went out to try it out. He came back in, smiling about the speed he'd found in it.

But in time trials, the two front-row starting positions went to Donnie Allison in a Chevy at 185.8 miles per hour and David Pearson in a Mercury at 184.4. And in his 125-mile qualifying race on Thursday before the 500-mile race, the engine failed in Parsons' Chevy; he failed to finish and wound up way back in the sixteenth row, thirty-second starting spot among forty starters. Pearson passed Petty on the last turn of the last lap of the other 125-mile qualifier, but that put Petty in the second row and all Richard really cared about was a start close to the front. "It's a long race and you don't win it in the first lap," Petty pointed out. On the other hand, Parsons was worried about starting so far to the rear. "It's a scramble back there and it's easy to get shoved into a wall," he sighed. "It's tough to get to the front from so far in the back."

As the big day drew near, Parsons found it hard to eat or sleep. He stayed up until four-thirty in the morning on Friday night and hoped he would be so tired he'd be able to sleep on Saturday night before the race. He slept some, but on Sunday morning when he sat down to breakfast on ham and eggs, he found he couldn't eat. "I took one bite and thought I'd throw up," Benny admitted later.

Petty never eats much at any time, much less anything the morning of a race, but he had slept well in his room at the Reef Motel, and when he got to the track he seemed rested and relaxed and sure of himself.

The infield had filled the night before, beginning at midnight, when the gates were thrown open and a long line of cars, campers, trucks, motorcycles, and other motorized machines ended their wait outside, rushed inside for the best parking spots, and started the long, cold wait inside around campfires, portable stoves, and cans of sterno. They ate cold chicken and ham sandwiches and drank beer and Bourbon. Some slept, while some danced to music which blared out of transistor radios. The Daytona 500 is a happening as much as it is a race. Some who were content to be part of it would see little of the race.

By race time the expensive seats in the stands were full and more than 100,000 persons packed this sprawling arena to see this celebration of speed and danger. Petty and Pearson and Parsons and the rest waited out those last, long hours before finally climbing into their cars as the fans stood and hollered for their heroes. The engines roared these gleaming machines to life, and the cars started around the oval, falling into their proper places on the preliminary laps. With the waving of the green flag, the big cars blasted into the first turn with a deafening sound.

Petty pressed his red-and-blue Dodge right to the front and started to pull away from the pack in the early laps. On the fourth lap, almost a fourth of the field was finished. Already far arear of the leader, Jim Vandiver lost control of his car in the third turn and his car turned and got rammed from behind to touch off a chain-reaction crash that sent cars crashing and spinning all over the oval. By the time it was done, nine cars were bent too badly to continue. Petty and the other leaders were slowed by the time they got to it under the yellow caution signals. Somehow Parsons escaped it, snaking through to find himself a lot closer to the lead than he had been.

J. D. McDuffie suffered a broken breastbone, but that was the worst of the injuries. Grumbling, the defeated drivers retired to the sidelines. Some watched the race, while others packed up and proceeded home. If they couldn't win, they didn't care who could.

It looked like Petty could win. He built a big lead, which disappeared when Johnny Rutherford spun out and the cars bunched up under another slowdown period. And Richard lost the lead on the seventy-fourth of the two hundred laps when Buddy Baker barged in front. But Buddy was the sort of driver who had to lead as long as he was in it, while Richard preferred to protect his equipment, stay close to the lead, and wait for the later laps to turn it on.

However, on the seventy-seventh lap, Petty's chances began to disappear. A cylinder head cracked and he began to lose water. His engine overheated and he had to pit to replace the lost liquid. He kept driving hard, but his engine kept overheating and he kept having to go into the pits for more water. Despite his sprints between pit stops, he kept falling farther and farther back.

Baker led until only 145 miles were left, but he had been running hard and his engine just gave up. As Buddy drifted off the track in despair, Pearson, who had been saving something, found himself in front. Baker later said sadly, "We had it won. All I had to do was keep the car between the walls. But it quit on me and it beat me." Pearson later said, "It was ours to win then. All I had to do was to avoid making any mistakes."

He was not a driver who made many mistakes. He was forty years old, he had driven Grand National for fifteen years, and he had won more races and more money than anyone other than Richard Petty. He always said all Richard had on him was a better team and a better car. Now that David had what he considered the best team, the Wood Brothers, and the best car, a mighty Mercury, he did not, he said, expect to be bested very often.

He'd had some bitter battles with Richard over the years, including a couple in recent years when their bitterness became almost too much to handle and they had driven dangerously against one another. Now, however, Petty was eight laps back, while Pearson was almost a lap in the lead. Second, surprisingly, was Parsons, who'd ground down rivals slowly, relentlessly through the long, grueling race, which sidelined twenty-six of the forty starters.

Finding A. J. Foyt's Chevy two laps back in the standings but right in front of him on the track, Pearson pulled in right behind him and started to draft him. Drafting is a specialty of stock-car racing. The big cars break the air resistance in front of them, creating a vacuum directly behind. Pulling right behind a car, another car is sucked along. If the first car is faster, the second car finds himself getting towed to that speed. Also, the second car's engine does not have to work as hard as the first and conserves fuel. Finally, by steering his car to the side, the second driver is pulled alongside. He gets a sort of slingshot effect briefly, which makes it easy to pass the car in front of him. Which is why it is said that in a two-car race to the wire, a car drafting the leader is in the best position to win because he is in a position to pass on the last lap of the last turn when there is not time left for the other car to follow suit.

Parsons tried to tie up to Lennie Pond's car, but Pond's car was not fast enough to pull Parsons along at a speed comparable to the Pearson-Foyt pairing, so Parsons pulled out and tried to go it alone. He was ten seconds behind with ten laps left when he saw Petty pull out of the pits and motion for him to follow. Gratefully Parsons put himself on Petty's rear bumper and found himself drafting at dizzying speed. Petty had by far the fastest car on the oval. His car refreshed by its latest gulp of water, he pulled Parsons along at a rate that reduced Pearson's lead one second every lap. His crew warned David he'd have to pick up the pace, which put a lot of pressure on Pearson, who had won just about every big race except this biggest of races on this circuit. Pearson pulled past Foyt and pressed his car to its limits, but Petty kept tugging Parsons closer and closer. By then the crowd was standing and screaming and all was madness at old Daytona.

On the backstretch of the 197th lap, Pearson threw caution to the winds and went to pass the slower car driven by Cale Yarborough. As David tried to duck under Cale's Chevy, Cale's car drifted down and the two came close. Suddenly Pearson's Mercury was spinning in a smoking slide toward the grass at the bottom of the track, and he was still spinning even as Petty pulled Parsons past up on the banked oval. Those who could see it, couldn't believe it. Seemingly certain victory had been snatched from Pearson just as he was about to win this one he wanted most to win. As he was straightening his car out and starting out again, Parsons already was out of sight.

On the last lap, Parsons pulled free of Petty and drove home alone, taking the checkered flag and coasting around to Victory Lane. One of the most surprising of winners, he climbed out of his car and stood in the sunshine shaking as his crew fell on him in joy and the officials and reporters there surrounded them. "Maybe I'm too big to say this, but I feel like crying," he confessed. "The Good Lord let me win and I'm grateful. Richard Petty had a part in it, too. When he waved to me to join him, it was like the answer to a prayer. I don't know what I'd have done without him."

In his graveyard of a garage, Pearson said, "He'd have lost, that's what." As to his mistake, David denied it had been that. "I had to take a chance. I couldn't just fall in behind Cale and wait to get caught by Benny. I guess Cale could have just let me go by, but he didn't, did he?"

Cale said, "You don't just let anyone go by you, no matter where you are in a race."

Petty said, "I could outrace everyone out there, but my radiator ruined my chances. I saw Foyt let Pearson draft him. And I saw Dave Marcis refuse to let Parsons draft him. When I pulled out from my last pit stop and saw Parsons coming along I decided to let him draft me. I didn't think a lot about it. It's something you do in racing. It wasn't done to defeat David. I think if David had come along with Parsons in front, I'd have let David draft me.

"I will admit"—he smiled—"that on my last pit stop Dale suggested if I could get in a position to help Ben a bit I might want to do that. It seemed like a sort of a good idea. I don't know anyone deserves a little help more. He's had a hard time and he's a good guy. All I wanted to do was give him a chance. Frankly, I figured if it came down to the two of them the last lap, Pearson would outsmart Parsons. David's been there before and Ben hasn't."

Later, Parsons sighed and said, "I don't know what would have happened but I'd have given him a go for it. I don't know what I can say about the lift Richard gave me. It is extremely odd for one driver to help another, except it exemplifies Richard Petty. That's why he is The King and will be that to the end of time. Maybe some can compete with him in cars, but no one will ever be in his class as a person."

Parsons pulled out of his pocket a string of beads. He said, "A little girl gave me these before the race. They're love beads. Her name is Audrey; she's from Richmond, and she scores for me in my pits. She sent the beads down with a message that maybe they would bring me luck. I just stuck them in my pocket and never gave them another thought until now. But I'm a little superstitious so I'll carry them with me awhile now. Maybe they'll win me some more races." He smiled.

That, however, would be the only race he would win all season.

The next race was at Richmond, Virginia, the following Sunday. While nineteen of the Grand National events in the 1975 season would be on superspeedways of a mile or more at distances of four hundred miles or more and two would be on the Riverside road course, the Richmond race was the first of nine short-track events at shorter distances. This was a .542-mile oval and when it was billed as the Richmond 500, the "500" meant laps, not miles, and the actual distance was 271 miles.

"Two hundred and seventy-one hard miles," Richard Petty observed. "The smaller the track, the tighter the traffic. You may not run as fast, but you run just as hard and you never relax. However, this is a real nice race track and I really like it here." There was no reason why he would not. He had won a dozen races here while others had won one or two. He had won eight of the last ten events here since they went to two races a year. The shop in Randleman is called "the Petty Place"; a rival referred to the track here as "Petty's other place."

Petty swept around the half-mile in about twenty seconds in time trials to put his Dodge on the pole at a speed of better than 93 miles per hour. He leaped into the lead at the green, led for 440 of the 500 laps, led the last 286 laps, lapped everyone else at least six times, and after 3 hours 37 minutes and 3 seconds of hard driving won by as big a margin as is recorded in NASCAR record books.

The only time he lost the lead was on the restart from a slow-down when Richard Childress tried to pass him and Petty pounded into the Childress Chevy, spinning it out. Petty in turn slid into the rail with a flat left rear tire and had to pit to replace it. Ben Parsons took over the lead, but, after Petty returned to the track, he ran down the Daytona winner within sixty laps, passed Parsons, pulled away from him, and started to lap him and all the others. Parsons fell back, permitting Lennie Pond to take second place, the highest finish in three years on the tour for the 1973 "rookie of the year."

For Petty it was the 165th victory of his career and he took it in stride. "Keep countin', 'cause I'm not," he said, grinning.

"I popped the tire before I hit Richie. That's what made me pitch into him. But neither he nor anyone else was going to beat me here today. This is my track and unless something goes wrong we're gonna win on it. Two races a year since 1970 we've run every cotton-pickin' lap here, which is a lot of laps. It's a flat track, a driver's track, and it gets slick, which is good for a good-handling car, which is good for us. It fits us fine. We've come up with the combination."

He won only $6,200 compared to the $41,000 he would have won at Daytona, but seemed content. "Yeh, it's unusual to win any race by six laps," he admitted. "Cale hit the wall, which is no way to win. Another guy got tire trouble. Another got transmission trouble. All the good cars got trouble, and soon I've got the race with no one good enough left in it to run with me. They don't all run these short-track races and there were only four or five to fear to begin with."

David Pearson, Bobby Allison, and Buddy Baker were the most notable absentees.

He shrugged and said, "Well, they could run 'em if they wanted. These races count, too. Not as much as the big ones, but the points add up. That's one reason we kept running at Daytona. Not to help Ben. He was there to be helped, so we helped. But what we really wanted was to pick up a position or two and some points. We passed Richie Panch, picked up a position to seventh, and picked up points. With luck, we coulda' won there, but we didn't. So we won here. And with the points we picked up here and there, we're back in front in the standings. With a little luck, we can win the driving title again. That'd be nice, you know. Like it's an honor. It's pride and prestige. It's also"—he grinned—"a lot of loot."

With his first victory in the third race of the new season he was back on top and on his way to his sixth championship in eighteen years on this tough tour.

Puffing his small cigar, Petty packed up for the drive home from Virginia to North Carolina, a contented king.

3

THE BEGINNINGS

The Pettys were born and reared and still live in Randolph County, North Carolina. Their part of the world lies about fifteen miles south of the "big city" of Greensboro, just off U. S. Highway 220. It is wooded countryside with a tiny community here, a small town there. As recently as ten years ago it was a remote area of dirt roads but in recent years a lot of it has been developed and many of the dirt roads have been paved over. There still is not a lot there, but there are churches, community centers, ball fields, country stores, and gas stations here and there.

The Pettys have given this place prominence. The Petty compound, where racing cars are readied to win championships, has grown year by year into a sprawling complex of garages and storerooms. It is located in the community of Level Cross. Across the road, Lee and Elizabeth Petty live in a large white house with an expansive grassy lawn that stretches to distant trees. At one time, their sons, Richard and Maurice, had houses on the property, but now they have built newer houses a few miles away. Coming from the compound, you pass cousin Dale Inman's house on the way to Richard's new place.

Richard's new house is tucked away down a dirt road and behind a bank of towering trees. On the way there you pass an old trailer in the woods where Richard and Maurice lived a lot of their youth. They are not far from where they began. "I don't think we ever thought of moving to the big city," Richard says. "Why should we? There is more there, maybe, but not for us. We can go there to do what there is to do there, but we don't do a lot and we don't want to live there. We like living here, where we always been. We like the country. We like being where we began.

We got a whole mess of relatives living around here who like it here. The Pettys stay put. This is our place."

Richard is supposed to be from Randleman, but it is difficult for him to pin it down. He says, "What Randleman really is is a township. We live in Randleman, but what we really have is a route number. Our garages are in Level Cross. Always have been, from before they was a garage. That's our mailing address, but what telephone calls we get come through the switchboard in High Point, down the road a bit. They have a downtown there, and that's where we bank and shop and go to the picture show or go out to eat when we want to do those things. There's nothing fancy there. The fancy stuff is in Greensboro.

"What we have is a collection of communities is what it amounts to, none of 'em big enough to amount to much. I went to Randleman High School, which is in the community of Piedmont, which is where my older kids go now. My mother's parents had the house in Level Cross my parents live in now, across the road from the garages. When Mom and Dad got married, they moved into a little house in the near countryside. They was livin' there when I was born and two years later when Maurice was born. But in 1943, when I was six, our kerosene stove exploded. No one was hurt, but the house caught fire and burned down. Dad was gone and Mom had all she could do to get us out. I remember standing outside it and watchin' it burn and not believin' it and wonderin' what was gonna happen to us. I remember goin' back that evenin' and looking at the smoulderin' embers and wonderin' what had happened to my clothes and toys.

"Maybe it was lucky that we didn't have much because we didn't have much to replace. We moved into the big house with my grandparents and lived there about three years. I really liked that place. But Mom and Dad wanted their own place. Daddy made us a home out of an abandoned construction trailer in the woods. He made three rooms out of it—a living room, a bedroom, and a kitchen—and we moved in there. It's so tiny it's hard to believe now we lived in that thing then, but we liked it well enough. The kitchen roof was so low Daddy kept bumping his head when he stood up, which we thought was funny. All of us slept in the same bedroom. Mom and Dad had a double bed, and Maurice and me had Army bunk beds. There was about a foot between beds, but we squeezed by. The bathroom was out back—an outhouse.

"Things started to change for us when Daddy started to race. Not at first. Not for a while. But after a while he began to make money at it and we began to get things we never got before. In time we moved into the big house. When Lynda and I got married, she moved in with us. Then we got us our own trailer. Then we built our first house. I was racing by then and Lynda moved us in all by herself, carting our stuff by wagon and wearin' down the road. We lived there fifteen years and it was fine. But Lynda's been wanting something better, so we built the big, new house we have now and jus' moved into.

"Her father built it. It's big and it's fancy, but it's not far from our other homes. Maurice built his own new place a year or so ago. Dale has a nice new place, but it's where he's always lived, near his mother and daddy. We may live a little fancier these days, but we don't move far from where we was. All the Petty places is within a few miles of each other, and every day going to where we are we pass where we were. The racing changed our lives, but it didn't change us," he concluded.

Men have raced cars since the horseless carriage came into existence in Germany in 1885. The first real race probably was a road race in France in 1894. The first real race in the U.S. was the Vanderbilt Cup event on Long Island in 1904. The first Indianapolis 500 was in 1911, but a championship trail for specially constructed racers had begun before that. Sports cars were raced in Europe in the early 1900s and eventually were raced around the world. The worldwide Grand Prix tour of sophisticated cars similar to those raced in Indianapolis started in the 1920s.

There was little racing in the South until the 1930s. Stock cars—the kind ordinary people drove on the city streets and on the highways—had been raced only occasionally and irregularly in this country until then. The South did not have enough people in enough big cities to make it worthwhile building car-racing tracks until then.

Prohibition, which lingered longer in the South than elsewhere, gave the sport the push it needed. Stills were commonplace in the backwoods. Bootleggers souped up their cars so they could outrun the law during their dark-of-night deliveries. With nothing better to do, they raced their cars on Sunday afternoons. These were wild races because the bootleggers had become skilled drivers with daredevil abilities. Crowds started to convene for these events. Seeing another way to make money, some converted horse-racing tracks or carved tracks out of the countryside, erected wooden bleachers, surrounded these dirt arenas with fences, and charged spectators to get in.

This is the legend, and there is more fact than fancy to it, though the Pettys and others of today hate to hear it: They are tired of it. Richard Petty says, "I wish people would quit talkin' about it." His mother, Elizabeth, says, "That may have been the way it was, but it's not the way it is." Well, that is the way it began, but it has changed. It began with bootleggers, and some of them, such as Curtis Turner and Junior Johnson, raced into the 1960s. Turner lost his life in a plane crash, but Johnson still runs a racing team, providing a link to the garish past of this sport.

Turner once talked of selling "white lightning" to the sailors in Norfolk. He talked of furious chases through the hills of Virginia, bullets whistling about his car: "Some ol' state trooper ran me thirty-nine times, but he never come close. I used to talk to that ol' trooper and he'd say, 'I'm gonna catch you if it's the last thing I do.' Later, that ol' boy committed suicide and some people say it was because he never could catch me. I don't know about that, but thirty-nine times sure's a lot." One did catch him, but he got off with a suspended sentence and went straight . . . in racing.

Johnson got caught, too, and served time in prison. He never was ashamed of it. "Ah'd say most folks in this part of the world was into bootleggin' one way or another at one time or another—makin' it, sellin' it, or buyin' it. It was a business, like any other business, far as we was concerned. During the Depression here, people either had to do that or starve to death if they didn't have a better business. My father was a hard worker. There ain't no harder work than whiskey work. Gettin' caught and pullin' time was part of it."

With hands like hams and a big belly that bulges beyond his belt buckle, ol' Junior remains a living legend in the Deep South, discussed by old-timers sitting in front of country stores to this day. He is a folk hero, called "the last American hero" by journalist Tom Wolfe. His arrest was as recent as 1955. Stock-car racing was beginning to boom by that time. He started racing before he went to jail and resumed racing after he got out.

He has seen stock-car racing grow into maybe the most popular sort of automobile racing. Indianapolis remains the single biggest event by far in racing, but its championship trail is crumbling around it. The Grand Prix circuit is struggling. The recent rise of drag racing has leveled off. The cost of constructing and racing special, sophisticated cars is rising beyond reason. Adapting stock cars to racing is more reasonable. The sponsors prefer supporting the kind of cars and equipment the public purchases.

In its beginnings few foresaw that stock-car racing would become the busiest and best-paying of all auto tours. One little dirt track was built after another. In 1936, the city of Daytona Beach conducted its first race on the long, hard stretch of sand at the beach where speed records had been sought for many years. Big Bill France, a banker's son from Horse Pasture, Virginia, who had worked as an auto mechanic and car dealer before he began to race on the side, finished fifth in it. It did not make money at first, but two years later France took it over and started to promote the annual event to profits. Then World War II interrupted all racing in this country.

Lee and Elizabeth Petty both came from farming families, large families. Lee explained, "Our pas did whatever they could do to get by. My pa did a little bit of everything. He farmed a little. I worked on the farm when I was growing up. Back in my day, Depression days, boys worked, and worked hard. We didn't have much time for playing games. I went to school for a while, but when it came time to quit school and really go to work, that's what I did. Like my pa, I did everything and anything I could to get by. I farmed a little. I got a little trucking business. My brother and me we got us a little garage. We worked on race cars. Then we went racing."

It is said by some that Lee's trucking included a bit of bootlegging, but Lee denies it. In any event, when the bootleggers started to race, Lee and his brother, Julie, started to watch the races, going to Greensboro and Martinsville and other area tracks. They liked it and talked of trying their luck at it. They thought they might make some money at it. When the war ended and racing resumed, they bought a 1937 Plymouth and put a Chrysler engine in it. Richard recalls his father was always tearing down and rebuilding every car he had his hands on anyway, so readying one to race was easy for him.

"One day in 1946 we decided to just do it," Lee said. "I told my wife I was goin' racing and she didn't say not to." A tough, flinty sort, Lee would not have listened to her if she had. She was tough, too. Feminine, but firm. But she did not tell Lee what to do or what not to do. He was born in April 1914. He was twenty-two when they were wed in 1936. He was thirty-two when he went racing in 1946. "I guess that was old, but a lot of old guys were going racing in the South in those days," he once said. "There were young guys going into it, too, but the sport was young for all of us. None of us knew what we were doing. Young or old, we were all equal."

She said, "I told him, if that's what he wanted to do, to go ahead and do it. But I'll admit I thought he was just skylarkin', and I had no idea what it would come to. I thought it was just something he wanted to try which he wouldn't stick to. And at first that's all it seemed to be."

He won his first race, in Danville, Virginia. He was second in his second race, in Roanoke. And he was third in his third race. He explained, "What happened was I could race with any of 'em right off, because no one knew how to race, but racin' took more out of my car than I could put back into it. We jus' didn't have the dough. We added it up and found we'd won nine hundred dollars and spent four thousand. There jus' wasn't enough in it to keep us in it."

Elizabeth said, "Times was tough. My dad had a sawmill but he didn't turn much of a profit on it. Lee's dad worked on the roads. We lived better than some, but we didn't live good. We didn't think about it much because we didn't know any better, just like Richard and Maurice didn't think about it when Lee and I were married and times were rough. We come from working class and Lee was willing to work but there wasn't a lot of work to be had. He was a salesman for a biscuit company and a deliveryman for a bakery before he got his own truck and started to haul all over the South. He put in a lot of hours on the highways and I put in a lot of lonely nights and we had a lot of thin meals before racing paid off for us."

In December of 1947, the year after Lee Petty's aborted try at racing, Bill France got a group of racing men together at the Ebony Bar of the old Streamline Hotel in Daytona Beach to discuss the formation of an organization to operate a stock-car circuit. Most were skeptical of its chances for survival, but France found an ally in Bill Tuthill, a small-time promoter from the East. They enlisted a lawyer, Lou Ossinsky, who patronized France's service station in Daytona Beach. They formed the National Association for Stock Car Auto Racing, formulated rules, and incorporated it in February 1948. France owned 50 per cent, Tuthill 40 per cent and Ossinsky 10 per cent. France and his son, Bill France, Jr., who has succeeded him as president, have ruled NASCAR with heavy hands ever since. Occasional efforts to overthrow them or compete with them have collapsed, possibly for the best. They have presided over a rise from rags to riches unmatched by the sometimes strife-torn efforts of other racing circuits.

NASCAR's first race was France's Daytona Beach race that February of 1948. Red Byron won it with a Ford coupe and with it won $1,000 of the $3,000 purse. That year NASCAR sanctioned fifty-two races at a handful of tracks with pennies for purses. Half of them were in North Carolina, with seven in Greensboro, six in North Wilkesboro, five in Lexington, four in Charlotte, even one in Occoneechee. Lee Petty went to some of these races and his interest in trying racing again was rekindled. Julie was not so sure of its future, but Lee had been hooked. He felt he could beat the best of the barnstormers of those days. Fonty Flock won fifteen races, Red Byron eleven, and Curtis Turner seven that first season. They drove battered old cars on their gypsying tour of rough races on dirt tracks. They did not dare risk new cars.

However, France figured a lot more people than had been patronizing his races might pay to see races run with new cars such as they drove themselves every day. He announced a new division, the Grand National, for new cars, with the first race at a three-quarter-mile track in Charlotte, North Carolina, in June of 1949.

Lee liked a 1948 Buick Roadmaster he had been borrowing from a friend, and he asked to borrow it for the race. He talked him out of it on a promise of rich returns, took it, took the exhaust off, tuned it up, took it on the back roads at night and practiced it. With Julie's help he had it ready, and on the morning of the race they loaded half the Pettys in North Carolina into it— including twelve-year-old Richard and ten-year-old Maurice—and drove it to the track.

To their surprise, to everyone's surprise, there was a tremendous traffic jam outside the track. It seemed like everyone wanted to see a new-car race. More than 13,000 paid to see it, and they overflowed the wooden bleachers of this old oval. And a lot of drivers wanted to try it. Some thirty-two turned up, some of them with cars right off the showroom floors. After they all got inside and got on the track for a little practice and got qualified into starting spots, they got the race under way.

Richard remembers it well. "It was one of the wildest races I ever saw—all those big cars on that little-bitty track. They were all over the place—up in the fence, down on the grass—making the dangdest racket you ever heard. I don't know how anyone knew where anyone was in the standings, but it sure was thrilling. I remember being amazed at how well Daddy drove until he started to roll over and over and over and over. It scared me half to death and I remember how relieved I was when he climbed out okay. He wasn't relieved. He came back so angry he like to cried. He tole ol' Uncle Julie they'd just have to get them a better car."

Lee Petty was thirty-five years of age when he drove his first —*the* first—Grand National race. He had just moved into the lead when the sway bar on his car broke and the machine rolled over four times. He escaped with a cut that required some stitching, but, though he denies it, there are those who say they saw him sit down and cry that day, the only time they saw this tough fellow let a tear go. Though he never admitted he did it for more than money, he found he loved it and couldn't let it go. He was an intense person, prideful, who wanted to be the best, who watched with angry envy as Jim Roper ran off with that first Grand National event in a Lincoln.

His brother Julie dropped off at the side of the road, but Lee Petty picked up a Plymouth coupe and drove in all eight races on the Grand National tour that year. He won some and lost some and finished second to Red Byron in the drivers' point standings. Richard remembers, "Pa paid cash for that car. It was the best he could afford. It was the lightest car on the tour and had the least horsepower. But it was a dependable car and Daddy drove it smart. People laughed at him when heavier, faster cars boomed right on by him, but most of these would break down. Pa kept plugging and after a while he'd find he'd fallen in among the leaders.

"People began to think of his driving as miraculous, but it wasn't a miracle; it was just a case of a good driver outsmarting a lot of other drivers. I was a boy, but, watching him that first season, I learned a lot that has stuck about taking care of your equipment and not running it so hard it breaks down and being patient and waiting for your time to move up."

There were wild drivers on the tour in the early years. Glenn "Fireball" Roberts, who got his nickname as a softball pitcher in Florida, was one. He did as much to glamorize this sport as anyone, though he was an introvert—tight-lipped and tough—who had few friends. He drove like a demon. At one time or another he held the qualifying record at almost all the tracks on the tour as it expanded. In the races he led twice as many laps as anyone else and he won thirty-two, but he broke down in most of them and was never consistent enough to capture the championship.

When the first big paved track opened at Darlington, South Carolina, in 1950, Roberts started sixty-third in the first Southern 500 and finished second. Five years in a row he was the fastest qualifier there, and in 1958 he finally won it. As other big paved tracks opened, he dominated them. Three years in a row he was the fastest qualifier at the new Daytona Speedway and he won more superspeedway races—eight—than any other driver.

Some were as wild off the track as they were on it. Joe Weatherly, known as "Little Joe" and called "the Clown Prince of Racing" was one. A short, husky, homely fellow, he always wore bright-colored sports shirts and saddle shoes when he drove. He drove hard. Once at Savannah he somersaulted his car six times, soared over a twenty-foot fence, and walked away from the wreckage in a drainage ditch with nothing worse than, as he put it, "two bloodshot eyes." He drove all night—five hundred miles —and the next night drove in a race at Moyock, North Carolina. "If you want to cash in, you got to be there when the man puts his hands out with the money," he explained.

Little Joe and "Pops" Turner became buddies. They'd party away the nights before and after races, and race in between. Little

Joe once put gin in the water bottle Pops kept in his car so he could refresh himself during races. And he once drove a new car right into a swimming pool after Pops and he held a race to see who could get back from the track to their motel first. Little Joe won more races than Pops on the new tour. Little Joe won twenty-four races and the driving title two years in a row, while Pops, who was primarily a dirt racer, won only seventeen and never won the title as paved tracks started to pop up all over the tour.

Pops made and lost several fortunes in the lumber business. He spent one fortune trying to build one of those newfangled paved tracks at Charlotte, but went broke before it was finished and lost it to others. He had sought a loan from the Teamsters on their behalf and tried to unionize the drivers. Furious, France suspended him from the circuit. After four years, on the eve of the debut of a rival circuit put together by Turner, France permitted him to return, and the new circuit was allowed to die. At forty-one Pops still was good enough to win the inaugural race at the new North Carolina Motor Speedway in 1965.

They were rough characters with rough reputations, the kind that captured the hearts of the "good ol' boys" who sat around the country stores and gas stations swapping stories about them. Junior Johnson said, "They'd just as soon fight as race. They'd stop the race and fight."

At Charlotte in 1959, Junior was leading a race and taking up a lot of the track to hold back Lee Petty, so Lee started to ram his car into Junior's. A fender bent in, cut a tire, and blew it, causing Junior to spin out into a guard rail. Junior limped into the pits, grabbed a pop bottle, got his tires changed, got back onto the track, chased Lee, and ran him into the infield. The two drivers scrambled from their cars and came together. While Junior waved his bottle, Lee lashed out with his fists. Before it was over, the Charlotte chief of police and other cops had to break it up. "I could take care of myself," comments crusty Lee Petty.

He could, of course. He was one of those for whom racing was not so much fun as it was a way to support a family. He did not admire the wild bunch. He once said, "I never saw many heroes in this sport. I've seen drivers with all the money, some with some of it, and some with none. There were times when I was getting started in racing when we hardly had enough money to buy the groceries. It took time before we started to live high off the hog." As Richard would say, he just kept shoving.

Lee finished second in the standings the first year of the new tour, third the second year, fifth, fourth, and second before he finally finished first in 1954. He did not have the best equipment, and while he won a lot of races, he did not win many big ones. They ran fifty races a season in those early seasons, sometimes two or three over a three-day weekend. Lee seldom won as much as $20,000 a season. The season he won his first title, he won only a little more than $26,000. "You worked for what you got and risked your neck for a little return," he once commented.

Elizabeth points out, "What Lee did win, we lived on part and put the other part back into the business. The other drivers, they spent their money and some of 'em were supported by sponsors, but we was our own sponsor and supported ourselves and our cars, which was the way we started our company. For us it was not so much a sport as it was a business, a family business, just like a mom and pop store. We were always there, all of us, putting ourselves into it, even the kids from the time they were old enough to help. They always went with us even before that. We went to the races together as a family—all those that were close enough to drive to, which was most of them at that time.

"We always packed a lunch and saved something back from it for dinner in case we didn't win any money. That way we was sure we'd have something to eat no matter what. A lot of the others they went home hungry. I mean that truly. It was a fact of life. They went to the track without a spare penny and if they didn't win any money they couldn't even afford to stop for a hot dog on the way home. Today they spend sponsors' money or they won't go racing. Yesterday a lot of the drivers ate peanut-butter sandwiches and slept in their cars. There were no fancy restaurants in no fancy motels for them. They were making a living if they could. We made a living. When he first started winning he'd make maybe eight hundred dollars a race. When it went up to a thousand, boy we thought we was really making money."

As a family, they stuck together. As Richard and Maurice followed their father into racing, the bonds between them tightened. Tiny Lund, who drove a second car for the Petty team in the middle 1950s before Richard began to race, once said, "I never felt part of the team because I wasn't part of the family. Me and

Lee never did get along. He was a clannish, tight, selfish man back in the beginning and I don't see he's ever changed much."

Tiny recalled a time in 1957 when he was driving a Petty team car but was treated like a rival. He said, "Lee hated for anybody to pass him on the race track. He had an Olds with wing nuts and plates on the side of the bumpers. He could brush up against another car and ruin it. He tried to get me, and I retaliated. He didn't like that.

"After the race, he came up to me at the payoff window on an elevated stand. He told me I'd torn up the side of his car and that I should pay for it. I refused and he hauled off and punched me in the eye. As we started down the stairs, I kicked at him and he sailed off. I followed and we wrestled on the ground.

"Speedy Thompson tried to separate us but couldn't. Pretty soon Maurice and Richard joined in, and I was battling all three of them. But the clincher was when Mrs. Petty joined in and hit me over the head with her pocketbook. It was like a scene from a slapstick movie, but it's true it happened. When you beat the Pettys, you have to beat them all."

It was always that way, right from the beginning, from the time Richard and Maurice were working in pa's pits, getting kicked out for being too young and sneaking right back in. Pops Turner once commented, "Them Pettys—never could figure 'em out. Lee didn't have no fun. He wasn't free and easy like the rest of us. He was always with his family. Why, any time Lee was runnin', all you had to do was look in the pits, there'd be Richard and Maurice hanging onto the fence, tryin' to pull themselves up just a little bit higher, tryin' to see how their pappy was doin'. They was too young to be allowed in the pits, but they was already working on Lee's cars and ready to go racin' as soon as someone would let 'em.

"Now Lee was a helluva driver. I'm not trying to take anything away from him, but Jeezus God, every race he went to there'd be Elizabeth and the kids. Lunchtime they'd be off somewhere together. After the race they'd pack up and head home. How'd he ever get any fun out of life? And, you know what, that kid of his, Richard, turned out the same way! A family man. A real racer, but no fun at all."

To Pops it was positively ridiculous, but to Richard it was reasonable. "Daddy cared for our family that way and I care for my family the same way. We have fun, but in a different way from those other dudes. We don't get it partying with pretty ladies or drinkin' or drivin' cars into swimming pools. We get it by working hard and racing hard and winning more than the others win and enjoying our winnings by living a good life. I don't guess they was wrong, but it would've been wrong for Daddy and it would be wrong for me. Everyone's got to find his own way to live, and the way we was raised you worked hard, did your best, and lived decent."

Richard remembers boyhood days before his father went racing. "We had a simple country life—fishing and fighting, swimming and going to school. Maurice and I used to fight a lot—like most brothers, I guess. I got more scars on my body from rock fights than from racing. When we did something wrong, we both paid. Daddy or Mother would whip both of us without waiting to find out which one did wrong. They always wanted us to do right. But we did our share of wrong. I remember my teacher in the second grade made me stand out in the hall so often for doing wrong the older kids got to know me by name. I was always out there when they were changing classes.

"We used to have a lot of good times playing in a big hay barn Dale's father had. We'd make tunnels through the hay bales and have forts and all. We went to Level Cross Methodist Church most every Sunday morning and we'd play kick-the-can in the field out front afterwards. When they had homecomings they'd have a lot of food and boxes of soft drinks, and we could eat and drink all we wanted and we really liked that. I remember drinking eight or ten bottles of pop. We didn't have television when I was a kid and a soft drink was a treat you enjoyed maybe once a week. I was fifteen before we got our first television.

"I was about eight when Daddy started racing. I always loved driving cars. Almost always, anyway: as soon as I found out what they were. When I was a boy, people used to ask me if I wanted to be a race driver like my daddy when I grew up. I would always say, 'No, I'm going to work on the cars and let Daddy race them.' I think maybe I was buildin' up protection inside myself in case it turned out I wasn't going to be good enough, but I think I always wanted to try.

"I remember the first time I drove anything at all and how thrilled I was. I was, let's see, five years old mebbe, and it was a

1938 Ford pickup truck, all beat up don'cha know. Everybody was putting up hay, so Daddy had me drive. They put that ol' truck in granny gear—that's extra, extra low. I had to stand up on the seat to see over the top of the steerin' wheel. But that was enough. That did it. I was hooked right then. Still am.

"It ain't the money. Nor the glory. I just like to drive. It's that simple. Some cats, they like to watch cows eat grass. That's their thing. Me, I like to drive. It's my thing. I like the feel of metal around me, the feel of tires under me.

"My brother, Maurice, and my cousin Dale and I used to race everything we got our hands on. I can remember playing in the dirt when we were real little, maybe seven or eight. We'd carve a race track into the dirt and push the cars around them. We'd turn the cars over sometimes, too, just like they was wrecked. When I was ten or so I'd organize wagon races from our house down to the swimming hole, which was downhill all the way. I wanted to win so bad I'd pull the wheels off and grease 'er every day so it would coast smooth and fast. I'd win, too, with about ten wagons comin' in behind me.

"Then I got my first bicycle. Dale already had one. So we went racing. But that downhill course was too fast and it was too hard to stop at the end of it. We skinned ourselves good before we decided we better set up another course. We made one up on a road we cleared that ran up and down through the woods behind the barn. After a while we added a mudhole to splash through. It was wild. We raced hard, crashed a lot, got skinned up and dirty. We used to go to the swimming hole to wash up. We'd wash our clothes, too, and wait for them to dry before heading home. Mom never could figure out how we'd get so cut up and beat up and never get dirty. But sometimes we ripped our clothes and got lickin's for it.

"For a while Daddy tried to keep his trucking business going, though the garage was gone by then. We still farmed on the side, and Maurice and I had a lot of chores to do. We also had to work on the race cars. We didn't have help, so we had to help. I remember when we built our first garage right where our whole mess of garages is now. It wasn't a garage like we have now. We put up siding and put the race car in between it. It was an open-air affair with a dirt floor. Later, we mixed concrete and laid our own floor. Then we put a roof on it. Like Topsy, it just growed.

"Maurice and me we washed the car and changed the oil and packed the bearings and in general did what we could do. Daddy worked all day, then came home and worked on the car all night. Some nights and most weekends except midwinter we went racing. Where he went, we went. I was an apprentice mechanic at twelve, and I thought that was just about the most anyone would want to be."

He was thirteen when he went into his first real race. It wasn't the way he wanted it to be. He was helping out in the pits at a track in High Point. It had rained and the track was muddy. Lee's windshield coated over so he could not see. He pulled into the pits and Richard grabbed a rag and wiped the windshield clean as far as he could reach. Then he hopped on the hood so he could reach the rest of the way.

At that point, Lee had turned to see if the track was clear. He slammed the car into gear and roared back into the race before he realized his son was still on the hood, hanging on for his life. Lee was not about to stop racing, so he sped all the way around before he darted back through the pits, slowing just enough for his son to hop off. "He had no business being on there," Lee grumbles, still angry about it many years later, "and I let him know later."

Richard laughs and says, "I was scared to death, but less of riding the hood in a race than of what my daddy might do to me later. But he just hollered some, he never hit me."

When Richard entered Randleman High School, he went out for the athletic teams. He was tall at about six-two and heavier than many others, though skinny at 160 pounds. He was center on the basketball team, first baseman on the baseball team, and an all-conference guard on the same football team on which Dale was a halfback. By the time Richard had filled out to 180 pounds his senior season, he was good enough to get some small-college scholarship offers for football and he thinks he might have made it in small-time college football, but he had no interest in trying to make it in college.

"I was good, but not as good as Dale. He was bigger and tougher," Richard recalls. "I was an average student, but I wasn't much on studying. I did go on to take a business course in junior college for a year because I thought it might help me with what I did with my life later on, but all I really wanted to do was race cars."

Red Byron, Bill Rexford, Herb Thomas, and Tim Flock all won driving titles before Lee Petty won one. That was in 1954, when he was forty. He won the beach race at Daytona that year for the first time. It was a 250-miler in which the lead changed hands thirty-five times. He had crashed in the first race he had tried there in 1949, and he finally conquered the course in his sixth try. He has said, "It was a different kind of racing than the boys do today and a lot tougher."

Richard remembers, "It was the wildest sort of racing I'd ever seen. They had this circular course on the beach right by the ocean with stands and all and those cars would fishtail through the sand and bang into one another, and if they got into a slide, they just slid a fur piece, I want to tell you."

That was the year Richard got his first car, a two-year-old Chrysler his father figured was too heavy to continue in racing. Before he even had his driver's license, Richard ran it over the red-clay back roads of Randolph County. Wanting something superior, he saved his money and bought a year-old Dodge. He set it up right, souped up the engine, painted it black and white, and practiced driving it at top speed and sometimes "broadsliding" it sideways through the turns of the off roads.

The police in that part of the world let him run as long as he stayed on the back roads. "We had a deal. We never discussed it, but it was understood. They'd chase me. If they could catch me, they would. They never did. If I made it back to that big ol' tree over there, I was home free."

The Pettys put in a lot of work tuning up the cop cars. But when brother Maurice came up with a car and ran even faster over regular roads, a cop cracked down and booked the boy, costing the family a fine. That particular cop later mourned, "From that day on I had the slowest police car around." Maurice smiles and says, "We just stopped hanging goodies on his car."

Hudson cars, which are no more, dominated stock-car racing until the middle 1950s. Lee Petty turned from a Plymouth to a heavier Dodge in 1953 and took his family on a cross-country tour with it, towing it to races in a dozen states. Richard recalls, "We slept in cabins along the way, which was before there were many motels. Sometimes Maurice and I slept on the floors, which we thought was great."

Lee turned to a Chrysler in 1954 and it took him to the top.

The next year he took it to a new track in Memphis, blew a tire, crashed through a fence, and landed in a lake. As his sons watched in shock as the car sank from sight, their father reappeared to the side and pulled himself from what they came to call Lake Petty.

That year Tim Flock won his second driving title. He often drove with a pet monkey in uniform by his side. Tim drove himself so hard he developed an ulcer. He was typical of the early NASCAR kings who grew up in hard times. He says, "We was born on a farm near Fort Payne, Alabama. My daddy died when I was a child, leaving nine little Flocks and Big Mamma. She worked in a mill for nine dollars a week and nine little Flocks almost went to an orphanage." Their father had been a tightrope-walker at one time, and the other Flocks followed in his daredevil ways. Four became race drivers—Fonty, Tim, Bob, and sister Ethyl, who was named after the high-test gasoline. Another brother, Carl, raced boats. Another sister, Reo, made thirty-nine parachute jumps. Tim and his brothers broke away from running liquor to running races. A ladies' man, he once said, "It was all right. Plenty of doll babies."

Buck Baker won the title in 1956 and 1957. Lee Petty finished fifth one year, fourth the next. A former bus driver for Greyhound, Elzie Wylie "Buck" Baker was fearless. He once said, "I never saw nothing out there to scare me much." He scared others the way he drove cars and flew airplanes. He was one of the first to buy and fly his own planes. NASCAR's good ol' boys were becoming affluent.

The Pettys still were struggling. After graduation from high school in 1955, Richard became a full-time employee of Petty Engineering Company in 1956. When he turned eighteen, he asked for a chance to drive a Petty car. As he remembers it, Lee looked at him and said, "Wait till you're twenty-one. You'll be three years older and I hope three years smarter by then." Rather than rough it, Richard decided to wait to race with the family behind him.

He had learned a little about engines. His father then set out to teach him a lot about them. They'd buy a production engine, tear it down, hand-tool and machine-work each part, and then put it back together with precision to give it the balance, strength, and consistency it needed to produce racing speeds and endure. He began to feel more a part of the team's successes and failures. He recalls, "The first time I saw Pa blow an engine that put him out of a race, I felt responsible, really rotten. But he just told me, 'Boy, I've blown a lot I built myself. We build 'em as good as we can, but sometimes we ask more of 'em than they've got to give. If one comes apart, we put it back together again. Or build a new one. We just try to make them better and better.' Which we did. But we didn't have the equipment or facilities or manpower we have now. We had a low-buck business."

Lee drove a Dodge in 1956, but when Oldsmobile offered him factory support, he switched to an Olds in 1957. It was the first time the Pettys tried anything other than Chrysler products. They went to Detroit, picked up three new cars and sufficient spare parts to get them through the season, and set about learning the new chassis and engine. That was the year Maurice graduated from high school, and Lee put both his boys on the new engine. Richard remembers, "Maurice had more of a feel for engines than I'd ever had. I liked driving more, so I had more of a feel for chassis. I encouraged Maurice to take over most of the engine work while I started to take over some of the chassis work. But what I was doing was waiting to drive."

4

LIKE FATHER, LIKE SON

In 1958 Richard Petty started his career as a professional race driver at the age of twenty-one, at a time his father was not only still competing but charging toward his second driving title at the age of forty-four.

NASCAR still sanctions competitions in several classes besides the glamorous Grand National division, with divisions for late-model modified cars, sportsman cars, and street stockers. In 1958 it introduced a convertible class, and the Pettys found a way to double into both divisions by bolting a hard top onto a convertible. They would take it off to run a convertible race, then put it back on to run the same car in a Grand National event. If there was a conflict, the car ran Grand National because that's where the money was and that was what Lee wanted. So when Richard ran, he started competing in the convertible class.

"I think it was the day after my twenty-first birthday when I walked up to Daddy and said, 'Pa, I'd really like to go racing.' He was working on a car and he turned his head and looked at me a little bit and motioned to an Olds convertible we had in a corner and said, 'All right, we'll fix this one up for you.' Then he asked me to hand him a wrench, and that was that. Daddy wasn't much for much emotion. But we had two races to run on the same night, so I went to one while he went to the other. He didn't even see me run my first race. Anyway, I didn't win. I didn't win one for a while."

Richard's first race was on the twelfth of July 1958, just ten days after his twenty-first birthday. It was at Columbia, South Carolina. Dale had come into the company and served as his crew chief. "Dale was a lot more worried than I was. He like to worried himself to death. I wasn't worried at all. I'd been going to races ten, twelve years, watching Daddy win a mess of 'em, and I figured I could do it, too. But the funny thing was I hadn't raced at all and I didn't know what I was doing and it was a few races before I found that out and started to worry some myself.

"Daddy wasn't much for giving advice, but he told me one time, 'Richard, if you expect to make it in anything, you have to try a little bit harder than the rest. I don't care if you're a clown in a circus or trying to sell pots and pans, you have to work harder than the next man if you want to be the best.' And Daddy always worked hard at racing, we could see that, so we was always willing to work hard. I worked my fanny off getting my first car ready for my first race and Daddy didn't do much more than come over every once in a while to check her out and make sure I wasn't making any mistakes.

"When I left for my first race, all he said to me was, 'If she runs right, run hard. If not, don't be afraid to back off. You won't win 'em all anyway.' When we got on the track to practice the car wasn't running right. It wasn't handling at all, so Dale and I had to change the sway bar real quick. I qualified thirteenth, I think, right in the middle of the pack. I remember sitting in the car real calm. Then the race started and all hell broke loose. Cars was passin' me right and left and dirt was flyin' through the air. I blew my cool.

"I drove that car every which way but straight. I never did spin out, but I bounced off the wall a bunch of times. I run real high anyway and did it just natural right off the first race, but at that time I couldn't keep the car off the wall. We had big ol' bumpers on the car and I tore the right rear bumper right off it.

"The big deal I remember about that race, we was coming off the number-four corner down the straightaway and Joe Weatherly blew a tire and went right through the grandstand fence. There was boards and things flying everywhere and I put my hands up over my face. It was just an automatic thing, and when I realized I'd taken my hands off the steering wheel I couldn't believe it and it like to scared me to death. I said, 'Man, I can't be doing this!' But I just kept on doin' it.

"That was the roughest sort of track to start on. It was real slick dirt like it was wet, and everybody seemed to run sideways the whole time. They'd broadslide through the turns so they'd be pointed straight when they accelerated down the straights, but by that time on that little ol' track they was in the next turn. I didn't know how to go or where to go, so I just started following the fast cars. I'd follow one for a while, then when a faster cat came along I'd follow him. I couldn't keep up with the fast cars, but as soon as one would get away from me, I'd find another one.

"I lost about six laps to the leaders, which wasn't too bad on a short track in a two-hundred-lap race. Joe Weatherly went into my pits hopin' to drive relief for me, figuring I'd never last I found out later, but I lasted. As I remember it, Fireball Roberts won the race. And Bob Webber, who was convertible-class champion, ran second. So it was a strong field. So it wasn't too bad when I finally finished sixth. I was too dazed to decide how much I'd liked it, but when I got home and Daddy asked me about it I said I figured I'd keep trying it awhile. I remember it now as an enjoyable experience."

It was a year and six days later before he won his first race, the same Columbia contest in a convertible. "I learned a lot from my first race to my first win. I learned by watching those other cats and trying to do what they could do. After a while, I could see when I made a mistake and I could try not to make the same mistake again. Of course you're in fast traffic and you can't always do what you want to do, but it's best to know what you can and can't do.

"Daddy saw me race for the first time my fourth or fifth race and he told me I'd run too low when I'd already realized it. Usually what he told me I'd discovered for myself already. You can't tell anyone else how to drive, really. Everyone has his own style and his own abilities and limitations. Everyone has to discover how he can drive.

"No matter how much ability a driver has, it's a slow learning process before he can really use it. With experience he starts to react the right way without having to think situations through. There isn't a lot of time to think things through out there, but the thinking driver is the one who wins most often.

"My first win, I was finding my own groove by then. I was starting to find the places on the track I could go the fastest. If somebody ran another groove better, I figured he was faster than I was. At Columbia I came into the last lap with some cat and we was about even, but he may have tried to go faster than he could to keep me off because he made a slide and I just ran right by him real smooth and took the checker. It was a thrill, but it was something I was sure was going to happen sooner or later anyway. By then I was confident I could cut it."

The first ten years or so of NASCAR's Grand National tour produced tremendous changes. Harold Brasington, a construction man from Darlington, South Carolina, returned from the Indianapolis 500 in 1949 with the idea of building a big, paved track in his hometown. He purchased some farmland and carved a squared oval 1⅜ miles around with 26-degree banks in two corners. It opened with a race named "The Southern 500" on Labor Day in September 1950, and because it was the first long race and a long time before another "superspeedway" was built, this became the granddaddy of southern race tracks and the most treasured of races.

Richard remembers the inaugural: "We'd never even heard of the place till we heard about the track. When we got to the track, they had the biggest traffic jam outside you ever saw. Everyone wanted to see seventy-five cars trying to go five hundred miles on one track at one time. No one thought they could. Well, they couldn't. Only a few could. We got inside the place and I never saw so much asphalt in my life. The track just staggered us. When Daddy got on the track, he found out two turns was banked and two wasn't and a couple of the corners got real crowded. It was something.

"They had twenty thousand people there hollerin' all at once, and the drivers turned a lot of nice machinery into junk before they was done. Daddy and Johnny Mantz battled it out for the lead almost all the race, but we ran into problems and Mantz was prepared and he went on to win while we settled for sixth. There were a lot of firsts for NASCAR that first race. It was the first one we spent four days on—qualifying on a different day than we raced. And the first one with organized pit stops. The Mantz crew had brought a pneumatic lug wrench and, while everyone was popping tires the whole race, Mantz got his changed a whole lot faster than the others. Grand National grew up that day."

Still it was 1959 before Bill France opened the second superspeedway—a 2½-mile paved layout modeled after Indianapolis, but wider and with much higher banking—at Daytona. The next year, paved 1½-mile tracks opened at Atlanta and Charlotte. In 1965 a fifth major track opened in the South—a one-mile paved oval in North Carolina, near Rockingham. In the last year of the 1960s, a 2½-mile track was opened at Talladega, Alabama, and two-mile tracks in Irish Hills, Michigan, and College Station, Texas. The southern stock-car circuit was spread across the country. NASCAR already was competing on the road course at Riverside, California, and in the 1970s the tour started to make stops at such new tracks as the one-miler at Dover Downs, Delaware, and the 2½-milers in Ontario, California, and Pocono, Pennsylvania.

Richard observes, "With the big tracks came the big crowds and the big sponsors and the big bucks and everyone wanted in on it. A lot of Northerners came into it and it stopped being just a southern thing. I had an advantage in that I came into the tour the same time as the big, paved tracks. I ran the short, dirt tracks only a year or two before I moved up to stay. I didn't have habits to unlearn; I just had to learn. Pretty soon there were more big-track races than small-track races, and they started to pave over the small tracks we raced at. A lot of small tracks couldn't compete and went bust. A lot of old cats couldn't adjust, and a whole new bunch began to run at the top."

When General Motors, Chrysler, Ford, and other automotive companies got competitive in stock-car racing by sponsoring top teams and drivers and providing them their equipment, NASCAR flourished.

Richard ran his first Grand National race at Charlotte in 1958 and finished far back. He ran nine races on the top tour that year and didn't come close to winning one of them and won only $760 in prize money. However, he ran twenty-one races the next year, and while he didn't win any, he placed in the top ten nine times and earned more than $7,800. While it was his second season of driving, it was his first full season. He was still regarded as a rookie and was voted Rookie of the Year in NASCAR ranks.

That was the year the Daytona International Speedway opened with the inaugural Daytona 500 in February. That was Richard's first race on a superspeedway. "I fell out of it fast and finished fifty-seventh, so it wasn't much," he says, smiling. "It was so much longer and wider than Darlington that the speed didn't seem so much more.

"I had run against Daddy in this race and that race and I didn't even think much about it, though a lot of the newspaper guys tried to make a lot of it. I never felt a lot of pressure being Lee

Petty's son. I know a lot more was expected of me than of the other young drivers, but I didn't expect any more of me than they did of themselves. I just tried to do my best. I just tried to beat Pa every time, and he just usually beat me. I wanted to win, but after me, I wanted him to win. If I fell out of a race, I went into the pits and pulled for him and tried to help out any way I could. We were teammates, after all. And he was paying my way and letting me pile up big bills banging up good equipment, which was something young guys didn't usually get.

"After I fell out of the first Daytona 500, I pulled for Pop to pull it out. And I want to tell you Daddy provided a wild ending."

To say the least. The first Daytona 500 remains the most controversial. More than 50,000 fans flocked to the fancy new track and saw a stirring race. Cotton Owens was the fastest qualifier in a new Pontiac with a speed above 143 miles per hour, but he never led the race. Seven other drivers exchanged the lead thirty-four times through the long afternoon. Lee Petty in an Oldsmobile and Johnny Beauchamp in a Thunderbird traded the lead thirteen times over the final fifty laps. With the crowd roaring, the two cars crossed the finish line side by side along with a third car, Fireball Roberts', which was a lap back but confused the issue. There were no sophisticated electronic photo-finish or slow-motion movie cameras at that time, and officials were left to their own judgment.

Lee once recalled, "Most people thought I had come across first, but the officials somehow figured John had won. They handed him the trophy, and when I went into Victory Circle they told me to go away. I protested and they agreed to study still photos of the finish to make sure they had called it right. I was mad as a hornet, but I had to settle for that. We packed up and headed home, as down as down could be. I have to hand it to them: they were men enough to reverse themselves when the pictures showed them wrong, but we sure had a long wait."

It was three days after the race before the officials found a still photo that had been taken at the finish line at the moment of the finish, and it showed the Petty car in front. They telephoned the Pettys, who let out a happy holler.

That was Lee's first and only superspeedway victory, but with it he went on to his second straight and third driving crown at the age of forty-five.

King Richard the Racer in radio-equipped helmet, ready to roll. FRANK MORMILLO PHOTO

Lynda and Richard with Rebecca on Lynda's lap; behind them, Lisa, Kyle, and Sharon.

Lee Petty. DAYTONA SPEEDWAY PHOTO

Elizabeth Petty.
SUCCESS PROMOTIONS PHOTO

The young Richard Petty. DAYTONA SPEEDWAY PHOTO

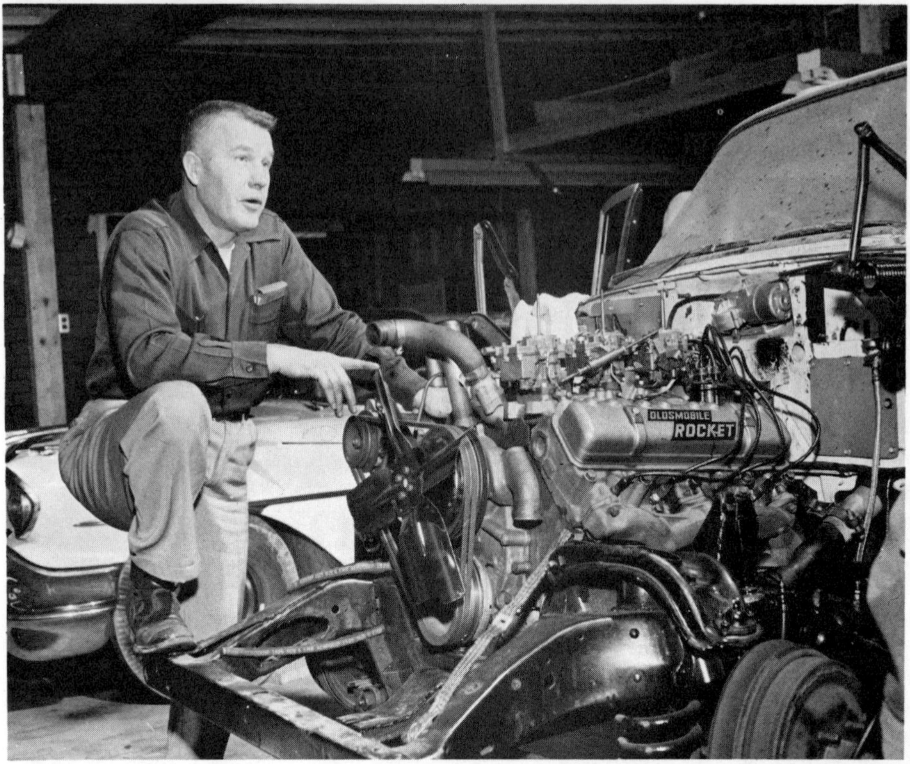

Above, Lee Petty the racer.
DAYTONA SPEEDWAY PHOTO

Right, Lee belatedly receiving his trophy after the controversial first Daytona 500 in 1959.
DAYTONA SPEEDWAY PHOTO

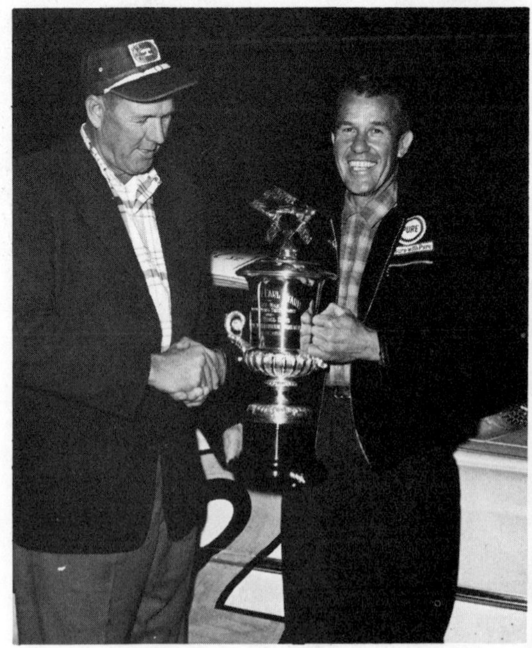

John Beauchamp (73) rams Lee Petty (42) from the rear, knocking him over the fence and following him, in the serious wreck at Daytona in 1961 which led to the end of Lee's racing career. DAYTONA SPEEDWAY PHOTOS

Richard after his triumph at Daytona in 1964. DAYTONA SPEEDWAY PHOTO

The ill-fated Plymouth Barracuda Richard campaigned in drag-racing exhibitions in 1965 while temporarily out of NASCAR. VICTORY LANE ENTERPRISES

Fireball Roberts with Miss Georgia.
DAYTONA SPEEDWAY PHOTO

Tim Flock. DAYTONA SPEEDWAY PHOTO

Curtis Turner. GOODYEAR PHOTO

LeeRoy Yarbrough with wife Gloria, left, and race queen. FORD PHOTO

At Atlanta's Lakewood Speedway in 1960 Richard almost won his first Grand National event. He finished first, took the checkered flag, and coasted into the pits. Lee kept charging around for another lap, then went up to the officials and demanded a recount, claiming the checker had come out one lap too early, that the race really hadn't been finished until he finished it. They checked the scorers' summaries and, sure enough, Lee was right. So they took the trophy from Richard and gave it to Lee and declared him the winner.

Questioned about his act later, Lee snorted, "I don't reckon I regret it. When he wins, he can have it, but he ain't gonna have it given to him."

Richard smiles and says, "Dad didn't give anyone a break, not even his son. He taught me you have to earn everything you get. They were hard lessons, but I learned from them."

Richard finally got his first Grand National victory that year at Charlotte, whipping Rex White at the wire with Lee running in relief of another driver and placing third in a futile attempt to catch his son. "Winning was a thrill, but not what you would expect I guess," Richard says. "I'd spent a lot of years watching Daddy and others win and a couple of years winning lesser races, so I sort of took it in stride. I was always sort of unemotional. I always expected to win. When I didn't, I was disappointed. When I did, well, I expected it.

"I won two other races that year and brought about $35,000 back into the business. We figured out I'd cost them about $20,000 up to then, so they got ahead on me that year. I was on salary and a percentage of winnings at that time, just like any other working driver. The company was what counted."

Family, too. It was at this time Richard had taken on new personal responsibilities. He started to date Lynda Owens in the late 1950s and had married her and had their first child, son Kyle, with her by 1960. "When I get my mind made up, I can never see no reason to wait around," he grins. "The folks started wondering why I all of a sudden started to go to all of my old high school's games that I could get to. The reason was Lynda was a cheerleader and I volunteered my jalopy as the cheerleaders' bus and chauffered them all over. When there were no games, me and Lynda went to movies. Sometimes we'd get out of one and go into another. Pretty soon I started taking her to our nearby races.

She'd help Mom fix the food. She fit in real well. She saw what a racer's life was and she saw she could live with it. So we got married. Real fast, because she was still in school. We moved in with the folks at first and then into a little old trailer. We made do, but it was good that I began to make some money in 1960 because we were beginning a family."

Richard ran forty times for those returns; expenses were high and profits were low. Maurice tried his hand at driving that year and there were three Pettys on one track at times, but his competitive career did not last long. Richard says, "It's a shame he didn't stick to it because I believe he was more of a natural and maybe a tougher competitor than I was. And Daddy thought he showed more promise in his first few years than I had. But Maurice had some physical problems, including poor eyesight. He had to cock his head to see straight. He tangled with another car at Columbia, South Carolina. That's where I started and he finished. He flipped, crawled out of the racing car, and never got back in one again. I did the driving after that.

"Daddy lasted a little longer, but he didn't finish the following season. He became the boss of the team before he quit that, too. Maurice became engine man. Dale took over the chassis. And that's the way the team has stood ever since."

Although he won only three races, Richard finished in the top ten thirty times in forty starts and finished second in the standings to Rex White. Meanwhile, Lee slipped to sixth and may have been headed down even if his career was not doomed at Daytona the following year, 1961.

In the first hundred-mile qualifying race, Richard was trailing Fireball Roberts and Junior Johnson on the last lap when Johnson's right front tire ran over a piece of debris from an early engine explosion and blew out, spinning his car to the right. Richard yanked his car to the left to avoid him, but Johnson's car careened off the wall and caught Richard's in the rear, spinning it back up toward the wall. Richard remembers, "When we reached the wall, my car seemed to lift right up and it started to ride the wall. I could feel the concrete ripping everything right from under it. Then, suddenly, the car slipped off the wall and went sailing way down into the parking lot below the bank. The car hit with a terrific crash and I could see the metal tearing apart all around me.

"I was stunned at first, then I came to and thought I better get out of there in case there was fire. The windshield had been knocked out and I climbed right out through there and fell to the ground, spraining my ankle. The ironic thing was that that was the only thing I hurt. I sat there still stunned looking at that wreck and listening to it before I realized the engine was still running. I limped away and they got to me and took me away to the hospital at the track. They couldn't find anything wrong, so they let me go.

"When I got back to the pits, my daddy was getting ready to run his race and he asked me, 'You want to run this one, too?' and laughed a little. I smiled and said, 'No thanks,' but I wasn't shook up, I remember that. The accident hadn't scared me. That meant a lot to me. That meant I could handle that. You never know until you have to find out. But even before Daddy got going my eyes started to hurt real bad and water up so I could hardly see. Daddy made me promise to go back to the track hospital before he took off. I did, and when they looked, they found out when my windshield shattered it left maybe a million little-bitty pieces of glass in my eyes. It took them a long time to pick the pieces out. Luckily, none had stuck.

"By the time I left the hospital they were in the last lap of the second hundred-mile qualifier. Sure enough, just as I looked up, Banjo Matthews got sideways and Daddy got sideways trying to avoid him and Johnny Beauchamp bashed right into him. Maybe, like was said later, Johnny just froze on the throttle, but all I know is Daddy's old Daytona rival never let up, he rammed him at top speed and sent Daddy out of sight, crashing right through the first-turn fence. I ran for him but because of my bad ankle I kept going down in pain and getting up and going on. I was scared to death. By the time I got there, they were lifting Daddy out of the car. I couldn't believe that car. There was just no car left. It was opened up like a sardine can. Both sides were gone. The engine sat smoking a hundred yards away. There was blood everywhere.

"After they took him to the hospital, I went there too. You could follow where they had taken him by the trail of blood. I found him in the emergency room lying still, cut up, beat up, bruised, his uniform tore. They were working on him and one of the doctors chased me out of there. Mom was sitting there in the corridor, pale and praying. Maurice was there. And Lynda. A doctor came out and told us it would be a while before they could tell us anything.

"Lynda talked me into going back to the motel to clean up and tend to my ankle. I was a mess. I put on some fresh clothes and a fresh tape on my ankle and then I wanted to get back there. Believe it or not, we ran out of gas on the way back. We walked to a service station—I hobbled—to call the hospital and found we had no money. Lynda borrowed a dime from the boy there and lost it in the phone, which didn't work. We went to a nearby house and asked to use their phone. We called and Maurice came for us.

"It turned out Daddy had a punctured lung and a mangled leg and they were working on him trying to save him. A doctor hinted he would not live. It went on and on, hours and days. He was slipping in and out of consciousness. They were transfusing blood into him, but they didn't do anything else, not even set his leg, except to try to keep him from dying.

"It was a nightmare, but, believe it or not, Maurice, Dale, and I went back to the track on race day. I hung around the pits during the race and I even drove relief for a neighbor from Level Cross, Bob Welborn, when he came in and said he needed a rest. I drove so well I forgot who I was driving for and didn't notice their sign saying I should come in until they gave it to Maurice to hold. Bob went back in the race and we went back to the hospital.

"Maybe it says something because it just didn't occur to me not to go to the track and not to race when the chance came. We didn't hold Daddy's accident against racing. Accidents are part of racing. Either you can accept them or you can't. You go on or you don't.

"Daddy did a lot to prevent accidents. He introduced roll bars in the cars, for example. They said they were illegal. Daddy refused to run without them and warned them they'd look bad if they were against a safety feature. So they let us use them and soon everyone was using them. Racing has become safer and safer on our circuit. We have all sorts of safety features including visors in front of our faces so a man won't get glass in his eyes if something smashes. But they were just learning what they could do then. And an accident like Daddy's might have happened at any time.

"In a few days, Daddy began to get better. He sent for me because he had something he wanted to say to me. He talked in a whisper so low I had to bend close to him to hear him. He said, 'Son, you go on home. You and Maurice start working on a car for the next race. Your mother and me will come home Friday.' Right then and there I broke out in a big grin because I knew he was going to be all right. What a tough old man! But it was six or seven Fridays before he got home.

"It took two operations to save and set his leg, and they warned him he'd have to wear a brace and might limp the rest of his life. But there isn't much limp left now. He drove the doctors crazy until they let him come home. He knew we needed help. He was supposed to stay in bed but Mom couldn't keep him there. He kept sneaking into the garage to see how we were doing. We weren't doing very good.

"It was a struggle. We didn't have much help. We had to handle all the paper work as well as get cars ready to race. I never knew how much paper work there was. We had picked up Plymouth sponsorship and we had to account for all we spent. Dad said it was up to us to keep the business going until he could get back into it, and we felt that load of responsibility. It made me grow up real fast.

"Maurice and Dale got the cars ready and I drove them. I won only two of forty-two, but I finished in the first five in almost half of them, mostly in short-track races, and earned about $22,000, which was enough to keep us in business. In fact, at year's end Lynda and I had our own house built. Our second child was born that year, a daughter, Sharon, and we needed the room.

"Over the winter we worked on our new equipment for 1962, and by the time the new season rolled around I was refreshed. The only real problem was that Daddy had decided to drive again, and while we knew there was no stopping him, we didn't want him to. We didn't tell him that, of course. But we were relieved when after a couple of races he called it quits.

"I suppose he just wanted to prove he wasn't afraid, though he wouldn't admit that. He just said it wasn't any fun anymore. Well, he was forty-seven, almost forty-eight, and it was time for him to step aside and time for me to take over."

In a dozen years on the Grand National circuit, Lee Petty had finished first three times, second two times, and third three times in the annual driver standings. He had won more titles, three, and more races, fifty-four, than any other driver to that time—records which would stand until his son surpassed them. As he stepped to the side of the road, the old was giving way to the new. Junior Johnson would still run a few years, and Curtis Turner would come back briefly before he was killed in the crash of his plane. Red Byron, Herb Thomas, and Tim Flock were long gone, and Rex White would leave soon too. Joe Weatherly would be killed at Riverside and Fireball Roberts at Charlotte in 1964 in awful accidents.

"Fast Freddie" Lorenzen, a long-track specialist from Chicago, and "Gentleman Ned" Jarrett, a short-track specialist from Camden, South Carolina, came into it and shot to stardom. "Li'l" David Pearson was Rookie of the Year the year after Richard and on his way to the top. A new group of drivers dominated the tour who knew nothing about bootlegging, who were professional racers and brave businessmen.

In 1962 Richard Petty won eight races, finished in the first five thirty-two times in fifty-two starts, and earned more than $50,000. In 1963 he won fourteen races, finished in the first five thirty times in fifty-four starts, and earned almost $50,000. In 1964 he won only nine races, but they included his first Daytona 500 triumph, his first superspeedway success. He placed in the top five thirty-seven times in sixty-one starts, and earned just under $100,000. He finished second in the driver standings in 1962 and 1963 and first in 1964, his first title coming exactly ten years after his father's first. That year brother Maurice was voted NASCAR Mechanic of the Year too.

In seven seasons Richard had reached the top in his perilous profession, and in the next ten or so he would attain heights neither he nor anyone else had ever dreamed of.

Richard had made the Petty-blue Plymouth 43 such a formidable force on the tour that its hemi-head engine was doomed by new restrictions imposed by the powers-that-were under pressure from rival teams prior to the 1965 season. Rather than seek another sponsor, the Petty team loyally stuck by Chrysler and stepped to the side of the road awhile, waiting. Restlessly Richard converted one of his cars into a drag racer and made appearances at drag strips throughout the South. Dissatisfied, he prowled the Petty compound between trips. I visited him at this time, in March 1965.

Richard took me behind the single garage they had at that time and showed me where in a weedy hollow lay a large pile of twisted and broken cars and metal debris that would have gladdened the heart of a junk dealer. "Any time I get to feelin' too cocky, I can always come back here and look at this and sober up," he said. How many wrecks had he put there? "About half. And I'm just beginnin'," he grinned. "I just started to do my share of winnin', which is why I hate layin' out. But I already done my share of losin'."

In a magazine article he had been described as a sort of rattlesnake—cool, coiled, waiting to strike. It was said he had a "feel" for his perilous profession. An admirer asked, "Ever see a good bartender pour whiskey without using a shot glass? He doesn't have to look and he can pour a hundred and you ain't never gonna git a drop more than what's comin' to ya. He has the feel. Richard, he has the feel, too."

Richard said, "It's something you can't learn. If a boy told me he wanted to be a race driver, I'd say forget it. It's tough to break in and it's dangerous while you're learning and it takes a long time before you know if you're any good or not. In the end, I think, you've either got it or you don't. You can't train for it, and all the learning and practicing in the world won't help you if you don't have it.

"It's not only raw ability but a sort of instinct for knowing where to put your car on the track and when to pass and when not to pass and when to charge and when to lay back and just how much your car can take. It is a 'feel' I guess. You can't have any fear in you at all. Like they say, if you hesitate, you're lost. The only time we think about fear is when writers ask us about it. If we even thought about being afraid we couldn't be race drivers. Not good ones anyway."

He was wearing a sports shirt, Levi's, and high boots. He stood in the cool of a shade tree, breathed in the fresh air, and squinted into a setting sun. He said, "We run this thing like a business. We run every race we can. We're out to make money. If we could make more money doin' somethin' else, we'd do it. We work eight or nine hours a day, five or six days a week, just like anyone else. We all pitch in. It's a business, like any other business. For us, a family business. We're all in it, except Lynda, and she's sure a part of it. Her part," he smiled, "is keepin' house."

He was tougher than he seemed. After one rough race, he and Ned Jarrett had a fist fight. After another, when the event was called off, angry spectators closed in on the drivers and track officials and some drunks began to swing tire irons. Richard waded into them. An official observed, "He's as good a fighter with his bare fists as I ever saw."

He had a sense of humor which could handle hard times. After winning a race in horrid, humid heat at Nashville, he collapsed and had to be revived with oxygen. The promoter asked Richard if he wanted to take a victory ride around the track in a convertible with some attractive ladies. Richard said, "No, thanks. I just want to lie on the ground so they won't have far to go to dig me under."

Now, in the middle 1960s, with his career just turning into what it would be, he said, "It's a tough life, but a good life. I started a lot sooner than my daddy and I got a lot longer to go. The house is all paid for. The kids is all paid for. I'm still young and I'm having myself a high old time. The sport used to be rough, but it's cleaned up a lot. The fans are clean and real sportin'. The drivers are clean and real businesslike. We're all a better class of people now."

"Ain't no way they could be worse," commented Lee with a laugh. Lean, mean, close-mouthed, cigar-chewing, Lee said, "I'm right proud of Richard, of course. If I could've won more races, I'd've won 'em and maybe Richard never would catch me. This racing came along too late in my life. I got a late start. I laid the groundwork for youngsters like Richard. He's buildin' on our bones. It's a brand-new ball game now. Nice cars, nice big tracks, clean-cut kids. It's sort of soft," he complained.

Off to the side, Lee's wife said, "I'll admit I had no idea it would come to all of this. When Lee had his accident in '61 I wasn't surprised. I always knew it could happen. That was a hard time, but it could've been worse. And I was upset when Richard was startin' and Lee was so hard on him and so many people expected so much of him. But it's worked out."

She sat down and sighed. "I'm afraid for them, certainly. It's hard on any woman in any race family. There's nothing we can do except wait and hope it works out for the best. But it's no good trying to make a man not do what he's bound and determined to do. And my men are good at this business and have worked hard at it and don't take any unnecessary chances in it.

"And it's a nice sport. People have the wrong impression of it. Maybe it started out wild with a bunch of bootleggers and all, but it's a real clean sport now. There's a lot of manliness to it, and my family has been something special in it and has been able to stay real close because of it. I feel real proud."

Richard's wife said, "His job is racing and my job is to raise his family right and be a good wife to him. I want Richard to go to each race knowing his family is well cared for. We go to as many races as we can because we want to be together as much as we can. That's the way it is with the Pettys, and I'm a part of them now. And I get a real kick out of the race, just like any fan. Maybe I get more excited because my husband is in them. Sometimes in a long race when nothing's happening I get bored by them, but it's not a boring business."

She sighed and said, "I don't worry about him getting hurt. He told me not to think about it, so I don't think about it."

Richard said, back in that time more than ten years back, "I wonder sometimes what the next ten or fifteen years will be for me, but for me the future is no further off than the next race. I live life one day at a time and I take each race as it comes. After a while mebbe I'll add 'em all up and see what they amount to."

5

MARCH

In the spring of 1975, as February turned into March, winter was still in the air as the drivers gathered in Rockingham, North Carolina, for the Carolina 500 on the 1.017-mile, mildly banked North Carolina Motor Speedway.

Fresh from victory in Virginia on the short track in Richmond, Richard Petty, at thirty-seven the King of NASCAR, spoke about his chances of winning on this short superspeedway in his home state.

"Maybe it means a little more to me than most because it's a home-state track. I've won here a bunch of times. I like the track but I used to like it better before they banked it. When it was flat it wasn't quite as demanding on the driver or the car. Now it's a track where the handling of the car is important because it's quicker, but so short you're still always in traffic.

"I think we can handle this track better than any of the other teams, but we still haven't sorted out the overheating troubles we had at Daytona. If it holds together we'll win. We won't qualify the fastest probably. We don't qualify the fastest at most tracks. Our Chrysler engine just isn't as powerful as the Ford and Mercury engines, but it's more reliable. And our car handles best. We got a shot."

As he got up to walk away, someone thrust a piece of paper and a pen into his hand and he stopped, smiled, signed his fancy autograph and spoke with the fan for a moment before moving on. Someone else stopped him to ask him to pose with them for a picture, so he paused. This fan put an arm around Richard's shoulders as if they were old friends and Richard flashed his teeth while the fellow's wife snapped the photo. Then the fellow exchanged places with his wife and snapped her photo with him while she giggled. An official came up to talk to Richard about something and Richard threw his arm around the man's shoulder as they walked toward his car. The official said something funny and Richard laughed, slapping the fellow's shoulder.

Big Buddy Baker in a Ford turned the oval in 26.6 seconds for a speed of 137.6 miles per hour to take the pole on qualifying day, but Richard ran second in the time trials to put himself on the front row for the start of the race. Although the sun was shining, race day was cold at less than 40 degrees, with a chill wind blowing over the 31,500 fans who came in off U.S. 1 to take in the show, fourth of the new season. The Petty family drove sixty-five miles south to the event, which was practically in their backyard.

Richard had won six times and was the defending champion here but he did not win this twentieth of the races run here. He took an early lead and was so much quicker than the others that he passed every car at least once and some cars two or three times in the first 185 miles. However, his engine started to overheat. He was a lap ahead when he went in for an unscheduled pit stop to repair his radiator 194 laps into the 492-lap event, but by the time he got back out he was a lap behind. He passed the leaders and unlapped himself and was closing in on the lead again when his car started to overheat again and he had to pit again.

"After that I didn't do no more racing," he said later. "All I done was watch the heat gauge and run according to what it done. We kept running and we could still outrun most of those cats out there, but we couldn't run with the best of them without roasting our engine, so we cooled it and kept pitting. It was a shame because once I got tired of messin' with them in the early stages, I just went out and put a lap on them as easy as could be. It was a cold day, just miserable, but we were hot. Too hot."

Baker led before Richard, but after Richard fell back, Buddy's engine broke. Lennie Pond ran near the lead until the 307th lap, when his car and Dave Marcis's car came on a tangle between Benny Parsons and Darrell Waltrip. Running alongside Waltrip, Parsons hit his car and they spun. Coming up on them, Pond's car crashed into Waltrip's, and the Marcis car crashed into Parsons. The only one hurt was Parsons. The surprise winner at Daytona, Benny Parsons was carried away unconscious on a stretcher at Rockingham, but came to at the track infirmary and after being taken to a nearby hospital was judged to be all right.

"I was better at Daytona," he said with a smile.

Cale Yarborough in a Chevrolet prepared by team boss Junior Johnson at Junior's shop in Ronda, North Carolina, led by a lap with less than fifty miles left when his right front tire came apart and he had to slow down and limp to the pits for a replacement. He came out twenty seconds behind David Pearson's Mercury, but caught up with thirty laps left and pulled away to win by thirteen seconds after four hours and fifteen minutes of racing, with Petty placing third a long nine laps back. The winning team won $14,200, the Petty team $7,925. Junior put his big belly up to Cale's car and leaned into the cockpit to congratulate his chauffeur on their first victory of the young season. They had taken ten events the previous season and thought they were on their way for this season. They had no way of knowing it would be a season of struggle and few celebrations.

William Caleb Yarborough was almost thirty-six years old and had been driving race cars half his life. Before that he was an all-state schoolboy fullback in South Carolina, an amateur boxer, and a semipro football player. He flew his own plane, taking one up and landing it safely before he even knew how or had started to take lessons. Once he learned how to handle planes in the air, he started to jump out of them, sky-diving for kicks. "Whatever there is to do—on a dream or a dare—I want to do it," he drawled. "But from the day I hung on a wire fence and watched the Southern 500 at Darlington, fifteen miles from my farm, that's all that I wanted to work at."

He starred on the southern stock-car circuit for ten seasons before he left to try Indianapolis and that tour. He didn't have a competitive car and didn't win there, so he had returned to the Deep South, hooked up with Junior Johnson, and was trying to hit the heights again. He had earned more than $800,000 in racing. He and his wife, Betty Jo, and their three kids had an ancient mansion on their thirteen-hundred-acre farm in Timmonsville, where he doubled as a county commissioner. Short, stocky, straw-haired, Cale commented, "I'm not ready to retire to the tractor yet."

As for this, his twenty-eighth Grand National victory, he said, "The only reason Richard ran away from us was he was in the pits a lot and came out with fresh tires every time. I could run with him otherwise."

Told this, Richard Petty smiled and said, "There was no way he or anyone else there could run with me today any more than they could at Daytona. We're gonna spend a long week licking our problems and then you'll see. But, for now, let ol' Cale laugh and live it up. He and Junior won it and they're entitled to enjoy it." And he headed for his family and the drive home, while Maurice and Dale packed up.

Bristol is brutal, a .533-mile cement saucer in northeastern Tennessee, near the Virginia border and about two hundred highway miles west of the Petty place. Richard had nothing good to say about it. "It's the only race track we run I don't like. I even like Talladega compared to Bristol. And it's not because I only won there once, because there's places where I never won. It's because it's a barrel like those motorcycle cats run at fairs. It used to be a real nice, real wide, sort of flat half-mile track, and they decided they wanted it faster so they banked it up and made a speed-dome out of it. It's so short and so steep that when you go into the corners all you can see is concrete and you can never see more than about seventy-five yards in front of you. If something happens in front of you, you got to hit it."

He ran five hundred laps flat out in his short-track car, and he didn't relax a second that third Sunday in March. Again Baker beat him in time trials and took an early lead in his Ford. They started under the yellow to dry the track out from morning rain and snow. Some seventy-eight laps into the five-hundred-lap event, Cale Yarborough came on to take the lead in his Chevy. Baker and Benny Parsons pressed him as the three raced in front until Cale's car quit on him on a pit stop on the 155th lap. Petty, who had been laying back, took the lead then and held it for about fifty laps. Baker began to drop back, but Parsons stayed in the running and swapped the lead with Petty twice for a 150-lap stretch. Then, on the 371st lap, Petty reclaimed the lead for the last time and started to pull away, lapping everyone again and again, despite a pinched nerve in his right shoulder that put his arm to sleep and put him in agony. Parsons almost passed out, pulled into the pits, and requested a relief driver. Walter Ballard got into his car and finished second in it, a long six laps back.

Chilled, worn out, and nursing his sore shoulder afterwards, Richard sat in his garage and admitted, "I stayed away from

Buddy, Benny, and Cale when they were racing in the lead because I feared they'd hit and have an accident. I decided to run high and away from them, lay back, and wait awhile. It worked because Cale broke down. I could outrun Buddy and Benny. My pit crew put pressure on Parsons with faster pit stops. No matter how good he ran, he kept falling farther behind and finally quit. I wasn't going to give up with the lead, but it took a lot out of me.

"I have a wire that runs from my helmet to the inside of the car to keep my head straight but we didn't get it tight enough. That track isn't anything more than one long left-hand turn and the force keeps pushing your head to the right and my helmet started to cut into my right shoulder. Soon, I lost all feeling in that arm and had to steer strictly with my left arm. My arm got so bad I'd prop it onto my knee to hold it up, but then I'd have to give the steering wheel a jerk and the arm would flop down. It was a long, hard run. It always is, here."

He lay down, massaging his arm, which began to return to life with pinpricks of pain.

It had been 266½ miles and 2 hours 43 minutes and 53 seconds of wearying work, but it brought him his first triumph at Bristol since 1967 and his second in twenty-eight starts here. It earned his team $5,350 and increased his lead in the driver standings.

Parsons settled for $3,825 for his car's second-place finish. "I hated to call for relief, but I was just plain worn out. I just couldn't make it anymore," he apologized. Darrell Waltrip, who also received relief, complained that his right arm had gone numb. Told that Petty had proceeded with the same problem, Darrell admitted, "He's some man then because I don't know how he did it." Then he caught himself and added, "I don't know if his arm was as numb as mine."

Maurice drove home to let Richard rest.

Before the following Sunday's Atlanta 500, a cracked cylinder head was discovered to have been to blame for the overheating at Daytona and Rockingham, and Maurice angrily went to work to replace the part and correct the problem. At the 1.522-mile oval twenty miles outside Atlanta in the countryside around Hampton, Petty drove his Dodge almost 160 miles per hour in the time trials to top David Pearson's Mercury by a few ticks of the electronic timers in the qualifying runs. The two bitter rivals, sponsored by rival liquid additives—Petty by STP, Pearson by Purolator—were ready to run for victory from the front row.

Richard is so relaxed that it sometimes seems he would sleep all day if he was not awakened. Often he sleeps until a few hours before a race and arrives at the track just in time to get into his car. Unwilling to take any chances on Richard getting caught in a traffic jam on the long drive to the track this race day, Maurice and Dale decided to take him to the track with them when they went, which as usual was early. At five in the morning Dale shook a protesting Petty awake, and Richard rode grumpily in the back of their rented car as they drove under dark, threatening skies to the track. Once there, Richard located a cot, stretched out under a wool blanket and went back to sleep while his crew readied his car for the event.

It was one he had never won, though he had won the later event of the season at Atlanta, the Dixie 500, four times, including the last time it was run, the preceding season. Refreshed after a couple of hour's added sleep, Petty sat on a workbench in his garage sipping a soft drink as the race drew near. "It doesn't matter that I haven't won this race. I've won races at this track. It's the track that counts. A race is just a name. I wouldn't even know I hadn't won it if you didn't tell me so. If it's one I haven't won, I want to win it. There's only a few like that left. But I want to win 'em all, you see," he said, smiling.

Some 55,000 fans flooded into the grandstands surrounding the course. In the garages within the oval, the drivers pulled on their fire-retardant coveralls. The pit-to-car radios inside their helmets were checked out. The crews buttoned up the cars and pushed them out onto the asphalt mainstretch, the drivers following with their helmets held in their gloved hands.

"It's a good, fast, safe track," Richard said. "I'd rather run a handling race track than a horsepower race track and this is a handling race track. I count on my car more than my engine. The way this track is set up with two long corners and two short straights it's more important to get through the turns smooth than it is to go down the straights fast, and that's my kind of race course."

The drivers got into their cars and moved away. The green flew and Bobby Allison burst past Petty and Pearson to move his Matador into the lead, but he fell from the front, tearing up his suspension as he yanked his car around to avoid a spin by Rich Rudd in the early going. Indianapolis 500 champion Johnny Rutherford bounced off a barrier into Joe Mihalic's car, eliminating both. Three-time Indy king A. J. Foyt's Ford threw a bolt from its water pump, sidelining him.

Early on, the race resolved itself into a Petty-Pearson match, with big Baker hanging on. The leaders darted in and out of the pits in swift stops to resume racing on the track, unable to gain any real advantage as the miles fell away and the long, swift race wore on in a thundering duel. They swapped the lead seventeen times in 450 miles, with Petty leading for 163 laps and Pearson for 142. As the race closed, the crowd was screaming for their favorites in this classic test while the crews of the STP Dodge and the Purolator Mercury worked and worried the day away.

Pearson led with seventy-five miles left, but a tire flatted on him and he had to make an unscheduled pit stop fifty laps from the finish. He lost not only the lead, but second place also as Baker barreled by on the track before David could get back to speed. Petty led by thirty seconds and seemed safely on his way to winning when the engine exploded in Lennie Pond's Chevelle, causing an accident and dumping oil on the track. The yellow signals slowed the sliding cars with eight laps left, and Dale advised Richard there was no way workers could clean up the course before the finish, meaning he would win under the yellow with no passing permitted.

However, as they counted off the last lap and then another lap, and the checkered flag did not fly, the crews started to holler at anyone who would listen to them. Then, suddenly, the green and white flags flew simultaneously, signifying racing was resumed with one lap left.

Baker, who had closed in during the slowdown, suddenly shot his Ford up to the Petty Dodge. Richard accelerated, and they roared around the oval on the last lap with the fans hollering at them. Slowly Petty pulled away, and as he came around the last corner and flashed under the checkered flag, he was three lengths in front of his foe.

After three hours and forty-six minutes, Petty pulled his Dodge into Victory Lane with his third victory of a season that was just six races old.

"We run two laps too many," Maurice observed as he poked his head into his brother's cockpit.

"Dang right," Dale agreed.

"Somebody goofed," Richard said, and shrugged. "As it worked out we won her anyway."

As it turned out, other crews agreed with them. Each keeps his own count. Only the officials did not agree. They keep their count, and that is the one that counts. Of course, it is difficult to keep track in long races such as these with cars coming in and out of the pits and passing and being passed and slower cars getting lapped. Mistakes are made, though maybe not many major ones.

"I would have hated to have had Buddy beat me because of the way it worked out," Richard told the reporters later. "I could outrun him all day. It wouldn't have been so bad if David had done it, because he ran with me all day and I don't know what would have happened if he hadn't had tire trouble."

He said he was happy to have won the Atlanta 500 at last, but just as happy to have a check handed him for $17,000. He had then, three months into the 1975 season, boosted his eighteen-year take to $1.8 million, which worked out to an average of $100,000 a year.

Undressing in his garage, Richard observed, "A lot of struggle went into those winnings."

6

TO THE TOP

In 1958 and 1959, his first two years on NASCAR's Grand National tour, Richard Petty entered thirty races, did not win any, and earned less than $10,000. In his next two years on the tour he entered eighty-two, won five, and had enough high finishes to place second in the driver standings for 1960. His earnings for 1960 and 1961 rose to more than $55,000.

Richard was only twenty-three years of age and his brother, Maurice, a year or so younger when they had to operate their team alone most of 1961 after their father's accident. Richard responded with eight victories in fifty-two races in 1962 and fourteen victories in fifty-one races in 1963, earning more than $100,000 for the two campaigns.

He finished second in the driver standings in both 1962 and 1963 and won his first title in 1964, when he won his first superspeedway event, the Daytona 500, and eight short-track races in sixty-one starts. He earned almost $100,000 for that one campaign alone.

His third child, Lisa, was born in September 1964. He was a young family man on the move, and it hurt him to have to sit out much of the 1965 season at the request of Chrysler after its powerful engine was outlawed.

"It's hard to get to the top and harder to stay there," he said at the time. "I'm twenty-seven years old and just approaching my peak. By not defending my championship, I'm losing five hundred dollars a race in appearance money alone, to say nothing of what I would win. Do I get the itch to run? Man, I itch a whole lot. But I am not going to break trust with my sponsor."

So he went drag-racing across the South. "We have just jumped right in," he said. "We're running that newfangled class they call funny cars—stock cars all tricked up. We built us one and are building another. We're working real hard on it. It's as much a challenge to make this kind of car faster than the others as it is our Grand National cars."

Then he sighed and confessed, "It's just something to do. It's not what we want to do. It can't make us the money we're missing out on."

After his racer ran amok into a crowd in Georgia and a little boy was killed, Richard retired the car. "I felt so bad about that I just didn't want to do it anymore after that. I just lost interest. When my crew saw I lost interest, they lost interest."

So they parked it and waited. To their relief the restrictions were altered in midseason, and the Pettys returned to NASCAR racing in June. By that time, Ford was the dominant car in the competition. Driving Fords, Ned Jarrett was on his way to the title, Junior Johnson was on his way to the most victories, and Freddie Lorenzen, Dick Hutcherson, and others were on their way to major victories. John Holman and Ralph Moody's Holman & Moody racing team were also readying Fords flawlessly. The Petty team of Chrysler cars had some catching up to do.

In his second start of the season, Richard Petty's number 43 pale-blue Plymouth surpassed the Nashville Fairgrounds Speedway qualifying record, led most of the race, and survived a torrid duel with Junior Johnson to win the 400-lap event on the half-mile oval. Climbing wearily from his car, Richard said, "I have not run such a long race in a long time and I'm plumb worn out."

Without waiting to celebrate his return to Victory Lane, he went to his truck back by the garages and stretched out on the front seat with a cool, wet rag on his forehead. When a young man asked why he hadn't bothered to kiss the pretty Miss Fairgrounds Speedway, who was left with only a trophy in her hands, Richard giggled and said, "I figured if I couldn't do it right, I'd rather not do it at all."

Plagued by mechanical troubles, he would win only three more races the rest of the year, but he wound up with four victories, three second-place finishes, and two third-place finishes in his fourteen starts. He earned $16,000 despite missing most of the tour. "Heck, we missed out on that much in appearance money alone," he sighed sadly. "I'm just glad to be back."

In 1966 Richard got back in the groove. Up until that season all of his victories except the one in 1964 at Daytona had been on short tracks, but in 1966 he became the first driver to win the Daytona 500 a second time. He did so with a tremendous comeback after tire troubles put him two laps back. He won the Rebel 400 at Darlington by four miles over Paul Goldsmith, and the Dixie 500 at Atlanta by four feet over Buddy Baker.

Petty explains, "I think I had proven I could drive with anyone by winning on the short tracks where the driver matters more than the car. But it wasn't until I got a more powerful car that I could start to win on the long tracks where the car matters more than the driver. You have to be a good driver in a good car to win on any track, short or long, but it's a matter of what matters most. My ability was wasted on long tracks until we got something that could go with the good cars."

He won five short-track events that season. However, he hurt the ring finger of his left hand and had to sit out a few races and was handicapped in others. "I didn't hurt it in no wreck or nothing like that," he confesses sheepishly. "I hurt it playing touch football back of the garage before dinner one night. It gave me a whole lot of trouble in the long races, so I had it checked by a doctor. He discovered torn ligaments and said if I didn't have an operation I'd wind up with a stiff finger the rest of my life. So I went into the hospital and had it fixed. I lost two weeks, but in the long run I guess I made the right move."

It dropped him down to third in the driver race and he had to settle for less than $80,000 in winnings. He had only eight victories in thirty-nine starts that year, while David Pearson went fifteen-for-forty-two for his first title. But once Richard healed, he was hungry, and in 1967 he all but ate up the opposition. Ford had pulled out of racing because of restrictions on its engine in 1966, but it was back bigger and better than ever in 1967. However, it just couldn't keep up with the Pettys and their Chrysler cars.

This was the year Lee Petty resigned as racing chief of the team. As Richard remembers it, "Pa had picked up a few golf clubs and golf balls and had started to practice with them on the Petty Country Club course, which combined the front yards of his house and my house. One day he went to a real golf course to play a real round for the first time and he shot an eighty-eight. He didn't think there was anything unusual about it at all. That was the kind of athlete he was. And that hooked him.

"He started to sneak out of the shop to play. He was sitting in the shop one day, sort of staring into space, thinking, when suddenly he got up, got his golf clubs out of the office, and went to the garage door. Maurice and me were watching him. He just turned around and said, 'Okay, boys, it's all yours. If you need me, I'll be at the golf course.' He left and in a way he's never come back.

"Oh, he still has a say in anything he wants to have a say in. He's around a lot. After all, he lives next door. But he's usually on the lawn hitting golf balls. Or at one course or another playing around in the 70s and wondering why he didn't take up golf instead of racing. He doesn't even come to many races anymore. He just leaves it to Maurice and me and Dale."

Lee laughs a little grumpily and says, "They can take care of it. They don't take my advice anyway."

So in 1967, with Maurice building powerful engines and Dale and Richard tearing down new Plymouths and building them back up with strong, nimble chassis, the Petty team hit the heights. Richard won ten straight races to surpass the previous record of five in a row, and twenty-seven in the season to surpass the previous record of eighteen. These may remain in the record books. It takes a lot of opportunities for a driver to win twenty-seven events; they are running a lot fewer races now than the forty-eight they ran that year, and the mechanical magic it takes to win ten straight is almost miraculous.

"It is unbelievable that the car didn't break down somewhere along the way," admits Richard. "But we finished forty-one of the forty-eight races and finished in the first five in thirty-eight out of forty-eight, so obviously Maurice and the crew gave me cars I could go with. The credit is as much theirs as mine, maybe more. Most of the ten straight were short-track races, but we still had to hold together for more than two thousand miles to win 'em. We ran around ten thousand miles at racing speeds that season and only once in a while did we have any trouble."

It was by far the greatest year he'd had, maybe the best season anyone ever has had up to now. It started slowly. Richard lost Riverside to Parnelli Jones and Daytona to Mario Andretti, but after that the Indianapolis invaders returned to their regular tour and Richard started to trim the NASCAR regulars. His car had caved in at Daytona, but once it was beefed up, he could have beaten almost anyone, including the Indy crowd, almost any time.

His first big victory of the season was the fourth in his streak. He led all but 25 of the 291 laps of the Rebel 400 at Darlington to defeat David Pearson by a full lap. This was the fifty-fifth victory of Petty's ten-year career and surpassed his father's six-year-old record of fifty-four established over thirteen years in the hard days of stock-car racing. Richard refused to make much of it. "Daddy didn't have the best cars and he didn't have as many races to run. You can't compare records. Our years were different."

This was Richard's year. In succession he scored victories at Winston-Salem, North Carolina; Columbia, South Carolina; Weaverville, North Carolina; Darlington, South Carolina; Hickory, North Carolina; Richmond, Virginia; Beltsville, Maryland; Hillsboro, North Carolina; Martinsville, Virginia; and North Wilkesboro, North Carolina. When he won the Sandpiper 200 on the half-mile at Columbia, where his career had begun back in 1958, he surpassed the single-season standard for victories set in 1952 by Tim Flock.

Richard's streak was snapped in disappointing fashion in the National 500 at Charlotte. He was running with the leaders when Paul Goldsmith's car blew a tire and swerved into Richard, crashing him out of contention. "It had to end some time," he shrugged. "We'll just have to start a new one." He could not get another one going like the first one, but he did continue to win more than his share of races as the Sundays slipped away.

Following his second successive victory in the Rebel 400 at Darlington, Richard won his first Southern 500 there to give him a sweep of the season's races at the South Carolina arena. He also won the Carolina 500 in his home state at Rockingham to give him three wins on superspeedways for the season.

"Winning the Southern 500 may have meant more to me than any other race this year," Richard remarked at the time. "It has a special place in the hearts of stock-car racers and I've tried seven times to win it before. This place has just lived and breathed bad luck for me.

"Just last year I led this race with five laps left when I blew a tire and had to settle for second place. A few years before that I led with four laps left when I blew a tire again. Another year I led another four laps from the finish when another tire blew. I've had my battery break and my ignition wires burn off when I was on my way to wins here.

"This year I led this one by five laps and still I feel lucky to have won," he said with a sigh. "I kept waiting for something to go wrong."

There was not much that went wrong with Richard's racing in 1967. "It was one of those years when most things went right for me," Richard recalls. "Twice at Darlington accidents happened right in front of me and I got by 'em both. Sam McQuagg rammed Dick Hutcherson and flipped all over that track one time. Another time, Bobby Isaac sideswiped a car and two cars ran right into them. Both times there were spinning cars and wreckage all over and debris just raining out of the skies. It was scary as could be, but I got by.

"At Nashville I was leading when I blew a tire, hit a fence, and bent my car all out of shape. I went to the pits figuring I was finished, but the boys went to it and hammered this and hammered that and told me to take it back out. It looked awful, but it worked. It was still the fastest car, but I had lost eight or ten laps. I stood on it and started to pass cars. I never could have caught the fast cars, but one by one they broke down. Winds up, I win by five laps. Just unbelievable!

"At about that point I got to thinking that there weren't no need for those other cats to keep on running. We outrun 'em in some and outlucked 'em in others, but one way or another we like to beat 'em to death. When I was winning the ten in a row, I began to believe I couldn't lose. That helps because you drive with confidence. I had confidence in my car. And in myself.

"Now I'm not the kind of cat who believes he's better than anyone else. I believe my team is the best, but I believe we've got to get the breaks to win any race, and I never expect to win every race. There's too many good drivers and good cars out there; you can always make a mistake and your car can always fail. That's racing. But '67 was just one of those years when my ego got swollen a little. Everything worked for us. Charlotte brought us back to earth, but we just went back to work harder than ever."

Among other records he set that year was a single-season standard for winnings, $130,000. By that time he was a one-third partner in Petty Enterprises. The partners sunk a large slice of their returns back into the business, making a massive addition to their compound in the form of an outsized garage. It was so big it was termed a "race-car preparation center."

The most modern facility in car racing, its opening was celebrated with an open house to which fans were invited for a fee to be donated to charity. The state police were stunned by a turnout of around 14,000 fans, who clogged the highways and side roads. Richard sat for four hours straight signing autographs.

With his second driving title he had become the brightest superstar in stock-car racing. The nation's motorsports press voted Petty the Martini & Rossi Trophy as "Driver of the Year" in all racing.

Ford went to work that winter and produced a superior engine that surpassed the Plymouth in power. Cale Yarborough swept both races at Daytona and won one at Darlington in a Mercury. LeeRoy Yarbrough and David Pearson won other major races in Fords, and Pearson drove his Ford to the driving title.

Richard had one of his most impressive performances, though he settled for third in the final standings. He won fifteen short-track events and capped his campaign by winning the American 500 at Rockingham. He admits, "I may have won that last one on determination alone. We were outclassed on the superspeedways. I had to hang it all out and take chances I don't like to take to win on the short tracks."

He won $80,000, which wasn't bad, but would be the last time up to the present he failed to win at least $100,000 on the tour.

Prior to the 1969 season, the Petty team startled the stock-car racing world by switching from Chrysler to Ford. Chrysler wasn't catching up to the Fords and the Petty team believed they would get a better deal from Ford. A lot of fans who perhaps picked up on Petty because he drove a Plymouth were disappointed, but those who rooted for the driver, not the car, remained loyal. However, Richard and the rest never were comfortable with the new car.

Richard recalls, "When the trucks started to pull up to our plant to unload Ford cars and equipment I had the funny feeling they were making a mistake, that all the stuff was meant for Holman & Moody Ford in Charlotte, not Petty Plymouth in Level Cross. I felt like telling them to take it back.

"Maurice and Dale did, too, after they started trying to put together all that strange equipment. They were about the best in the business at the stuff they knew, but this was a whole bunch of new stuff. For them, it was like starting all over again and it was tough.

"I found out how tough it was when I took those new cars out on the track. They were better cars, but they handled different than our old cars and I had to find a feeling for them. It was a lot more different than you might think."

In their first race for Ford that season, on the road course at Riverside, Richard lost control twice. Once he went backwards through the S's. But he wanted so much to do well that he drove hard enough to make up the ground he lost. He won, but it was downhill after that.

It was a remarkable feat, Richard winning his first race in a new car on a road course. He says, "It was my ninety-second win, but my first at Riverside and my first in anything except a Plymouth. However, wins were hard to come by that year after that, so maybe I was trying too hard. Maybe it was me. It wasn't the car. LeeRoy Yarbrough won the Daytona 500 and other big races, in a Ford that year, and David Pearson won the driving title in a Ford."

Riverside is not a true superspeedway, but it was the only long race Richard won all season, though he won ten out of fifty events he started, finished in the top five in more than half his starts, finished second in the standings, and earned almost $110,000. His most memorable win was at what he called "little-bitty" Bowman-Gray Stadium in nearby Winston-Salem, because it was the hundredth of his Grand National career.

"It was 250 laps of the quarter-mile track, only 62½ miles and so no one noticed much. We throw those kind back now," he notes. "I was lucky because Bobby Isaac led 240 laps and ran out of gas. I remember Daddy came up to me afterwards and asked me what I was going to do now that I had broken through the hundred-win barrier. I looked up at him and smiled and said, 'Go for two hundred.' It was just a joke back then, but then one hundred had seemed impossible when I was starting."

At one point he won two races within eighteen hours in Tennessee—the Smoky Mountain 200 at Maryville on a Saturday night and, despite collapsing from heat exhaustion after that one, the Nashville 400 on a Sunday afternoon—each by a car length.

He recalls, "We went to Nashville the previous week but got rained out, so we had to double up the following weekend. I needed oxygen in Nashville. Woooeee, it was hot. We were pushing awful hard to make it all year. Every dime counted because we weren't making many dollars."

At the time he told a reporter, "I guess I got all the money I'll ever need, but I'm too young for rocking chairs, and they don't go fast enough for me anyway."

When Chrysler came up with faster cars, the Dodge Daytona, and then the Plymouth SuperBird, they pulled the Pettys back into their fold for 1970. "We were going where the money would be," Richard remembers, "but we were ready to return to the kind of cars we knew best, anyway. Plymouth paid for two cars for the big races, so we put Pete Hamilton in one and it paid off when I broke down at Daytona and Pete went on to win it."

For a few years the Pettys put two cars in the big races. Hamilton drove some. Buddy Baker drove others. Tiny Lund drove some. They won some, too, but not enough to cover costs. And dividing the crew into two and taking on new members hurt Richard's chances, so the doubled effort was discontinued. However, it helped in 1970 when the Dixie 500 at Atlanta and the Carolina 500 at Rockingham were the only other superspeedway events the team took.

The Dixie was a drag race to the wire with Buddy Baker and was Richard's first victory at Atlanta. "I'd run there about twenty times without winning one, so I was real happy about winning it," he recalls. "I don't know why I didn't win there before, but those things happen where you just don't get the breaks at a track that seems perfectly fine to you. Buddy could run with me in the straights, but not in the corners. I got through the turns better and I got away from him at the finish. Buddy run a bunch of seconds that season. It was one of those years for him."

It was one of those years for Richard. He has few fears, though he does have some fear of heights. He is not especially superstitious, but he was bothered by a bad dream. He dreamed he, Maurice, and their mother and father were flying through a thick forest in a small plane and kept hitting trees until they crashed to the ground, alive, but battered and with their craft torn apart. "Man, I woke up in a cold sweat," he remembers. It stuck to him like a stain.

The dream came the night before the Carolina 500. He worried about it before the race. And when he lost control of his car in the race and went into a sideways skid, he thought, "That dern dream. I'm gonna crash." But after he regained control of the car and went on to win, he dismissed the dream as meaningless.

However, the dream returned to haunt him in the next major race, the Rebel 400 at Darlington, his "hard-luck track." His car got out of control and struck the concrete wall coming out of the fourth turn, skidded sideways into the mainstretch, took off, rolled in the air, and tumbled end over end wildly before pounding to a halt along the pit wall in front of the main stands. The car was upside down with Richard hanging half out of it.

It was the worst accident he has had in racing and it left him unconscious. Francis Allen of the Junior Johnson crew was the first to get to him, followed by Buck Brigance of Charlie Glotzbach's crew, and driver LeeRoy Yarbrough, who was in the pits after his car was sidelined. They pulled Petty from the cockpit in case the car caught fire.

"It don't matter what team you're with, when a driver is hurt, you help," points out Petty, whose cousin Dale would dart from the pits to rescue a rival from his wrecked racer in 1976, just before it exploded in flames.

Petty was placed on a stretcher as the crowd of 42,000 fans watched in silence. He was hurried to the hospital in the infield, but he came to swiftly and soon was found to have only a dislocated shoulder, cuts, and bruises. When Lee Petty told the track announcer the good news and it was passed on to the crowd, the fans stood and cheered.

He was supposed to be sidelined six weeks. He did miss six races. But he was back racing in four weeks and back in the winner's circle within six. Despite an aching shoulder, he drove determinedly to win on the road at Riverside in the late-season event there. Awkwardly, wearily, he worked his way from the cockpit. "The accident shook me up, but it didn't shake my desire to race," he said.

"Maybe it scared my family or my fans, but it didn't scare me. I just got back in and began to drive harder than before. I always knew it could happen any time and I never gave it a second thought. If you thought about those things, you couldn't, or shouldn't, drive racing cars." Laughing, he added, "One thing though, I don't plan to dream anymore."

He wound up with eighteen victories in forty starts and finished fourth in the driver rankings, led by Bobby Isaac, which probably would have been led by Richard except for the races he missed. As it was, he won almost $140,000 to shoot his career earnings near the million-dollar mark.

Entering the 1971 season, he reminisced, "I remember the first money I ever made. I earned about a dollar a day working in the tobacco fields when I was seven or so. I never even knew there was a million dollars anywhere. I read about millionaires. Me, I just wanted to make a living some day."

Winning his third Daytona 500 by ten seconds over teammate Baker near the beginning of the 1971 season, Petty picked up the fattest purse of his career—$46,450 from a total prize list that topped $200,000. Weaving through a series of wrecks two laps from the finish, he won the Carolina 500 at Rockingham to tie the record of twelve superspeedway victories established earlier by Freddie Lorenzen.

He had led the last 143 laps at Rockingham. He led the last thirty laps at Atlanta. The lead changed hands twenty-seven times, and he had to survive a stormy battle with Bobby Allison over the final forty miles to take a dazzling Dixie 500 by a single car length, with the fans standing and shouting at the finish. This gave him his record thirteenth superspeedway win.

The $20,000 payoff put Petty over a million dollars in earnings. Only A. J. Foyt among car racers had beaten Richard to it and Foyt had benefited from three fat winning purses at Indianapolis. If Daytona paid off as does Indy, Petty's earnings would have been out of reach. Richard had won more than twice as many races as A.J.

"I don't want to make too much of the money," Richard said with a big grin. "After all, it took me fourteen years to earn it. And we spent three million winnin' it. It's not all mine, anyway. A right good piece of it, mebbe, but not all of it. I'm still just a poor ol' country boy trying to keep my head above water." He was thirty-four and he could swim in wine if he wanted.

He was just back from an eastern swing that produced three short-track triumphs in four days and nights in New York and New Jersey in which he picked up purses of $1,500 and $3,800 and

$6,700; and Atlanta stretched a new winning streak to five races in a row. Maurice and Dale just put the Plymouth on the track and Richard brought it back first Sunday after Sunday.

He also won the American 500 at Rockingham, the Texas 500 at College Station, and the first Delaware 500 at Dover. In all, he won twenty-one races, finished in the first five thirty-eight times, and failed to finish only five of forty-six starts. The car, prepared by Maurice and Dale, endured a record 12,870 miles and earned a record of almost $310,000. To top it off, Richard matched his father with a third driving title.

King Richard opened the 1972 campaign by conquering Riverside in his old Plymouth, but it was not a Petty-blue Plymouth. As Chrysler and other car companies withdrew from the expense of sponsorship, the teams sought other backers and Andy Granatelli's STP Corporation got behind the Petty team.

Andy wanted the Pettys to take on STP red, but was refused. They compromised on a combination of the two colors, as it is today. And as they moved into the season, the Pettys switched to another Chrysler car, a Dodge, which they deemed aerodynamically superior though similar to the Plymouth.

When Petty put STP in Victory Circle in his first start, Granatelli's grin was as big as his belly. Richard won only one other superspeedway event that season, however—the Alamo 500 in Texas—and only six other races. However, to go with his eight victories were nine runner-up finishes and eight third-place finishes.

With the withdrawal of the car companies, a lot of teams cut back to a single big-track car, and a lot of small-track events were canceled. The schedule was cut by a third. In a reduced slate of thirty-one events, Petty piled up enough points to capture an unprecedented fourth driving title.

The big money remained. All but ten of the events were big-track classics. Richard earned more than $225,000. STP's veteran publicist Bill Dredge remarked, "Richard's like a slot machine. You put some money in, pull the crank, and more money comes out."

At the conclusion of his fifteenth year on the Grand National grind, on the eightieth lap of the last race on the schedule, the Ontario 500 in California, Richard completed an unprecedented 100,000 miles on race tracks.

But it was a tough season for the Petty team. Others won more major races. Bobby Allison and David Pearson won six super-speedway events each. Others were earning big money now, too, and Allison led in winnings for the second straight season, following a $235,000 season with a $270,000 year.

Another difficult year followed for the Pettys in 1973. Fooling around with a riverboat gambler's long hair, long sideburns, and Fu Manchu mustache, Richard flew to his fifth Daytona 500 victory, but followed with only one other superspeedway win—another Alamo 500 triumph in Texas. He won only six of twenty-eight starts, settled for second in the standings, and fell a little short of $150,000 in earnings.

It was not a bad year, but others did better. Benny Parsons parlayed one first-place finish and twenty-one top-ten finishes into sufficient points to pick up the driving title. David Pearson won ten superspeedway classics to set a single-season record. He took the career lead with twenty-three, to twenty-two for Richard. And Pearson soared into the big-money class with almost $215,000 in earnings.

Many rated Pearson's crew, the Wood Brothers team, superior to the Petty team. The rivalry between the teams was as intense in the garage and in the pits as it was on the track. On the track, the thirty-nine-year-old "Old Gray Fox," Pearson, and the thirty-six-year-old "King Richard" dueled dramatically in the big events. Bobby Allison and Petty had been roughriding one another.

"Some seasons everything seems to go right and some seasons everything seems to go wrong," Petty pointed out. "Every year the cars are changed. No sooner do you get ahead than the other guy catches up and passes you. There's only a few top teams and drivers, but it's hard for one to dominate the others. Consistency is what counts the most. Over a stretch of seasons the good guys will get most of the gravy."

In 1974 most of the gravy went to the Pettys, who pocketed almost $300,000 in winnings compared to $220,000 for Pearson and $115,000 for Allison. The surprise of the season was the comeback of Cale Yarborough, who earned $255,000.

Petty won ten events and finished in the first five twenty-two times in thirty races. He swept to seven victories on superspeedways, dominating Daytona for the fifth time and the second in succession and winning also the Talladega 500 in Alabama, the Dixie 500 at Atlanta, the Delaware 500 in Dover, the Carolina

500 in North Carolina, the Purolator 500 at Pocono, and the Motor State 400 in Michigan. He won his fifth driving title.

Meanwhile, Pearson rested between big races, passing up most of the short-track events on the tour. In His Purolator Mercury, Pearson won seven of nineteen starts, six on superspeedways. Allison won only two of twenty-seven races, only one on a superspeedway. He drove an undersized American Motors Matador on the track, prepared by Roger Penske and sponsored by Coca-Cola. Cale Yarborough came through with ten wins, four of them on superspeedways, in thirty starts in his Junior Johnson Chevy.

Entering the 1975 season, Petty had won 164 races to 84 for Pearson, 43 for Allison, and 28 for Yarborough. Pearson, however, had won 30 on superspeedways compared to 29 for Petty. Pearson and Allison had become million-dollar winners, and Yarborough was closing in on his first million, but Petty was pushing toward the two-million-dollar mark. "I just keep on shoving," pointed out Petty as he started his sixteenth tour at the top.

7

APRIL

The first Sunday of April 1975 found NASCAR's Grand National gypsies in North Wilkesboro, North Carolina, on their seventh stop of the season. Here was scheduled the fifteenth annual Gwyn Staley 400, a 250-mile race over the five-eighths-mile banked asphalt oval.

The track was known by his rivals as another "Petty Place." No one else had won at this track more than twice, but Richard Petty had won here eleven times and said he thought he'd make it twelve: "It's a real nice track. It gets greasy and slick so the car really has to handle right, which works out well for us."

As usual, David Pearson and Bobby Allison were passing up the short-track event, but Buddy Baker was in, as were the regulars such as Cale Yarborough, Darrell Waltrip, Dave Marcis, and Benny Parsons. On Friday afternoon Waltrip had surprised, outrunning Richard by a few ticks to take the pole position at 105.5 miles per hour with a run around the oval in 21.3 seconds.

On Sunday afternoon, Richard remained confident. Less than one hundred miles from home, he said, "I can usually win this one and get home in time to cut all the grass, but I got too much grass now." He grinned. His wife and kids were with him, watching him. A few more than 15,000 fans worked their way into the grandstands of the old oval and set up a whoop and a holler when the big cars roared away at the start of the race and Petty passed Waltrip right away.

On the fourth lap, Waltrip took the lead. On the eighteenth, Petty took it back. Waltrip started to drop back then as the power plant in his Chevy started to sputter. Petty made no effort to pull away from the pack at that point, preferring to save his stuff. He held the lead for about eighty laps, but lost it on a pit stop.

Yarborough led for a couple of laps, Baker for a couple, Parsons for a couple. Even Lennie Pond led for seven tours.

Petty flashed in front again on the 112th lap, but five laps later Bruce Hill lost control of his Chevy and spun in front of Richard, who could not avoid him and sideswiped Hill's car. The yellow caution signals came out and Richard limped into his pit with the left side of his car crumpled. His crew rushed repair work, but bent metal was all it amounted to.

So as not to lose a lap, Petty darted his Dodge out on the track just ahead of the leaders during the slowdown, then went back into his pit for a second time for further repairs before going out again. He fell to fourth, but avoided losing a lap. When the green signals sent the field racing again, Richard ran hard to make up the lost ground and gobbled up the asphalt.

Yarborough swapped the lead back and forth with Marcis and Parsons for about sixty laps, but Petty passed them all to reclaim the lead on lap 179 and started to pull away from the pack. Neither Cale nor any of the others could keep up with him after that. Richard lapped them all. By the time he took the checker after 2 hours 46 minutes and 39 seconds of racing, he led by three laps, with Cale coming in second in his Chevy and Baker booming up in the late stages to take third in his Ford.

Richard had led 310 laps, including the last 22, and he picked up a paycheck of $6,675 for the STP team and 185 points to pad his driving lead to about 200 better than Benny Parsons. As Dale loaded the damaged Dodge on the trailer, he laughed and said it sure looked like a loser. Richard grinned and said, "You can make it purty again. It'll give you something to do next week."

They had something to do, but it was not to fix this short-track car, which would not run again for three weeks, but to prepare their superspeedway car for Darlington the following week.

Darlington's second race, the Southern 500, over Labor Day weekend, is its biggest one, but the Rebel 500 in the spring is big, too. A purse of more than $110,000 was set out for the thirty-six drivers who would qualify to start the event and a crowd of 40,000 or so fans was expected to turn out.

All week, as the crews arrived and unloaded their cars and started to ready them to run and the drivers fidgeted and took them out to practice and then fidgeted some more, it was gray and gloomy and splashed from time to time with rain showers.

"The Old Lady," as the narrow track was called, loomed as imposing as ever. Richard Petty, who had won this race twice in the middle 1960s, nevertheless seemed as gloomy as the weather. "This isn't my favorite track," he said of this place where he had crashed so spectacularly a few years earlier. "This was the first big track built for us, but that was back in 1950, and now, twenty-five years later, it's outdated. It's like Indy, built to race half as fast as we go now. It was built for speeds of 75 or 80 and now we run it at 150 to 160. It's like a half-mile track only you have to go twice as fast as we go on the half-miles.

"It's a one-groove race track and the guy that's got the groove owns the track. You have to get out of the groove to pass and there aren't any good places to pass. You go high and you get right up to the wall. Turn one is one of the worst places to pass, so when the field takes off, it's right tight.

"Turn three is probably the toughest turn we have on the entire tour. Just getting through it is tough. If you've got a car on either side of you, it's scary. Usually you get so high you brush the wall. So many cars have brushed the wall and rubbed paint off on it that they call the streak of bare metal on our right sides 'the Darlington stripe.'

"They reworked it a few years back, but it's still bad. It was built as a mile and a quarter without much banking, but they pushed out most of the turns and banked it a bit more and it became a mile and a third or so, but it's still sort of flat and nasty narrow.

"You got no room to go anywhere. You can't get out of the way of anything. You make a mistake or someone makes a mistake near you and it becomes a demolition derby. I really feel it takes more luck to win here than any other track we run. I seen so many sure winners look good all day and wind up looking bad at the end of the day it's disgusting."

Dale said, "The turns here are all different and each one is cockeyed. The driver is never satisfied because you can't set up the chassis for any one turn, you have to compromise, so the car rarely handles right. It's a bitch."

Almost all of the other drivers agreed, with similar gloom, but David Pearson, who had won this race three times straight, disagreed. "It's a race track like any other race track. They're all different. You run 'em all different. You can learn to run this one just as good as any other."

The Wood Brothers' forty-year-old veteran driver seemed somehow even more determined than usual, maybe because he had not won a race yet this season, while Petty had won four, including the last three events on the schedule. "I told Glen and Leonard I was a little tired of hearing about Petty outrunning everybody and I was going to go hard," Pearson said privately.

Pearson, small and strong, was born and reared in a small mill town near his adult home in Spartanburg, South Carolina. As a boy, he built powerful hands, arms, and shoulders hefting heavy spools of cotton. He quit school at sixteen to get married and became a race driver.

Four months after his first child was born, he bought an old car for forty dollars and told his wife he was going racing. She offered to go to work to support him if he'd forget it, but he wouldn't. His mother offered him thirty dollars if he'd sell his car. He took her thirty dollars, sold the car for seventy dollars and bought a better car for a hundred dollars.

There was no way he wasn't going to race, though he admits he knew nothing about it at the start. He learned fast and moved up fast. He fell into a factory ride with Pontiac and won three superspeedway events in his second season in Grand National competition in 1961. "I don't know how I did it," he admitted later. "I had a good car, but I wasn't that good."

During the next six years David did not win a single superspeedway race, and for a couple of years he did not win a race of any kind. It was assumed his luck had run out. The good teams did not want him. He bounced from team to team, until he landed on a team with which he could win in 1968. He won sixteen races and was on his way to the top at last. However, he still had trouble sticking with his teams.

Almost painfully shy much of his life, he admits, "I had so little education and spoke so poor there was a time I hated to open my mouth." Life educated him, and gradually he began to emerge, though he still detested the spotlight and refused most of the public-relations appearances most sponsors expect of their drivers.

Dark and handsome, with a face that showed his Cherokee Indian heritage, David and his wife, Helen, had three sons and lived quietly away from the track, but he was a terror on the track.

The Wood Brothers of Stuart, Virginia, used him as a backup driver to A. J. Foyt when the Indianapolis superstar was busy with USAC events. Wanting someone who would give everything to Grand National, the Woods made David their regular driver and parted from Foyt in 1972.

Since then, these mechanical marvels and this driving daredevil had been enormously successful, but there were rumors flying around Darlington in the spring of 1975 that they were dissatisfied with David because of his Daytona mishap and might part from him because he drove too daringly.

In his garage, Glen Wood growled, "I have never heard any rumor so ridiculous in my life. We have never had a cross word with David. And we have won more than twenty events on the big tracks and more than $600,000 during the short period we've been together. Pearson not only is skilled, he's smart. There isn't a better driver on the circuit today, and that includes Richard Petty."

Leonard Wood added, "When people start rumors like this, they create trouble where there wasn't any before. We're happy with Pearson and he's happy with us. It's not true that he takes foolish chances. He takes chances, but you have to take chances to win. He wins, even if he hasn't won yet this year. He'll win our share for us, you'll see."

By Friday the skies had cleared and a fired-up Pearson thrust his red-and-white Purolator-sponsored Mercury around the egg-shaped 1.366-mile strip of asphalt at 155.433 miles per hour—faster than anyone else had ever threaded this thin track. His gun was cocked. Petty, Waltrip, and young Dick Brooks also bettered the old mark, while Allison, Parsons, and Yarborough also put their cars high in the starting lineup.

Fifteen laps into the 367-lap grind on Sunday, Yarborough's engine expired and his day was done almost before it had begun. Pearson and Baker led early. Petty stayed close to the top pack until a series of spins and crashes brought out the caution flags, sent the cars darting into the pits, and swapped the lead around among numerous drivers.

"Some of those cats who lead early never have run an entire race," Petty points out, shrugging at the foolishness of it.

Richard took the lead about two hundred miles into the event as the others stretched out behind him, bumper to bumper at high speed, like an express train, rolling round and round the treacherous track, cars uncoupling just long enough for pit stops, then rejoining the roaring ribbon of expensive machinery.

A couple of crashes and two blown engines littered the track with some debris the cleanup crews missed. On the 188th lap, Petty's tire was slashed by a stray piece of metal. As the tire popped, Petty's car careened front-first into a wall and spun off it. He got it stopped, then started and took it into the pits, pulling his hurt machine behind the wall for Maurice, Dale, and the rest to wrestle with.

They pulled off the hood and tried to straighten the front end while Richard sat and watched the race get away from him. His crew sent him out again then, but he ran only a couple of laps before he brought it back in and parked it, finished for the day. "Most others would have left it the first time, but we're hard-heads," shrugged Richard. They were packing up while the rest were still pursuing the Rebel rewards.

Pearson, Parsons, and Waltrip were racing for the lead. Allison had fallen two laps back, penalized one when he passed the pace car during a caution period. His team manager, Roger Penske, radioed him, "We're beaten. Just do the best you can." Bobby made up one lap: as another caution bunched up the cars, he came up behind the bunch, and passed them when the race was resumed. But he still seemed beaten with forty laps left.

A cut tire took Pearson into the pits and out of a ten-second lead and into a twenty-second deficit. He came out charging, caught Parsons and with fifteen laps left went to pass him in the first turn. Parsons had the groove and would not give it up. Pearson put his car below Parsons', then drifted up into his car; the two banged together, their wheels locked, and they went sideways up into the outer barrier, where they came to a screeching stop, torn apart.

While their crews cursed and the cleanup men came to the rescue, the caution signals came out and the remaining runners bunched up behind the pace car again. Making up another lap, Allison caught up at the tail end of the pack, then passed six cars to streak into the lead as green showed and racing resumed. Waltrip was right behind him, but he could not get by him. Bobby led the last eight laps to the checker, the only laps he led the entire race.

Following his incredibly lucky come-from-behind triumph, Allison smiled and said, "You just don't never give up in a race, especially here where anything can happen." It was the first victory of the season for the thirty-year-old father of four from Hueytown, Alabama, who had won more than forty races in fifteen years on the Grand National grind, including victories on every superspeedway except Daytona.

Waving the $15,080 first-place check which went to his Matador team, he was on his way to his sixth straight season with $100,000 or more in earnings, including two seasons with $200,000 or more. "I remember years when I won nothing, nights when I went hungry," admitted the slender Alabaman. He now raced everywhere appearance money was offered him, including sportsman races other Grand National stars did not bother with.

The Penske crew packed up happily, while the Pearson and Parsons teams wrapped up their equipment unhappily.

Poor Parsons said, "I had the groove and I wasn't going to give it up for anybody. What was I supposed to do—go high and drop back and settle for second, or hang in there and hustle for first? All of a sudden he was alongside me, he hit me, and I lost a car and the race. There's no need to blame anybody. David was trying to win. That's racing and racing luck for you." Benny's crew chief, Travis Carter, said, "Things like that happen, but I saw it coming and I hated it."

Pearson, holding himself as though he were hurting, sat in a dark corner of his garage and said, "I thought Benny would back off and let me by. I had no idea there would be any problem. There just wasn't enough room. There was oil on the track, too, and I may have slid some. It's hard to tell sometimes when you're inside one of those cars and they start to move on you and you don't have complete control. I hate that it had to happen."

Having seen his driver crash out of the lead trying to pass another car for the second time in three major races, Glen Wood growled, "I have nothing to say. I've said it all already. Pearson's still our driver."

Driving home in his pickup truck, Glen Wood struck and killed a six-hundred pound Black Angus bull on the highway near Parsons' home-town of Ellerbe, North Carolina. At least it didn't belong to the herd owned by L. G. DeWitt, Parsons' sponsor, as first suspected amidst some hard laughter.

Back home in Randleman, Richard Petty commented, "Once I crashed out of it, I couldn't've cared less how many times Parsons and Pearson crashed as long as they wasn't hurt none. Once we're out of a race, we get out of the track and go home. We're racers, not fans. We got another race to get ready for."

The Petty-STP team was ready for Martinsville's Virginia 500 the last Sunday in April. He won for the fourteenth time there where two times was tops for anyone else. And with it he won his fourteenth grandfather clock promoter Clay Earles awards each winner. "We got 'em all over," grinned Richard afterwards. "We got a couple or three at our house, a couple at Pa's place, a couple at Maurice's. Dale has one or two. My in-laws have one. Just about everyone I know has one."

Earles has an outstanding operation at his half-time. Offering $70,000 in prizes—more than any other short-track, more than some superspeedways—he pulls an impressive array of drivers and draws around 35,000 fans, who fill the grandstand at a top ticket price of ten dollars.

The place was packed on race day and the fans were roaring from the first. "They are maybe the most enthusiastic fans of any track we run," Richard Petty remarks. "It makes you want to run here. Along with the money and the clocks," he smiled. "It is a bad track, but it has been good to us."

He held back in the early going of this 262½-mile tour of the .525-mile oval. The asphalt surface started to tear up early, tearing chunks out of the tires of the cars who careened around. Two long delays created in an effort to clean up the surface failed to improve matters.

Parsons, who put himself on the pole with a speed above 85 miles per hour, paced the pack for the first thirty miles; but once the track tore up, the race became a scramble. It seemed as though everyone except Petty led for the first two hundred laps. Racing conservatively and carefully, Richard did not take the lead until the 201st lap.

He led all but thirty-seven of the remaining three hundred laps, though he was pressed by Waltrip for a while. With fifty laps left, Petty pitted and took on four fresh tires, allowing Waltrip to take the lead. However, Richard then caught him with twenty laps left and was pulling away through the last laps to win by almost twenty seconds.

In this 3-hour-37-minute-20-second short-track marathon, it was a matter of mind winning over matter. Sitting in Victory Circle later with the applause of the audience washing over him, Petty pointed out, "The way things were going, I wasn't sure I could outrun Darrell, but with fresh rubber I was sure we could. So that's what we decided to do and that's what won for us."

In his garage, young Waltrip admitted, "I knew the fresh tires would win for him, but there wasn't anything I could do about it. I didn't have time to take on tires, too. I was slipping and sliding all over that track those last laps. I had all I could do to hang on to second place. I know I couldn't have lasted another ten laps or so without one of those tires going for good."

Petty picked up the winner's check for the fifth time in the eight Grand National events run through April in the 1975 edition of the circuit named after the cigarette sponsor, the Winston Cup tour. He also picked up 185 points to clinch the lead in the first phase of the season's driving competition, worth a $10,000 bonus to him. And he picked up $19,250 in prize money, including a $5,000 bonus for leading the most laps, 263.

He also was hugged by Be-Bop Hobel and Doshia Wall, tall, long-legged gals in shorts and tops, who shivered as late afternoon brought cool winds across the Virginia countryside. Be-Bop, an advertising saleswoman for a television station who doubles as Miss Winston weekends, parading around in a checkered costume that says "How Good It Is" all over, said she was happy her long weekend was over. Doshia, a model who becomes Miss Union 76 Oil on weekends, said we wouldn't believe the hours they put in touring the circuit.

Be-Bop said, "The last Miss Winston left to get married. I'm a new sort of Miss Winston—sort of unbusty, more like a sister than a sex goddess." Doshia said, "I suppose we're selling sex, but we're really just supposed to be something nice to look at." They swore they didn't care who won. The winner, Richard Petty, didn't give them a second look—well, maybe just one little-bitty one—as he left on the less-than-a-hundred-mile drive home to the wife and kids.

8

THE RACER AND THE RACES

Former Indianapolis champion Parnelli Jones once said that when he started driving recklessly in jalopies it was because he wanted to prove he was braver than the next guy, and when he started racing cars professionally it was because he wanted to do something most others would be afraid to do.

Grand National king Richard Petty says that he never felt the need to prove his bravery and that it never occurred to him when he went into racing that he was doing anything unusual. The fact is all kinds of fellows enter racing for all kinds of reasons.

"Maybe it was different for me because my daddy was a racer. I grew up in racing, it was my way of life, and it was sort of natural for me to go into it. I'm not sure if it's that way for all the sons of racers, but a lot of 'em do follow their fathers.

"Maybe some of 'em want to prove they're as brave as their daddies or maybe some of them are scared off by this dangerous thing their daddies do, but me, I never thought about being brave or about having to prove anything to anyone. It's just something I thought I could do that I wanted to do.

"I didn't do it for money or anything like that. I mean when I was starting no one was making a lot of money in stock-car racing. My daddy never did. He made a living at it and I thought maybe I could do that, too, but that's as far as it went.

"Maybe if the life had been dull I'd have been turned off of it, but I didn't think about it being exciting. I mean it was the only life I knew, just like being in the restaurant business is the only life the son of a man who owns a restaurant knows.

"I know most people wouldn't do it, but I know a lot of people who are doing it. I'm around them every week at the race tracks. They're the people I know.

"As far as that goes, I don't think I could throw a football the way Kenny Stabler does or run the way O. J. Simpson does. As an athlete I feel like one of 'em, but I admire their ability to do something I couldn't do the way maybe they admire a race driver.

"In fact"—he laughed—"most people drive cars, but few play football and a lot of us never skied or ski-jumped or skated or played ice hockey."

Is a race driver an athlete then, as some seem to doubt?

"You better believe it. I'm not much of one for tooting my own horn, but I'll speak for my sport. It's as tough as any sport and it takes an athlete to compete in it.

"The race driver has to have the reflexes, eyesight, strength, and stamina of any athlete.

"He has to wrestle a car that weighs three to four thousand pounds for three to five hours, and I want to tell you it takes all the physical strength a man can have to keep it on the track and under control. And to last all the way. It gets roasting hot in those cars sometimes. There's no air-conditioning and no oxygen breaks.

"If he gets involved in an accident, the driver really has to wrestle that thing. That's when reflexes matter most. Whatever you have to do, you have to do right then.

"And driving in tight traffic, speeding up and slowing down at just the right times, passing and being passed, there isn't a time your reflexes aren't important.

"Also, eyesight. You have to see it to handle it. And you have to see it before it's too late. Eyesight is as important to a race driver as to a baseball batter. You have to see everything that's going on, and it's happening fast. If you see it soon enough, you give your reflexes the extra split second they may need to take care of it.

"And you have to be mentally alert. I can 'see' things sometimes before they happen. Experience is in this, too. What I mean is because of a certain way a driver or a car may be behaving or the way a situation develops, I can anticipate something that's going to happen before it does. I often know when a driver is going to lose control of his car or something's going to give on the car or a tire's going to blow.

"And, except for fifteen seconds or so on our pit stops, we don't have time-outs the way football and basketball players do. We don't have breaks between innings or periods or at half times. We can use relief drivers, but we seldom do. We don't use substitutes the way football teams do or play in shifts the way hockey players do. We go as far as our cars will take us almost every time out.

"Near the end of long races I'm sometimes so tired I may say to myself I just ain't gonna turn that wheel when I get to the end of a straight. But I always do.

"The strain is just tremendous, both physically and mentally. We can't afford to make mistakes. If a football player fumbles or a baseball player makes an error, it may cost them a touchdown or a run. If we mishandle our cars, we'll wind up on a wall and that could be the end. If a basketball player or a hockey player isn't alert, it could cost him points or goals. If we're not alert, it could cost us our lives. If a basketball player lets up on his concentration it won't kill him. We can't let up at any time.

"Some say we're not athletes because we depend on our cars. Well every athlete depends on something. Did you ever see a golfer without a club? The club is no good to him if it's not the right one for the job or if he doesn't use it right. Well, our cars are no good to us if they're not right and we don't use 'em right. You don't just climb into a car. You're fit into it. You wear it. Like you do a glove. It does what you make it do.

"Ours is a team sport. If you're going to be the best, you need the sponsor with the money behind you to buy you the best equipment, and you need the best mechanics to put the car and engine together right and keep it running right and give it what it needs in a hurry on pit stops. But, out on that track, the driver is all alone. Unlike most sports, he has no teammates to help him or hurt him, he has only himself to account for his driving performance.

"In football you maybe need the emotion to go out there and hit harder. In baseball you maybe need control of your emotions to hit a hard, curving pitch. In golf you have to be calm under tension; you need just the right touch. In car racing, you need to absorb the bumps, keep calm, control your car, and handle it with just the right touch. It's all athletics. And we're athletes as much as any others, maybe more than others."

Richard grew up in racing and started pretty much at the top "I had done every kind of a job a man can do on a car except drive it in a race before I went racing, so I knew a lot about what I was driving. Some men know nothing about mechanics, but I know what's happening in a car and I can explain it to my crew so they know. Sometimes I can even tell them how to fix it.

"A lot of the boys we race with were winners in sportsman ranks, but when they come into Grand National it takes them two or three seasons to start winning; it's that different. I got into Grand National right quick and it took me two or three seasons to start winning, so I was even with them without their background. We had to learn new things and I didn't have to unlearn any bad things.

"I learned a lot by watching, but mostly I learned by doing. Pa never had time to teach me a lot, but when I first started drivin', he'd tell me I was doin' this or that wrong. Never that I was doin' this or that right, of course. He still tells me sometimes, but I don't listen so much anymore. We all have to have our own ways of doin' things, anyway.

"I used to find the fastest groove by following the best drivers around and going where they went, and when I got to where I could go by one of them, I'd pick up on another one of 'em. But, gradually I began to find my own way. Everyone has his own style and he finds the places on the track he handles best.

"Most drivers run high but Pa preached to me to run low on the short tracks, and I listened. Every time I'd get to goin' around on the high side, he'd just ream me out. He said that on a short track the more you ran the shortest way around, the shorter you made the track. He ran down in the infield half the time to save time. He was about the best there ever was on the short tracks, so I did as he did.

"He never said much about the big tracks because he never ran them that much or pretended to know them that much, and after a year or two I knew more about them than he did. A lot of us young guys came in and just blew the old guys off on the superspeedways because we came in when the new tracks did and we learned on them, whereas the old guys had to unlearn everything they'd learned about racing.

"You can't drive the long tracks the way you do the short tracks. You can't drive the low groove on the long tracks because you're not going the same speed all the way around and you have to come out of the corners hard in order to speed up to top speed down the long straightaways. I tend to drive the high groove on the long tracks, but it depends on the track. You go the same groove as everyone else, you won't go any better than they do. You have to find a better groove.

"You find your groove running by yourself in practice because then you can put yourself anywhere on the track you want and you can experiment. I'll take one line for a few laps, then try another. It's difficult to guess your speed sometimes, so I'll have my crew tell me my speeds. It's funny, sometimes a line that doesn't feel as comfortable will be faster.

"If the car isn't handling right, I'll come in and Dale and I will talk it over and decide to try this or that to make it handle better and I'll keep taking it out to see how it works. As the handling changes, I'll have to try different routes around again to see if the speeds have changed.

"I've run all the tracks, so I know them all, but from race to race and from year to year they change. Maybe because the asphalt has altered. Or cracked. Or weather has affected it. And your car is always handling different. So you have to try things out until you find the right combination.

"But I probably run less laps than any other top driver. I just don't believe in overdoing it. I can find out fast what's happening out there. And depending on what's happening, I'll adjust to it. I want to get the car the best it can be before I adjust to it. When I get into a race and the crew can't do much more to the car, then is time to adjust to it.

"When you're in a race, you can't always run where you want to because someone else may be there. But by then you know where you want to be, so you do the best you can to be there as much as you can. And you adjust to the traffic the rest of the time. You've figured out where it's best to pass and where not to and you keep this in mind, then do what you have to do.

"Car-racing is not an exact science. You're out there with a lot of cars and they keep changing and the track keeps changing all the time you're out there. You can't predict exactly how your car or any other car will run, so you can't get a game plan and stick to it. You have to make adjustments as you go. So you decide what you want to do and then you go out and do what you can do. And I do different things unexpectedly to give the boys things to think about. I throw out a line to see if the boys will bite.

"I like a loose car. It's set up and sprung loose to move around a lot. I learned by driving loose cars, moving around a lot, because

I learned in cars that weren't as powerful as some and I had to handle 'em better to beat the others around. I like a loose car because I can hang it high all the way around. I like it high because it's cleaner up there and my tires stick better and I go faster.

"Most drivers don't like to run as close to the wall all the way around as I do. I scare some people I run so close to the wall. It's my trademark. But it's not as risky as it seems. When you're a few feet off the wall and something sends you up into the wall, you whack it good. But when you're within a few inches of the wall, a cushion of air develops between your car and the wall and you couldn't get through it to turn into the wall if you wanted to. I feel like I can control my car as well a few inches off the wall as a few feet from it. And if I do scrape it, that's all I'll do," he concluded.

Several drivers have said they started, or have been said to have started, the practice of drafting, which is peculiar to stock-car racing. Richard Petty never has said anything about this before, but he now says he started it back in 1962 at Daytona.

"I got caught close behind cars a couple of times and I noticed some strange things happening. I experimented with it a little and I found a way to go faster. I didn't win that race, but it was probably the best race I ever drove because I made the most of what I had.

"I experimented some more in the following races and soon I saw others following my lead. I can't say for sure I started it, but I never saw anyone else do it before I started to do it.

"It looks a lot hairier than it is. When one car is drafting another, front bumper to back bumper, inches apart, at 150 miles an hour, it's no riskier than at 50 miles an hour because if they came together the impact would be the same.

"Only a bad driver drafts a bad driver. I'll draft David Pearson and a couple of other cats any time, because I figure they won't do anything foolish, like suddenly stop or swerve unless they have to. And if they do, I'll just do what they do.

"I'd follow David down into the infield because I figure if he's going there, it's the only place to go.

"Except in an accident, the speed doesn't bother us as much as the average fellow figures. Our cars are so well balanced and handle so good and our tires get so much traction and our tracks are

so good that we can handle our cars at 150 better than the average
guy can handle his car at 50.

"We go better than 200 on the straightaways at a couple of
tracks such as Daytona and Alabama, but you get used to it so the
world slows down. You can pick out your pit or a person in your
pit as you pass because you're concentrating on it and you don't
care that the rest is a blur. You can see the marks on the wall
you want to see.

"In an accident it's something else, because you're out of control then and everything the car does is exaggerated according to
how fast you're moving. The faster you're going, the harder you'll
hit when you hit something. So as the speeds rise, so do the risks.

"Sheer speed is one thing, and acceleration is another kettle of
fish. An engine that responds real quick is as important to you as
straightaway speed, because you can make the passes you want to
make when you want to make them without too much trouble.
When a driver starts to pass and stops and then tries again and
again, he's wasting his car and hisself and his time.

"It's important to pick the right spots to pass and to pass
smoothly.

"It's as tough to run a short race as a long race, a short track as
a long track, a high-banked track as a flat track.

"The short race is all out all the way, with little time to make
up for any time lost. The long race tires you out eventually, but if
your car holds up, a lot of the cars that might beat you will have
broken down by the end.

"On a short track you're in traffic the whole race and turning
all the time, while on a long track you have to go faster and run a
lot longer.

"On a high bank the car sticks better, but it is still trying to go
straight when you turn, all the force goes down onto the track,
the car becomes heavier, and it steers harder. On a flat track you
lose traction when you turn and it's like steering on ice.

"They all have their problems for the drivers.

"I never worry about winning the pole position because we set
up a car as much for handling as for speed. You have to give up
something somewhere. I run as fast as I can when I qualify, so I
sometimes take the pole, but all I really care about is getting a
place near the front so I don't have to work too hard to get up
with the leaders.

"The race is not won the first few laps. The race is won by the car that runs the fastest and finishes. If you run too fast, you won't finish. There's never been a car fixed so you couldn't break it. It's your job as a driver to figure out how fast you can run and still finish. You have to have a feel for it and you have to find out early and run accordingly.

"Some drivers are too racy. They can't stand to be second. They have no patience. They not only want to lead, they want to get as far in front as they can. They usually don't finish, so they usually don't win. A lot of cats lead, but not many win.

"If the pace is slow, I'll take the lead. I want to find out what my car can do and what the cars of the other contenders can do. I want to know what Pearson and Parsons and Cale and Bobby and Buddy got on a given day. Most of the others I don't even give a thought too, whether they're first or last. I know who's gonna be up front at the finish if their cars hold up.

"Most of the time I'm content to stay near the front and keep my car together so I can race for the lead near the finish. That's what I call racing.

"There are better drivers than me, but I don't know if there are better racers. There are cats that can outdrive me for fifty miles or a hundred miles, but they push themselves past their limits or they use up their cars, and at two hundred miles or four hundred miles or six hundred miles they're long gone while I'm still in the race and racing when it counts.

"When the track gets slippery and hard to handle late in a race, that's when I like to race.

"Consistency counts. I drive deeper into the corners than most drivers. It's just my style. I get on the brake later and on the accelerator earlier than most drivers. A lot of drivers will drive in deep for twenty laps or forty laps or sixty laps, but the longer the race goes, the less deep they go, while I'm still driving deep at a hundred laps and two hundred laps and so forth. Pretty soon I'm getting through the corners faster than they are and picking up on them every lap.

"A lot of drivers will beat me down the straights but will be beat by me through the corners. They may be able to go faster, but I may be able to get around faster. In racing, the race is not always won by the fastest. The difference between drivers a lot of time is knowing what you and your car can do in a race and not

Part of Richard's wild crash at Darlington in 1970. GREG FIELDEN PHOTO

Below, the 1974 Darlington crash.
GREG FIELDEN PHOTO

A smile even after defeat at Riverside, 1969. DARRYL NORENBERG PHOTO

43—*The Petty Story*, later known as *Smash-up Alley*, with Darren McGavin as Lee, Kathie Browne as Elizabeth, Richard, Lynn Marta as Lynda, and Pierre Jalbert as a friendly rival. VICTORY LANE ENTERPRISES

Richard, sporting riverboat-gambler mustache, and Andy Granatelli sporting comb in Victory Lane following the 1973 Daytona 500. NASCAR PHOTO

Richard at left and Bobby Allison at right lead into the stretch in the 1972 Atlanta 500. NASCAR PHOTO

Allison has a slender lead at the race's end. NASCAR PHOTO

The Petty pit crew in action. Bottom photo is at Michigan in 1974 and Dale Inman, Barry Dodson, Wayne Dalton and Maurice Petty can be seen on far side of car, ill-fated Randy Owens to rear right. TOP PHOTO, STP; BOTTOM, DORSEY PATRICK

An anxious Richard Petty, wet rag stuffed in his dry mouth, prepares to take off from pit stop. DAYTONA SPEEDWAY PHOTO

The 1975 Daytona 500—Buddy Baker's Ford drafts the Petty Dodge. NASCAR PHOTO

A dented Petty Dodge slingshots inside Cale Yarborough's 11 Chevy en route to victory at North Wilkesboro, North Carolina, 1975. DOZIER MOBLEY PHOTO

Part of the Richard Petty pit crew prior to Talladega tragedy: Left to right, Maurice Petty, Randy Owens, Wade Thornburg, Richard, Barry Dodson, Dale Inman.

Richard talks things over with Cale Yarborough before the World 600 at Charlotte.

One of the critical pit stops in which the STP Dodge 43 crew outsped the Coca-Cola Matador 16 crew, credited by Richard Petty with narrow victory over Bobby Allison in the Tuborg 400 at Riverside Raceway, 1975. TOM SHAW PHOTO

knowing. Maybe I think about it more than most drivers. Track and car conditions change as the race goes on. You can't race like a robot. You have to keep thinking. And making adjustments.

"Now I know David is always thinking. And Bobby, for example. I don't have any advantage over them in this. But we have an advantage over a lot of the others, which is maybe why we win more. Of course we've got the good equipment, but four out of five drivers out there could take my equipment and not make anywhere near as much of it as I can. David could, maybe. And maybe I could take David's and do as well as he does. Most of them, forget it. It's just an excuse for most of them. Sponsors aren't stupid. Sooner or later most of the good drivers are going to get the good equipment.

"You have to keep thinking and working at it and improving what you've got. We can win Daytona with a car and if we don't make it better by the time we get to Darlington we'll wind up down the track, because the top teams will have made the changes they had to make to catch up and pass us. If we aren't getting better, we'll be getting beat," concludes the driver.

Richard can be, has been, and will be beaten many times, but his winning percentage of 25 per cent for his career and 35 per cent the last ten years was by far the best in the history of this circuit. Pearson, for example, had winning percentages of 19 per cent and 27 per cent for these periods. On the championship car circuit, A. J. Foyt's career percentage of wins is just 22 per cent.

"It's been said I've been beaten on the last laps more than any other driver, but that's because I've been running for the lead on the last laps more than any other driver. I've also won more on the last laps than any other driver," Richard remarks.

"Our rules have been set so there is not much difference between our cars. Many times every season, a few inches, a few feet, maybe a car length is the difference between winning and losing. It's exciting, for the driver and his crew as well as the fan."

I recited from a list of some of the close finishes Petty has lost on the last lap: "In 1971, you lost a lot of races on the last lap. You lost a wheel-to-wheel duel with Foyt by two seconds in the Atlanta 500. You lost a duel with Bobby Allison by one second in the very next major race, at Talladega. At Daytona you lost the Firecracker 400 to Bobby Isaac by four seconds. You lost the Firecracker 400 four straight years by one to four seconds. You lost this race to Pearson in 1972, 1973, and 1974. You couldn't get past him in 1972, and he got past you in 1974. He held you off by less than a car length in the World 600 at Charlotte in 1974."

Richard replied, "I think if you check the qualifying times in the trials in the race you'll find that every time we lost a close one to David, he had the faster car. I feel we were doing well to be so close to him we could push him at the finish and beat him if he made a mistake.

"He makes mistakes, but he never seems to make 'em when I'm the one he's got to beat. Maybe I bring out the best in him. He's tough though. And he's always got a quick car. And he's always willing to shoot the works when a win is in sight. Give him credit.

"But we won some close ones from him. And from some of the others. We won some on the last laps."

I pointed out, "You held Pearson off in the Motor State 400 in Michigan in 1974. You beat Bobby Allison by less than a car length in the Dixie 500 at Atlanta in 1971. . . ."

He said, "You could go on and on. There's been a lot of 'em. It's tough to run four hundred or five hundred or six hundred miles and lose by less than a car length, by a few feet or a few inches, by a second or two seconds or three seconds or four seconds, but that's our racing. It happens so often it's just part of it, and you learn to live with it. Like baseball, it's a game of inches. And if a cat beats you, it doesn't much matter whether it's by one foot or one lap."

"But couldn't you make up that foot somewhere?"

"It looks like it, doesn't it?" Richard laughed. "You think if you run five hundred miles you could make up a foot or two to win somewhere. But the kind of deal it is, the other cat run five hundred miles, too, and he wasn't giving away any ground if he could help it. Maybe you had a slower pit stop here and he made a bobble there. A lot of things tend to even out over a long distance if two cars are competitive.

"Of course, when it comes down to the last lap, it looks like the driver you want to win should be able to put just a little more into it and win. But the other driver is putting everything he has into it, too. Probably you've both been running flat out for a while and there just isn't any more speed in the cars than you've already gotten out of them and neither of you has been able to open up a real lead.

"Now when you are in the last lap and close, you might take a chance you wouldn't take a lap earlier and maybe one of you makes a mistake or one of you lucks out and that's it, but you've both driven into the turns as deep as a man dares go and you've both got your foot to the floorboard as you charge down the stretch and the one car can either catch the other or he can't. If he can, he's still got to pass him.

"Last-lap races are drafting duels usually. Most times they seem to be won by one car slingshotting around another at the finish. That's why we say it's better to be second than first going into the last lap in this kind of finish. But you've still got to make your move just right or you won't catch the slingshot just right. And the leader may be moving around to break up the draft, and he'll take up as much of the track as possible to stop you from passing if he can.

"You've got to use your judgment if he's the sort of driver you can draft and slingshot around and if your car and the conditions are right for it. Or maybe you'd rather get the lead when you can and hold it and let him try to pass you. You got to decide where and when to pass. It's like a football play. You can call it ten times and maybe it's a good play, but no one time will it work exactly like any other time. You got to be good, but you got to be smart. And sometimes the best thing you can be is lucky."

I said, "Luck has run against you a lot of times. In 1960 you led Darlington until your battery failed, got up to lead again, and a tire failed and you were beaten by Buck Baker. In 1962 you led Darlington when a tire failed with only four laps to go and Larry Frank went on to win. In 1964, you were leading Darlington by four laps when your ignition failed and Buck Baker beat you again. . . ."

He said, "You could go back to Darlington and look at every race and find where bad luck beat someone. That's that track.

"I remember my first race there—'59, I guess. I led the race, but I was a rookie and they thought they better turn the car over to someone with more experience.

"They put someone else in it and I watched him lose the lead in a few laps, and I said, 'Heck, I can run that good.' So they put me back in the car and I caught up near the end and I was coming up to pass the cat leading the race and the dang right front tire blew on me."

I noted, "In 1969 you lost to LeeRoy Yarbrough when your right front blew twenty-two miles from the finish of the Firecracker 400. In 1971 you lost the Southeastern 500 at Bristol when you lost the right front sixty-three laps from the finish. You lost to Lorenzen at Charlotte in 1964 when you hit a wall while leading near the end. That year you led Bristol about 450 out of 500 laps before your engine blew up. . . ."

"Hey, you're making me cry, here."

"In that Bristol race, you got back out there and caught up to within four seconds of Pearson before you ran out of laps. In the Riverside race in 1974, you were ten seconds behind Cale Yarborough with two laps left and you closed to within three seconds before time ran out. And as he crossed the finish line, his fuel ran out."

"But, we were catching it," Richard replied. "Boy, we were really coming on it. The deal was, I decided there was no way Cale could finish, as hard as he was running, so I let him lead. Then as we got near the finish, I decided he wasn't going to fall out after all, so I got to pumping on him. I just didn't start soon enough.

"I should have won that one."

"In the Miller 500 at Ontario in 1971 you led by twenty-five seconds with fifteen laps to go when you went to pit, missed your pit, had to go around and go back in again, and lost so much time you lost the race."

"I should have won that one, too. I came in too fast and blew right by my pit before I realized it. You know, you pit different places different races. It can confuse you, but it's your job to know where to go and there's no excuses for a driving error on that. Dale had something to say to me about it, in fact."

"Twice in two weeks your crew left the gas cap dangling when you left the pits, and you lost time having to go back in. Did you have something to say to Dale and the others about that?"

"Well, one time I just left too early. They weren't done, so they weren't none to blame. The other time maybe they were. But we all make mistakes. It's a game of mistakes. We make less mistakes than most, so we win more than most. None of us is perfect. We're racers, but we're human."

He added, "Like I said, between being good and being lucky, maybe being lucky is best. Being good, maybe you make your own luck. But if you make a mistake, you have an accident, and if you're lucky, you may miss it."

"It hurts, though, doesn't it, losing races that might have been won?"

"Sure it does, but you forget. Well, you don't ever forget, but you put it out of your mind. If you only run ten to fifteen races a year and Indy is the only big one like those USAC cats usually do, you remember the details of every 500 and it weighs on your mind, maybe. But when you run thirty or forty races a year and half of 'em are big ones, you can put 'em out of your mind, those you don't want to think about.

"Remember," he continued, "something's gonna happen every race. You keep plugging, and if you've got the goods, you're gonna do all right over the long haul. Whatever happens at Daytona, forget it, you got to go on to Richmond and Rockingham. Whatever happens at Darlington is history; you got to go on to Martinsville and Talladega. You don't keep count. You add it up at the end and see where you stand.

"One man's bad luck is another man's good luck."

"You've had some good luck, too," I said. "You won your one-hundredth race at Winston Salem when Bobby Isaac ran out of gas two laps ahead with two laps left. You've overcome bad luck. In 1970 at Rockingham you spun out twice and still came back to beat Cale. In 1973 at Pocono you fell a lap behind after a flat tire and came back to beat Butch Hartman. Lots of times you made up one or two laps lost early to win late. Once at Daytona you had to make more pit stops to replace more tires than anyone else and came from far back to win. . . ."

"Yeh, well, see, you keep pluggin' and you never know what will happen. Lots of times I was tempted to give up on races I wound up winning, so I learned never to give up. You put my pit crew behind a car and they can make miracles sometimes. So I always drive hard no matter where I am in the standings.

"The thing is, we rarely break down early in a race like a lot of cats do. As long as you're running at the finish, you got a chance to win or at least make some money. A driver can't abuse a car in five or ten laps. He can wreck it, but he can't abuse it. If a car fails that fast, it's the crew's fault. Of course it happens to all of us. We're dealing with a mechanical thing and sometimes a ten-cent part will fail and you're finished. But if a car finishes race after race, the driver has been given the chance to win and the credit is the crew's.

I pointed out, "You've won a lot of races by large margins. In the Old Dominion 500 at Martinsville in 1967 you won by four laps. In the Southern 500 at Darlington in 1967 you led 345 out of 364 laps and won over Pearson by five laps. The year before, you won the Rebel 400 there by four miles. In 1970 you led all but five of 153 laps to win the Falstaff 400 at Riverside. In 1971 you led the last 143 laps to win by a full lap in the American 500 at Rockingham. In 1974 you led 491 out of 500 laps to win by three laps at Delaware. I could go on and on. . . ."

"Could you?" he said, laughing. "I don't remember those races as well as I remember the others. It seems like there have been a lot more hard ones than easy ones. And I guess you remember the hard ones you lost a lot longer than the easy ones you won.

"From what Maurice and Dale and the boys say and the way they act, I think they feel the worst about the ones when you break down because maybe they could've done something to prevent it, whereas when they keep you running to the finish you're more to blame for losing than they are."

"On the other hand, " he concluded, "the hurt lasts longest for the driver when the crew and the car didn't fail him, but he maybe failed himself and he maybe feels maybe he was outdrove by another driver. The thing to remember is you're not the only good driver racin' out there. Some of those other guys are good, too."

9

———

THE RACER AND HIS RIVALS

Richard Petty spoke of his rivals: "Before I even started to race, I watched racers, and respected some and didn't respect others. But, I got into it so close to the beginning of southern stock-car racing that I raced almost all the greats, though some of them were past their peaks.

"I'm serious when I say my daddy was as good as any. His record speaks for itself and it says he did more with what he had than anyone ever. He started late in life and he may not have had the natural talent of some and he sure didn't have the equipment of some, but what he had, he put to good use. I think Lee Petty was the smartest race driver I ever saw.

"When I raced Daddy, he beat me like a dang drum.

"Jim Paschal was just about as smart as Daddy or anyone else. Now there's a name you don't hear much anymore because he didn't do that much. He hardly ever had a hot car, but when he had good equipment he won. There are drivers that impress other drivers even if they don't impress fans or writers. He was one.

"Now when I talk about natural drivers, I mean men who act like they were born in race cars. They drive it, they don't let it drive them. They sit in it and they have the touch to put it where they want it, the strength to get it there, and the smarts to know where it should be. Paschal was smooth and smart.

"Tim Flock was smooth and smart, too. He got the good equipment in his day and he won with it. It was his record of eighteen victories in one season that I broke, but maybe it was tougher in his day than mine. Or maybe not as tough. I don't know. I know he was a real racer.

"Flock and Paschal never looked like they were racing. They

never fought a race car and flung it this way and that way on a race track. They made it look easy and I know it's *never* easy.

"Flock was mostly a short-track racer because the big tracks didn't come along in time for him. When I was breaking in, Ned Jarrett was about the best there was on short tracks. He just did it on dirt. He was smooth and strong, a real racer. But he never did as well on the big, paved tracks as he did on short, dirt tracks.

"When I was a young driver, Fireball Roberts was the biggest name in racing. I was just getting going on short tracks and wasn't doing much on the long tracks, while he was mainly a long-track driver, so I didn't really race him that much. He was speed— qualifying and racing. I really respected his ability to flat run faster than anyone else.

"I don't think Fireball was the best because he wasn't as good on short tracks as he was on long ones and because he broke cars, but he was about as hard a man to beat in a big race as anyone ever was.

"Back then, Freddie Lorenzen was the best on the long tracks. He hooked up with Holman & Moody when their Fords were the classiest cars on our tracks so he had that advantage, but he made good use of it. He was smart and smooth; he didn't break cars and he took advantage of every opportunity that presented itself. He was lucky, but he took advantage of his luck.

"But Freddie wasn't the best because he never raced short tracks and he didn't know what dirt was. Fred never got dirty. He raced clean and neat.

"Now I don't think Junior Johnson was the best on either dirt tracks or paved tracks, short tracks or long, but he was one of the best because he won on them all. Most cats can't drive all kind of cars and courses, but all you had to do was give Junior wheels and a clearing and he'd race. He won a lot of races, but not a lot of big ones. He came along a little early.

"Junior was a tough competitor, too. All race drivers aren't tough, you know. Some don't win what they might because they're not tough enough. Daddy was tough. He'd do almost any- thing to win. He didn't care how much he won by, just so he won. If he didn't have to dent you to win, fine. If he did, he'd do it. Junior would do it anyway, just for fun.

"Buck Baker was as tough as anybody, but he wasn't choosy about what he drove. He'd get in any old car without worrying about how it was fixed up. He'd win with good cars and lose with bad cars. He just loved to drive. I'm not surprised to see him coming back into racing at fifty-seven or whatever he is. If anyone would, he would.

"Herb Thomas was tough, a real competitor, a real winner.

"Curtis Turner was a character, not a real racer. He's the most overrated of the old racers. He was a showoff and he didn't show me much. He could drive, but he couldn't race. He was so anxious to run up front all the time that he didn't finish half the time. It was as important to him to show everyone he could lead as it was to win. With a race car, he was a kid with a toy. As long as he was flat out, he didn't care if he was sideways or heading backwards. He didn't respect cars.

"Curtis wasn't trying to impress the fans. He was trying to impress himself and his buddies. He was the opposite of smart.

"Joe Weatherly went down that road with him. They cared more about the parties after the race than they did about the races. But Weatherly was a better driver than Turner. Little Joe went out to win and the parties were just icing on the cake. He was a good driver and he drove hard, but he tried to keep his cars in one piece. He respected racing more than Turner and didn't hurt it the way Curtis did.

"I think the drivers of those days were a tougher lot than those of today. They had to put up with more to get to the top. They'd had harder lives. But the good athlete wasn't going into the racing game in those days; there wasn't that much money in it. A lot of guys got into it late in their lives. Today the money attracts the young athlete. Today's drivers are probably better athletes.

"One thing, though, there's less room at the top. Before we got good cars and good tracks, the drivers were more important than the car and a good driver sometimes could win in a bad car. Now we got good cars and good tracks and the cars are more important than the drivers. Only the equipment and the cost of running it is so expensive that there aren't many competitive cars available.

"There is no way a good driver in a bad car is going to beat a Petty or a Pearson in a good car. I can go down the line at any race and eliminate half the field because both the cars and drivers aren't good enough and another fourth simply because the cars aren't good enough. There are only six or eight cars and drivers for me to worry about in any race and, depending on the race, only three or four I have any real concern about. And unless these all break down, there is no way an outsider is going to sneak in. He can't even stay close.

"Now, that's all right. How many good teams you got in football? Or basketball? Or baseball? If you got six or eight can win it all, you got a lot. So it's no different in racing. Maybe they make a mistake on a driver here or there and maybe a good guy gets overlooked, but for the most part the good teams take the good drivers. And because the drivers don't quit so fast, because the Pettys and Pearsons keep racing, there's not a lot of room for a young guy to get a break.

"Most of the best drivers today are the same guys I've been racing for six or eight years and they compare favorably with the best drivers of any day. I know I could run with any driver of any day, and David could, too. I won't say I'm the best driver, but I'll say that I'm as good a driver as there is in stock cars. I don't know about the drivers in other kinds of cars, but I don't think any of them are any better than any of the best drivers in stock cars.

"I won't say who's the best driver ever. I will say I think David Pearson's a better pure driver than I am and probably the best pure driver ever, but I think I'm as good a racer because I work better within a team and put the combination of driver and car and crew together better. That's what produces the end results. You could say I won the most so maybe I'm the best, but maybe I had a better chance than David did.

"The fact is, I think I have more confidence or desire than David or anyone else. I think most of the drivers are beat before they begin. They think they're going to lose, so they're going to lose. Some of the others may think they can win, but they don't expect to win. I know I'm not going to win every race, but I expect to win going into every race. If I lose it, I figure I'll win the next one. I don't think since we hit the top we've ever lost ten in a row. Everyone else has, more times than once. I'm the only one ever won ten in a row. Next best, I think, was Bobby, when he won five straight. So I won the next five straight.

"When I put the hammer down, some of those cats scatter. Not David. Or Bobby. Or some of the others. But a lot of them. They say, 'Uh-oh, here comes 43.' They been waitin' for it to come and when it comes they scatter. I think even David wants to beat me so bad that he doesn't drive the same against me as he does against the others and it takes something away from him. But he's beaten me a lot, so he knows he can. The other cats haven't, so they don't think they can, and it takes something away from them.

"As for desire, I'm not talking about winning. We all want to win. But when it looks like we can't win, we're all different drivers. I'm the kind of a driver that runs hard and never gives up. If I get five or six laps behind, I run harder than when I'm in front because I know I got to, to catch up. And sometimes because of this I do catch up. And other times I take a second instead of a third, or a third instead of a fourth. Which is why I'm always up there in points and in money over some drivers that maybe are winning more in a given year.

"I think there's only one or two others that run this way. Cale is probably the closest to it. He'll race anywhere on the track for anything he can get. And Buddy. Buddy will run hard all the time, though a lot of the time he won't get anywhere. I run hard under control, but Cale and Buddy are out of control half the time. Cale is a tremendous competitor, but he runs so close to the ragged edge that he'll spin cars more often than most good drivers. Buddy breaks cars he pushes them so hard. But these guys are physically stronger than anyone else on the tour, so they go hard and can outlast a lot of cats. They're strong-willed, too.

"Now David wants to win as much as anybody, and when he's in a position to win, he's the hardest driver I've ever had to beat. He doesn't always drive hard, but he drives smart. When he has to drive hard, he does. He's strong, so he'll last. A lot of drivers may be tough for twenty laps or two hundred miles, but David is one of the few you have to figure will still be tough at two hundred laps or five hundred miles. That matters as much as anything. When he has a tremendous team like the Wood Brothers behind him, you know he's going to be hard to beat. As for his pure skill, well he always knows what he has to do and when to do it and how to do it. He can handle a car so smooth it's a pleasure to see.

"Foyt is the only driver I put on a par with Pearson on pure skill. Foyt can do anything any man ever could do with a car. He's as strong as any driver ever, yet he's got a light touch and he knows how to win races. Any time I beat Foyt, I figure I beat the best, and any time he beat me I figure I was beat by the best. I don't know about the other Indy drivers because the few times I raced against them they were in stock cars and they didn't have the best equipment. Mario Andretti had a good stock car one year and he won Daytona, so I know he can go, but I really don't know that much about him. Foyt is the only one who's run stock cars enough so I know what he can do, yet he doesn't run them enough so he's done all he could do. If he ran them full time, I'm sure he'd be close to my record.

"I don't think he'd be better for two reasons: "One, he feels he has to do it all by himself. He builds and mechanics his own Indy cars, and while someone else builds and mechanics his stock cars, he's always putting his finger in the pie. When he was with the Wood Brothers, he won a lot because they wouldn't let him mess in. They had him ahead of Pearson, which shows how good Foyt is. But Foyt figures he can only count on Foyt. I don't just depend on Richard Petty, I depend on Petty Enterprises. I'm a team man, and in the long run a team man will win more than an individualist.

"Second, Foyt, and Pearson too, want to win too much. By that I mean they lose some races because they won't settle for second. They don't care about second or third, they only care about first. They don't care about a race once they find out they won't finish first. If they see they've got a better car and can beat you, they'll beat you. Put it in the bank. But if they see you've got a better car, there's no way they're going to beat you. They'll race you for a while, but if they see you're not going to give up, they'll give up.

"A lot of times when I don't figure to finish first and still run hard for second or third, I'll finish first because the car or the couple of cars in front of me will break down and I'm in a position to pick up the win. Foyt and Pearson don't pick up many scraps like that, but I'm not too proud to do it.

"I guess from what I hear Foyt was a great dirt driver. As strong as he is, I guess he really could wrestle his cars around. But he never drove stock cars on dirt against me. David did and he was sort of special on those old tracks, the best I ever saw. But we don't drive dirt much anymore. David doesn't drive short tracks any more. Depending on his sponsorship, he has driven the whole tour some years and only the big tracks other years. He's just been driving the superspeedways the last few years.

"There's some plusses and some minuses to this. David and his team can take more time preparing and pointing for the big races and they're fresher when they get to them. On the other hand, David lays off a lot and he may not be as sharp as I am. It's tough, but we only race once a week, not every day, and I think it keeps me and my crew sharp. I get to know the other drivers better. And when I get David on a short track I'm more comfortable than he is and usually can beat him.

"Now Bobby Allison drives more than any of us. He doesn't always drive the whole circuit, but he drives other circuits. If you offer him appearance money, he'll appear. And they'll offer it to him on the sportsman circuit because he's the only name driver they can get and he gives them a name to promote. He gives them their money's worth. He's a winner. But when you drive Saturday or Saturday night, you got to be tired on Sunday, and Bobby's tired a lot. He drives too much.

"One of the things I admire about Foyt is he won't even go to a race unless he's got a car ready to win. When he was young he'd race anything anywhere, but we're none of us as young as we used to be and we've learned not to waste ourselves. Allison jumps in and out of all kinds of cars and it has to hurt him. He's a good driver, but he hooked up with a car, the Matador, that was so underpowered he didn't have a lot of chance to do good the last couple of years.

"Bobby's brother, Donnie, is a good driver. He's a fast driver. He's fast more than smooth. He's better in time trials than in traffic. At least it looks like that to me. But maybe he hasn't had a real chance to show me. He hasn't had real good cars. He qualifies them fast and they break down fast.

"LeeRoy Yarbrough was stung by one of those Rocky Mountain spotted ticks or whatever they are and had yellow jaundice or something and was sick for a while and maybe it took something out of him.

"Now there's an interesting case. A lot of years you get a hot car or a hot engine that's so much better than anything anyone else has that it's going to win almost everything until the next year when the others catch up. One year—1969, I think—LeeRoy hooked up with Junior Johnson and they had by far the best stuff going for them and they won seven superspeedway races, which was unheard of in those years, and a pile of money. But the next year the rest of us caught up and passed him.

"He hadn't won much before and he didn't win much after, and now, when he should be at his peak, he's long gone. I don't know where he is or what he's doing. He was always a fast driver, and he was good or he could've never won what he won. But he wasn't that good. He wasn't as good as he thought he was and it hurt him when it went bad for him. He didn't come up slowly, learning, and he went down fast, without having learned.

"The sickness greased the skids for him. He was already on his way down, but he wouldn't have gone as fast. I think he started messing with booze or some sort of stuff and soon he couldn't get a good ride or any kind of ride at all and he just dropped off to the side of the road.

"Now you put some drivers in a Petty car or a Pearson car and they'll do better than they've been doing, but they won't do as well as we would unless they're better, which I doubt. There's a lot of guys always got excuses. This wasn't right or this isn't right. They blame everything but themselves. But if they show something, they'll get their chance. Most of them, when they get a good chance, they blow it.

"We put Pete Hamilton in a Petty car at one time and he made the most of it. He won a couple of big races, including Daytona. He had to be good to do it. But I don't know how good he was. When we couldn't get the sponsorship money to support two cars, we had to drop him, no one picked him up and, now he's in the minors. On the other hand, we had Buddy Baker in a Petty car and nothing much came of it. He ran exactly the same stuff I was, fixed exactly the same and he broke his while I won with mine. I believe Buddy is unlucky. He needs a stronger car than most drivers. When he gets one, he will win with it.

"There's a lot of drivers around like Cecil Gordon and Elmo Langley and Jim Hylton that have hardly had good cars at any time and it's hard to judge them. They don't run hard because they know their cars can't take it or their sponsors can't afford to replace anything they break. They don't dare qualify fast because they can't risk blowing their only engine. And they can't race fast because they can't risk ruining their equipment. They stay in the middle of the pack and they just try to make a living. Jim Hylton's won one or two big races, but he hasn't been a big winner.

"Dave Marcis has been around awhile without winning anything at all. Dave will drive hard and run fast, but he's so erratic on the track that drivers dread racing him and the top sponsors hate to take a chance on him. But if Dave will steady down, he's capable of winning.

"The most promising young guy may be Darrell Waltrip. He has ability and drives hard, but breaks cars so he hasn't gotten real good cars. He has a lot to learn and he's so sort of cocky I don't know if he'll take the time to sort things out, but if he does, he could be a comer. There's nothing more important to a driver than knowing your limitations and your car's limitations and I don't think Darrell is driving within those limitations.

"In Benny Parsons you've got a guy who has learned his trade and knows his limitations. He's no kid and he come along late, but he'll drive as good as his car is. He won a driving title doing that. He won one race, I think, but he piled up the points placing as high as he could in every race. I don't know how far he can go. Everyone can go just so far. But if you give Benny a good car he'll do a good job for you, and when things go his way he can win.

"I think the thing that happened at Darlington is that Benny is such a sportsman he will move over for a faster car because he can't win anyway, but when he was on his way to winning, there was no way he was going to pull over to permit Pearson to pass him no more than anyone else would. David was so surprised that Benny wouldn't just let him by that he went in tighter than he should have in an effort to squeeze by and he ran out of room and ran right up into Benny.

"Earlier at Daytona, I think David made a bad move trying to pass in a tough place to pass while leading late, but he probably made a wrong move four or five times in the race; we all make wrong moves four or five times a race and we usually get away with them, and this time the circumstances were such that he just didn't get away with it and he spun out and it cost him a win he wanted more than most.

"Maybe he wanted it too much. He's smart and maybe he did a dumb thing because he was so anxious. We all run into that, but maybe I don't as much as some because I don't get too anxious about anything. I take one lap at a time, one race at a time. I don't build myself up for a big fall before any of 'em. I have a race every week and if I don't win one week I look forward to winning the next week. David's running every other week or so, only the big races, so he may figure he has to win when he runs.

"I don't think it's a matter of me wanting to win any less than anyone else. I want to win every one. But I've won so much more than anyone else, I'm more in control of my emotions than the next guy. I've won the Daytona 500 five times. David's never won it once. I think I wanted to win it this year as much as he did, but maybe I could have played it cooler than he could.

"I think one reason I've won as much as I have is I'm hungry by nature. I don't think about the ones I've won as much as the ones I've lost. I love to win, but hate to lose. Because I've won so much, I can handle losing. But when I win one, I want to win the next one. The more I win, the more I want to win. And the more I lose, the more determined I get.

"I guess when you haven't won much, you have to be desperate and you get so determined, when you get a chance to win you take chances. David's won a lot, but he does take a lot of chances. David's done some things I wouldn't do."

"Like in the Firecracker 400 at Daytona in 1974?" he was asked.

"Right. I was drafting David going into the last lap in a position to pass him with a slingshot for the win. I guess I was where he wanted to be. So he put me there. We came down the stretch 190 or 200 miles an hour and, when we went into the first turn of the last lap with me right behind him, he suddenly let off the accelerator and slowed and I had to swerve as hard as I could to avoid running right over him and couldn't help running right by him. He accelerated and got right on my tail and drafted me around until he made the slingshot pass I'd wanted to make on the fourth turn, and passed me and won.

"It was smart, I suppose, but it wasn't right. We have unwritten rules we live by and he broke one of them and could have killed us both. I don't know that I've ever known him to do something like that any other time, but he wanted to win so much that time he did it. And he's lucky I didn't hit him or do the same thing back to him when he got behind me or swerve over and knock him into the infield when he went past me. I was so mad I might have done anything. I was too mad to drive right, or I might have had a chance to hold him off.

"The thing that hurt is I trusted David more than any other driver. I had complete confidence in him when I drafted him and I know he had complete confidence in me when he drafted me. When I'm drafting him, he could make a right turn or run through a fence and I'd follow him. I trust him that if something, cars spinning or something, happens in front of him, he'll make the right move, so I'll move with him. When he's drafting me, I know he'll work with me and try to make me run fast so he can run fast. He don't try to move around to mess you up or slow you down or any of that kind of stuff. We just get out there and run, man. And that's what it's all about.

"I don't mind getting outrun. He's outrun me before and he'll do it again. If he'd just outrun me, that'd've been fine. I'd just try to outrun him the next time. I've done that, too. But this was a dirty trick and the only reason he had the guts to do it was because he trusted me so much he trusted that I'd react fast enough to cut left and go around him rather than ramming right into him. He took advantage of our trust in each other. It really hurt because whenever you think you know someone and you find out they're different than you thought it's a hard thing to handle. I mean I lost a lot of my liking and respecting of David that day. But I've been getting it back. It hasn't happened again."

"It stirred up a storm of sorts?"

"Oh, sure. You know, we went up into the press box to talk to the writers and broadcasters the way the one-two finishers do and I said something to him and he said something to me and the press picked up on it and made a lot of it. The next day we was booked for a special appearance at his home-town track in Spartanburg and some photographers talked us into posing with our fists up. Those fans were hanging out of the rafters. The pictures were spread all over, but we never came to blows. We was sore for a while, but the press made more of it than there was."

"You turned the tables on him a week or two later."

"Four or five weeks later. As luck would have it, we wound up in the same situation at Talladega except I was leading and David was drafting. I didn't stop in front of him, but I slowed and he went on by. Then I picked up and laid on him. When we came out of the last turn, I slingshot around him. He moved over to try to make me back off, but I didn't move. Our sides scraped and sparks flew off the cars. There was no way I was going to give a foot and I just kept scraping past him and was four feet in front of him by the finish line."

"So you got even."

"That's what they said then. I said then, like I say now, no way. You never get even. You might have won this one anyway. The one you lost is lost forever."

"But you're all right with David now."

"Yeh. I mean we ain't buddy-buddy, but we can talk to each other, we respect each other, we enjoy racing each other. We don't do dumb things week after week in an effort to beat each other. It was something that happened and it hasn't happened again and it's history. You can't carry a grudge around with you and race the right way. I don't race David or Bobby or anyone else. I really race myself. I figure if my team puts everything on the track right, we can win no matter what anyone else does. When the time comes that what we put out there ain't good enough, then is the time to worry."

"You did have a dangerous series of duels with Bobby Allison a few years ago and it lasted a long time."

"Yeh, we did bend some metal back around '71 and '72. It really started a few years before that when he was breaking in and I was better than he was. He won a race at Rockingham and I think he thought he should win them all. One race, he had a quicker car but I was smoother so I could keep up with him. He went to pass a slow car and he made a bad move and I went by him without touching him. There were only eight or ten laps to go and there wasn't any way I was going to let him get back by me. The first thing I knew I was going into a corner sideways. When I let up, he kept coming and rammed me right out of it. Maybe you do that with $5,000 sportsman cars, but not with $40,000 Grand National cars. I wasn't too pleased.

"I was loading our car on the trailer when I realized Maurice and Dale were gone. There was a big crowd of people around the Allisons, and then Bobby burst out of it and ran down the road and here comes Chief, who can't hardly run, runnin' right after him. It seems like Maurice was so mad he'd gone over and thrown a punch at Bobby, and Bobby just took off. By the time I got there, Bobby's brother, Eddie, who worked on his car, had said something to Dale, and Dale threw a headlock on him and threw him to the ground. I never got to take a punch at no one. It didn't come to much anyway. Maurice and Dale were fined for it.

"There were hard feelings between us, but nothing came of it for a few years. Bobby began to do good and in 1971 he really got going. We whopped one another in races from time to time, but I swear I never hit him until he hit me first. Of course, that's my side of the story. You can go get his side too. In '71 we wound up racing up front a lot and neither one of us would give the other any room. You can bend fenders in stock-car racing without killing one another and we was bending fenders.

"We got into it at North Wilkesboro and we just beat on one another until by the time the race was over our cars looked like they came from a demolition derby. A sort of angry group gathered around us afterwards. I had taken off my helmet and handed it to Maurice and he was holding it. Some cat put his hand on my shoulder and Maurice turned around and swung that helmet and hit him alongside his head and laid him low. Everyone scattered. No one was going to go after Chief while he held that helmet in his hand. So that was that. But Bobby kept coming after me race after race.

"I think what it was is he was king of the sportsmen and I was king of Grand National and the guy coming up wants to knock off the champion. I was king of the hill and he wanted to knock me off. He had a Petty complex, but he didn't mean anything to me. I never had no trouble with no one else, so why should I pick on him unless he started it? But once he started it, I had to retaliate. I couldn't let anyone run me off the race tracks. So race after race we started to bump and bend metal. It was fun for a while, but then it got to be plain pitiful. I think we both got scared. Like someone was bound to be hurt if we kept it up."

"You've bent metal before in your day."

"Sure have. I'm no saint and never pretended to be. I've drafted cars that slowed down so I pushed 'em a spell to get 'em going better. A bunch of times I've come up behind somebody I've lapped ten or fifteen times, and deliberately tapped 'em or maybe run 'em off the track because they didn't belong on the track. Now, you should be ashamed of doing something like that, because that poor fellow probably is running as good as he can and he'll get out of your way. But you do do that, I must admit. We all do.

"I can remember one race, Cale was coming up on me and I was coming up on another cat in a corner and as he turned I tapped him and got him sideways. Cale had to slow sharply to avoid him and I picked up three or four car lengths on Cale. I can remember going under a car, and him dropping down to block me. The next time he dropped down, I knocked on his rear and turned him around into the infield.

"You have to know when you can and when you can't do things like this safely, but I'm as guilty as anyone of doing them. With our big old cars we can get away with it. But what Bobby and me was doing wasn't safe. It was becoming clear we couldn't get away with it forever. We was trying to knock one another right off the track at top speed and that's dumb. We could both see it, I'm sure.

"But every time we'd cool down, the press would write something about it and it would heat up again. Finally at Riverside in '72 or '73 Allison told his side to a writer and it came out in the newspaper like he was all innocent. Maurice and I read it and it teed us off. That night we ran into Eddie and Bobby at a restaurant. So both sets of brothers went at it, mouthin' off. Until then, I never had said anything to them or anyone else about it. This time I did.

"I said, 'I'm not the sort of person who argues a lot and I don't intend to get into any arguments now. But I got somethin' to say and I'm goin' to say it. I'm sick and tired of leanin' on Bobby out there and I think he's sick and tired of leanin' on me. I think we both want to get back to racing. And we sure don't neither one of us want to get hurt. The next time I hear one word about Bobby and me beatin' on one another, I'm gonna kick the hell out of whoever said it, and I don't care if it's Bobby or Eddie or Maurice or Dale.' And I just turned around and walked off.

"Next thing I know we're around the garages and Maurice has his arm around Bobby and they're just buddy-buddy and Eddie is talking to Dale about something. Well, I'll tell you, that's all it took to end it, but Bobby and I still don't talk to each other sometimes. That's just what it amounts to. But at least we're not playing games out there that could get us hurt anymore. The funny thing is it's always the crews that stir up the trouble while the drivers race."

"You've had your fights, though?"

"Oh, yeh. Well, I've thrown some punches. Not many land. Maurice and Dale get heated up a lot faster than I do. But I get hot at times too. I remember one time when I was working in Daddy's pit on a quarter-mile track around a football field. Rex White ran Daddy into the wall and won the race. I was only sixteen or so, but I was already a six-footer, while White was a little-bitty guy couldn't have gone more than five-four or so. When he came out of the clubhouse after washing up, I just picked him up this far off the ground and held him and I started to give him this 'You son of a gun' stuff. He was saying, 'Go ahead and hit me, you're bigger than me,' and stuff like that. All of a sudden some cat come over my shoulder with a right hand and knocked White into the dadgummed bushes. Bloodied his nose and knocked some teeth loose. Turns out he was no bigger than White, he lived right across the road, and he was a fan. A fan of Daddy's, I guess.

"I remember another time, I was runnin' that little ol' track at Asheville years ago and I had flat run off and left everybody behind when a wheel bearing went out. I slowed way down, but it took time for the field to catch me. When Ned Jarrett caught me, he ran right through me instead of going around me. I was beat. I would have let him by. But he wouldn't wait. So he sent me into the wall and tore the right side out of my car and cost me second place. I waited for him to win. When he stopped by the starter's stand and took his helmet off, I reached in and grabbed him and pulled him half out of the car. And I laid a little speech on him. I had no respect for my elders, you see.

"Comes a commotion and I see Maurice and Dale have some cat from Ned's crew up against a wall and they are putting it to him. It turns out he'd pulled a knife and was coming up behind me when Chief and Dale intercepted him and put him on the sidelines.

"Well, that was the old days."

"You don't do much of that anymore?" he was asked.

"Not much." He smiled.

"You're all friends."

"Well, not exactly friends. Some of us are friends. Some of us aren't. Like in any group. When a group of guys are competing with one another, friendship goes just so far. You don't want to like a guy so much or feel so sorry for him you don't want to beat him. When you get in a guy's way he's bound to be upset by it. When you beat him he's not gonna like it. And if you're one of the good ones and he's not, he's gonna be jealous of you.

"Still, we're sort of set apart from other people. The things we feel about this sport, no outsider could know. So we sympathize with one another and we understand one another and we stick together a lot. I feel like I have friends in this sport, but no close buddies."

"The other drivers say none of the top drivers treat the bottom drivers as well as you do, that you'll always help anyone whenever you can," it was noted.

"Well, you know, I try to treat everyone decent," he said. "Not just drivers. Even writers. I don't feel like I'm any better a person than anyone else just because I may be on top of this sport and he may not be. He may be a better person than I am.

"You can call this book 'King Richard' if you want, if that's the way people see me, but I don't feel like King Richard.

"I hesitate to give advice, because what works for me may not work for another driver. I wouldn't want to be responsible for anything that happened to him. But there isn't a race goes by that four or five drivers don't come by to ask how I drive the track or how we've set our car up. I always tell 'em, because, like I say to 'em, if their car handles better, they'll be better able to get out of my way when I come by.

"Dale is decent to everyone. So is Maurice. Maurice is kind of tough and standoffish with fans and writers, but he treats the other mechanics and the drivers like family. He's comfortable with them. He'll give 'em equipment, anything they need.

"That's sort of traditional in racing. I think if I asked Allison for something, he'd give it to me in a second. The Pettys have picked up parts from people, too, you know. We're rivals, but we're in this together.

"The poor boys will kid me that they'd like half my appearance money, but I never had a one of them really ask me for money. I get touched up all the time by people who figure I got so much I should give it away, but never by drivers. I'd help a cat if I could, and I have.

"I think David and Bobby treat people decent too. I think they're good to the other drivers. I don't see them lord it over others. I don't know what they think of me. What do they say?"

David Pearson

"The thing about that Daytona race is you do almost anything to beat the other guy and you do different things different races. What I did in that race was I made Richard pass me so I could draft him and slingshot around him coming off the fourth turn to win, which is what I did.

"In a race when one of us is a lot better than the other, well it's no race. But in a race when one of us is just a little better, well to win the race you got to outfox the other guy and that's what I did in that race. I slowed when he wasn't expecting it and he had to go around me. Nothing wrong with that.

"The writers made a lot more of it than there was.

"Richard was mad because he got beat. And maybe because I did the unexpected. It's no good if he knows what to expect from me every time. I haven't done it since, because I know he's looking for it. The situation doesn't come up a lot, anyway. I mean it's only a couple times a year maybe that it's just me and him together at the end.

"I don't take him for granted, so there's no reason for him to take me for granted. If he trusts me, fine. I trust him. But you don't trust an opponent to the point where you don't watch him every turn of the way.

"To tell you the truth, I'm more relaxed runnin' close to Richard than anybody else. He is smooth. He'll run the same groove at the same speed all day long if he can. He's consistent. He'll take the turns the same way all day. A lot of those other drivers, you don't know what they'll do. They'll go in hard one time, back off another time. Not Richard.

"But when we get down to the last laps, I don't take nothing for granted. It's not like he'll let me past him. He'll use up a lot of track. And if he wants to pass me, he'll go low one time and high another. He'll put the pass on in a turn one time and a straight another.

"He tries to fox me too. That's racing. When I'm racing Richard, I'm really racing. I don't know who's better, me or him, but I'd rather be me than him. The last ten years or so I've won my share. Since I got with a top team, I've won more superspeedway races and more of those close finishes between us than he has.

"He runs more races. He has that sort of sponsorship money. I've run all the races when I've had the money, and I've won the driving championship when I did. He has more money to put into his racing than any of us. But he doesn't have any better team than I do right now. The Petty team is good, but I think most people around our racing will agree the Wood Brothers is the best.

"I'm sure it wasn't easy, but Richard didn't have to come up the hard way like the rest of us. He inherited his pappy's stuff and he never had to struggle or go hungry. But I don't begrudge him any of the breaks he's had. It's just that he got the chance to win before we did. So he got ahead of us. But he's not ahead now. We start out every season even now. And we're winning our share.

"He runs for points as much as for victories now, I think. He'll settle for second sometimes, too. It's tirin' to run all the races. I know it because I've done it. It's up to the sponsor. If he wants me to run 'em all, I will. But I'm most concerned with winning the big ones. And I think Richard really is, too. Bein' tired never stopped Richard. I don't think he's physically as strong as some of us, but he's mentally as strong as any of us. He just makes up his mind he's gonna race five hundred miles and at the end he's there.

"He's consistent is what he is. He's a good driver with a good crew and good equipment and he's consistent. Others may be better on a given day, but it seems like Richard is there every day. He drives smart and hard and he has to be one of the best ever. I respect his record, which is the best ever.

"I think we're friendly, even if we're not friends. I mean maybe after all of this is over for us, we can be friends, but it's hard now when we're racing so hard against each other. Yeh, he treats everyone nice. We all try to treat everyone nice. He's got a nice family. I got a nice family, too.

"Richard's like the rest of us. He ain't perfect. None of us is.

"I don't know if you could say he got back at me at Talladega after that Daytona race. He didn't trick me into passing him. I took advantage of the one chance I had to pass him. My back window was coming out. My car was a mess. I couldn't keep up. I thought my best chance was to try to hold him off. I couldn't. So he won that one, that's all.

"He was so mad he didn't just drive by me, he scraped by me. But I'll tell you, I'd rather rub fenders with Richard than compete clean with some of those other cats, who are crazy at times. If Richard was scraping my side, it was because he wanted to scrape my side. I always know he knows what he's doing.

"We all take chances at times. We all go where we shouldn't go. We all make mistakes. But you shouldn't be racing if you aren't willing to take a chance and go at times, if you're afraid of making a mistake.

"I made a couple of moves lately I wish I hadn't made. They cost me a lot. But that doesn't mean I shouldn't have made those moves. It just means they didn't work.

"I had to take a chance to beat Richard at Daytona that day. There'll come another day when Richard will take a chance to beat me, you'll see."

Bobby Allison

"Anybody, I mean anybody, who runs hard consistently is going to run into another driver at times. Especially on short tracks. We have big, heavy cars and we can bump and bend a little metal at times without anyone getting hurt. I have seen Richard wreck cars on short tracks and win with them.

"The root of the situation that developed between Richard and me was it came at a time when we were the only two people who were totally competitive race after race. He was established as the top guy and I was just coming on and he seemed to take the attitude he shouldn't be challenged.

"It doesn't matter to me who he is. When we're equal, I'll race him lap after lap, mile after mile, short track or big track. While there are guys who get cars who can blow the rest of us down, he is the only guy besides me who runs a five-hundred-mile race for five hundred miles. Nobody else will run him door to door for five hundred miles.

"The fact is, we're not often equal. I haven't often had the equipment he's had. But I go into every race with the intention of doing whatever it takes to win, and so does he. And our talent is close enough so, if our cars are close, sometimes he'll win and sometimes I'll win. We got to leaning on each other for a while, but I still respect him and I think he respects me.

"For a few years there we did bend each other's cars. Some races were worse than others.

"The one race in North Carolina, I led almost all the race. He took the lead coming out of the pits on a restart after a caution flag. I was quicker so I was set to repass him. When I come up behind him, I bumped him on the back bumper twice.

"You can decide for yourself if it was misjudgment on my part. The fact is, he slowed down in front of me both times. You know the fuss he raised about Pearson braking in front of him at Daytona? Well that's what Petty did to me.

"I backed off and made sure he was still straight both times. The third time he went one place to block me and I went another place to pass him and it surprised him. I made my pass and won my race. See, I felt like it was my race. I sideswiped him going by. He didn't give me the room I needed to get by.

"Every driver feels he has a right to a certain place on a track, and when another driver tries to take it from him, he may get mad.

"That was 1967, the year he won twenty-seven races. I don't think anyone had even really raced him on a short track all year and it upset him to get competition.

"The next year we had another rough race. He had the field beat bad. I was way back in second, but I was still running hard in the hope that something would happen to him that would let me win.

"I was passing a slower car on this short track on Long Island and we was two abreast in tight quarters. He wouldn't move over for me. Then Richard came up to pass me and I wouldn't move over for him. They gave me the move-over flag, but I decided I'd gotten there first and I was as entitled to make my pass as Richard was to make his.

"Richard ran right into me and bent his fender in on his tire and had to pit. Well, I feel like he decided to hit me, so he decided to take his chances. I don't think it was supposed to be tap-tap-tap: it was supposed to be a CAH-LUNK, you know what I mean?

"After that I didn't hesitate to CAH-LUNK him when the opportunity arose. I wouldn't back down no more than he would. And we got to looking for each other, if you know what I mean. It just went on and on. Not race after race. But year after year as certain situations developed in certain races.

"The fights? Well, they weren't between Richard and me. They were between Richard's crew and me. Not Richard's crew and my crew, Richard's crew and me.

"The thing is, I think third parties steamed Richard up. I think they were on his crew. I don't think they were unbiased. Right after races Richard would act like maybe he'd made a mistake or maybe there wasn't much to what had happened, but by the next week he'd be angry and making a lot of it.

"Maurice and other members of the crew were always shouting stuff. One time Maurice said he wanted to talk to me and the talk turned out to be a swing. I can accept that, but he knocked me down and while I was down another member of the crew kicked me several times.

"Who? I don't want to say who. Dale? I don't want to say. I will say I got up and fought and held my own with Maurice fighting, but it's hard to hold your own when you're down and being kicked.

"Actually, Maurice knocked me down two times and this other guy kicked me the other time, too. I don't recall ever running, but I never pretended to be a fist-fighter. I'm not afraid to fight, but it's not the way I want to earn my living. I don't think it settles disputes on the track.

"I don't remember if my brother Eddie fought too, but I do remember our crew members were madder than Richard and me were. And the press built it up bigger than it was. I remember after one race when we didn't do nothing but pass each other three or four times the stories made us seem like we was firing from machine guns mounted on our cars.

"The thing kind of came to a head when a story in the Los Angeles *Times* steamed things up. A writer named Shav Glick had asked me for the inside information on it in confidence. I told him my side as you would to a friend. To my surprise it came out in the newspaper.

"Well, facts is facts and you know everybody's got a little history that's unpleasant. But Richard felt enough was enough. I kind of agreed with him when he stood up and said his piece. So that was that.

"It was dangerous when we carried it to the big tracks where we're running at top speeds. At Talladega, I was racing Richard and Pete Hamilton tight, and they made contact. That threw Richard into me, but I got the blame.

"I'm going to say this straight out to you. I never distrusted Richard. You know, I felt like some of the things he did as he went along were wrong, but I never felt that he was going to go too far or cross over the line to where it got touchy.

"He'd put a move on me and that was all right, but then I'd throw the same move right back at him and that wasn't right as he saw it.

"On more than one occasion we raced each other straight up and then laughed later when they wrote it up like it was war. It wasn't as bad as it seemed. It's history now anyway.

"We're not best buddies, but I think when we quit racing we will be. I don't like all the people around him, but I don't dislike them all, either. And he's good people.

"I think his crew is the best in racing. The Wood Brothers may be more effective, but the Pettys are more dedicated. The Pettys may have more money than anyone, but they run more races too.

"Richard had the best opportunity of anyone in racing, but the fact is he's taken it and multiplied it a hundred times, whereas many others would not have made nearly as much of it.

"He says he's not the best driver? Well, I'm not sure he's not. At least he's as good as the best of us. Of course, I'd have liked to have had a go at it with his equipment.

"I had a hard time on the way up. I went hungry a lot of times. I almost quit Grand National racing as recently as 1971. When you know you're not going to be competitive, it's hard to go racing.

"I've thought about sticking strictly to sportsman racing. I can make a good living at it and I like it. I don't have to travel all over the country and I have several days a week to be with my family and to fish. As it is, I still race sportsmen because I make money at it and enjoy it. It doesn't hurt me. It keeps me sharp.

"What with endorsing equipment and doing advertisements and speaking and promoting and getting ready to race and racing all over the country, Grand National is eighteen hours a day, seven days a week. I admire Richard for puttin' up with it and still racing as well as he does. He's more in demand than anyone.

"But Grand National is the major leagues and when you know

you can compete up top it tempts you. The one year, 1971, I raced Fords for Holman & Moody, I won ten big races and $300,000 in winnings and sponsorships. But they broke up. When John Holman ran the show, they didn't win anything. When Ralph Moody did, they won everything. Holman didn't like that. They were always in the parking lot, like teen-age kids, fist-fighting.

"The next year I drove for Junior Johnson. I owned the Coca-Cola sponsorship and I pitched that in along with a piece of my own money. It paid off, because we won a bundle.

"But Junior sat in the pits and drank Pepsi, while his crew members wore dirty old overalls instead of the uniforms Coke sent. I never did fit in with those back-country buddies of Junior's. I formed my own team the next year and won two races, but it was tough.

"Then Roger Penske came along with the backing of American Motors to run Matadors. Becoming competitive with those cars was tough. We ran nineteen races and blew eighteen engines in one stretch. Penske's crew had skill, but were unfamiliar with stock-car racing and wouldn't work together. It's been the biggest heartache of my career.

"I'd just love to race the Richard Pettys straight-up. It's hard not to be jealous of him, but he's put everything he has into it and I admire him for it. If he's in front of you, all you can do is chase him and hope. If he's behind you, you keep lookin' in your rear mirror cause you know sooner or later he'll show up.

"He takes everything he can from every race. He has the most help, but he makes the most of it."

Cale Yarborough

"You're not competing with Petty so much as you are the Petty team, the Petty family, really. Lee laid it out for them and the boys picked it up and went with it. They've always had the best sponsors and the most money, so they've had the best and most of equipment. Fair is fair. They use it right. They run a classy operation.

"Maurice and Dale have been with Richard for fifteen years or more, and by now they know what one another is thinking. They work well together. They put together cars that run fast for five hundred miles.

"There's just no way of knowing how some of us would do with the same operation. But from year to year the Wood Brothers are almost always competitive with them, and my boss, Junior Johnson, has been at times, too.

"It's hard when you're trying to beat someone who is no better than you but has more. They say I run too hard at times, but I have to run harder than Richard to keep up with him. If my car was equal to his, that would be something else. At times when it has been, I've been able to run with Richard. He's as good as there is, but there may be others as good. I think I'm as good as any. If I didn't, I wouldn't be running. I run hard from the start to the finish of a race. So does Richard. I respect him for that.

"I don't care if it's Richard or David or Bobby or me or maybe some others. If our cars are equal, you won't see much difference between us. We'll all win some. I think I'll win more, but that's me.

"The thing that sets Richard apart is his dedication to stock-car racing. He's been at it a long time, he knows it as well as anyone, and he works just as hard at it today as he did ten years ago.

"I took a couple of years off to try Indy racing. The challenge and the big bucks tempted me. But I never had a chance. I never had a car that could compete. I came close in some 500s, but the car finally failed each time.

"Coming back to NASCAR, I was set back a bit. Richard's never left. He's on top and he aims to stay there. He's a good guy —I'll give you that—but he won't give you a thing on a race track. He may have been handed a silver platter, but he piled a lot of dough on it.

"Others have driven his cars without being half as successful as he's been. Some don't see that. They're just jealous."

Buddy Baker

"I drove for Richard, but I never really drove Richard's car. It's hard to believe Maurice and Dale didn't put a few extra pats on Richard's car. But they gave me a good car and they treated me good. It was my fault if I didn't make more of it. I won two races.

"It was too early for me, maybe. I had a lot to learn. I have learned. There have been times in recent years when I wished I could put a Petty car on the track again and see what I would do. I think I'd do all right now.

"Bud Moore is fixing me some Fords now that I think I'll really run to the bank in. I'm a big man, but I can't carry a car to the finish line. Because I'm big, people think I drive too hard. Don't they think Richard and David drive hard? How do they think they win? I can't help it if my cars break while I'm running right with them.

"I've raced for the lead in almost every race I've run. Any race you can lead, you can win. I've led a lot and won some. But you have to lead to win. And if my car breaks down while I'm leading and on my way to winning, it's the car's fault, not mine.

"Richard is a great race driver. So is David. And Bobby. And Cale. And Buddy, too.

"The Pettys treated me fine while I was with them. I consider Richard a real friend. He's one of the great racers and a super person. You've just gotta like a guy who'll go into the Stork Restaurant and order a bowl of butter beans and a slab of corn bread."

Benny Parsons

"Richard is just folks. I don't know anyone who treats people better. I don't know a driver who is so decent to other drivers, to the press, to the fans. I can't imagine a superstar in any sport as humble as he is. He knows he's good, but he doesn't act like it.

"He may be the nicest man I've ever known. The whole Petty operation is A-Number 1. Maurice acts tough, but his heart is soft. He'd do anything for anybody in racing. Dale is always kidding around, but he's also the first to help someone who needs it.

"I don't know why Richard gave me the lift at Daytona. It was extremely odd. He says he'd help anyone the same way. Maybe. He says he didn't just want to defeat David. Maybe. We're friends, of course.

"All I know is when he could've driven off and left me, he gave me the follow-me signal.

"It's very delicate to discuss it. All I know is drafting him gave me the chance to win the Daytona 500. He pulled me to the thrill of a lifetime. No stock-car racer could want to win any race more.

"My record shows I get the most out of my cars. I won the driving title with a car when I couldn't win a race. Maybe with his cars I could win the races he wins. I'd like to think so, but I don't think so.

"There are a lot of great drivers, but I think he is the best. He's the best at finding the best line around and at lasting.

"Helping a fellow driver exemplifies Richard Petty. He does things like this, which is why he is the King and will be to the end of time. No one else ever will do what he has done, and no one ever will be in his category."

Darrell Waltrip

"There are a number of drivers in Grand National racing as capable as Petty. He's been successful because he's a good driver who has good help. He's had the same chassis, the same crew, and the same operation year after year after year. Give me the same car and the same crew for ten years and I'll be just as successful.

"When David Pearson or Bobby Allison or Cale Yarborough have had equipment as good or better, they've been as good or better. The same guys have had the good stuff too many years now. It's time for some young guys to get a good chance to show what they can do. I'm just beginning to get good stuff and so I'm just beginning to go good.

"Myths build up around the Richard Pettys. He's a good driver with a great record. He's a nice person, but maybe it's easy to be nice when you're a winner. It's a lot harder to be pleasant to people when you're losing. Let me win a couple of hundred races and you see how nice I'll be. Of course, I have to win them, while he already has."

Dave Marcis

"Richard was my idol. I still have his picture up on my old garage wall. I don't envy Richard. When you're on top, everyone wants to knock you off. He may have had a car handed to him, but he didn't have victories handed to him. His pa winning didn't help Richard win. He did his share of losing while learning.

"I started with fifty bucks and an old car. He started with more. But he still had to work his way to the top just like any of us. He put his winnings back into his racing. He paid the price to reach the top. I have a long way to go.

"Of course I'd like to have his crew. Who wouldn't? But if they could stick together, other teams could, too. They just don't. I know Richard and Maurice and Dale were always willing to help me with advice and parts whenever I've asked.

"I'm driving a Dodge and the Pettys handle all the Chrysler equipment, so I have to go to them for anything I need. As far as I can see, they've always given me things as good as they take for themselves.

"But it has been tough to compete as an independent with the top teams. I've gotten a little sponsorship money and blown it in five or six races. I've put my cars together by myself and gone to races without a crew.

"There've been times when blowin' a tire blew me right out of a race because I didn't have another one to put on. There've been times when I felt I had as tremendous a year as Richard just by finishing in the top ten of ten or fifteen races he won.

"But he got to the top and so can I. I never considered quitting and now I'm getting the kind of support I need. Are some racers afraid to run with me? Not that I ever heard of before. I race hard, but not beyond myself. I try to stay out of trouble. I like to run around Richard or David because if I can stay with them I can be in contention at the end.

"Maybe I had to run a little harder than them to keep up with them, but I've always tried to keep my cars under control and not push them past my ability to handle them. Maybe my cars didn't handle as well as theirs.

"I think Richard and David are the best drivers in our racing. Richard may be a bit better right now because he runs all the events and is sharper, but when it comes down to one race David may be just as good. On hot days, the heat seems to take something out of Richard. David may be stronger.

"I wish I was as good. Maybe I am. But I have to prove it. I just hope I get a good chance."

Cecil Gordon

"How can you envy a person as decent as Petty? He deserves every good thing that comes his way. I'm proud that he's a personal friend. He and Maurice and Dale and all are all friends. No one in racing ever asked any of them for a favor or advice that didn't get it.

"It is impossible for me to compete with him. I don't have his kind of crew or car or ability. But I do have a good crew and we put the best car we can on the track and I run it to the best of my ability. My ability is close to his, but it's not his.

"I love racing and I'm happy to have made some kind of a living at it. I'm proud just to have run with a Richard Petty. I'd like to have won a race in Grand National, but I'm proud to be a part of it. Maybe he's won too much, but it hasn't changed him.

"I don't think he'd be any different if he was a loser."

Lennie Pond

"It is frustrating to know you have the ability to win but not the equipment. Take Dave Marcis. A year ago he was driving his own car. Now he's running a sponsored car and is running fourteen miles per faster. He had trouble getting into races. Now he's on the pole. He's the same driver. The car is different.

"I respect Richard Petty as much as anybody, but he can win races walking. He wins because he has cars that can win. He could take a tenth-place car and maybe finish eighth. Maybe his ability would move up a car a couple of places, but he still wouldn't win if he didn't have winning equipment.

"One reason Richard wins so many races is his cars run five hundred miles. And they run them fast. We can't go too fast in our cars, and if we do they won't last four hundred miles. You can't win a five-hundred-mile race in the first four hundred miles. Richard is as good as anyone, maybe the best, but we'll never know because we'll never all race the same cars."

Elmo Langley

"After twenty years of racing, a lot of the fun has gone out of it. I still love it, but an independent can't make it today the way he could yesterday. It's too expensive to put a car on the track that can compete with a Richard Petty car.

"In twenty years in Grand National, I've run five hundred races. Only Richard has run more. I've won two races. What's

Richard won, amost two hundred? I don't even know if he knows what it's like for an Elmo Langley. But then I don't know what it's like to be a Richard Petty."

James Hylton

"We just don't have the kind of money it takes to compete against say Petty or Pearson or the million-dollar operations. I do a lot of my own mechanical work. I know Richard could, but he doesn't.

"In ten or eleven years, I've led a few races and won two. I won Talladega. Maybe me just winning that one with what I have was worth a lot of wins by a Petty or a Pearson. I'm consistent. I've come close to winning the driving title a couple of times.

"But I admire Richard. He's a tremendous driver. We all talk a lot about what we could do. He's done it and he keeps on doing it."

A. J. Foyt

"There are drivers who get the equipment Petty does and they don't do with it what he does. He is as good a driver as I've faced in any form of racing. He is so smooth that when he sneaks in behind you, you can hardly feel it. He sneaks on by so you don't notice until too late. He can also ride rough. He has the feel for it. He's a real race driver."

10

MAY

The month of May means Indianapolis to most of the car racing fraternity, but to the Grand Prix group it means Monaco, and to the NASCAR crowd it means Talladega and Charlotte and a couple of stops in between.

No classic is comparable to the Indianapolis 500 in racing. It has a historical tradition dating back to 1911. Between a half-million and a million persons pay to see the practices, time trials, and race during the month of May, and more than a million dollars in prizes are paid out.

A race-day crowd of around 300,000 fans and a first-place prize of close to $250,000 have lured Bobby and Donnie Allison, Cale Yarborough, and LeeRoy Yarbrough off the Grand National tour. But, notably, Richard Petty and David Pearson have resisted this temptation. Pearson says, "Drivers die every couple of races at Indianapolis. It's an accident when a driver dies at Daytona. I'll stick to what seems safe to me."

"No racing is safe," says Petty, "but ours is the safest of all. If you wanted safety, you wouldn't race. But a man is a fool for running unreasonable risks.

"Billy Foster died when he came half out of his car and whacked a wall at Riverside. After I came half out of my car in an accident at Darlington in 1970, we rigged up a netting on the driver's side to keep me in my cars. Now everyone uses the same sort of setup. You learn from experience. Jim Pardue died because he went right through a flimsy fence. They put up a retaining wall so no other driver would die that way. The next year I hit the wall right where Pardue had hit the fence, but I was fine.

"There was a day when drivers didn't wear hard helmets or seat belts or shoulder straps or flameproof uniforms, and a lot of lives were lost that no longer are lost. Drivers still get hurt and killed in our racing, as well as other racing, but we don't want anyone to die, and we remove all the risks we can. Race after race, drivers are so well protected they walk away from wrecks that would kill a man on a highway.

"I'm a race driver, like my daddy was. I'm sure if Daddy had driven Indianapolis, I'd be driving Indianapolis. Whatever the risks were, I'd accept them. But Daddy drove a safer form of racing and I can see how much more dangerous other racing is. We're enclosed in a lot of strong metal and our heavy cars don't turn over easy. The driver is much more exposed in those flimsy little open-wheeled Indy and Grand Prix cars and they're so light they bounce all over a track.

"I've thought of giving Indy a go, but I never give it a second thought. It's a great race, but we have some great races too. I don't know that the Indy 500 means more to them than the Daytona 500 or the Southern 500 or the World 600 means to us. I don't know that their 300,000 crowd looks like more than some of our 100,000 crowds. You can only see so many people at one time. The kind of money they pay appeals to me, but money doesn't mean that much to me. They don't just give it away, you know. Cale and a couple of our other boys found that out.

"You have to have a car capable of winning to make the effort worthwhile, and there aren't but a few of those. I'm sure I could have one. Foyt keeps offering me one of his whenever I want it. But I'd still have to learn to drive it. Indy cars and Indy racing are different. It's a different game. Joe Namath and Catfish Hunter both throw balls, but they're different balls thrown different ways. I'm sure if they'd started soon enough and stuck to it long enough, Catfish could throw a football fine and Namath could make money pitching baseballs, but you never know.

"I've been to Indianapolis a couple of times, but I never got to see the race. I didn't like the looks of those little old June bugs. I don't know if I'd like laying on my back so close to the ground with those wheels all around me and the wind in my face. Foyt showed me the little-bitty shoes he drives in even though he has feet as big as mine. He said I'd have to squeeze into the same sort of shoes because the pedals was so close together you couldn't wear big boots.

"I've driven around the track in a passenger car, but I've never driven an Indy car. I was offered a ride, but I didn't take it. Yeh, I suppose it's strange, but I just never did. Maybe I was afraid I'd like it. Built just for racing like those cars are, I'm sure they work well and feel fine. Actually, Maurice, Dale, and me, we've talked about building an Indy car. They fool around with their cars so much I'm sure we could build a clean car that would beat them at their own game. But we won't. It costs too much to build a car these days. It costs too much to build a car just on the chance of winning Indy, and with the rest of the championship trail shrinking, I really believe Indy will be a stock-car race within ten years. I also believe we'll be running smaller cars, like compacts, within five years.

"Indy is interesting, but, driving or building, I wouldn't want to take all the time away from our tour it would take to do the job the way it should be done. My sponsor, STP, might go for it, but I don't want to give up a steady income for a potshot at a pot of gold. And I really don't want to run the risks they run for their money. One year one of our boys got into one of those wild accidents they have there. I took a newspaper full of photos and spread it in front of Lynda and I said, 'Good news. I just got a ride for the next race at Indy.' She like to killed me right then and there."

Syndicated columnist Jim Murray of the Los Angeles *Times* was surprised when he met Richard Petty. "Where are your scars?" he asked the racer.

Petty says, "I raced stock cars at a USAC event at Pocono and I couldn't believe my eyes when I saw the Indy drivers coming out of a meeting. There wasn't a one of them that wasn't scarred from burns or wasn't missing fingers or a hand. And they talk about their accidents like they were war stories. They're proud of their injuries. They wear their scars as if they were medals of honor. Well I don't dig that. I don't have a death wish or anything like that. I don't think they do, either, but I think they brag about their accidents as a defense against feeling like fools.

"You just don't see scarred and broken bodies driving Grand National. We get drivers hurt or we lose one here or there, but it's rare. We prove it doesn't take death to draw crowds to races. You don't dare touch in Indy racing. We rub metal all the time. They wouldn't dare take the chances we take. They can't race the way we race. To us, a race is a race, it's not an accident. I'll just stick to the kind of racers and the kind of racing I know best."

The one time he went away from the racing he knows he will regret as long as he lives. That was in 1965 when Chrysler withdrew from NASCAR and the Pettys picked up eating money drag-racing a Plymouth.

At Southeastern International Drag Strip in Dallas, Georgia, on the twenty-eighth of February, Petty pulled a standing-room-only crowd of approximately 10,000 fans into an arena designed to seat 2,000. Richard got off to a slow start in a match race with Arnie Beswick. As Richard accelerated, a wheel flew off his car, it swerved left, then right, dove into a ditch, rode up an embankment, and landed on a fence against which many fans were crowded.

An eyewitness reports, "As I ran over there, I saw people running right over one another to get out of the way. As the area cleared, I saw people lying on the ground, bleeding. I saw a lady holding a baby that looked like it was hurt. The lady was hysterical. Then the ambulance came to take away the hurt people."

Petty unbuckled his harness and tumbled from his car to the track. As several persons rushed to his aid, he was heard to say, "The heck with me. Get to those people I hit." They did, but an eight-year-old boy, Wayne Dye, was dead, and six or seven others were injured, some seriously. Petty was uninjured. His crew took him and their wrecked car back to their truck and they loaded up their equipment and left.

He says, "I don't know what happened. They say a wheel flew off. The suspension may have broken. Later, there was too much damage done to the car to tell. All I know is I lost my steering and went out of control and when I hit my brakes I didn't stop. When I went into the ditch, the car went straight up and laid down on top of this four-foot fence, half on one side, half on the other.

"I don't think the people were where they shouldn't have been, but that fence may have been too close to the track and they may have been crowded against it too tight. There just weren't any safety features. I hit so hard and was so shook up I couldn't feel if I hit people, but I guess I did. I couldn't see much, but I think some of them may have hurt themselves running into each other.

"When I got out of the car, I was still on my side of the fence away from the people. I never did look at the people. I went down and got into the truck. The others, they just throwed everything up on the truck. We took the wrecker and pulled the drag car out of the place and three or four miles down the road before we even stopped to load it up. After that, it was a long, hard trip home.

"There wasn't anything we could do for those people and we just wanted to get away from there. When we found out a boy had died, we felt terrible. None of us wanted to go drag-racing again after that and we never did. I lost all interest in it. Oh, it wasn't drag racing's fault. I don't know if it was the track's fault. I don't think it was my fault. It was just one of those things. If it had happened in Grand National, maybe I'd have lost interest in that.

"I don't think of it as something that happened because we'd been squeezed off the Grand National tour and had taken to the drag strips. I'm a fatalist and I think of it as something that was bound to happen wherever I was and wherever that poor boy was. But I think most of that big crowd was squeezed in there to see me. That poor boy, too, maybe. I hate for it to have happened and I wish it hadn't.

"It doesn't do that poor boy or his parents any good, but it's the only thing I really regret from my life and my career. It's something else when a driver dies. We all accept the risks of this sport and we've learned to live with death. Not like it, but live with it. I guess we're a bunch of hardhearted people, but if we weren't I don't guess we could be racers.

"You try not to get too attached to other racers so you won't feel too bad if something happens to them. You can't get too involved with other people's problems. Like if you're driving down a highway and see an accident, it bothers you, but five miles down the road you've forgotten it. The only way you can tolerate the hard things of this life is to keep going.

"I don't feel any fear for myself at all. If a racer does, I don't think he should race. I'm sure he's not a good driver. If a racer does, I think he's young and just starting; I don't think he's a veteran or he wouldn't have lasted. You can't have fear affecting your judgment and interfering with the moves you have to make right now.

"I don't think a driver thinks about accidents much. It's only the other people—the press people and the fans—who think about it and make us think about it and talk about it. When drivers are together, they talk about winning, not about getting hurt. I think one of the reasons I'm a good driver is that I'm not out to impress myself or anyone else with being brave. I'm not out to go as fast as I can, only fast enough to win. I'm only out to drive as best I can. I accept the accidents I've had and they don't affect me. When my time comes, it's just as likely to be when I'm crossing a street as when I'm driving a car."

However, when asked which of his many records and accomplishments gave him the most satisfaction, he has been known to smile and say, "I guess in still bein' alive."

His worst accident was in the Rebel 400 at Darlington in April 1970. It wasn't his week. He wrecked the car that had been readied for the race during practice.

They rushed his short-track car in as a replacement, and then he really wrecked that in the race.

While contending for first place just past the midway point in the race, he lost control of the car coming off the tight, tricky fourth turn. It glanced off an outer barrier, skidded sideways down the straightaway, smashed so hard into the reinforced concrete wall along pit row that it caved in, came off it flipping end over end, then rolled side for side before it stopped in a steaming heap upside down.

The first person to get to him was Francis Allen from the Junior Johnson crew followed by Buck Brigance of another crew and LeeRoy Yarbrough, who had wrecked out of the race earlier. Wiping a bloody finger he'd cut on torn metal, Allen said, "He was out cold, just hanging in the straps. As I unstrapped him and we started working him out the window, he came to and complained about his shoulder."

As the 42,000 fans watched in stunned silence, the superstar was put on a stretcher and taken by ambulance to the track's medical office. There the doctor diagnosed his most serious injury as a dislocated shoulder and tended to his cuts and bruises. Papa Petty, Maurice, Dale, and Lynda rushed in to find Richard recovering, though suffering. Maurice said, "The car just took off. After it hit the wall, it really took off. I thought it was bad.

Thank God, it isn't." When Lee emerged smiling, the gathering around the office relaxed. When Richard waved to the fans as he was returned to the ambulance to be taken to a local hospital for the first time in his career, the crowd roared its relief.

As Richard recalls it: "The car we took there was really ready. We qualified fast. As I practiced it, it got faster and faster until it was the fastest car there. But I went too fast with it. It didn't stick comin' off a corner and ran right into an inside wall, which tore the side pretty bad. We decided the best thing to do at that point was go get the short-track car, which we did.

"When I put it on the track it was a second slower a lap and that bothered me. We put the good engine in it and it handled all right, but it just didn't get through the straights quick. I qualified it into the race all right, but in the race I was driving it harder than I should have to make up for my loss of speed.

"About eight or ten laps before my wreck, I got into a turn too high and tapped the wall with the right front wheel, and my steering got messed up. I kept going, slower for a few laps, then faster. Like I say, in a few laps you can learn to drive anything. Soon, I had it going as fast as ever.

"But then I come tearing out of the fourth turn and I got a little behind in my steering. It was pure driver error, just like the other times I hit the wall. I got too high and when I tried to correct, the steering response wasn't there. I hit the outside wall hard and completely lost control.

"I was trying to steer it, but I had stopped being a driver and become a passenger. It went where it wanted to, which was down into the inside wall. I remember it starting to take off into the air and that's all I remember. I didn't hit my head, but I blacked out. I think when things get bad the good Lord gets your mind off it. He pulls a plug. It's like a built-in buffer zone.

"It happened so quick I didn't have time to think about it. My life didn't flash before me or anything like that. The last thing I thought was I didn't want to go over that wall into the pits where all those crews and cans of fuel were, because I could have wiped out the whole place.

"The next thing I know I'm hanging in the car upside down and sort of coming in and out of consciousness. I've seen films of those flips and they're really something, but it's like it's happening to someone else because I don't remember any of it.

"That boy Francis from Junior's crew, he reached in and grabbed my left arm and it hurt like heck. I said for him to take it easy because it was hurt. I guess they did because they got me out of there. They said I was moaning something awful. I'm glad I can't recall it, because I might wake up at midnight screaming and hollering if I could.

"I vaguely remember them moving me here and there, pitching me back and forth from stretchers to tables. I guess they had a nurse cutting my uniform off, but all I know is I woke up and this gal was coming at me down there with the biggest pair of scissors you ever saw and I thought, 'Oh, my God,' and I passed out again.

"I remember them giving me a shot with a big ol' needle, and the next thing I know they've got me on a stretcher and they're trying to put me in an ambulance and one cat dropped one side of the stretcher and I had to hold on with my good arm or I would've fallen off the thing.

"They got me in there and Lynda and one of her buddies, Martha Jane, jumped in with me and we took off. I was alert enough to realize we were going out pit road backwards, against traffic, I raised up and I asked where the hell the driver thought he was going. The driver said to Florence Hospital. I said you ain't gonna get there this way. I offered to drive, but he turned me down.

"I can still see the faces peering in at me through the window every time we slowed down. I waved my foot at them to let them know I was all right. The next thing I know they're rushing me into the emergency room in the hospital and some gal is hollering that they can't take me in there until I was signed up and the doctor is hollering that he'd fill out those fool forms later.

"They just throwed me on a table and X-rayed me from head to toe. All they found was that shoulder injury. A bone that holds it in place had broken and there was a whole bunch of them trying to get it back into place. They was a-pushin' and a-shovin' and it hurt so they had to hold me down. I heard one say, 'Man, it won't go in.' And another one said, 'It will if we shove harder.'

One gave a pull and one gave a shove and I came about a foot off the table and blacked out again.

"They fixed me as fast as they could and it wasn't long before I was ready to leave. Only I didn't have anything to wear. The boys were headed back home with my suitcases in the truck. Lynda had come down on race day without even a toothbrush. My uniform had been cut to shreds and my boots disappeared. I was left with my underwear. I borrowed a pair of britches and a slipover sweater and I walked out of there in my bare feet.

"Daddy and Maurice and Dale took it so much in stride it almost made me mad, but Lynda was scared, I could see. She was sitting in the scorers' stand when it happened and as soon as she ran to the hospital, she kept running into people telling her I was fine. She knew they didn't know, and that made it worse. She wasn't interested in being consoled, only in seeing for herself how I was. When she saw I was all right, she was all right, but it shook her.

"It was a reminder that this was racing and these things happen in racing, in case things went so smooth for so long that she'd forgot.

"It reminded me, too. It didn't scare me, but what I can remember I can't forget. I don't think about it exactly, but it's in the back of my mind. To this day I drive slower through that corner than any other, and a little more carefully on that track than any other. It's an old, hard place, very unforgiving. If you miss your line, you're in trouble and I know it as well as anyone alive.

"I'm not sure if it was my worst accident, but it was my most spectacular and it's exciting to see on film. Sometimes an accident that doesn't look like much does more damage if you happen to hit just the wrong way. But I didn't lose any part of me; I'm still here.

"The thing that hurt worst is it cost me a driving title. I was leading when it happened and I missed just enough races to miss out. I got back to racing as soon as I could, and, even though the shoulder hurt, I did as good as ever. Actually, it was my third best season. I won eighteen races. The next season I won twenty-one. I averaged almost twenty wins a year for five years, the late sixties through '71.

"I think the accident made me run harder than ever. You talk to anyone who run against me and he'll tell you I'm running harder than ever."

In the spring of 1975, he was nearly thirty-eight years of age and had been hunched into hot noisy racing cars under severe strain for four or five hours at a time almost every week since he was twenty-one. He ate irregularly. During pit stops an aide would push a tray full of pills at him to gulp down.

His listed measurements of six-two and 195 pounds suggest a sturdy man, but, stripping to shower after races, he looks terribly thin and pale. He was so hard of hearing he often had to ask you to repeat what you said and sometimes seemed to be reading lips.

He seemed relaxed around racing, but rumors persisted that he had stomach trouble and had never shaken off the effects of being "gassed" by carbon monoxide which leaked into his car during a race about ten years ago. A couple of times he had staggered from races run in humid heat requiring oxygen and cold compresses to bring him back. As though insulted, he denied he had any special problems: "A long race takes a lot out of a driver. Any driver. I'm not the only one needed oxygen at times. I'm not a bull like Buddy Baker, but no one ever has run five hundred miles as many times as I have, and there's no way I could run thirty or forty races a year, year after year, if I wasn't fit.

"Everyone has problems. People say I'm hard of hearing from the roar of the engines. The fact is, when I was in the third or fourth grade of school, a nurse coming around to test the kids' hearing found out I was hard of hearing. I was sent to specialists, but they couldn't correct it. I've been to Duke University, where they're researching hearing problems, and they couldn't help me. I've been told I have old ears. As I understand it, the feelers inside the ears that help you hear are going away as they do as a man gets older.

"It doesn't bother me much, but when a man is standing behind me, talking to me, there's no way I can hear him. I have to turn around to look at him while he talks to me. I halfway read lips. I have a hearing aid, but I only use it when I'm watching TV or at a movie or at some meeting where I figure it won't embarrass me if people notice I'm not hearing. It's funny, but in the garage, the guys talk loud when they're cutting up, but start to whisper when they get down to business. It drives me mad trying to hear what's happening.

"Maybe being around loud engines made it worse, but Daddy was around racing a long time listening to engines and he can hear as well as anyone. And there's lots of deaf people out there never heard a racing car in their lives. I've learned to live with it.

"I do get headaches, but they don't come from racing. Mother always had a lot of headaches. Dale's mother has tremendous migraine headaches. I don't know if mine are migraine, but I think my headaches are inherited.

"They are hard to live with. I get them so bad that three or four times a year when I don't have to I won't even get out of bed. When a headache happens during a race, I'll take a couple of aspirin at a time to ease the pain. I'll wind up taking ten or twelve aspirins in a period of three or four hours and that has to be hard on your stomach.

"I get upset stomachs from the aspirin, so I take Di-Gel pills to soothe my stomach. I guess it takes my appetite away because I don't feel like eating later. But then I don't feel like eating earlier either. I just don't like to eat a lot. Food doesn't mean that much to me. A hot dog and a Coke are fine as far as I'm concerned. I don't drink whiskey or even beer except seldom, and don't smoke except for cigars.

"I did get gassed back in 1966 and for a year or two it really bothered me. The doctors said it takes six months or so to get that stuff out of your system, but it took me three or four times as long because I constantly was exposed to it. We used to get a lot of carbon monoxide coming into the cockpit, and three or four times I had to quit races because of it. It just made me sick to my stomach. But they construct the cars better recent years and that stuff doesn't get through and it's not a problem anymore.

"A lot of heat builds up in the cockpits. You lose a lot of weight in a hard race and it takes a lot out of you. I sweat a lot and take salt pills to make up for it. A couple of times I had to quit races I was so tired. All drivers do at times. Sometimes it gets to you more than other times. But most times I don't feel it till the race is over. Maybe for the first time I realize I have to go to the bathroom bad. You don't think about it when you're concentrating on the race.

"I believe in mind over matter. Most of the time I won't give in to being tired. I won't even let my body know it's tired. When I relax and let down later, that's something else."

Richard rejects the notion his age is beginning to go against him. "Most top drivers reach their peak in their thirties. The thing people don't think about is we have no Little League or high-school or college car racing like in baseball or basketball or football. You can't even drive a car until you're almost an adult and you can't race one until you are an adult. That's when we first start to apprentice in our profession. We learn on the job. It takes a while. If you lose a little on your reflexes, your experience makes up for it.

"I don't hear good and that don't hurt me in racing, but I see good and that helps me. I have outstanding eyesight and I think that's the single most important thing an athlete can have. I may not be muscular, but I'm wiry and strong enough to do the job. I know how to do the job. I don't see that I've slowed down and I expect to be on the job for a few years yet.

"I really like what I'm doing and something's going to go out of me when I can't do it no more. I think it eats at Daddy that I'm doing what he can't do no more.

"I look forward to every race. Before a race, I'm relaxed. Ten minutes before a race, you can talk to me about anything. The crew is cutting up, it doesn't bother me a bit. During the race, they tense up more than I do. I'm busy doing my job.

"The short race is tough physically because you're always in traffic and turning. The long race is tough mentally because, while you can relax in the long straights, you have to stay alert. If anything is going to happen, it's going to happen at top speed.

"After a race, I may be worn to the bone, but I'm not wound up or anything. After a race, I relax, win or lose. But, of course, I feel better if I win.

"Driving is what I do. I don't even think about accidents. When a baseball batter is standing at the plate, is he thinking about getting hit in the head with a pitch? When a race driver is racing, he is not thinking about wrecking. When I'm racing, I'm thinking of how I can win. I'm an addict about winning. I'm hooked on it. I'm anxious about it, but I try to keep the nervous tension at bay because it can drain you faster than anything. Worrying can get you tired before you turn a wheel.

"I don't want to die. I'd like to live forever. I know I can't. When my time comes, it will come. It may or may not be in racing. Most drivers don't die in racing, you know. I'm not going to worry about it. If we prepare properly, we reduce our risks of accidents. I'm not going to wait for them. When they come, they come unexpectedly."

They raced for $200,000 in the Winston 500 at Talladega, Alabama, on the fourth of May 1975. The prize was second only to the earlier Daytona 500 in NASCAR Grand National history. As the leaders charged around the sprawling 2.6-mile layout at speeds of close to 200 miles per hour, there was one mishap after another.

After leading the first three laps, Donnie Allison's Chevy blew an engine, spewing oil on the oval. Benny Parsons' Chevy slid on the slick surface into a wall. Two lesser drivers also slid and wrecked. Cale Yarborough charged his Chevelle from far back to near the front until the front windshield twisted out. Bobby Allison led a lap before his Matador engine broke. The 1975 Indianapolis 500 champion, Gordon Johncock, retired when his Chevy engine failed.

Ramo Stott's Chevy blew an engine, dumping oil on the track. Country singing star Marty Robbins, who races for fun, spun his Dodge on the oil, hit the wall hard, and bounced off to hit James Hylton's Chevy. Robbins was hospitalized briefly but was not seriously injured.

The most serious accident occurred in the pits, and it was truly an accident. A right front wheel bearing began to burn on the Petty Dodge and Richard drove into the pits after 140 laps. As he got out of the car, one of his crew members, his brother-in-law Randy Owens, went to squirt water onto the flaming wheel from a pressurized tank and it exploded. The bottom of the tank came off and hit his chest and head with such force that it fractured his skull and drove him twenty feet into the air. He fell down into the scrambling crowd, dead. His body and the tank narrowly missed Richard and Maurice.

Most of the crews had similar tanks, which are supposed to operate with twenty pounds of air pressure and are used primarily to put water into radiators and to wash gasoline and oil off the sides of the cars and the ground around the pits. Apparently, the pressure had built up past the point of tolerance. When the twenty-one-year-old Owens, Lynda Petty's brother—married, and the father of two young sons—started to use it, it tore apart. The sound of the explosion startled everyone; a piece of shrapnel cut the head of Gary Rogers in Benny Parsons' nearby pit; and everyone around was left stunned by the sudden unexpectedness of it. Richard jumped to the pit wall to call for help, but it was too late.

"It was just a freak thing," Richard says, sadly. "It happened right in front of me and I knew he was a goner the instant it happened. I don't know how you know those things, you just know. It was so quick it was hard to believe, a little like lightning hitting a boy in the field. Then came the hard part, having to tell Lynda. But by the time I got to her, she already knew. She had a bad feeling about this race and didn't come. She wasn't even listening to the radio, but our girls were and they were the ones broke the news to her. But they didn't know how he was, so Lynda and Mom called the hospital and got the bad word.

"He just loved racing and being around us and he'd been working with us at one thing or another since he was sixteen. He was in this because of me and I felt real bad about it as if maybe it should have been me. We were running with the leaders, but there was no thought of running any more that day. We just packed everything up and left. I went to the airport with my friend Bill Frazier, a Petty employee, 'the Reverend of Racing,' to accompany Randy's body back home."

At Alabama International Motor Speedway, the race went on. Buddy Baker and David Pearson dueled for the lead through the last hundred miles. Pearson drafted Baker through the last lap and tried to slingshot around him coming off the last turn, but Baker kept his Ford in front to the checkered flag. Pearson put his Mercury almost even as the two drove almost abreast across the finish line.

It was Pearson's third second-place finish of the season, and David admitted he was depressed afterwards. Baker, by contrast, was elated with his first victory in three years. "It's the happiest I've felt in fifteen years," he said. Bud Moore, his car owner, also was satisfied. "We've worked and waited a long time," he sighed. Though well-known and well-regarded, this was his first victory in more than ten years.

They did not mention the accident that fatally injured Randy Owens because that was not their problem, but their crews conceded they would be keeping a closer watch on those water tanks in the future. Meanwhile, Richard Petty was on his way home with Randy's body. Despite this setback, the Petty STP team completed the first third of the campaign, the first phase of the Winston points series, more than two hundred points, in front, worth $10,000 to Richard.

He was not thinking of that when they buried Randy on Tuesday with his wife, Jan, weeping. Their sons, Travis, two, and Trent, one, were too young to know what had happened. But, while racing pauses to bury its dead, when that deed is done, it goes on. Racing is a business, like any other business. Richard Petty says he did not even think of the next race until someone said, "Let's go," and then they just began to get ready to go, preparing their short-track car for the Music City USA 420 on the half-mile at the Nashville Fairgrounds Speedway the following Saturday.

In Nashville, where Marty Robbins had made big money as a singer, he announced his retirement as a racer, at least for the time being. He'd had accidents in three straight races and said, "I think that's enough for now. It's fun racing, but not crashing. After the last mishap I was so shook when I got out of the car I sang a few bars of 'El Paso' just to see if I could remember how." His country music could be heard in the cars and bars, homes and motels of this Tennessee town as the other racers resumed.

The Petty team had prepared their car and took it on the long drive to Nashville with as few words as possible. "There was the sound of silence around us," Richard remarks. Arriving, he asked the track operator, Bill Donoho, to ask his friends of the press not to ask him about the accident of the previous Sunday for a while, and they agreed and did not bother Richard.

"We had to reach down into ourselves and try to charge ourselves back up," Petty said. He qualified his car fourth fastest for the race and was second in the race until his Dodge developed carburetor trouble. He lost twenty-one laps on a seven-minute pit stop for repairs and after that he just ran for points.

Darrell Waltrip from Franklin, Tennessee, who had been coming closer and closer to Victory Circle week after week, finally landed there in this home-state event, earning $6,500 for winning by two laps. After five years on the tour, it was his first triumph. "I expected to win one a lot sooner than this. I expect to win a lot more from now on. It's time the Pettys moved over," he said.

Petty pocketed $1,350 for finishing seventh and left quietly with his brother, his cousin, and the rest of his crew. "We noticed someone missing," he said. "Like having an empty chair at the table."

The following week was worse. Work on the car did not go well. Then there was the long drive to Dover, Delaware, for the Mason-Dixon 500 on Sunday. The race itself, five hundred one-mile laps on an oblong layout, is one of the harder ones on cars. The Pettys could not get their car to handling right. Richard encountered tire trouble and fell a lap back as the event started under dark clouds and was stopped in a downpour short of the halfway mark, which would have made it officially complete.

The race was resumed the following morning. When Dean Dalton's Ford blew a tire and spun in front of him, Petty drove his Dodge right into him. Richard remained in the race, finishing third, ten laps back. "It was just terrible. I was outdrove. Then I hit someone I should have missed," Petty admitted later.

Cecil Gordon finished second, six laps back, and was ecstatic. "It was beautiful, my best finish ever," he beamed.

Making ten short stops under rainy, slowdown conditions to remove and replace a broken shock absorber on Sunday, David Pearson went on to win the race and $14,925 on Monday. "It's about time we won one," David said. "But the Woods won this one more than me." It was their first win in seven months.

Through the next week Petty team members told one another that it was time to get back to business. "We had to get our heads screwed on straight again. What's past was past. We couldn't brood away the future," Richard remarks. They were ready when they took their car on the short drive to Charlotte Motor Speedway. Richard was weary of hearing how he had yet to win here in sixteen years of trying, but he blew and had to replace an engine in practice this year.

Outside of the endurance events, the World 600 is the longest major race in this sport. Its four hundred times around the 1½-mile track is a tremendous test of men and machinery. On race day, the final Sunday in May, a heavily hot and humid day, it was a tougher test than usual. The Pettys met the test.

Pearson qualified fastest at almost 160 miles per hour, but Petty put his STP Dodge into the third starting spot. As 90,000 fans filled the grandstands and grounds on race day, Pearson, Petty, and Cale Yarborough dominated the early running of the $175,000 event in 90-degree temperatures that reached 140 degrees at track level.

Pearson eventually lost time replacing cut tires and later admitted, "We was just out for a Sunday drive after that." Petty lost time with rubber tearing off his tires and fell a lap back in the first half, but wouldn't give up. "We wanted this one. We spent so much time replacing our blown engine and breaking in a new one, we had to sort out the chassis during the race. I got sideways and thought my right-side tires had flatted, but when we replaced them we didn't find anything there. When I came back in to replace left-side tires, we found them chunking up. We were running too loose and had to put more weight on the left side.

"Once we made the chassis adjustment, we had found the right combination. I don't think our car was the fastest, but it's been a long time since I could outhandle the others the way I could in this one. I could run well anywhere I wanted.

"I made up my lap and caught Cale. Once I passed him, I went on to put a lap on him. That gave me the margin to put on four new tires every stop and I could run faster yet. My crew made real fast pit stops. Once the track got slippery, Cale couldn't keep up with me."

While Tom Sneva was crashing in a fiery wreck and Bobby Unser was winning the Indianapolis 500, Richard Petty was winning the World 600.

Cale led seven times for about 225 miles. Richard led six times for about 350 miles, including the last 100 miles. He won by about two miles. He hugged Lynda and they had big grins on their faces as they stood in Victory Lane and he waved to the crowd.

The only driver in the race using one of the new helmets in which ice water is circulated to keep the driver cool, Richard insisted this one was so easy he would have won without that help. "It's just one of our $3,000 added attractions," he laughed.

While the other drivers were dragging in, sweat-soaked and weary from the sweltering, long afternoon, Petty hopped on the hood of his car and stood alongside the race queen receiving the cheers in front of an enormous laurel wreath.

Cale came in to his pit and pushed himself out of his car. "Lordy, it's hot," he said. "Somebody throw me a wet cloth."

Someone threw him a cloth, which turned out to be wet with gasoline instead of water. After rubbing it on his face, Cale threw it away angrily. "What's going on here? Somebody is trying to turn me into a human torch. Dumb, dumb," he muttered, stalking away.

After a cooling shower, he came out to say, "The man who invented a six-hundred-mile race ought to be hung on the square in uptown Charlotte where everybody could see it. This isn't anything but a torture contest."

An hour later, Petty was still talking to the reporters in the press box, relaxed and ready to celebrate. "Usually I'm tired after a race, but I don't feel tired at all," he said. "I'm just enjoying this." He held a check for $27,290, which put him within $60,000 of the two-million-dollar mark in career earnings.

Someone pointed out this was his thirteenth start, but a lucky one, his sixth win of the season. Someone else asked him about the jinx that had hounded him here. "There's no such thing as a jinx," Richard said. "If we could win at other tracks, we could win here. We knew if we worked at it, we'd win here. We didn't do anything different we didn't do here before or elsewhere. We've had bad breaks before, but this time the bad breaks went to others and the good breaks went to us.

"There's an element of luck in racing. You can't predict where a part will break. A lot of parts broke for us at Charlotte that didn't break at Daytona. It's no bigger deal to win here than anywhere else, except that I think this 600 is a bigger race than the Southern 500 or any race outside of the Daytona 500.

"The Petty team has won this race here before. We won with Jim Paschal in 1964 and Marvin Panch in '66 and Paschal again in '67, but I know it didn't mean as much to the team as when I'm driving. They were aggravated by my losing here and they wanted me to win here so much they worked harder at it than usual. The crew won for me as much as I did, or more."

Part of his prize money was paid him in silver dollars. He had them engraved "Charlotte World 600 Victory, 1975" and handed them out to his teammates who treasured them far beyond their real value. "A thousand bucks wouldn't mean as much to me," said one of them, who was proudly displaying his for months afterwards.

11

THE TEAM AND THE CREW

Richard Petty refuses to take credit for his success. Nor will he accept the blame for his failures. To him, racing is a team effort. It is a tribute to this team that its success has by far outweighed its failures.

To the Pettys, car racing is a business and they operate in a businesslike manner out of offices in their compound in Level Cross. The team effort begins with the cars that are built here, ends at the end of each of the races that are run across the country, and begins again before the next race.

Perhaps it is the family aspect of this team that makes it work so well. Lee Petty laid the foundation on which the business was built, while Elizabeth Petty looked after the business. Lee now is a sort of chairman emeritus, but Elizabeth still keeps an eye on everything.

Maurice and Dale have been with Richard since his racing career began. No other team is so closely knit and has been together so long. Glen and Leonard Wood have been a team a long time, but they have had many different drivers in the cars they put together. The same was true of John Holman and Ralph Moody before they broke up.

Also, there is a family feeling among the Petty employees who work in the offices or shops or crew the cars in races. The Pettys appear to be demanding but decent people for whom to work. Many of their workers remain with them a long time, though the ambition of the better ones and the restlessness of the younger ones causes some to drift away every year.

The Pettys have earned the success that has won them the best sponsorship in racing. All told, from STP on down, the Petty racing team receives about one million dollars in annual sponsorship.

Additionally, they have earned an average of $150,000 a year in winnings for ten years and around $250,000 a year the last five years. Then, too, they profit from cars built for and special parts supplied to others.

What sets them apart from most teams is that they put a lot of their earnings back into their business. What began as a tin-roofed, dirt-floored, one-car garage has become a compound of buildings, including a chassis shop, a body shop, a paint shop, an engine shop, and a collection of parts warehouses.

The compound collection includes 50,000 square feet under roof. The STP Racing Team occupies only 6,000 square feet of this sprawling layout. Generally speaking, on a day-to-day basis, Maurice is in charge of the compound and Dale is in charge of the racing portion, but Lee and Elizabeth oversee the lot of it and Richard has a hand in all of it.

Three large shedlike buildings occupy the most prominent part of the compound, which is encircled by a chain-link fence. Tours are taken around regularly and visitors are allowed in some buildings but not in others. They are welcome in one, which houses the winged Plymouth which was retired after the 1966 season and has walls lined with countless trophies, polished to a high shine. They are shown parts of other buildings where work is going on.

Unlike the average garage, all the buildings are spotless. Tools are put away in their proper places or laid out neatly. The workers' clothes are clean. While one car is ready to roll, has been painted, and is being polished, another is lying apart in pieces, and parts are being hand-tooled for it. The jet of blue flame glows brightly as an acetylene torch is applied to a piece.

Aside from the outer shells of the latest models, race cars are hand-crafted today rather than purchased off the assembly line. Chrysler no longer sponsors the Pettys, but the Pettys stick to Chrysler cars and parts because they have accumulated so many parts over the years that they have storerooms full of almost anything they need. What they don't have, they will make for themselves.

If you want to race a Chrysler car, the Pettys will sell you a used one for as little as $5,000, or build you a new one for as much as $35,000. They'll also sell you racing's version of the "Saturday night specials"—a cheap short-track car kit. If you can't assemble it yourself, Petty workers will do it for you for a fee. And the Pettys sell parts to a Dave Marcis or a lesser driver who uses a Dodge or a Plymouth.

The Pettys share decisions on gross expenditures and divide their net profits three ways. The parents get a third, Maurice a third, and Richard a third. Although they will not discuss their finances in detail, an educated guess is that they earn about $75,000 apiece annually.

However, Richard doubles his share because he can keep points money or other bonus money he makes in racing, and all the commercial money he makes in advertising and endorsements. The others do not get a lot of this, although Maurice has done a few advertisements.

Actually, several outstanding race drivers take home more money every year than Richard does. Fellows like David Pearson, A. J. Foyt, Mario Andretti, and Al and Bobby Unser have contracts calling for $100,000 to $150,000 a year to represent sponsors, and keep 40 to 50 per cent of their race winnings, as well as side monies.

However, aside from Foyt, none owns a share in a racing business, and even Foyt does not have a share in a business worth several million dollars, as does Petty. And no other driver has the long term security Richard has with his place in the Petty empire, which presumably will still operate after Richard retires.

The one oddity to the Petty setup is that Dale, while family, is not immediate family, and, though he bears responsibilities almost equal to the others, he is not an equal as far as profit-sharing goes. He is on contract and gets a flat salary plus car performance bonuses that probably earns him about $30,000 a year.

However, he has security, too—far beyond that of most mechanics in this sport.

Richard details: "In Petty Enterprises, Pa is president, me and Maurice are vice-presidents, Mom is secretary-treasurer. We all have a say in it when we contract with sponsors. All the sponsorship money and all the race winnings and all the business earnings go into one pot. We draw salaries. I get $36,000 a year, Maurice $24,000, Daddy $10,000. I get more than Maurice because I'm running greater risks. And I get to keep my bonus and side monies I earn with my driving.

"We all have a say when we spend money. Oh, if Maurice wants a piece of equipment, he'll just buy it, but if he wants another building, he'll put it to us and we'll vote. Daddy casts a vote here. Two out of three will carry it. Then at the end of the year we split our profits. And Maurice gets a bigger percentage than I do because he's the boss man of the business. He operates the compound. If Petty Enterprises sells an engine to a cat in Oshkosh, I could care less, because Maurice tends to that.

"Since we've won almost two million dollars in racing, I'd have made a million if I was on a 50 per cent contract. But I wouldn't have made it because we wouldn't have made it if we hadn't put a lot of our profits back into putting top cars on the track. And I wouldn't have one-third share in a business that is worth several millions. It would be hard to put a price on Petty Enterprises. What we have here is worth more than a million. And if our expertise went with it, that'd be worth some millions. We gross a million a year, on the average. But our payroll is half a million.

"Not many people in racing have put back their earnings into racing. Foyt has. And Dan Gurney. But not nowhere near the extent we have. Parnelli Jones has a team, but he mostly spends other people's money. The Unsers and Andretti and Pearson and Allison and Cale and the rest, they don't invest in their sport. Well, I've got a good investment here.

"What I haven't put in racing, I've put in land. I've bought a lot of raw land around here. I don't know whether I'll develop it or sell it in time, but it's improving in value. Pa doesn't take a lot out of the business because he doesn't need a lot. He has both developed and undeveloped land. He has a lot of offices and motels and other rental property.

"Because Petty Enterprises is such a close-knit family operation, we probably have a higher profit margin than most businesses, but you have to spend money to make money, and we're not cheap, as our championships show. We buy the best equipment and build the best cars we can. We completely tear down and go over and rebuild a car after every race. Not even the Wood Brothers do that. We hire the best help. We pay as well as anyone for the work we get and we have profit-sharing plans and insurance programs only the biggest businesses have for their employees.

"From time to time, we have thirty or forty employees at the compounds. Mother signs most of the checks, but any of the four of us can sign checks. When we want to hire or fire someone, we just do it. Mother runs the office help and the gift shop we have, and if she wants to make a change, she just does it, the same way Maurice does in the shops. As far as that goes, Dale can just let someone go or take someone on who works in his department.

"As far as the racing goes, Maurice is responsible for the engines and Dale for the cars. Maurice misses some small races or maybe just gets there the day of the race because he's busy bossing the compound and building the engine for the next race. Where the car goes, Dale goes. He's there from the time practice starts. Maurice is the boss, but Dale takes care of the crew because he's with them more. He's on salary, but Dale does all right, I guarantee you.

"Aside from driving, my responsibility is seeing that the team gets to a track when I want them to be there, and we have a good place to stay and things like that, although the girls do a lot of the detail work. If I don't pick up our check after a race and turn it in to the office, the girls will see to it that we get what's due us.

"Dale fits me into my cars. He makes sure my seat is right and I can reach the controls and all. From past experience, he knows how to set up a car for every track and how I like it, so there will only be small changes to make when we get to the track and try the car out.

"An advantage I have over most other drivers is I've worked on chassis and engine and I can tell Dale what a car is doing and suggest how we can help the car. An advantage we have is we've worked together a long time so we don't have to waste words. Dale has watched me so long he'll often know when something's wrong and what it is before I bring it in.

"There's not much I can do about the engines, but I can baby them the same way I baby the chassis. I drive a car loose, but not rough. I don't have a heavy foot on the accelerator. When you thump the throttle, raw gasoline jets into the carburetor and a lot of it is wasted. I try to maintain a steady speed and I'll let the car coast when it can.

"It's teamwork. In racing we have severe restrictions on fuel these days and the more miles I can get from a gallon, the better off we are. And the less revs I subject an engine to, the less it's apt to tear apart. The harder I am on tires, the more we have to change on pit stops.

"We've got a good crew. We ride herd on them, but we get guys we don't have to ride hard. Maurice is all business, while

Dale funs around a lot, but if Maurice is tougher, Dale is strict when it counts. They get the same job done in their own ways.

"Dale doesn't ask any of his workers to do anything he won't do himself. He gets down on his hands and knees to clean a car the way most won't. And when a car has to be trucked to a track, he's often one of those driving it, even cross-country. Most of the top drivers fly to races, but I'll drive with my team most of the time. And we'll switch off the guys so they take turns flying to the far-off races.

"We'll pay all the expenses for six, while we'll pick up room and meals for another five or six who get to and from races on their own. We try to keep our basic crew together. These are the guys who have the important positions. But we also have to have others to do the odd jobs and we have mostly the same ones from year to year. There's no shortage of people who want to be part of the Petty team if only for the fun of it or how important it makes them. But we don't want to pick up spare people we don't know like a lot of teams do when they get to a town.

"We run a tight ship. I don't care what our guys do on their own at home, but they have to do their jobs at the compound and at the races. From what I've seen, USAC crews really live it up at races a lot more than NASCAR crews. Some NASCAR crews run wild, but I believe boys in our part of the country party less than in other parts, and grow up more religious and straighter. The NASCAR crews that do run wild don't run well, I can tell you. The Wood Brothers' crew don't fool around, and neither do ours.

"Me and Dale don't drink at all, and Maurice might have a beer is all. A few of our boys will have a beer or two. We don't let a lot of ladies around our rooms before a race. The married men might have their wives with them, but we do not allow a lot of ladies lying around. Curfew is at ten on nights before races and we run bed checks. We work hard and most of us are flat out by eleven. I'll sleep in. Next to racing, sleeping's what I do best. Most of the boys have to be up bright and early. They have a hard job to do at the track, and if they don't do it right, we not only won't win, I may not make it.

"Most of the top drivers do not drink much, but there are a few who do. There are a few who go for wine and a few who go for hard liquor and they'll blow themselves out even the night before a race. Some may still run all right, but not as well as they would without the booze. Most don't care what their crews do and most crews do a lot of high-living. We figure we have to respect racing. This is what feeds our families, which maybe is why our families is fed better than most.

"I'm proud of our record and I know a lot of hard work and desire made it what it is. It didn't come easy. Over the long haul we may have had more sponsorship money to work with than anyone else, but we also spent more. From year to year there always has been a couple or three teams that had the resources we did, maybe more, and we just had to outperform them, and usually did. Some seasons one may have a hot car while we have a cold car, but they won't stay ahead long. We'll catch up.

"I don't know if I am the best driver, but I believe Maurice is the best engine-builder and Dale the best car-builder. I'm sorry that because they're so closely associated with me that they don't get the credit a Bignotti or a Wood will. I can't finish first if I can't finish, and no other team car finishes near as many races as ours—some years twenty-five out of thirty, or thirty-five out of forty, or forty-five out of fifty.

"Maurice is a lot tougher than I am and would have been a better driver, but he had physical problems that prevented it. He was born with a birth defect. He has to cock his head to get his eyes lined up properly. To adjust to it, he's thrown his body kind of off kilter. It shows when he walks. He went to specialists, but they couldn't help and eyeglasses don't help. Also, he had polio as a boy and he doesn't have a hundred per cent use of his legs. So he limps around crookedly and looks sort of cockeyed. But he does just fine.

"He played football and basketball in high school and he was a hell of a good player. He started to drive race cars after I did and did so much better than me that he was ahead of my pace. But in one race he hit a car and went over a bank and end over end. When he crawled out, he told me that from then on he'd work on 'em and I'd drive 'em. I said, 'Okay.'

"He said the one thing he remembered was his arm was flying out the window and he was afraid the car would land on it and crush it. But I don't think he was afraid. I think he saw he wasn't physically able to do the job with his eyesight and all.

"It's been okay because even if he'd've been a better driver, there was no way he would've won more with me building the engines. We get along real good. Oh, we have our knock-down and drag-outs and there are stretches we don't talk to each other, but that's like all brothers, I guess, like all chiefs and drivers. Chief, he ain't the easiest guy in the world to live with, like I am.

"As far as friends, I may be friendlier with Dale. I'm with him more. I'd trust him with my life, which I do every race. I don't think he ever wanted to drive, but he always wanted to build cars and he builds the best. Ain't no one in any form of racing ever built almost two hundred winners the way he has. The shame of it is he's not only overshadowed by me, he's overshadowed by Maurice.

"I don't think they care that much. They may drop in Victory Circle, but then they cut out and back to the garage as fast as they can. Neither one of 'em likes to be interviewed. Maurice hates it. Dale will talk to fans faster than Maurice will. If Maurice signs an autograph, he just scrawls M. Petty as fast as he can and you can't even read it. I take the time to make mine fancy. I could do interviews and talk to people in my sleep.

"I don't think they're jealous of me. They're just not cut that way. They kid about it, especially Dale. But I don't believe he'd trade places with me and put up with what I put up with. The crew guys, they eat up the association. Once in a while we'll send one or two of 'em to a show with a car. They'll sign autographs till their arms fall off and love every minute of it. When they get their pictures in the paper or they're mentioned in stories, they put it up on the wall, and they're proud as they can be about it. I always mention 'em when I can. I think they deserve it.

"The Wood Brothers are supposed to have the top pit crew, but ours is competitive with them. The Woods may be poetry in motion, but we get the same job done without being as pretty. Everything is organized and everyone has a job and everyone knows how to do it and does it. Even if the man sweeping the garage floor doesn't do it right, it will show up in the car somewhere. It's all part of our pride.

"We realize racing is a team sport even if most people don't. In football, O. J. Simpson doesn't run without a blocker to give him a hole. In basketball, the big tall player looks like a hero when he dunks the ball, but what about the little short player that got the ball through people to him? I get out of a winning car and I'm the hero, but what about the people who built the car and the engine so it'd perform perfect and stick together so I'd be safe, and what about those poor sons of guns who burned their hands changing tires or busted their fingers fixing up the sheet metal I bent? They're forgotten, but without them, there's no hero. Any way you cut it, I'm only part of a team.

"Sometimes I want to show the rest of the team I know this. So when we win Charlotte I wanted to cut up the trophy and give 'em each a piece of metal mounted on a plaque. But, it turned out to be a wooden trophy with a clock in it. You can't cut up a clock or give a guy a piece of wood. So, when they paid a prize in a hundred silver dollars, I had them engraved for the guys. I think they knew it meant more than money. Some of 'em had 'em mounted; others carry theirs with them for luck."

From Brenda Williams and Louise Laflin in the office to the lowliest sweeper, Petty employees express a pride in their employers and a loyalty to them that is impressive. One of those sweepers was Joe Millikan not so long ago. Today, the Petty's provide him a sportsman, which he races successfully. Tomorrow, he will be going after Grand National laurels. He says, "They start you at the bottom, but let you work your way up. I learned a lot from them because they let you learn. They are super people and I will always be grateful to them for treating me so well and giving me my chance."

Some of the workers want to drive; others want to be racing mechanics or car-builders. Most are just doing a job, some just in it for fun. Fellows like John Coble in the engine shop, Richie Barz in the build-up shop, and Curtis Wright in the machine shop are accomplished professionals who work behind the scenes and do not appear in the spotlight. Different workers such as Norman Hall or Billy Biscoe will get to perform in the pits from time to time, but Wade Thornburg, Wayne Dalton, and Barry Dodson were not only full-time compound employees, but regulars in the pits during the 1975 season.

Bob "Radar" Townsend, Jerry O'Donnell, Jim Martin, Billy Butler, Horst "Kraut" Fischer, John Hill, and Chuck Strabley are race-day crewmen, who come on their own and are accepted as part of the team. Townsend, a former pilot, is vice-president of a mobile-home firm, O'Donnell is vice-president of a Ford dealership. Martin buys tobacco and Strabley sells vacuum cleaners.

Fischer drives trucks, Butler delivers milk, and Hill supervises a maintenance team.

They are a varied lot but fit together as a team. Most of the time they are bossed by Dale, but when Maurice moves in, there is a subtle shift in authority. Once while Dale was directing practice prior to Maurice's arrival, I asked a crew member which of the two really was the crew chief. "You'll find out when Chief gets here," he grinned. When Maurice arrived, I found out. Even Richard refers to Maurice as "Chief" part of the time.

However, Richard grins and says, "I'm really the head honcho. They can decide between themselves what we're going to do, but I do the decidin' I want to do, because if I decide not to take the car out on the track, we ain't goin' nowhere. Ask Chief."

Maurice Petty

"Richard's the driver. We put it together for him, but if he don't put it in first place, our work is wasted. He's the one that has to win out on the track and takes the chances. So we have to do it the way he wants it. Yes, when you get right down to it, Richard has the final say. It's his right, as far as racing goes. But if he didn't listen to us, too, we wouldn't be able to do our jobs right and we wouldn't be able to work together the way we can. We all have to fit, Richard, Dale, and me. And we do.

"I'm chief because this is a Petty partnership and I'm a Petty, the Petty in the mechanical end. Someone has to be boss. Dale is family, but he is not a Petty or part of the partnership. But Dale has his department, I have mine, and we don't disagree. Every company has key employees and Dale is a key to this company's success. Without him, we wouldn't be anywhere near what we are. I hope we keep him happy.

"The times I take over is when someone has to holler. I have the best holler of any of us.

"As far as the family business goes, well Daddy is doing other things these days and deserves to, and Mother has her things to do, while Richard is too busy with what he has to do. That leaves it to me. I have to make most of the decisions here. It's become a big business and I can't take the time away from it to spend four or five days a week at the race track. I'm not needed there before a race, because Richard and Dale run a race right. Race day, I'm usually there.

"We have close to forty-five employees and someone has to keep track of what they're doing. I realize we're responsible for a lot of families eating. I don't take that lightly. Only ten or twelve of them are full-time on Richard's racing cars, but that's still the main thing. Without that, there's nothing.

"There always seems to be more to do than time to do it, but we always take time for Richard. His car comes first. We can have another car all set up, but if Richard's car needs something off it, we'll just tear it off. If Richard's car needs something, cost don't count.

"We tear our cars down completely after every race. I know the Woods don't do that. I don't think Junior's team does it twice a season. I won't build three or four engines in advance because if trouble turns up in one, it may be in the others, too. We may figure out something helpful in one race we can use in the next. But we take at least two to every race.

"I don't work alone. Take John Coble. He's been with us eleven or twelve years. The last couple of years he's assembled every engine Richard has raced. I'm in charge, but he could be, and he turns the screws. Others help in the shop. At the track, when an engine isn't working or breaks and we have to put in another, Dale helps me.

"Basically, we start with a 340-cubic-inch Chrysler engine and change the stroke and the bore to make a 355 out of it. I don't want to get too technical. We have machines to inspect and to test every part. If a part doesn't look right or doesn't fit right, we won't use it. We'll make our own if need be.

"Little by little, you learn how to make an engine pull a car faster and last longer. A lot of people use good parts and they assume it will all work together right, but they haven't fit it together right and don't have everything going in the same direction. It's easy to get one part fighting another. A racing engine is complicated.

"When an engine isn't running right at the race track, you have to know where to find the fault, and how to fix it, and you usually don't have a lot of time to do it. After a race, we tear the engine down and check every part to see if anything has cracked or bent.

You always find some things have. Racing takes a tremendous amount out of an engine.

"NASCAR keeps changing the rules on engines. This keeps us going just to keep up. No sooner do we get ahead than we fall behind. The more restrictive the rules, the more cheating goes on. You've got a lot of ingenious guys in this business and they're always looking for some way to get ahead of the other guys. The less they can do within the rules, the more they'll do outside of them.

"However, right now there probably is less cheating than there ever has been. The engines are so limited that the more horsepower we put to them, the more they're apt to break. We're working with a very delicate balance between speed and endurance. We spend more of our time trying to build engines that will hold together at a competitive speed than we do trying to develop power.

"Do we use STP? We sure do. We use the oil additive and the filter. You have to keep an engine lubricated and ventilated, and STP works and works well. Maybe if someone else paid us, we would use something else, but I don't know anything else that works better.

"If we can do something in an hour and do it better in two hours, we'll take the two hours. But once I feel I've got my engine running right, I won't fool with it. Some people can't let well enough alone. I have enough confidence in my ability that I'm not going to keep going back to try to tighten something one more turn.

"I know we have Richard's life in our hands. That's racing. We're dealing with mechanical things and metal parts, and they break sometimes under stress, but if you've checked them carefully and prepared them properly, you can't do anything else.

"Sometimes when things happen, you're thinking, 'Couldn't I have done something else?' But when something is done, it's done. All you can do is decide if you want to do it differently next time.

"I think our record shows we put the safest cars in racing on the track, but we're not running on our record, we're always trying to do better, and we never put safety second. If it's a choice between safety and speed, there's no choice.

"Richard takes races in stride. Dale acts like he does, but I think Dale and I both get tenser before races than Richard. You want everything to work right and you want Richard to run well. Every race is the same to us. Daytona sort of sets you up for the year and some of the short-track events don't pay a lot, but you can't concern yourself with that when you're readying a car Richard has to run on a track.

"When the race starts, you worry that everything will work right. If the engine isn't working right or blows, maybe it's my fault and maybe it isn't, but it hurts when Richard's chance to win has been taken away from him. We've been there and we know you don't leave a race with a winner every time, and you just have to try harder to win the next time. But, oh man, when we win, when Richard takes that checkered flag, that's just as good a feeling as there can be. I'd just as soon have that as anything.

"Winning is enough for me. I don't have to get into the picture in Victory Lane. I don't need a lot of front-runners glad-handing me. Oh, everyone wants respect. I don't like it when someone says so and so is the best mechanic in racing and they forget about me and what I've won. We all like a pat on the back now and then. But I don't feel like I'm competing with Dale or Richard for attention. If it would take away from my life, and it would, I wouldn't want it. I'm kinda' private and I dislike interviews like this one.

"I don't envy Richard one bit. I see how he runs around the country promoting our sponsor's products and racing, always surrounded by writers and fans, standing and talking to people while we're ready and waiting to go, and having to drag him away. It's all right for him. He likes it. I'd hate it. He can handle it. I couldn't. He's welcome to the spotlight. For me, the price would be too high.

"I did enjoy driving. I really did. I could do it, but it was hard for me. I was born with bad astigmatism and I can't see straight when I hold my head straight. And I had a little touch of polio when I was three and it settled in my left leg and left me with a limp. I found when I was driving, you had to run hard every lap to keep up with the leaders. It seemed to take a little more stamina than I had.

"I remember the accident as if it was yesterday. It was at Columbia, South Carolina. I came off a corner and another car hit my front side and run me off the track right at a series of sawed-off telephone poles. I was cool, not nervous, and I got through them, but hit something and started to turn over. I remember my hand hanging out the window, and landing with my head down in the dirt. I said to myself, 'What in the world are you doing here?'

"I don't know that it scared me so much as it made me mad. The car was totaled, which cost us a couple thousand dollars, which we could afford now, but couldn't then. I started to think that in our financial situation we couldn't afford to put two cars on the track. I was going to drive again at South Boston, Virginia. But Richard blew his car's engine in practice, so I gave him my car for the race. That was that.

"I figured he was better on the track than I was and I was better in the shop than he was, and, instead of fixing up two cars, we could take twice as much time to fix up one better and we'd spend less and win more. It was strictly a situation of finances at the time. If it had come along now, it would be a different story. But I never regretted it. I'm happy. I think if I knew I could live the rest of my life like I've been living it in racing I don't think a man could ever ask for more.

"One thing, I have more time for my family than Richard does. The details? I was born March 22, 1939. I'm married, my wife, Patricia, and I have five kids. Lynn is fifteen, Timmy thirteen, Elizabeth Ann ten, Richard eight, and Mark five. Will any of the boys be race drivers? I have no way of knowing. I wouldn't care one way or another. Richard's boy, Kyle? He might be. He's sharp as a tack. He's a lot like Richard. He can do absolutely anything, but he loses interest fast. Richard can put together cars and engines as well as anyone, but driving's the only thing that's held him.

"I'm not concerned with continuing the dynasty. We can always get a good driver. And it'll be a challenge to prove we can win with someone else. But I don't think it will be nearly as much fun as with Richard. There wouldn't be the personal involvement. I think me and Richard get along as good as any brothers I've ever known. And I think he'll miss driving when he's done with it.

"I'm not an easy guy to get to know, and Richard, Dale, and I have had something special. I'm comfortable with racing people. I hate it when I'm with strangers. I like the racing world. I don't know the other world. I don't know what I would do in it if I wasn't doing what I'm doing. I wouldn't want to do anything else."

Dale Inman

"As long as he's driving, I guess Richard is the boss, but I'll bet after that Maurice will be. They both have minds of their own and they're both really smart men, but Maurice lays it on the line, while Richard sneaks it across. They're both my bosses. Lee is, too. He doesn't have as much to do with the operation as he used to, but if he wants something done, he'll see that it's done. And Elizabeth is strong, too.

"There are a lot of times when I'm on my own and have to make decisions, but if one of them is around, I'll ask about any decision that has to be made. I don't mind. Everyone can't be a boss. They don't boss me around. The way we work it, there are no head coaches, but a lot of co-coaches, like offensive coaches and defensive coaches and so forth. It's no one-man operation.

"I wouldn't want a car of my own because I couldn't imagine anyone offering me the sort of sponsorship support we have here, and I like winning the way we do here. It's not just the money, it's the sort of shops we've built up, the equipment we've got, the teamwork between us. It's just a beautiful setup and I wouldn't want to break it up.

"No one here ever questions anything I do, no more than we question anything Maurice does. We respect one another and we know if something we put together doesn't work right, we'll work at it until it does work right. No one ever questions Richard's driving. He may say he's not the best, but I won't say it. I don't know anyone any better.

"Oh, there are times he makes mistakes and we jump on him about it. And sometimes he jumps on us about something we've done. We're not a bunch of back-slappers and yes men. But all the arguing we do on the outside doesn't change the feeling we have for each other on the inside.

"It's amazing how well we get along, especially considering how much time we spend together. And Maurice and I are both high-strung and hair-triggered. I like to fun more than Maurice, so it may not look like I have as much of a temper, but I blow up a lot.

Richard says I'm hardheaded. Well, he's soft-headed. Soft, anyway.

"It doesn't bother me being overshadowed by the Pettys, if that's what it is. I've won mechanic of the year awards and trophies, as Maurice has, too, so I'm known within racing, which is what matters the most. I don't need a lot of stories about me in the paper or anything like that.

"I wouldn't want Richard's life. I believe I could handle it, but I wouldn't want to. He pays a price for his fame with all those fans and reporters around him all the time and all the appearances he has to make. He just does it and does it and does it, but I don't believe down deep he always enjoys it all the time anymore. He's just never home and it wears him down.

"I think the only time he relaxes is in a race car on a race track. That may sound silly, but he's alone out there and doing what he likes to do and knows best how to do. I don't know how he or the others do it. He's taken me around a time or two running slower than he usually does and I can't see how he does the corners like he does.

"I've worked on these cars half my life and after riding with Richard I don't know how he takes it and the wheels take it and the lugs take it. You feel like you've got to be going out of control. The strain is just tremendous. It's a thrill I can live without. On the other hand, just going around and around a long race must get monotonous.

"I never thought of driving, myself. It never looked like it would be fun. And when I look at Richard when he's done with a race, all drawn up and all, it's just awful. I wouldn't want any part of it. I don't know whether I would have been scared or not, but I believe I would have been.

"Our grandmothers were sisters. Our mothers were first cousins. We're second cousins, so I can't claim enough family connection to cut into the family business; though if you can talk them into it, I'll go along with it. I guess Richard and me were in diapers together. We were born and raised within crying sound of each other. We're like brothers.

"I was born on the nineteenth of August 1936, so I'm a year older than he is, but we were always together. I was a year ahead of him in high school. I played football and I was a pretty good running back, but I was too small to be what I might be. I didn't spread out until I was in the service. I never played any other sports because I had bad eyesight. In baseball, I couldn't see the pitch. In basketball, I couldn't see the basket. It's a good excuse, anyway.

"I started going to the races when I was just a boy. Because of Uncle Lee, of course. I started going to the races with Richard and helping him and Maurice help their daddy work on the cars in the early 1950s when we were teen-agers and Lee couldn't afford hired help.

"I went into the Army in '59 and got out in '61. By then, Richard had started driving and Lee had stopped. There was a year there where I went to work outside of racing and just went to the races, but then in '63 I went with the Pettys full time.

"Maurice was on the engines and Richard didn't want to do the chassis, so that's what I started to do and have been doing ever since. I had learned a lot by then and I learned a lot more as I went along. Now I feel like I know what I'm doing, but I'm still learning.

"It would take a book to tell you how we build a car, but there are three or four things we work with mainly to make it handle good and run smooth and last long. We have torsion bars in the front and springs in the back and shock absorbers on each wheel. We have all different kinds and different ways we can rig them to make them stiff or soft or redistribute the weight.

"Let's say we raise the right front corner; that transfers weight to the left rear corner, which is called putting in some wedge, which is changing the balance of the car. Or we can put in stiffer springs on one side so the car doesn't roll as much to that side.

"Our cars last longer than the Indy cars simply because they're sturdier. But we get a lot heavier tire wear because our cars are heavier.

"We can put on softer or harder tires and these will change the handling characteristics of the car. They'll change the roll and the bite. We have to combine these changes with chassis changes. You're always trying to find the best combination.

"When Firestone was competitive with Goodyear, they both were spending a lot of money to develop better racing tires and we had a whole bunch of compounds to pick from. We tested for Goodyear, which gave us an advantage. We knew the tires and could get the best.

"Tires are more responsible for increased speeds than anything else. They're twice as wide as they used to be, and now they're running slicks without any tread at all. The idea is to put as much rubber on the track as possible so it will stick and run smooth.

"Actually, these have a tendency to slide when the track gets greasy, but it doesn't hurt us as much as it does others because Richard runs higher than others, up where the track is cleaner.

"The tires are tremendously important, because they're the link between the car and the track. But from a crew's standpoint they're not as important as they were before Firestone pulled out because Goodyear isn't turning out as many different compounds now and our choices are limited.

"Tires are important in pit-stop strategy. It takes time to change two tires and more time to change four, but a car runs faster on new rubber. Sometimes you'll take the extra seconds in the pit because you hope to gain more seconds on the track. It's a gamble and a lot of the time it depends on what your rivals are doing. We do whatever we can to make things more right for Richard.

"NASCAR has the strictest regulations in auto sports and it enforces them. They change from year to year to keep the competition close. They change as body styles change, but most of the changes are directed at the engines. When they thought we were going too fast, they cut back on some of the things in the engine and it slowed us down.

"Sometimes the changes hurt one kind of car more than another. Some of the changes have been directed at us because we win so much. We don't like that, but we have to live with it. One thing about NASCAR, the Frances set the regulations and you always know what they are. We don't have committees arguing endlessly over rules like in other racing bodies.

"The basic car I work with has to weigh 3,700 pounds. It has to have a wheel base of 115 inches. Our cars have to have a height of 52½ inches. They have to have four-inch clearance off the ground. There are a whole lot of technical details as to how big things can be and where they go. The engine has to be in a particular place. We are restricted to 22-gallon gas tanks.

"There are only so many things you can do different from other teams, though you can try to do the things you do better than they do, of course. I don't say we've never cheated. I don't think any team can say that. The name of the game is getting away with what you can get away with. We've been caught. So have others. But we don't cheat the way others say we do. We're just better and they're just jealous.

"Whatever we do, the idea is to make Richard happy.

"Richard likes a car set up loose, which means the rear end slides right when he turns left, so the car is pointed straight in the direction he's headed. He likes a soft setup, which means the car rides high on the left, but leans low to the right, so the tires get a good bite on the outside and push the car to the inside. But you can get a car too loose or a setup too soft.

"Richard likes to steer the car and he likes to be able to move it around on the race track. A lot of what we do is so that when Richard turns the steering wheel, the car turns in the direction he's turning. That may sound simple, but there is such a thing as a driver turning a steering wheel and nothing happening. The tires start to slide out and it takes time for the tires to catch and the car to turn.

"The quicker the response, the happier Richard is. That's the quickness he wants. That's the handling he wants. He would rather have quick handling than straightaway speed. He'll give up something in the straights if he can get something in the corners and on his passes. He's looking ahead to the end of the race when the track is slippery with oil and he can handle it better than others.

"A car may be faster with a tighter, stiffer setup and that's helpful when you're all alone out there on the track qualifying. But it tends to be quicker when it's soft and loose, and that's helpful when you're in traffic and moving around during a race.

"A lot of drivers just look for speed and they're so happy with good qualifying times that they won't change their setup for the race. Richard looks for handling as well as speed in practice. He's practicing to race, not qualify. He don't care if he don't qualify first, just so he's close enough to move up. He doesn't want to have to make changes between the time trials and the race.

"From past experience we know how to set up a car for him on each track, but we have never gotten to a track where the setup was perfect. There's too many variables. So Richard takes it out and runs a lap or two. If it's a track where I can get up on something and see him all the way around, I can sometimes tell what's happening. I know what he's trying to do. Then he comes in and tells me what he felt. We put it together and we figure out what we can try to make it do what he wants it to do.

"You can change the setup. You can raise or lower the spoiler on the rear deck—the thin strip of metal along the trunk which catches the wind that blows across the car and forces the rear end down. You can use softer or harder tires. Sometimes changing something on a car a fraction of an inch will make a lot of difference on the race track. We want to give Richard as much control of the car as possible and keep him as happy as possible. You keep searching for the perfect combination. Sometimes you come closer to it than other times, but Richard ain't never completely happy.

"During a race we communicate with the radio setup almost all the teams use these days. Maurice and me both wear headsets in the pits, but Richard and me do most of the talking. We keep him informed of how far he's in front or how far behind which cars, and what the lap is, and the speed he's turning, and when we figure he should come in for a pit stop.

"Maurice is figuring out according to the speed of the race how much fuel he's using. We can go about ninety miles on a full tank of twenty-one gallons, so we get about four to five miles per gallon, but it varies from track to track and speed to speed. Unless the car is handling badly and we're getting bad wear on our tires, we don't have to change the inside tires on most stops, but if we can risk the time, we'll change all four because the car runs faster on new, cool tires.

"The first one of us that sees something on the track, we'll tell the other so the driver can look for it or the crew can look for a pit stop under slow-down conditions when you don't lose as much ground on the track. If you wind up having pitted under green while the other guy has pitted under yellow, you've lost a lot.

"We used to spend so much time chalking messages on a blackboard we'd hold up for Richard to see that we couldn't keep track of what the other cars were doing the way we can now. But Richard used to be able to keep track of the other cars by reading their blackboards.

"He feels the best part of the radio setup is the safety factor. At times we can alert him to some trouble he's driving into. And at other times he can alert us to some trouble he's having with his car so we can be prepared to remedy it when he comes in if we can. Of course, we don't have time to make a lot of changes during a race.

"When the radio breaks, we go back to the old system of signs and hand signals. When Richard comes by holding his nose, that means the engine is overheating. When he swings his hand to the left, it means the car is pushing the front end. If he swings it to the right, it means the car is too loose in the back end.

"When he taps his helmet, that means he wants to be replaced with a relief driver when he comes in. That may not happen in an entire season. Richard drives so relaxed, he doesn't know he's worn out until a race is over. Maurice swears Richard fell asleep while sitting in the car during a pit stop in the World 600 at Charlotte last year. Richard denies it. I dunno, but he could've.

"Sometimes he gets so far ahead he gets bored and almost falls asleep in the late stages of races. We needle him to keep up his concentration. If he gets too far behind, there's no way he can sleep because of the cursing in his earphones. Maurice swears at him more than I do. He's got the right by blood.

"Maurice don't get on me if my car breaks and I don't get on him if his engine blows, and Richard is real good about it whatever happens. We all know it ain't easy what we're trying to do. What we're doing is pushing the man and the machine and the metal to its limits, and sometimes we ask more than they got to give.

"We're so far ahead of where we were, it's not funny, but we got to keep progressing to keep up with the competition.

"You'll just flat be beat sometimes, and you've got to accept that. The hard thing is when you've got them beat in a race and something breaks or you run over something on the track. If you're leading, it seems like it takes a year for a race to end. If you're trying to catch up, the race seems to be over in a minute.

"I'm nervous before a race, but I'm calm during a race because I'm too busy doing what I have to do to think about it. After the last pit stop, when it's all in Richard's hands and all we can do is watch, I get nervous again. It's hard on the heart. But I'm used to it. It's what I do Sundays.

"I like money as much as the next man, but in a race you're not thinking of the money, you're thinking of winning. You can't pay me enough money to make up for the suffering of a race.

"When we lose, it's a letdown. All that work down the drain.

When we win, it's a thrill. The work paid off. We've won so much, we're spoiled. We can't tolerate losing.

"When you get in a cycle where you're winning, you have to keep on yourself to keep working and not take anything for granted. When you get in a cycle where you're losing, that's when you work the hardest.

"We have less losing cycles than most teams, but we have them. Maybe the rules are against us and we have to figure out how to overcome them. Or maybe we can't figure out the problem and we have to keep pushing at it until we find it and fix it.

"I think winning the Daytona 500 is the big thrill. It comes early and you figure if you get nothing else out of the year, you've gotten the big one. But you can't think this way. Win or lose Daytona, there's a lot of big races ahead.

"Maybe it's the same with managers and coaches in all sports, but I don't think we take time to enjoy the ones we win for worrying about winning the next ones. No sooner is a race over than I find myself planning the next one. It's terrible.

"Sometimes I think of something that may help us in a big race a month away. Richard is always getting on me about my thinking three or four races ahead. He doesn't want me to forget the two or three in between. He wants to take 'em one at a time.

"Richard wants to win all the races, big or small. If you remind Richard of races he's won, he'll remind you about those he's lost.

"After a race, win or lose, we talk it over. He ain't gonna be completely happy even if he wins by four laps. He expects a car to handle like an extension of his arms and legs. Maybe we all do better when we set our expectations high.

"I take what he says and what I saw and I'll either use it to set up the car for the next track or file it away to use when we return to the track we just run.

"When we're back home and get to the car Monday morning, we tear it down completely in a couple hundred parts. We put the magnaflux, which is a sort of X ray, on every part. We replace everything and anything that's bent or cracked or crooked the least little bit or even looks suspicious.

"It's a boring job, but safety is our first consideration. We respect our responsibility to Richard. We make sure everything is in its place and buttoned down tight before he takes a car on the track.

"By now we know where the dangers are and we automatically

eliminate them as we go along so we don't have to worry later about having overlooked anything. You could become neurotic if you lacked confidence in your thoroughness.

"We have three cars we work with every year so we don't have to run a car on consecutive weeks, and almost never do. We have two long-track cars and one short-track car. While the boys are doing the basic work on one, I'm finishing off another.

"Wade Thornburg and Barry Dodson work with me on chassis and Wayne Dalton works on the bodies. And there are others.

"If Richard has wrecked a car, we don't have to rush rebuilding it because we have another car we're readying for the next race. He bends some metal in almost every race, and we straighten or replace it.

"We work steady and by Wednesday afternoon we have a couple of hundred pieces put together and a car ready to roll.

"We make sure it looks like it's ready, too. We sandblast the paint off the body and spray it with ten to fifteen fresh coats of lacquer paint. Each coat is hand-rubbed smooth. Then we put several layers of polish on it, until it shines like Richard's smile.

"This is partly to please the sponsor and partly to please ourselves. STP likes to see that fancy blue-and-red combination we worked out sparkling, and we like to see it too. Also, at the speeds Richard races, the dirt pockmarks the paint finish. He usually rubs some off on the walls or other cars, anyway. The smoother a car is, the slipperier it is. The easier it slides through the air, the faster it will be. This may mean only a fraction of a mile an hour, but we'll take it.

"We sometimes turn the spray paint and polish on the cockpit interior and roll bars. The interior is gutted of all but Richard's seat and safety features, but we take pride in the car, inside and out. We want it pretty. We run a clean operation from floor to ceiling. We don't do messy work. We have even chrome-plated the gear-shift lever, steering column, and engine parts when we had a couple of days with nothing to do.

"But we don't often have days with nothing to do. Our first race is in mid-January and our last race in late November. There are only a few times when we have a weekend off during the season and only about six weeks between seasons to build the new cars.

"We are not seasonal, we are year round.

"My wife's name is Mary. She is a skilled beautician and has a beauty shop. We have a daughter, Tina Dale, who is nine, and a son, Jeff, who is six. Mary knew what the racing life was like before we got married, but she still don't always take it real good. She don't like me to be away most of every week, but if the kids are not sick or there's not some special problem, then we get along pretty good.

"I wish she didn't have to have the responsibility of making so many decisions on her own. I feel that I'm missing something by being away from my family so much and I feel like I'm cheating them a little, but that's the life. She is starting to go with me more and as the kids get older they are going to go more.

"All I know is I look forward to resting during the off season, and before I know it, I'm restless. If it wasn't for pro football on television Sundays in the winter I think I would go crazy. I'm used to the life I lead, I like it, and I'd miss it if I left it.

"Someone has to tow the car to the races and it is usually me and someone else. Sometimes others will take it to California when we go three times a year, while I fly, but other times I help take it.

"Usually we drive straight through, stopping only to eat and wash up and use the restrooms. I think we have stopped only twice on the way to California. One drives while the other sleeps.

"It's a tough trip, especially if you have trouble with your truck or something. One year we blew the engine in the truck seventy miles from Riverside and had to be towed in. Lucky we were close.

"Another year, they'd had rains. The trailer came loose from the truck and went into a muddy field with the car on it. We decided not to just leave it by the side of the road. We spent hours digging it out. Put us behind for the race.

"We never stop on the way home. We're too anxious to get home. Most of our races we're home the night of the race, but some it's the next morning. We go home in a caravan of truck and trailer, station wagons and vans and cars.

"We use the CB radios a lot. We want to know where the highway patrol is at so we know where we can make time. We also fun with it. We have code names. Richard is Kingpin. When the people found out who he was on one drive, he couldn't get his fans off the air.

"We get in bone-tired and split up and head for our homes. But we get up fresh and ready to go early the next morning.

"I've got good bosses and we've got good guys working for us. We don't party, we race, but we have a good time in racing. We've got a top team and I take pride in being part of it. I wake up every morning wanting to go to work. Not many people can say that."

Wade Thornburg

"I like the work. I worked at something else for a few years and the days dragged because lots of times there was nothing to do. Here, there's always something to do and there's a point to it. You see the result every weekend.

"I make a good living. What's the national average—$7,000? I make more than $10,000 with overtime and all. We get paid by the hour and we get paid overtime for all the hours we put in on the road and it works out all right.

"I'm from Asheboro. I've been working on race cars since 1960. I know this fellow name of Larry Thomas who raced a car Grand National back then and I got to helping him and going with him. He got killed in an accident on the road back in '65.

"I'd interviewed with Richard about a job earlier that year. I went to the Petty place, just piddling around. They wanted to know if I wanted a job, so I told them I reckoned I did 'cause I was looking for work. I went with them then. It was a one-garage operation then.

"I got drafted into the Army the next year. I came back in '68 and decided to try something else. I worked for a firm in Asheboro that ran concrete trucks. But I was bored by it. In '73 I asked the Pettys to take me on again, and they did.

"I guess I do the job they want from me. I work on the chassis in the shop. I do whatever has to be done in the garage at the track. I change the right rear wheel on pit stops. If we change four, I do the left rear. The car is jacked up on your side and you get the one wheel off and the other on. You get the job done in ten seconds or so. We don't practice, but we stick together and work at it race after race. I think we're as good as any crew going.

"Barry and me, we work with Dale on the overall maintenance of our race cars and our two trucks. I drive the tow truck a lot. Dale and me once made it from Greensboro to Riverside in forty-four hours, even with 250 miles in snow and on ice in midwinter. It's hectic now with the speed limit so low. You just piddle along. You pass a car and you come to a hill and it passes you. You stop at truck stops for fuel and food and stuff, and feel like you're losing time.

"It was Dale put a truck in the field, not me.

"Chief is all right to work for. He don't bother me but once in a while. He can cuss and raise cain when he gets upset, but he's a pretty good fellow. Dale's pretty easygoin', but he gets teed off at times, too. Richard's real easygoin'. You can talk to him like you can't some of those star drivers. He's just a regular fella. The way he is with the fans is unbelievable.

"He's begun to give the crew more credit. The silver dollars was nice. It's nice to know he knows you're doing your job. I don't guess anything would change if he quit and another driver took over. The other driver probably wouldn't be as pleasant and the job might not be as much fun, but it's just a job no matter who you're working for.

"I'm thirty-four. I've got a wife, Connie, and two kids—Steven, who is six, and Susan, two. I'm away a lot, which is why I thought of doing something else. But I enjoy this.

"I don't like to go to tracks like Talladega and Darlington, which I consider dangerous to the driver. I've been doin' this so long I don't get too excited most places.

"I don't know what else I'd do. This hasn't made me a master mechanic on all kinds of cars. I only know the cars we work on and I don't do much with the engines. It's not like working in a regular repair shop where you learn to do all kinds of things on all kinds of cars. I'm a sort of specialist.

"We win a lot and I'm part of that. There isn't a lot of glory in it for guys like me, but a lot of guys would like to be me, working on the Petty team. I'm not looking to trade places with anyone."

Barry Dodson

"I'm young yet, only twenty-two, and I could do something else, I guess, but I think I'm doing what I want to do. I drove a jalopy for a while, and I think I could do good as a driver. I didn't feel any fear. I didn't have any success, but I didn't know what I was doing and I didn't try it long enough.

"I think about trying some more, but I don't have any money, and there's not a lot lying around. If you don't have someone who can give you a good chance, there's not much point in taking a chance and leaving a good job. I think it makes more sense to try to work my way up to where I'm doing what Dale or Maurice are doing.

"I work with Wade and Dale in the shop. We work together on a lot of things, but my main job is I build the front suspension under the car, take it apart after every race, go through it to make sure every part of it is right, and then put it back together again.

"In the pit crew, I'm the tire man. I make sure we have all the tires we need and they're all right. I see that they're aired right and have all the lug nuts on and are stacked where they should be, and then I see that the right people get them.

"When we're changing two tires, I go over the wall and get the right front to Dale and then run down and help Wade on the right rear. Only six people are allowed over the wall at one time and one of them is a catcher for the overflow fuel. On a four-tire change, I jack the car's left side from behind the wall.

"Dale has been quoted as saying I'm probably the busiest man on the pit team and do the most physical work, and I'm kind of proud of that. There are always changes on a team. Guys come and go, though they stay longer with the Pettys than with most. We lost Randy recently, of course. This particular crew is kind of close-knit and as good as any, I think.

"I've been around racing all my life. I'm from Winston-Salem. My daddy, Johnny Dodson, was a driver. He drove for Lee Petty back in the fifties. He was a good driver. He won some races and made some money, but he was also superintendent at a rock quarry and he always had that to fall back on. When his boss said he had to do one or the other, he settled for the job. We had a big family.

"I'm not married so I could take a chance, but I like racing work. I went to work for Richard Childress, who was a racer from back home. Then I went to work for the Pettys and you couldn't work for a better racing team or learn from smarter men. I think Maurice and Dale are masters of this trade, and I believe Richard is the best driver I ever saw. He says he's not. No way. He's the best by far. He's just being humble.

"I like to win, you see, and these fellows are winners. They treat me decent and I make good money for a young, single fellow—

more than $11,000 last year. I don't know if I have a chance to move up, but you never know. I can't imagine Maurice or Dale doing anything else, and Richard one day will be on the other end when he stops driving.

"It won't be the same when he stops, but it'll go on, I guess. I know what it'll be like because when the Pettys sponsored Buddy Baker I worked on his car and it was all right. But Buddy didn't do what Richard did with the same, exact cars.

"I suppose some guys envy me, especially guys on some other teams who really have ability but waste it on low-buck operations, poor cars, and bad drivers. I don't know what it would be like to lose all the time. I don't know how you could have enthusiasm for your work. I really feel elated when we win. We start to worry about the next one right off, but winning stays with me awhile— forever, I guess.

"It's not the same for me as for the other guys. Most of them go home to their families, who welcome them. They celebrate winning and get consoled over losing. I go home to an empty apartment. But I got friends who feel for me. I date during the week. I don't mind not partying on weekends. It used to be fun when I was high-living with different teams in a different town every weekend, but it's more fun winning with the Pettys. I could live without the curfew, but I think it's a good thing.

"There's a prestige to being part of the Petty team that interests people and a glamour to being in racing that attracts some girls, but not always the ones you want to attract. But there's a responsibility that goes with it. When I weld a part, I know Richard's got to live with it. You've got to keep things in their place. If you work hard and learn all there is to learn and do a good job, you can make something of yourself. Beneath the fancy paint there's a lot of hard work."

Wayne Dalton

"I'm twenty-four. I was married about a year when I was eighteen or so, but I'm not now. I have a son who will be four later this summer. Barry and I like to go out and date girls and have a good time, but the married guys on this team don't run around and they keep strict rules. I can see their point. So I go along with them. I can have my fun at home. It's a business deal.

"These are good people to work for and I enjoy the work. As long as you do what you're supposed to do, they don't give you any problems.

"What I do is I work in the body shop. I fix 'em when they're bent or wrecked, and I paint 'em. And in the pits I jack up the right side, check to make sure the lug nuts are on good, then let it down. They tried out everyone in the shop at everything—jacking and carrying tires and changing tires—and timed 'em and took the ones that did best. It's an honor, it's exciting, and it pays extra.

"You have to be fast but can't rush to the point where you get careless. We all make mistakes, but we're not allowed many. I can't jack up a car so it falls on the people who are working under it. I don't have the most important job on the team, yet I can lose 'em a race almost as fast as any of 'em. And when we win I feel like I won.

"The first year I was scared half to death, but I've calmed down now. I think I'm part of a crew as good as any. I wouldn't go as far as to say we're the best, but no one's any better, and we're getting better. Lately, Richard's been seeing to it we get a lot of recognition, which is real nice.

"A lot of people play up to me when they find out I'm part of the Petty team, but I can't say it's helped my love life. I enjoy meetin' new people and talkin' to 'em, but I feel a lot of 'em are usin' me to get to Richard. They always ask me to get autographs and photos, and I say I will, but I'm not going to bug him with that stuff.

"I idolize him, myself. He's always been my idol. Not that I wanted to drive. I don't believe my nerves could stand it. I believe a certain caliber of person is cut out for it and another is not, and I'm one that is not. But as a kid growing up, all I ever talked about was Number One, Mr. Petty, and it's been a thrill getting to know him and work with him. He's a down-home sort who treats all of us the same. It's not as though when we stop to eat returning from a race he says him and Maurice and Dale will sit over here and you boys sit over there.

"I'm so used to the life, travelin' all over half of every week, I'm bored to death on weekends we don't race. It's hard on a wife and family. I know from experience.

"I'm from Virginia. A good friend of mine, Freeman Treadway, builds racing cars. He used to do some work for the Pettys. I'd do some work for him. When he came to the Petty place, I'd come with him. One day I asked Richard about a job. He told me there weren't any openings, but to check back with him. I showed him I was interested by checking back, and he gave me a job.

"I worked here eleven months, but my old lady didn't like it. She didn't like being away from home and me being away from her. Some times we worked to ten or eleven at night and she couldn't understand that. I quit and moved back home with her in the hopes it would make things better, but it didn't, so we broke up.

"I came back and Chief was good enough to give me another chance. I got me a girl I'm going steady with now and she likes racing and is understanding of the racing life, but I don't know what it'll lead to. She's got a job and I've got this job and we both work odd hours and we're lucky if we can work it out to be together in between times.

"I have no plans of quittin' this job again soon, I guarantee you. I went to a technical school to learn body work, but after six months I realized the teacher didn't know as much as I did. I learn more here.

"I can't see that I can go too far painting cars, but I'm not interested in learning engines or anything like that. I figure as long as you're happy in what you're doing, it doesn't matter what you do. I never even finished high school, and I'm making about $10,000 a year, I have a paid-for car and I just bought a house.

"Maurice is moody. Sometimes you go to him and he's good to you and sometimes he flies off the handle. But he has a lot on his mind, and the times he was wrong he's big enough to apologize. He's a good businessman and runs things right.

"Dale is nervous around races and he gets excited easy. He doesn't always tell you what to do, so you have to keep your eye on him and keep on your toes and kind of figure it out and do it and hope you did right.

"Well, a job's a job and this one is better and more interesting than most. I can't complain."

Norman Hall

"I do this and I do that around the compound. Odd jobs. Yeh, I sweep. It's not that great a job. The money ain't that great. But it would be better if I could work myself up to something better. I'm twenty-one, I'm married, I have a baby.

"I had family went to school with Richard. I went to school with Richard's brother-in-law. I used to hang around the shop. One day I asked Maurice for a job and he hired me. It's a seven-to-five job. It's more interesting than working in the hosiery mill.

"I like it when I get to go to the races to help out on the pit crew. I help keep the gas cans filled and moving. We use ten-gallon and eleven-gallon cans. The ten-gallon weighs eighty pounds or so; the eleven weighs ninety. I had to figure out how to handle 'em. I heft 'em on my knee.

"If Richard left, it wouldn't be the same. Dale's a little tough, but I guess he's got to be. He tells you to do something, like all bossmen he expects you to do it if it takes all day. If you mess up, Maurice really gets on you. There are good days and bad days.

"I don't make any money when I go to a race, but they pick up my expenses. The last race, I brought three dollars with me and I brought two-fifty back.

"I'll tell you, all the times I don't go, I feel left out."

Bob Townsend

"The fueling is my responsibility. I see that the two fuel cans are emptied into the tank on each pit stop and refilled between stops. They're heavy and you have to move fast with them, without wasting much that's in them.

"Union Oil provides us all our fuel, but we're only allowed to store so much per race. It's not an exotic blend like the Indy boys, but it is a high-powered gasoline. We don't get many miles to the gallon and we have to stretch it to go the distance.

"I only work for the Pettys on race days. I'm a pilot. Which is why I'm nicknamed 'Radar.' I learned to fly in college and I'm a commercially licensed instructor. But now I have a corporate job with a mobile-home outfit in Raleigh.

"The firm had Richard representing them in advertising and I got to know him. He paid to have me fly him to a few races, which helped us have the plane, but it became a losing proposition.

"I was interested in the races. I started to go with him. If I saw something that needed to be done, I did it. The gas man hurt his back, and, before I knew it, I had a steady race-day job.

"The pay is fair, but I'm not going to get rich on it. The hours are rough. I'm away most weekends and if I get home five or six in the morning on Monday it's good.

"I'm twenty-nine and I'm married. Donna and me have no kids, but I should be home more. I spend the money I make taking her to a lot of the races. She enjoys getting together with the other wives.

"She worries about me some. Randy's accident made all the wives remember how dangerous it can be in the pits. We had one fire in the pits in Charlotte, but we got away with it.

"With the cars roaring in and out and all the fuel that's around, you know something could happen, but you don't think about it.

"If we had children or my wife couldn't go, I guess I'd stop going. It can't go on forever. It's not a full-time thing, and helping out on race days is really a job for a single guy who likes running around the country every weekend.

"The thing is, I know I'd miss it. And I know there's a lot of guys who would grab it the minute I left it. I'm not a hero worshiper. I just like the Pettys and I think they like me. And I like racing. But for a lot of young guys, a job in the Petty team would be a dream come true."

Jerry O'Donnell

"I'm thirty-six. I'm married. My wife and I don't have any kids, although I have two children—a boy, Rick, sixteen, and a daughter, Diane, nine—by a previous marriage. Mary and I live a long way from the Pettys, in Atlanta, but she works for the airlines so we get to fly to the races free, so we can go to all the races. It's our recreation.

"Depending on the race, I may have to miss a day or two of work so I take my vacations a day or two at a time. It's a labor of love. It don't matter if you're not a high-paid employee, the Pettys expect you to perform. Maurice and Dale are firm, but fair. I like playing a part in a winning effort.

"I'm a fan, not a mechanic. My wife knew some of them and I met some of them. I started to score for them and still score some. You have to keep track of the laps and the lap times so you can plan pit stops and strategy and doublecheck the official scorers. My main job on pit stops, I'm a gas-catcher. I catch the overflow fuel.

"The funny thing is I'm business manager for a Ford dealership in Atlanta. I help the Pettys promote Dodges in racing and I sell Fords away from races. When one of the Ford drivers wins, I'll say, 'Well, it's good for business.' But, really, racing is one thing, business another. When we're racing, I want Richard's car to come in first."

Jimmy Martin

"I just love it—the Pettys and the racing. I love it better than anything I've ever done. I used to drive dirt-track jalopies. Now I work in tobacco. We have a warehouse. We buy tobacco and resell it. We put it on the floor and auction it off. North Carolina is tobacco country. But it's also racing country. Helping the Pettys keeps me in racing.

"I'm thirty-seven. I'm married. My wife, Martha, and I have two girls—Allison, who is ten, and Mary, who is seven. Martha knows I love racing and she goes along with what I do. I go to almost all the races. I do what there is to do in the crew. I score. On pitstops I clean the windshield. There's a lot of jobs that have to be done.

"If I make expenses, that's all I care about. These are the greatest people in the world. I like being with them on the road, on the track, in the motels. I feel like family. The good racing team becomes a sort of family. If you can't work well together, you won't win. I don't think I'd like it if I was with a loser."

Horst Fischer

"Just call me 'Kraut.' Everyone else does. I've been driving a truck for more than twenty years. I run round-trip between North Carolina and New York every week now. I drive the Petty truck weekends sometimes, but they say I'm a bad driver. I don't know how they think I survive safely through Thursday every week, but they don't take chances with their cars.

"I was married. I'm not now. I'm divorced. I'm forty-one and I live alone. I like racing and I've hung around other racers, but from the time I started to hang around Richard I wanted to be part of this team. They're the best bunch of guys I've ever been around. Did you see the engraved silver dollars Richard gave us? I mean they're nice.

"Like the rest of the weekend crew, I do what needs to be done. I carry things here and there. On pit stops I take care of Richard. I don't go over the wall. I have a long pole with a tray on the end of it and I reach into the cockpit with it. I give Richard his cold cloth and cold drink and his salt pills and stomach pills and aspirin.

"I know what he wants. I'm happy to help. It's something to do on weekends instead of staring at four walls or a television set. It's something to do with decent people. It's an exciting thing to do."

Billy Biscoe

"It's been my dream to be like George Bignotti or Dan Gurney and build Indy cars. But I got into Grand National cars. I've raced hobby cars and I've worked with Hershel McGriff and Neil Castles, among others. Early in 1973 I asked the Pettys if there was a place for me with them. I got a trial to see if they liked me and I liked them. It worked out, but they don't want you if you don't fit in. There are a few other top teams, but none like this one. It's organized. Everyone has his job and every job is done. The teamwork is tremendous. It becomes more than just a job.

"I work in the machine shop. I work in fabrication and parts. I do a lot of welding. I work a forty-hour week, but average actually about forty-five hours a week with overtime. I go to a lot of local races and make a few trips as needed. There's a lot of guys in the shop who like to go when they can. For the Pettys it's cheap help, but there's a lot of laying around. They pay expenses, but if they paid full salaries to a dozen guys every race their profits would disappear. That's why we don't stop overnight on long trips to California, it saves motel money. I'm interested in truck driving and I drive some for the Pettys.

"I drove from Carolina to California. We left at 7:00 A.M. Tuesday morning and got in at 4:00 A.M. Thursday morning. We took turns in the sleeper in the truck. It's a tough trip, but somebody has to take it. You take turns. You talk. You listen to the radio. You stop at truck stops to fuel up and eat and wash up. It's the part of racing people don't see. But there's a lot of little people helping to push the big guy into Victory Circle.

"The Pettys operate a business in a businesslike way. But if you work for them, you're one of them. If they can, they'll help you. I know my limits, but they're helping me make more of myself. They show me my faults and show me where I can improve. I'm twenty-five and I'm single and I'd like to make a good life for myself. I like the racing life and I like being part of a team that knows how to win. There's a lot to learn in life. Learning how to win has to help."

12

JUNE

The advance part of the Petty team arrived in Riverside, California, for the fourteenth event of the 1975 Grand National tour, the Tuborg 400. As they sat around the motel, Dale was talking about the time they lost the trailer in a muddy field: "The car was on top of the trailer and it just buried it in the mud so we couldn't find it for a while," he was saying. "We finally got some wreckers and tow trucks out there and a bunch of people turned up to watch and to help.

"We'd been struggling for forty-five minutes and I said, 'Hey, we got to hurry before the law comes along.' And this cat who'd been helping us from the beginning pulled out a badge and said, 'I'm the law.'"

They all laughed, sitting there in various states of undress with suitcases opened on the floor and clothes strewn messily about and an old movie showing, unwatched, on a television screen. Dale asked if there were any football games on television that night in California. Someone said there were not any football games on in June in California or anywhere else. Dale and some of the others settled for talking and arguing about football, especially pro football and the Washington Redskins, who are considered the home club in the Carolinas and much of the South, even though Atlanta and New Orleans have brought the National Football League to Dixie. The Petty team talks about pro football all the time so they do not have to talk about car racing all the time. Not baseball or basketball, but football.

Richard flew in on Wednesday. He took a rental car to the motel and threw his suitcase in his room. With his handbag of racing gear, he went out to the track, where the car was signed in and inspected and cleared. He did not drive it but sat around and talked to other drivers while his crew worked on the car. Around six, they left to return to the motel.

There were several motels in Riverside where racing teams were staying. It is hot, desert country and the teams returned to their rooms sweaty and dirty. They stripped off their soiled, damp uniforms and started to drink beer and talk and raise a little hell.

At one motel where there was a slide leading into the swimming pool, some of the crewmen put on bathing suits and slid into the cool water with whoops of joy, like little boys, hollering how good it was.

You could hear music coming from rooms with open windows and doors, but no pop music. Country music was dominant, though one team with several Italian members was playing a radio station's operatic arias at top volume.

They gathered in little groups around the pool or around the second-deck walkway, talking and arguing, and you caught snatches of conversations:

Two fellows with beer in their hands and towels around their middles were talking and one was saying, "I love that man like he was my father. I'm no blood to him, but I respect that man. I want to be there when he dies. I want to hold his hand and look into his eyes. I want to be with him to the end. . . ."

Another fellow with his uniform hanging half off him was saying to a friend, "I got no brother. I had a brother, but he ain't no brother to me. But my brother-in-laws are like brothers to me. I mean we are brothers because we are a family. I got no wife, but I got sisters and brother-in-laws, so I got a family. . . ."

A tattooed fellow wearing only shorts was saying to another, "I love my wife. I mean going out with other girls doesn't mean I don't love my wife. You get on the road, you get lonely, don't you? I mean, I don't know what my wife is doing back home, do I? And I mean when they hand it to you, you gonna turn it down? But it don't mean I don't love my wife. . . ."

Sitting off in a corner, two parts of a team that does not win races were talking about why they do not win. The one said, "If he would let me fix it, I could fix it, but he has to do everything himself, you know, and he don't know what the hell he's doing. He's the boss, so what can I do?" And the other said, "Even if it was fixed, it wouldn't help. That driver would run it off the track even if you run rails around the track and attached him to them. . . ."

The Petty team went out to eat without Richard, who said he'd already eaten on the plane and wasn't hungry. He watched TV until they got back, then they watched together and talked pro football. Some of them drank beer.

After a while, Richard stood out on the balcony in the cool night air and looked at the stars. He was asked how much it cost to operate a team. He said, "We figure it averages about $12,000 a race, but it costs twice as much to come to California as it does to run Martinsville. It costs us about $20,000 to run in California and there is no way we can come out ahead here even if we win.

"The thing is, you don't know where you're going to win the most money. You can make more finishing second or third some places than you can winning other places. And it all counts toward the championship and the bonus money we can win. So we don't want to figure California on a profit-and-loss basis. This is just one of the thirty races we run and we add it all up at the end.

"Actually, if you add up the cost of putting the cars together and all, our budget is about a million dollars, but most of that is up front. We figure that the cost of getting the car and the crew to a race and operating it in the race and putting the people up in their rooms and feeding 'em is about $12,000 a race. But it's about $20,000 for the races out here, and if I win this one I'll win about $15,000.

"The sponsor wants us to run 'em all. They especially want us to run in California. It's one place we run outside the South where we can promote STP. So I make more special appearances out here promoting STP and doing other things I feel I should do than I do at most places. But there is always something to do every place."

He sighed and grew quiet. He seemed tired. After a while he left the pleasant evening and went to his room to sleep. Well before midnight, the motel was quiet and most of the rooms dark. Music and the sound of laughter came from a few of them, and a couple of fellows were still splashing in the pool. The Petty team was tucked in.

Richard got up late the next day and went to the track. The crew, led by Dale, was there already, and the car was ready. Richard took it out to practice it. Riverside's 2.6-mile, nine-turn track is a difficult one for NASCAR drivers. Petty had won the second race of the season here in 1970 and the first one in 1972, but he had lost the last six.

"It's the only road race we run, so the only place we have to set up to turn right as well as left. It's difficult to find the combination when you only do it two times a year," he said. "I find it fun, but it took a while for me to find out you have to race the track and not the other racers. You just have to concentrate on keeping the car on the track, and not wrecking it when you run off the track, and hope you're doing it better and faster than the others."

He practiced on and off all day, he and Dale making changes between tours of the track, seeking the combination they wanted. It went well and they were hopeful when they left the track and went back to the motel and showered and changed into civvies and went in a group to eat at a steak house across the street.

He gave a lot of interviews Thursday and again Friday, laughing about how he had run off the track and lost the race here in January and how he hoped to do better now in June. He qualified at just under 109 miles per hour, which was fast but not as fast as Bobby Allison, who made his run at more than 110.

"Bobby beat us in January and he acts like he wants to beat us again now," Richard observed. "His Matador seems to fit this track and he does a good job here. But the boys figure I blew it for them in January and I'd kind of like to make it up to them now. We'll give 'er a good go."

Lynda had flown in during the day and was waiting for Richard at the motel. That night they went to the steak house to eat and then to a meeting of STP managers at the Holiday Inn and then to a meeting of the Richard Petty Fan Club of California at the Ramada Inn. They stayed for several hours, eating cake and sipping soft drinks, talking, signing autographs, and posing for pictures with Richard's adoring fans. Petty was patient with the people, some of whom were persistent about what they wanted from him, and possessive of him, and Lynda was relieved when they left. "That was real nice," observed Richard.

On Saturday he taped a bit with comedian Jerry Lewis for screening on a later muscular dystrophy charity telethon. Lewis seemed impressed shaking hands with the champ and looking at his car. Richard rode as a passenger while Lewis took the car around the course. Richard did not say a word when Jerry ran it off the course between turns two and three. Later, Lewis said, "You knew I was going to go off the road, didn't you?"

"Yup," admitted Petty.

"Why didn't you warn me?" Lewis asked.

"You were doin' the drivin'," Richard said, grinning.

Lewis laughed and left, without having made any jokes or having clowned around at all.

That night Richard had to fly to Las Vegas for a taped dinner in which athletes were to be awarded trophies for being the best at their sports as a fund-raising activity of the City of Hope. Lynda and STP's Bill Dredge and several others went with him.

"Won't it wear you out, flying to and from Vegas the night before a race?" he was asked.

"It's something I'm supposed to do," he answered with a shrug.

They had told him they'd put his spot late in the program in case he got there late. Most of the other athletes there were between seasons. When the Petty party arrived at Caesar's Palace and went into the banquet room, the show was starting and there was no one there to take care of them.

Rather than make a fuss, Richard insisted they just sit down at a vacant table way in the back, which they did. They nibbled on hors d'oeuvres and some sipped some champagne which was on the table. A waitress came to get their tickets, and when she found out they had none, she not only wouldn't bring them food but took the champagne and hors d'oeuvres away.

Finally they were spotted and brought to the front, where there was a table with champagne and snacks. It took a long time to get around to Richard, but in time he was introduced and brought up to accept his trophy on camera. By then it was time to fly back to Riverside. They could not wait for the dinner which was to follow.

The City of Hope did have a plane waiting to fly them and some other special guests back to southern California. Ann-Margaret and her manager and husband, Roger Smith, were part of the group, as was actress Adrienne Barbeau of TV's "Maude" show.

By the time Richard and Lynda got back to the motel, it was nearly midnight. They settled for hamburgers at a joint near the motel.

The race, the Tuborg 400, was the next day, the second Sunday in June. Les Richter, the former professional football star, has been running Riverside Raceway since 1964, and has succeeded where similar tracks have failed. It is not a good track at which to see a race, but it is a good place to spend a nice day. Racing fans are more accustomed to good days at Riverside than at the more comfortable facility in nearby Ontario, and the crowd of close to 50,000 for this race was bigger than most the other track pulls to its events.

Before the race Richard sat in his casual civvies in the bright, hot sunshine outside his garage and commented, "My crew has been arguing about the race with Allison's crew. There's other good ones out here, like Benny Parsons and David Marcis, but not a lot, and it seems like it's between Allison and me. The pilot let the boys down in the first one here this year and they're on me."

He was asked if he was tired from last night. He just shrugged.

"I guess I better get to shovin'," he said, standing up and going into a dark corner of the garage. Here, he stripped off his civvies and put on his uniform. He picked up his helmet and went out and crawled through the window of the car into the cockpit. Hands reached in to help attach his harness and to pull up the netting over the window. He started up the gaudy red-and-blue car and drove it out onto the track, with Dale and the rest of the crew following on foot.

It turned out to be, as expected, a duel between Allison and Petty. George Follmer challenged early, but he crashed out of it. Jimmy Insolo led a lot of the early running, but his engine failed and he fell out of it. Petty ran right off the track in turn one early, but got back on it. He got caught in a sandwich between two other cars in a turn later but got out of it at the cost of only a little lost paint and bent metal on the side of his STP special.

Allison led most of the first half of the event, but Petty started to press him in the second half. Petty took the lead on the eightieth lap, lost it on the 101st lap, reclaimed it on the 109th lap, lost it again on the 129th, reclaimed it again on the 135th.

They dueled spectacularly. There was not much difference between them on the track. The difference built up in the pits. Each made six stops. Richard's stops took less than two minutes, while Allison's took a total of twenty-three seconds longer.

Richard received a chassis adjustment early after falling behind a bit, but made it up on later pit stops. Richard's last two pit stops took five seconds less than Bobby's, and when they went out to finish the race that five seconds was all that separated them.

Petty protected the slim margin through the long last laps as Dale paced nervously across the concrete at track side. He could not see all the way around and had to wait until the lead cars came into sight and the Petty car came out of the ninth turn and sped past his pit.

The crew waved him on until the three-hour-and-fifty-eight-minute ordeal ended. Richard charged across the finish line to complete the 153rd and last lap and watch the checkered flag wave at him. He came into Victory Lane and climbed from his car, looking tired, as the fans applauded him and hands reached for him.

Interviewed over the loudspeaker, he said, "The crew won this one for me. I lost the last one here and they won this one. They really wanted it, I guess. They really got me in and out in a hurry and they gave me the room I needed. I couldn't outrun him. My car was quicker, but his handled better. Credit the crew."

He was sweaty and stained with grime, but he had business to do. Les Richter wrapped a large arm around Richard's slumped shoulders and led him across the track to the press box, where the writers waited to interview him. "Oh, Richard, oh, Richard," some girls screamed as he went by. Richard said, "Another day, another dollar," to a companion as he walked up the stairs to the press box.

After the interview he went into the STP suite for more interviews. He was told they were waiting to interview him on radio station KLAC, so he started for that booth, but before he got there, he was told he had to go to the ABC booth first, so he was diverted there. When he got there, he was told he was too late, as if it was his fault. So he went on to KLAC.

In all the interviews he kept repeating that the crew rated the credit for this one. Flashbulbs popped in his face. Programs and pieces of paper were thrust into his hands to sign. Finally, Richter wrapped him in one big arm and shoved him through the crowd to a car. They drove through the tunnel of the emptying track, back to the garage where Dale and the boys were loading the equipment.

Dale was reminded that he had won and should smile. He

smiled and said, "We did win, didn't we?" And went on with his work. Richard went out to the dusty parking lot where Lynda waited. He sat down in the car in his oil-soaked uniform and said, "We won." And she said, "I noticed," and started up the car and pressed it through crowds of autograph seekers.

Back at the motel, he spent a half hour in the shower, soaking the soreness from him. Then they went out to get something to eat.

They had to go to Alaska. It was a charity affair for the Heart Fund they had agreed to attend. While the others were headed home, the Pettys were taking the long flight to Fairbanks. They stayed there three days. They were guests of honor at a banquet where Richard was given a watch.

They were guests of honor at a stock-car race the next day. Richard did not drive. He was asked if he wanted to, but he said he had not brought his helmet or boots or uniform with him and would not be comfortable without them. Bobby Allison had warned him not to bring his gear or he would have been pressed into the race.

Richard and Lynda saw some of the city, but they did not have much time for sightseeing. He had to race in the Motor State 400 in Michigan the following weekend. On Wednesday they took the long flight to Detroit. There, they found their bags had not made the flight with them. They walked all over the airport that night trying to find where their bags were, before, finally, putting up at a motel for the night.

The next morning, they found out their bags had been at Jackson and had been shipped to Adrian, near the track. They rented a car and drove to Adrian. Richard went to the track and practiced, while Lynda rested at the motel. They had dinner together that night, then she went back to Detroit for a flight home. Kyle was due home between summer camps and she wanted to spend some time with him.

Yarborough sped around the two-mile paved oval in 45.4 seconds to set the pace in time trials at 158.5 miles per hour, followed by Donnie Allison, Pearson, and Petty.

Before the race Richard refused to say he was tired despite the hectic schedule he had endured for ten days. "I'm used to it. Alaska or Atlanta, it's all the same to me. I go so many places and

Dale wheels hose out of the way while Maurice leans in to release the Petty car from pit stop during Dixie 500 at Atlanta. NASCAR PHOTO

The STP Special leads drafting pack through turn in '75 Motor State 400 at Brooklyn, Michigan. There actually are five cars following him with Cale Yarborough's car and David Pearson's so close right behind him they look at first glance like one. DOZIER MOBLEY PHOTO

Surrounded by fans at Daytona. RUSS ELDER PHOTO

Richard serves as best man at a wedding during a meeting of his fan club at Pocono, 1975. GEORGE HARVAN PHOTO

Richard's early finish with a blown engine after twenty laps of the American 500 at Rockingham. DOZIER MOBLEY PHOTO

A rare photo of the full Petty team, taken at Ontario, California. From left: Horst Fischer, Jerry O'Donnell, Bob Townsend, Wade Thornburg, Billy Biscoe, Wayne Dalton, Dale Inman, STP executive vice-president Paul Tippett, Richard Petty, Jimmy Martin, Maurice Petty, Barry Dodson. STP PHOTO

The treasured hillbilly hat. NASCAR PHOTO

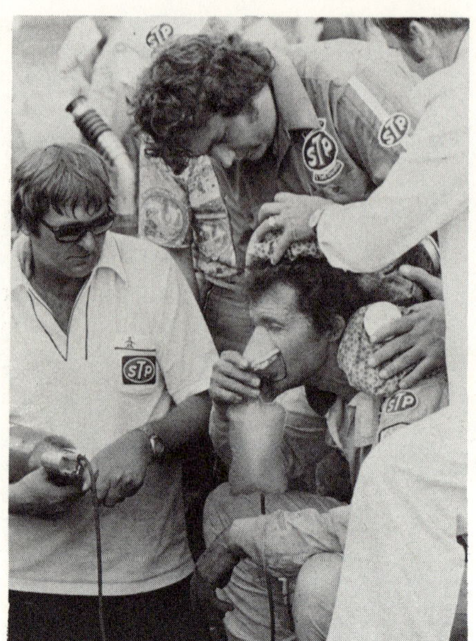

The flu, heavily humid heat, and the hot '75 Southern 500 at Darlington took a toll of Richard Petty, who had to be helped from his car and given ice packs and oxygen. Dave Marcis took over the car, but, after a rain delay, Richard resumed and finished. NASCAR PHOTO

After blowing an engine at Ontario, Maurice (left) and Dale lower a new one from the truck. BILL LIBBY PHOTO

STP's Bill Dredge with bearded Richard Petty in 1976. Bill Libby Photo

In the Petty office with business manager Bob Preddy.

The treasured hillbilly hat. NASCAR PHOTO

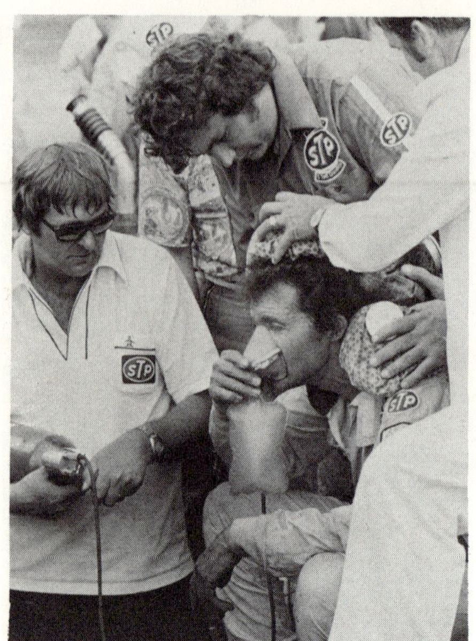

The flu, heavily humid heat, and the hot '75 Southern 500 at Darlington took a toll of Richard Petty, who had to be helped from his car and given ice packs and oxygen. Dave Marcis took over the car, but, after a rain delay, Richard resumed and finished. NASCAR PHOTO

After blowing an engine at Ontario, Maurice (left) and Dale lower a new one from the truck. BILL LIBBY PHOTO

do so many things, none of 'em stand out in my mind. On race day I'll be ready to race."

On race day, it rained, delaying the start a long, tiring 3½ hours. It cleared and the cars swung into action. Donnie's engine failed within fifty-five miles, but the other three top qualifiers—Yarborough, Pearson, and Petty—raced ahead of the others. It was an intensely competitive but cleanly run event before a record crowd of 53,000 in front of the Irish Hills on a track Richard considers one of the best on the circuit. The lead changed hands no fewer than forty-five times, and Dave Marcis and Bobby Allison got into it to lead late before Bobby's engine broke and Dave dropped back.

Cale fell from contention when he ignored a stop sign coming out of the pits during a caution period and was penalized a lap. He was so angry, he parked his car in the pits and got out of it to argue about the ruling. Told there'd been no penalty, he jumped back in and resumed the race. Actually, there had been a penalty. By then he was beaten anyway.

In the last laps as the sun set behind the hills, it was strictly a two-car race between the Pearson and Petty cars, but Petty seemed to tire. Pearson took the lead with eighteen laps left and held off Petty through the last lap. Richard was rapping Pearson's rear bumper from behind and trying to find a place to swing around his rival while David moved around the race track taking up as much space as possible. Pearson flashed across the finish line just two car lengths in front of Petty after more than three hours of dueling at 150 miles per hour.

The victory was worth $14,405 to Pearson, second place paid $10,130 to Petty. There often is not a lot of difference between first and second place money in NASCAR races, but Petty insisted, "There's a world of difference between winning and losing a race, no matter the money."

The win had put him within $27,347 of the two-million-dollar mark in career earnings and that meant a lot to him. "It's something else no one ever done," he said. "And, after all, it is a business."

He seemed worn through to the bone as he went to his crew and headed home for the first time in two weeks.

13

THE BUSINESS OF RACING

When Lee Petty started in racing in 1948, the drivers were on their own. They scraped up their own money to buy and fix cars and hoped they won more in races than they spent. Some drivers did pick up sponsorship support from local merchants who had their names painted on the cars, but if this amounted to fifty or a hundred dollars it was a lot.

As NASCAR's Grand National circuit began to boom and spread out, the automotive companies began to get into it. At first, they simply provided cars and parts to a few good drivers. When General Motors, Ford, and Chrysler entered into it enthusiastically in the early and middle 1950s, competition became intense.

The factories developed racing divisions and tested and turned out dynamic cars and engines to promote their products on the circuit. These were not exotic-looking Indianapolis or Grand Prix cars: they at least looked like the cars people drove in ordinary life. It became a byword that a win for a car on Sunday meant sales on Monday.

It became difficult for the independent to compete with the factory teams. The drivers vied for rides with the factory teams, and the teams vied for the best drivers. The teams began to back them not only with equipment, but with contracted money. The crews became sophisticated.

While not sponsoring individual teams at first, the people who produced fuel, tires, shock absorbers, and so forth became increasingly involved as the sport's popularity increased. At first, they merely provided their products to the drivers in exchange for the publicity they received. Then they began to pay premiums for the teams to use and promote their products, and threw in performance bonuses.

Under the close, continuing control of Bill France, Sr., and Jr., and their NASCAR organization, the Grand National tour has grown steadily. With the sprouting of the superspeedways in the late 1950s and early 1960s and the spread of the sport across the country in the late 1960s and early 1970s, and increasing television exposure, crowds swelled and race prizes escalated.

NASCAR has resisted efforts of the drivers to unionize, partly by insisting tracks provide drivers with fair purses for the races they run. These purses have multiplied to the point where the racers contest for about $2.5 million annually.

As the lesser races on the smaller tracks fell by the wayside, the tour was reduced from about fifty or sixty to thirty races a year, but those remaining promote major events. A few tracks are in trouble, but others flourish.

Crowds of 100,000 or so now are common not only at Daytona, but also at Charlotte and Talladega. Daytona's purse now exceeds $300,000, while those at Charlotte and Talladega exceed $200,000. A winner can earn $20,000 in many races, close to $50,000 in a few.

The R. J. Reynolds Tobacco Company took over the tour for a fat fee, which includes about $150,000 in drivers' bonuses, with the result that it is now the Winston Cup Grand National competition.

In 1963 Freddie Lorenzen became the first driver to earn more than $100,000 in a single season. In 1975 nine drivers would earn as much. One, Richard Petty, would earn close to $400,000. And surpass two million dollars in career earnings. Several had surpassed one million dollars.

As the cost of supporting teams soared, the automobile manufacturers withdrew from racing, although several of them continued to provide support on the side in the form of cars or parts so the top teams would continue to run their cars.

When Firestone and Goodyear were competing for the right to put their tires in the winners' circles and so promote them, they paid heavily for contracts with the top teams. When Firestone pulled out of racing, Goodyear's support decreased drastically.

Other sponsors have filled the gap, such as STP, which took over the Petty team. There are only a few financially fat backers who find racing rewarding, so there are only a few competitive teams. The others operate at a distinct disadvantage.

The tracks themselves have had to increase appearance payments to the drivers to insure full fields of the most competitive cars. The crowds come out to see the Pettys and Pearsons and Allisons and Bakers and Yarboroughs. There are a few others with followings on the fringe of the top ranks.

A Petty finds himself in an enviable position in which he has only to hold out his hand to have it filled with the money he needs to operate at the top, but he and his teammates are under pounding pressure from rivals. It was a hard climb to the top and it is hard to hold on.

At this point, Petty personally can command considerable side money from endorsements and advertising. He not only has been a winner but is a popular personality. He has a hold on his public that may exceed that of any other athlete in the nation. But he spends half his days promoting that popularity.

None of this has come easily.

In the early 1950s Lee Petty purchased his cars and parts from Chrysler. In the late 1950s Chrysler was giving them to the team. But by the late 1960s, Chrysler was only paying a premium of $25,000 a year to be represented by Petty Plymouths.

Ford went to something like ten times that much to lure the Pettys away in 1969 and Chrysler about doubled Ford to bring them back in 1970. Although the Pettys are reluctant to discuss details, it appears they were receiving about a half-million dollars a year in equipment and cash to conduct their racing operation for Chrysler in 1970 and 1971.

When the factory support fell out, in 1972, STP took over the team. STP representatives guard details of their financial tie to the Pettys as if their jobs were at stake, which they may be, but it appears that it ranges from $400,000 in a bad year to $450,000 in a good year because of bonuses.

The company may have started out paying $12,000 a race, which has been revised upwards until today it is around $13,000 a race. Since it wants the Petty team to contest all thirty races on the Grand National tour, this totals close to $400,000 and covers the Pettys race-to-race costs. Then STP pitches in with performance bonuses. The championship is worth $50,000.

STP was pitching pennies prior to its entrance into racing and today its sales average $65 million annually. It spends about a fifth of this in advertising to promote sales, and about a fourth of this advertising money is related to racing, most of it spent on the Pettys, but some of it spread around.

The Dodge division of Chrysler no longer contributes to the Pettys. STP executives concede they are frustrated that they cannot get their cars called the STP Specials, instead of the STP Dodges. Chrysler is getting free publicity for its Dodges from the Petty success, but STP sales suggest its investment does reap rich rewards.

Other sponsors such as Winston Cigarettes, Goodyear Tires, Union Oil, Champion Spark Plugs, and so forth pay from $2,000 to $40,000 to make moving billboards of Richard and his race cars by putting patches on his uniform and decals on the cars and using them in advertising. This amounts to about $300,000 additional money per year.

NASCAR reserves the front fenders of its racers for those who sponsor the Grand National events on a contingency basis. Depending on the finish of a car in a race, these pay prizes to those drivers who display their decals, thus saying they use the product. Some pay extra to get a Petty. Since STP is one of these, it poses no problem to the Pettys.

Other sponsors offer the Pettys premiums and perhaps performance bonuses to display their decals elsewhere on the car, but the Pettys have to get permission from STP. STP reserves most of the "paint," including the front spoiler, for itself, but does permit the Pettys to steal some space at an average of about $25,000 a spot.

Some are stuck so low you have to get down on your hands and knees to read them.

Appearance fees at the tracks average about $3,000 a race and add another $100,000 or so to the pot. Richard makes more for running than the tail-enders because he brings business to the box office while the tail-enders do not. There are fewer than ten drivers on the tour who mean money at the box office.

They are the winners.

Keeping their winnings, the Pettys attain an average annual gross of more than a million dollars. A large part of that is spent on winning and operating a mechanical compound with a half-million-dollar annual payroll for forty or so employees.

It is only operating as they do and winning as they do that the Pettys have put themselves in such a position.

Richard says, "I remember when we went racing on Pa's money and got home on Ma's money. Some of his best years, Daddy made maybe $25,000. With expenses, that didn't produce much profit. And when I started racing, I cost him money. I didn't make any money for us until he retired. We never really had double money.

"I remember back in 1953 when we thought it was great that Chrysler would let us come to their Dearborn factory and buy a chassis from them. When they started to give us stuff, we was happy like a hog wallowing in slop.

"My first year as a racer I made $760. My second year I made ten times that much and the family lost money on me. I averaged about $25,000 a year for a couple of years, then $50,000 for a couple of years, finally $100,000.

"But the costs of racing the tour are such that while we were real well off then, we weren't rich by any means. It was a while before we had the money to build up our shops the way we wanted, and we could be our own factory team.

"In the early sixties our engines were way underpower compared to other cars and we had to work extra hard to make up for it with a car that handled better. Ford was so much the most powerful that General Motors just left racing.

"For 1964 Chrysler came up with a hemi engine, which had a hemispherical combustion chamber instead of a wedge type. That's technical, but the point is it was powerful. For the first time, we were even with Ford. Not ahead. I didn't win that much. I ran the most races I ever ran, sixty-one, and won nine. I did win the Daytona 500 for the first time. I placed high most of the time. Jim Paschal had some high finishes in our second car. And he won the World 600.

"Ford didn't like it a bit. They hollered to high heaven about it. They said we had a smaller, lighter car which was aerodynamically superior to their cars and if we had a bigger, stronger engine we had an unfair advantage. They protested to Bill France, but he ruled our engine was legal under existing rules and refused to change them at that time. Ford spilled the secret it had developed a single overhead camshaft engine and asked permission to run it. It wasn't legal, so France refused.

"I should make one thing clear. I many times have disagreed with the rulings of Bill France and his son, but I always understood they have had a hard job. They have had to make rules covering a lot of different kinds of cars and engines to keep them competitive and safe, and they have done it better than any other racing body. The proof is in the closeness of our competition. It has been a sort of benevolent dictatorship, which has worked better than the committee system USAC has.

"Which is not to say NASCAR has not made mistakes. It has. But I don't think it has played favorites.

"In 1964 France found himself in the middle between Chrysler and Ford. He wanted to keep the competition close while they each wanted an advantage. Chrysler had it in 1964, but was afraid of losing it back in 1965. Before the 1965 season Chrysler said if Ford was permitted to run a single overhead cam engine, it wanted permission to try a double overhead cam it was working on. Instead, France decided to declare the hemi illegal. I think that was a mistake. I don't think he should ever have legislated against companies coming up with new and improved engines. That's progress and the company had paid a price for it.

"Chrysler was furious. We had been behind all this time and it had spent one heck of a lot of money catching up and it was told to forget it. This sort of thing is what eventually drove the factories out of racing.

"The companies would develop something that worked so well within the rules that the other companies would complain, and France would change the rules. A company would say, 'Hey, we've spent millions to build something better and build up NASCAR, so NASCAR says forget it? Well, if NASCAR doesn't want us to spend our money, we won't. We'll forget NASCAR.'

"There were a lot of things, little and big. One year Chrysler came up with special bodies and special fixtures for the bodies. After they ran them one year, they were told they couldn't run them the next year.

"You can't please everyone.

"In 1965, Chrysler was displeased enough to pull right out of racing, and they asked us to go out with them. We did. Out of anger. And out of loyalty. Chrysler paid us to soften the blow to us, but it hurt. I was just hitting my peak. I didn't want to sit on the sidelines wasting my time.

"That's why we took up drag racing. It wasn't our bag, but we got some offers so we took up the challenge to try to build a drag car that could beat the dragsters at their own game. It was just as much of a challenge as trying to beat the Grand National guys. It was fun for a while.

"Then that little boy got killed and the fun went out of it. Anyway, it wasn't what we wanted to do. We were itching to get back in Grand National. We'd beaten everyone on that drag tour, anyway, and were about as welcome by the other teams as a bee at a picnic.

"People were tired of seeing Fords race Fords. About halfway through the season, France announced new rules that we could run our hemi on the small tracks in our small car and on the big tracks in our bigger car, the Fury. Chrysler relented and agreed to run on the short tracks, but didn't consider the Fury suitable so we skipped the superspeedways. We did all right as part-timers.

"France's rules for '66 were we could run our hemi in anything anywhere. Ford had won the Daytona 500 with Foyt in '65, but Chrysler won it with a Petty Plymouth in '66. Ford pressed France for another ruling on its single overhead cam. After he had stalled and stalled, he said they could use it, but he imposed such restrictions on it they just disappeared from the tour.

"He said they could use it in '67 with restrictions and they came back. I mean this was a business to the companies. They were in business to sell cars. They could do it with winners. They didn't want to look bad by getting beat. The average customer could care less about hemi engines or single overhead cam engines, he just knows whether you look good or bad.

"During this time, Ford and Mercury came up with slick-bodied cars and Dodge had one with a wing on it, while our Plymouths had nothing. We went to the Plymouth people at Chrysler, but they said they couldn't build a slick-bodied car. We said, 'All right, we'll run a Dodge.' They said we couldn't. So we said, 'Well, then, we won't run any of your cars because we're shot down to begin with with a body that's five or six miles an hour slower than the others.'

"They said, 'Well, go across the street, and see what they'll do for you.' I don't think they thought we would do it. I think they thought the other companies already had their hands full of racing teams. What they didn't know was Ford had already come across the street to talk to us. Jacque Passino, Ford's racing boss, told us we were the top team in the sport and he would top any offer we had. He didn't know we weren't making any money with Chrysler. He offered us a whole pile of money. So we went across the street and took it.

"For the first time, we found out we were really worth a whole bunch of bucks to these businesses and we never forgot that from then on. We signed a one-year contract with a two-year option, knowing we could deal again the next year. Chrysler accused us of being disloyal. Maybe we were. We'd been with them a long time, almost ten years, and won a lot with them. It wasn't an easy decision. We worried about it a lot. But, the bucks being what they were, there was only one way we could go.

"For one thing, we worried about our following. The stock-car fans took their cars seriously. They drove what their hero raced. They got upset when their hero changed from one make of car to another. The Petty Plymouth was the most famous car in racing and our fans didn't want to switch to Fords. Neither did we, really. Maurice and me we weren't used to the Fords. We had our hands full with them. Fortunately, Ford had come up with a big, boss hemi engine. We won ten. We did well in others. We gave 'em their money's worth. But it was one of our worst years.

"Our fans stayed with us, but were happy when we went back to Chrysler the following years. They bid a bundle to get us back. They gave us all their racing parts business, which was a big leg up. And a contract that called for a first-class operation. They had a hot engine. And we went to town. We won eighteen races that year and twenty-one the next year when we went to a Dodge. But then they went out of the racing business.

"At first, the factories raced cars right off the assembly line. Then they started building their racers special. But NASCAR kept imposing new regulations on them. At first they had to market at least five hundred of any model they raced. Then the number moved up to two thousand. Along with everything else in the world, costs were soaring sky-high. One by one, the factories fell out. When you didn't have to compete to keep up publicity-wise, the last of them moved out.

"When Chrysler left, they took their parts business with them. We buy parts from them. We still race Chrysler cars because we have warehouses full of parts. The wheels, the brakes, the rear ends, a lot of the stuff stays the same. The middle sixties was the last time they delivered cars we rebuilt. After that for a while all we got was the body. Since the late sixties we've been building our own cars anyway. It just looks like a Chrysler car. Others do the same.

"We could market a Petty car, but the rules say we have to race what is for sale in this country. Besides, we ain't in the new car business. It would be hard to compete with the factories.

"STP doesn't like it that no matter what we call it, it's still called the STP Dodge, but there isn't anything we can do about it. If there was, we would. STP is our sponsor, not Dodge. And STP is about the best sponsor in the business. It markets quality products and gives us the dollars to race quality cars.

"They say the more money you have, the better you race. That ain't quite true. I don't know if there is enough money to put together a team that would beat the Pettys or the Woods. There is only so much you can do with a car and we know what to do with it. But money helps.

"Andy Granatelli developed STP as a liquid additive for cars and he sold it and himself along with it to a big outfit and sold the company on advertising the product in car racing. He'd been a driver, builder, and sponsor in Indy racing and that's where he put STP. He had a genius for getting publicity. Who else would've thought of putting a fat man in a raincoat and having him walk around a deserted race track doing a TV commercial? But it made him famous, and it made STP famous. He was STP.

"Actually, Andy never won a lot in racing. They banned his turbine before it could win, but by then it had added to him. When Al Dean died, Andy bought the Clint Brawner—Mario Andretti car and won the Indy 500 with it. They won it for him, but there was Andy in Victory Circle kissing Andretti and pasting STP stickers on the trophy and everything else in sight.

"I think Andy agreed he had gone as far as he could in Indy racing, though I'm sure he hated to leave it. But you can't sell car products with car crashes and death. Besides, USAC runs a limited circuit and doesn't operate half the races NASCAR does. It costs less to run a car in a NASCAR race and you get more back for your money. We race the cars the people buy and sell. So the sponsors are coming to us, not them. They're in trouble. And the only solution may be to bring us in.

"I honestly believe our stock cars will be competing in the Indianapolis 500 in a few years.

"Andy came to us. So did others, but not with the numbers Andy offered us. When Chrysler left, we wanted to take the best deal. Andy gave us the best deal in racing.

"Actually, as good as it was, it almost fell through for a reason that may seem foolish to some, but wasn't to us.

"He had approached us a couple of years earlier, but he didn't want to just put STP on the cars, he wanted to control them, and we were happy with Chrysler. When Chrysler announced it was leaving, he came back to us at the end of the '72 season with a proposal to take over our operation.

"We met in Texas after a race late in the '72 season, then again in Chicago on the way to California for the last race of the season. Maurice, Dale, and me met with him and a couple of other cats and we both compromised here and there until we reached an agreement on money.

"Then, just when we were going to go and let them draw up the contracts, Andy said. 'Of course, you'll have to paint your cars red.' And we stopped and said, 'Our cars are blue.' He explained to us his cars were red, and we explained ours were blue. And no one would give an inch.

"Actually, I've heard his color called 'Day-Glo orange' and described as a sort of orange-red, almost a pink, but whatever it is, it's associated with Andy's STP teams. And since the day we didn't have enough paint to paint our car and mixed blue and a little white, pale blue has been associated with Petty teams.

"The 'Petty-blue Plymouth' was famous. When we switched to Ford and later to Dodge, as long as we kept the blue and the 43 we were recognizable. We weren't about to change no matter how much Andy argued. I said, 'We ain't got nothin' else to talk about it,' but Andy, he can talk.

"The team had to take off for Riverside, but he talked me into staying a day or two. He called his aide, Basil Bacon, to drive them to the airport and I went along. I've been in some rough races, but that was the wildest ride I ever took. It was snowing and we clipped a couple of curbs in a mad dash to the airport and just made it in time to get Maurice and Dale onto the plane.

"I spent two days with Andy at the STP offices outside of Chicago. He brought me part of a contract that said the car would be half red and half blue. I looked at it and figured, fair enough.

"Then they got into the rest of it. He'd go into another room and dictate part of the contract and they'd type it up and I'd check it out and OK it or ask for changes on it. They'd go back and type some more. And I'd look at it some more.

"I'm a race driver become a businessman. These contracts are complicated.

"Finally, he brought me a complete contract and it said at the bottom that if I'd paint the car red he'd pay me $50,000. He said, 'You can do it before Riverside.' I said, 'I'm not doing it before, or after.' And I didn't.

"I think he thought we'd change our mind. He found out he could back us, but not buy us. Maybe we were foolish. It was a lot of money. But Maurice and me talked it over and decided not to do it. It was a pride deal.

"We worked out a pattern with most of the sides red and most of the top blue and STPs and 43s all over the car, and we never collected the $50,000.

"I've heard a lot of people say they suggested the compromise, but that's the way it really was. A lot of people said we was going to ruin our operation going with the Granatellis, but they never once tried to take over.

"Andy and his brothers may have messed with their Indy teams, but they never messed with us. They knew Indy cars and racing, but they didn't know our cars and our racing. Andy said he was buying the best when he bought us, and just wanted us to do our best for him.

"He'd call up every once in a while and he'd say, 'Hey, how's everything going? You need anything? Can we do anything for you?' And if there was anything, he saw that we got it. Contract or no contract, he wasn't stingy. And when we had to renegotiate a new one, he was fair. He was always fair. Hey, they were paying us and it was we shoulda' been calling to see what we could do for them.

"When we won the Daytona 500 for him right off the bat in '73, he was thrilled. He hogged the spotlight, but I been there before. I guess he was the first owner to win both the Indy and Daytona 500s and he had a right to ham it up.

"We won it again the next year. And we won the driving title that year, too. But, actually, we didn't have our best years before Andy and STP reached the end of the road. I'm sorry about that. There was a time that I worried whether I could live with him, we were so different. But he just did his thing and I did mine and there was plenty of place for both of us.

"He has a big ego, but so do a lot of us. He just shows his more than most of us. I really like Andy and I was sorry to see him go. I don't know why he went. We were no part of that. I think they thought he had become more important than the product he was selling, and maybe they were right. But he was a supersalesman and the best businessman I've known and I wish he was back in racing because he was good for the sport.

"He got STP stickers all over our car and my uniform, but I never had to have it tattooed to my rump. He'd say the STP people are having a little get-together and if we got a chance we'd be welcome to stop by—never that they expected us or that we'd better be there. And his successors at STP have been the same way. They always have seemed to see that we're not partying people, we're racers, and we don't want to take time away from winning. But I usually stop by. I do what I can do. I'm only asked to take two or three trips a year to major meetings. I've cut a few TV commercials for them. Not many. They don't ask anything of us they don't deserve.

"When Andy left, there were a lot of changes in management, but we didn't feel any of them. I don't want to name the important people in the company that we've dealt with because some of them come and go, but they've all been beautiful. Bill Dredge has been boss of publicity since we've been with them and he's been beautiful. He's helpful and understanding.

"We had some anxious moments after Andy left, wondering what would be with our deal, but nothing changed except that it's been bigger and better for both of us.

"Our STP contracts cover our basic costs, which are real heavy these days. We can put a stock car together for about $35,000. Throw in a $10,000 engine and you've got $45,000. But we put together three cars and we have to keep taking them apart and putting them together again. And we have to have spare engines in case we blow one. Sometimes you blow two or three preparing for one race. Sometimes you go a season without blowing more than two or three.

"We get some of our parts for free, representing the manufacturers. That's not really for free. We're giving 'em something to get something. The most important thing is the tires. We used to just buy our own. Firestone was in USAC racing, not NASCAR. When Goodyear decided to compete with them, they went to NASCAR first, in the middle sixties, before going to USAC. Then they began to bid for the best.

"We tested for Goodyear from the first. We used to get paid to test for them, then we wound up getting $50,000 a year to drive their tires, and they gave us all the tires we needed. Now, a racing tire costs close to a hundred dollars and we may use ten to twenty in a race, so we're talking in the many thousands of dollars for a season of thirty races.

"Since Firestone pulled out, Goodyear stopped paying, except to those of us they want to use their emblems. It ain't the same as before, but they still give us a lot of tires. We have to race their tires because they're the only ones producing a racing tire, though they're not producing nearly as many types as they used to.

"They have a formula which changes from year to year. On a typical year, they give twenty tires to the first four qualifiers for a race, twelve to the next four, and so on down the line. It may not be fair. Maybe it should be based on finishing, not qualifying. But if you win, they don't charge for any tires they gave you.

"That helps us because we finish first a lot more than we qualify first. It does not help the ordinary cat who qualifies and finishes in the middle or back of most races. Our sport is like golf and a few others. It is not like most professional sports. No one hands us a fat contract before we perform. We get only what we earn and any expense money we can get from a sponsor.

"The tracks help the independents and little guys. You have to have a field, so they'll guarantee everyone who runs regular five hundred dollars a race. That's $15,000 a year a cat who runs the full circuit knows he's gonna get no matter what. So they start off with that much to spend. You don't eat high off the hog on those dollars, but it's something.

"The drivers today forget that when we started yesterday we had nothing. My daddy gave me something, but he started with nothing. We used to tow our racer with the family car, but the drivers today won't go without a truck. We didn't have a dyno to test engines for years, but today's young driver gripes if he isn't with a team that has a top shop. I went hungry more times than most of today's young drivers, I guarantee you.

"Sure, it's tough to beat us the way we can outspend most of 'em, but if the lesser teams work at it, they can impress the sort of sponsors who spend money. It was tough for us, too, until we impressed the big-buck boys.

"When STP first came with us, they spent for a second car and we were willing to give a good driver a good ride, Buddy Baker. The economy was against it, however, and they had to cut back. It's just as well, because we had to hire other people and we were dividing our effort.

"The thing most people forget is, even if there were enough Maurice Pettys and Dale Inmans and Wood Brothers to go around, every driver couldn't be a Richard Petty or a David Pearson, and all the bucks in the world won't buy that.

"The average racer wouldn't win in our cars, and he doesn't expect to win in his cars. He doesn't dare risk his equipment by running hard, so he just goes steady. If he did run hard, he not only couldn't keep up, he couldn't keep on the track.

"The average racer likes the life and he just wants to make a living at it. It's a job, just like other jobs. He works at it and he wins two hundred dollars here and three hundred dollars there and at the end of the year he's paid his bills and fed his family and maybe put a couple bucks in the bank, just like any other working man. Every salesman in the world can't be the world-champion salesman. But there are those that think they can be, and those that can be.

"I do feel for the fellow who has the ability to race well but lacks equipment. I also feel for the fellow who has a hard time making ends meet. If it was just Petty versus Pearson in a race, we wouldn't draw flies, and if it was just the top ten, it would still be tough. To have winners, you have to have losers. We need full fields to put on the sort of show that pulls spectators. All the entries are of value.

"But it has taken time for the little guy to get his fair share of the returns. He risks a lot to get a little.

"From time to time, the drivers have tried to unionize. When Curtis Turner was constructing the Charlotte track, which he never finished, he got a loan from the Teamsters. To repay them, he tried to organize the drivers. Bill France simply suspended him. It was unfair, but that's a dictatorship for you. The thing fell through.

"In the late sixties they organized the Professional Drivers' Association and I was elected president. I didn't want it, but I took it. The feeling was I was a big winner who didn't need much help, so it would swing weight. The idea was primarily to increase the drivers' share of the track money, and also to provide pensions and insurance. We wanted a say, okay?

"It was slow going. Bill France remembered me as a twelve-year-old boy running around the pits and he couldn't imagine talking business with me.

"In '69 when the Talledega track opened, the surface was unsafe. Testing, the tires tore right off the cars. We asked France to postpone the race until they improved the track, but he refused. He said we should run slower. Well, that ain't racing. Some of us said we wouldn't run. He said they'd have a race with or without us.

"We got together and a lot of our guys said, 'Let's leave.' They was looking to me for leadership, so I said, 'Load up.' Most of us loaded up and left. Others raced. They had a yellow flag every few laps. They were lucky they didn't have any bad accidents. But when they didn't, they said it proved we were wrong. Lordamighty, does a driver have to die before they'll do what has to be done?

"France put in a rule that once a car is at a track, it can't be taken away until after a race, but I don't see how he could stop me if I decided to leave. He could suspend me, of course. He or his son, now. They have the power. But the point is not to suspend the Pettys but listen to them to see if they make sense when we get into a dispute.

"He also got the tracks to put up $250 to every driver who showed up, made the field, and started a race. It's since doubled, but that was enough to guarantee most drivers would run. And it has helped a lot of little guys, even if the idea behind it was wrong. I think now though they would listen if we said a track was unsafe.

"We tried to work some other stuff out for the drivers, but it didn't work. They didn't know what they wanted. The independent drivers wanted one thing, the factory teams another, and they couldn't agree. The little guys thought the big guys were against them. They put me in power and then accused me of trying to run the show. They spent all their time trying to figure what I was getting out of it, so I got out.

"I was doing it for them, not for myself. Richard Petty didn't need pensions. He didn't need insurance or stuff like that. I spent five or six thousand dollars of my own money and all I got in return was a bunch of bellyaching. Finally I figured forget it, and I quit.

"I was going to quit sooner, but when STP took over our operation, Andy Granatelli asked me to resign because he didn't want bad publicity and thought I'd get bad breaks bucking the establishment. I saw the sense in what he said, but I couldn't see someone else telling me what to do. So, I waited awhile. When I went, the group gave up. I guess they couldn't live with me and they couldn't live without me.

"They're talking about getting another group together now, but let 'em get together before they get me into it. If I agree with 'em, I'll go with 'em, but I will not lead 'em. I am not going to lead any more cavalry charges only to find my own troops sniping at me from behind.

"I'm not sure how well it would work, anyway. If me and David Pearson sit down to have a meeting with France Junior, I am going to try to get a rule in for me, and David is going to try to get one in for him. If Maurice and Dale meet with the Woods, they are going to be looking out for themselves.

"We work too hard to give anything away. If we bend rules in order to win, how are we going to vote in rules that will let the other guy win? Winners are selfish. If we could be unselfish, we still couldn't agree on what's best for racers and racing. That's the USAC system and it doesn't work real well.

"There is not much I wouldn't do for another driver, but I have learned that the best thing is to do for yourself. I've been lucky in life, but I've risked a lot and worked a lot for everything I've got and I don't want to give it away. I'd rather be rich than poor. I've had it both ways and rich is better. I am not really rich, except by a poor man's standards. But I will not apologize for being well off.

"Most of the money I make, I invest in racing. Racing will remain my future even when I am finished driving. I will represent my sponsor and my team. I will chief the chief. I will tell Maurice how to build engines and Dale how to do chassis. We will get a driver and I will tell him how to drive. Maybe I'll tell Daddy how to play golf. But, whatever, I will not retire from racing. And right now I don't even want to think about retiring from driving.

"I suppose I could retire. I've invested a lot of loot in land. I've invested in my home. You are sitting on a pile of Petty money. I have an air-freight depot at the airport and a motel lease for a Ramada Inn in Charlotte. I also am on the boards of banks in my home town and in Charlotte. But I am not going to be a banker. I feel like I should contribute to my community. I also contribute to Richard Petty.

"I fly all over the country to speak and give interviews. I am paid well for some and not for others. Some, I just get expenses. I will make appearances for charity. I think I owe that to my good luck in life. And I will go to a town ahead of a race to promote a race for a fee. Racing has given me a lot and I want to give something back. But if I didn't charge for some and say no to some, I would be busy every hour of every day.

"I have a business manager, Bob Preddy, who screens requests for me and arranges stuff for me. I do magazine ads for NRI Automotive Schools. I do ads for this and commercials for that. Not a lot. I could do ten times what I do. I won't do what I don't like. I won't do what takes too much time. I don't have the time, and I don't need the money. You can buy me, but only if I want to be bought.

"Preddy has a lot of ideas about business things we could go into, and I may go into some and I may not go into some. I don't like to run risks off the track with money that came so hard on the track.

"We've done books and cut records. A bunch of us drivers cut a record called *NASCAR Goes Country*. I sang with some of the others and sang one solo. Made Sinatra real nervous. But Hollywood never called. The fact is, neither did the producers. None of us has gotten paid yet. A lot of this sort of stuff looks better than it is.

"With Preddy, we made a movie. We called it *43—The Petty Story*, but the Hollywood types retitled it *Smash-up Alley*. Darren McGavin played Daddy. Noah Beery, Jr., played Uncle Julie. Actresses played Mom and Lynda. I played myself, but never was nominated for an Oscar. Maurice played hisself, but didn't have a lot to do or say. Dale played hisself, but never said a word.

"A French actor played a sort of friendly rival of mine, which was sort of silly since he was supposed to be a good ol' boy from the Deep South—I don't know who. A lot of the names was changed to protect the guilty. The story was half true and half made-up. Some of it was right and some of it was wrong. But it was sort of fun. I played a love scene; I liked it better than Lynda did. It drew pretty well in some places, but we didn't know what we were doing and got taken in places.

"When you get right down to it, racing is the only business we really know and the only thing I'm any good at," Richard Petty concludes. "We have a simple system. We're paid so much, we spend so much, and we live on what's in between. Like any business, racing is a good business if you're good at it."

Bill Dredge

"We would like to turn Richard Petty into an STP decal. He knows that and he goes along with it. We are in business to promote a product, and there is not a better way to promote an automotive product than through an association with Richard Petty. We pay for the privilege and he gives us our money's worth. Not only through winning, but also through a winning personality.

"I have been in publicity and in racing for a long time and I have never dealt with anyone as agreeable as Richard Petty. There are things I will not ask him to do because I know racing comes first. What I ask him to do, he does. Except he will not tattoo the STP logo on his hide. Andy Granatelli stuck a sticker on his forehead, but Andy and Richard are different people. Both will do business for you, but they do it in their own ways.

"Andy was all ego. He sold himself, but by selling himself, he sold STP. When he was criticized for stealing the show in Victory Lane at Indianapolis, he produced two thousand tear sheets to prove the publicity he brought his company as well as himself. Andy was hard-sell. Richard is soft-sell. The results are all that matters. Richard gets results by being himself. He gives of himself. He pays a price.

"Richard swears he is not a businessman, but he is. He wants you to think he is not smart, but he is. He uses that southern slang, but he is as sharp as they come. He is country folk, but he has been to the big city. He is humble but honest. He has the most appealing personality of any athlete I've ever known. For all of pro football's popularity, Richard prints as well as Joe Namath, O. J. Simpson, or anyone.

"Richard goes to places like Seattle and Portland, where they have never had a big race, and he wins the people over. I have never seen anyone who was as good with the press and the public. I have never met anyone who met him who did not like him. He is such a winner off the track that he does not have to be a winner on the track. Richard sells as much STP with defeats as with victories. He is always the same, win or lose.

"He is that rarity of rarities—a real sports hero. Because he is a real man. And a gentleman. And he is a winner. He has promoted our product and his sport through the persuasiveness of his personality. It is no put-on. He is a natural. He is almost too good to believe, but I believe in him.

"In the years we have worked together there has not been one single cross word between us, and that is a rare thing, believe me. Race drivers are rough. Richard is smooth. Only Foyt is comparable to him as a national name in car racing and Foyt can't compare to him in public relations. Foyt, of course, could care less. Richard cares.

"I'm no rookie. I'm sixty-five. I was in the newspaper business, but I was also a racing fan. I was with the L. A. *Times* when I started to race sports cars as a hobby. Hell, I never won a race, but I had fun for five or six years and I got to know about cars and drivers. I became automobile editor of the newspaper and that led to a job as public relations director with Studebaker. Andy Granatelli sold STP and himself to Studebaker and I drifted into his division. Now, STP is self-sustaining.

"I learned a lot from Andy, who was a born promoter. I learned you had to have something to sell if you wanted space in the press and time on the air. Andy sold his bosses on car racing to promote his product. He didn't just take any car to Indy, but brought the most interesting cars at the time, the Novis. No one ever figured out how to harness their power, but they were the most popular cars in the field. His driver was Bobby Unser, who was braver than he was good, at that time.

"Andy bought a pile of junk and came closer to making it win than anyone, but it just wouldn't work. So he went to England and he hired Colin Chapman to run his great Lotus cars with the great Jimmy Clark to drive, and we were second in 1966. All this time he was behind the development of the turbine cars and they commanded more publicity in defeat than any car ever had in victory there. It's a shame they legislated them out of existence after we ran them two years. The breaks beat us both years, but the payoff was soaring sales for STP.

"One thing Andy never was, was cheap. He spent a lot of money, but he spent it wisely. He invested heavily in the turbines, but got a large return on his investment. He paid a top price to Parnelli Jones to drive the first turbine when Rufus was going to retire. When Rufus did retire the next year, Andy got him in a hotel room and laid bills on the bed until there was a hundred grand lying there. It was a bid to get him back, but he wouldn't budge. They're still buddies though. So Granatelli got the world champ, Graham Hill, and Joe Leonard, who put us on the pole.

"After the turbine was shot down, Al Dean had died and Clint Brawner and Mario Andretti were desperate for a sponsor, so Andy got behind them. He gave them a Lotus that was the fastest thing there, but Mario wrecked it, so they dug Brawner's old Hawk out of the garage and Andretti won with it. It was Brawner's first victory at Indy and he was angry when Andy shoved him out of the spotlight, but Andy's position was that STP had bought and owned the whole team and was entitled to the publicity he could get from it.

"That's one problem he never had with Maurice Petty or Dale Inman. They're the best mechanics in the business and they know it and they don't have to be warmed by the spotlight to be reassured about it. Mechanics don't sell cars and car products, and Andy couldn't be concerned about the bruised feelings of the trusty old wrench-turner. They have a job to do and Andy asked them to do it. Despite what you may have heard, Andy never interfered with the mechanics.

"We were in Grand Prix racing all over the world, but left. Then we left Indy. Andy hated to leave Indy. That was home to him. And he stayed a couple of years with cars like the McNamaras, which were at least innovative, if not winners. Andy always figured if you can't win, you can be interesting. But the time had come to leave USAC and go over to NASCAR.

"The handwriting was on the wall. You can't put all your advertising in one race. After Indy, there wasn't much that mattered on that circuit. The kind of cars people drove could be found in Grand National racing, and they had big races almost every weekend in almost every part of the country.

"We'd have gone sooner except that Union Oil had an agreement with NASCAR to supply gas and oil that were not to be altered by additives. A few additive companies had gotten in but had been discouraged. In 1971 we went in with a radiator product that we've since discontinued. We've stayed in with the STP gas and oil additive and oil filter and we've been extremely successful, but it took a little time.

"We went in originally with Ray Nichels and Paul Goldsmith, who operated Chrysler cars. We brought Freddie Lorenzen out of retirement to drive them. He drove the hell out of them, but they weren't worth a damn. It looked like the crew couldn't have cared less whether they won or lost. Lorenzen left and took another ride. He was so anxious to prove he could still drive he drove the car right into a spectacular wreck and was lucky to live.

"The whole operation lacked class and our concept was if it wasn't classy, it wasn't for us. We looked around for the right team, but there were only a few who fit. The Wood Brothers team was one, but it was tied to a competitor. The others were all locked up, too. Then I heard from a friend that Chrysler was leaving racing and the Petty team would be free. I laid the word on Andy and he made his move. No one had to tell us they were the best and could be better than ever with help.

"We came to terms without any problems until we got into the dispute over the car's color. Andy wanted STP red and Richard wanted Petty blue. I know Andy offered Richard a lot of money to change his mind, but Richard refused. I also know that Basil Bacon and I spent an afternoon with colored felt-tip pens sketching every conceivable color combination on Xerox copies of the car. It was one of these compromises they eventually bought. Our idea was the fans up in the stands would see the Petty blue on top, but the photographers shooting pictures from trackside for the newspapers and magazines would pick up the STP red on the sides.

"It's funny, but as famous as the all-blue Petty Plymouths were in their day, few people remember how they looked. I've been asked to settle arguments between people who can't decide if the Petty cars always had just a little red on them or this kind of red and blue combination. Also, everyone forgets that our agreement called for the Pettys to run an all-red car for us in ten races that first season, and they did with Buddy Baker as the driver.

"We cut back to one car after that, but we continue to count our investment in racing in big numbers. I don't think there is the slightest doubt in the company that it has repaid us many times over. I don't think there was the slightest doubt that we would stay in racing after Andy left. I think we will stay in racing, though I cannot speak for the company or for an officer who may come into power and may feel there is a better way to promote the product.

"I think all at the company agree Andy did a marvelous job for STP. He took that logo, which, by the way, was designed by some country printer in St. Joe, Missouri, and made it among the most famous in the world. I think the TV commercials were his idea, though the ad agency of Stern, Walters, and Simmons had a heavy hand in it. I think I helped create him as a celebrity with personal appearances all over the country and a lot of TV exposures. But Andy had an instinct for promoting himself.

"I'll tell you, he had absolutely the largest ego of any man I've ever met, yet I miss him. You get used to ego in my racket, but you don't get a lot of honesty. Andy always treated me fair and I never knew him to play anyone unfair. I don't know why he and the company parted company. I really don't. I think there were a lot of little things. Maybe money. Maybe image. I think they agreed they were in disagreement. But they made a lot of money for each other.

"The thing is, the company has become so big that it is bigger than any one man. I'm nearly in retirement, so I don't have to butter up anyone. It's not my style anyway. Craig Nalen and the rest of the STP people are super. They put out quality products and they put a fellow up in first cabin while he's promoting them. I've worked for a lot of companies, but none with their class.

"That's why Richard is so right for us. STP people spend a lot of money and time and effort to sell their products through glamorous people and no one we've had has approached Petty. We have helped Petty because a few years ago he was simply not well known in New York or Chicago or places where there are not a lot of races, but he has made the most of the exposure we have given him.

"We have used him in television and print ads and made promotional movies with him, but, frankly, I don't think we use him enough. I don't think anyone has ever done a bad interview with him. I don't care how tired he is after a race, whether he wins or loses, he'll talk to the press guys as long as they want to talk to him. They run out of questions, they ask him about recipes or radios until I rescue him.

"They want to see him in the Winston suite and they want to see him in the Union 76 suite and this PR guy wants to take him here and that one wants to take him there and Richard just goes. I feel for him because he doesn't drink and these people have been drinking all day and they're all over him, but he's just as polite to them as he can be.

"He knows there's five hundred people waiting outside for him and another five hundred at the camper. They'll wait three hours, so when he gets to them, he takes care of them. He's hot and tired, he hasn't had a shower, he hasn't even gotten his uniform off, he hasn't eaten for twelve hours, but he'll stand with a sandwich in one hand and a pen in the other signing autographs and posing for pictures.

"I tow him here and I tow him there. I took him to San Francisco the other day to a dinner. After dinner everyone else was drinking and they kept talking to him so he kept talking to them until by God it was damn near midnight and I had to close the joint down to get him out of there. Still he wound up walking down the corridor in a crowd still talkin'.

"He is completely clean. He will never ever do a single thing to embarrass himself, his family, or his sponsor.

"When we talk terms, he takes it all in and talks when he has something to say. Maurice knows his numbers, he can add and subtract, and he has his say. And old Lee is always along and always adding right along. He can count, too. Maurice is tough, but Lee is tougher. Lee's the dealer in this family, and when we put our cards on the table, he knows how to play.

"Well, I've enjoyed the game. It's time to take it easy, though I don't know if they will let me. I'm supposed to stay on as a consultant, but I will move from my place near their Fort Lauderdale base back home to California. I have six grown kids, though two of them are still in college, and I'm a grandfather. One of my kids is a foreign-car mechanic and trying to break into racing. They're great kids.

"I feel like a father toward Richard. But Richard has a father. And Richard is his own man."

Bob Preddy

"It's my business to bring business to Richard, but he is selective. He will not represent a product he does not believe in and use. If he is sponsored by STP it has his approval. And he will not accept a cent from any company that is in any way competitive with STP.

"I could get a hundred grand for Richard to race another company's tires and they'd make them special for him. He will not go for it because the tires are not available to others and Goodyear was good to him for many years. He is loyal to them even though they are not doing a lot for him these years.

"He smokes Muriel cigars, but he will not advertise for them because he worries about kids smoking. He does not smoke cigarettes and he will not endorse cigarettes, even though he feels loyalty to R. J. Reynolds Tobacco Company because it sponsors Winston Cup competition.

"He does not drink whiskey or beer, so he will not endorse any of these despite big money bids. But he does not turn anything down without telling us to ask the company to offer it to other drivers. He wants the other drivers to get their piece of the pie too.

"He tells us to use STP products, but he also tells us that if we need an oil filter, say, and they do not have an STP oil filter, to ask if they have a Purolator filter. They may be our biggest competitor, but they support racing, so he wants to support them.

"I don't know how STP will feel about this, but it's typical of Petty.

"I was born in Louisburg, North Carolina. I was a basketball player in high school and still hold the state scoring record, but this is car-racing country and I was turned on to the sport. I began a Bible-recording company. I got together with Richard when I did a record and book which we called *Meet Richard Petty*. We printed a hundred thousand and only have about ten thousand left as collector's items.

"I formed Victory Lane Productions primarily to represent Richard in public relations and business, seven or eight years ago. My partner is Jack Carter. He's president of firms and organizations all over the country. He's an educator and produces educational films. We have a newspaper-sized printing press and our own recording and filming studios.

"We are associated with Matt Merola of Mattgo Enterprises in New York, who represents Reggie Jackson, Tom Seaver, and several other superstars, and Neil Jones of Jones & Company in Denver, and among us we can reach a wide variety of prominent athletes with business. But Richard Petty personally takes up most of my time, so I've never taken on other race drivers.

"I produced a film on him for the Coast Guard and have since done many films with him. And we did the one big movie, *The Petty Story*, which became *Smash-up Alley*.

"The one thing Richard said was, 'If we do it, let's do it right.' I flew out to Hollywood where I have a friend who wrote *Mission Impossible*, *Mannix*, and others, and he put me in touch with top people. We bought the best, from the director through stars. We rented thirty rooms for three months at a motel here. We went first class.

"We were budgeted at a half-million. When they explained to us that we were going to be spending $1,250 an hour and if one man got lost and held us up a half-hour it would cost us $625, it scared Richard and me near out of our wits. And they told us we were considered low-budget.

"We brought in a beautiful picture at $566,000, which wasn't bad. We finished it in 1972 and released it in 1973. We opened in Canada and did $110,000 business the first week. We figured that was fantastic.

"Then we found out half went to the second feature on the bill, which was nothing, but which they said we had to have. Then we found out the distributors took 10 per cent. And the subdistributors 10 per cent. And advertising came off the top. We came out with $11,000.

"We knew nothing about distributing and promoting a commercial movie, and that hurt. We got great reviews. Richard received great reviews as an actor. We opened in Raleigh and the house was sold out. Where they advertised that this was a real movie, we had long lines. Where they didn't, we didn't draw customers.

"Anyway, we've done three-million-dollars business and we're still $46,000 short of coming out even on it. But we're still doing business with it; we're selling it to TV now, and we may rerelease it in theaters. It was an entertaining and enlightening experience.

"The most profitable project I developed for the Pettys, and I really represent all of them, was the association with STP. Richard had a business manager before I took over and he had talked to STP, but it's easy for a guy to hit the telephone and call fifty companies, and if one of them later sees the success of the Pettys and says he wants a part of it to say, 'I did it.' Richard and I don't have that kind of relationship. We know who did what and it's not who asked, but who came through.

"The STP tie-up was started at Dover, Delaware, between Bill Dredge and me. We talked there and elsewhere, but the hangup was that Bill said Granatelli insisted on a red car while I knew Richard insisted on a blue one. About five months later I wrote a letter suggesting a marriage with half STP red and half Petty blue and Andy agreed to it and Richard went along with it.

"When I pitched our price at them, they couldn't believe it and they asked me why I thought we were worth it. I pointed out that out of their $40-million advertising budget they spent $40,000 to $60,000 a minute for prime-time television sports, while with us they got, among other things, ninety minutes of stock-car racing on *Wide World of Sports* twelve times a year with Richard's car usually leading and the STP logo on camera.

"When I first started with Richard, I'd try to arrange an article on him with a magazine and they weren't interested. Now they come to us and there isn't a major magazine we haven't been featured in from *Reader's Digest* to *Playboy*. *Time* was the most recent. He has become a major name and I'd like him to cash in on it.

"He owns a freight depot and a motel and part of a bank. We're real close to opening some Dodge dealerships and a string of self-service gasoline stations, both under Richard's name with the mechanics and attendants wearing Richard Petty uniforms, and the cars going out with stickers saying 'Bought from Richard

Petty' or 'Serviced by Richard Petty.' Dodge may put out a special 'Petty Dodge.'

"We have offers to merchandise Petty products from every kind of company you can imagine. We do have a deal with a key-ring company and others, but we're selective. I am getting some of this for Maurice and Dale, but they don't want to get too involved. Richard really sells. I know STP pays a lot for him, but he pays them back a dollar to a dime. They are just a terrific outfit to do business with and they have a priceless property in Mr. Petty.

"We always co-operate with the news media because Richard feels he is representing not only the Petty team but STP, and wants to return their investment in him every way we can. We send a different tape recording around to all the news outlets every month. We're available for interviews all the time. We charge a track five hundred dollars and expenses when Richard goes to town ahead of time to promote a race.

"There is just so much time. Richard has to race. He has to be at the track three or four days before a race to prepare for it. He has to have rest. We try not to take advantage of him, but we do, and he lets us. When it comes to personal appearances, he says, 'I'll give you this day or that day, but don't tell me where we're going or what we're going to do or what I'm supposed to say.'

"He leaves all the decisions up to me and never has questioned a one of them. I have to turn down nine out of ten requests. If it's for money, we charge $500 an hour, half-time going and coming. In other words, if it takes an hour each way, that's $250 each way, and if he's there three hours that's $1,500. But he only does four or five of these a year. I know he likes to do charity things, so we do these for free, excepting expenses maybe. He does these ten to one over the others.

"Richard receives hundreds of fan letters a week. We do not have a form letter and every letter is answered. Lynda has some high-school kids come in afternoons to help. Richard signs as many as he can. He has such a ridiculous signature it's hard to imitate, but I can come close. Lynda signs all their personal checks. Richard just doesn't want to be bothered about house payments and insurance and stuff like that. STP provides us thousands of eight-by-ten glossy pictures to send out.

"Richard is fantastic with his fans and they respond with a personal feeling for him that goes beyond anything I've ever seen.

"I started his fan club and I think it's the biggest any movie or television or sports star has. We have about fifteen thousand paid-up members. I'm not sure of the number because it keeps growing. We have about three hundred chapters in forty-eight states. I don't know why we're not in North Dakota or Arizona, but no one has come to us and we have never asked anyone to start a chapter anywhere.

"We even have chapters in eleven other countries, including England, Australia, South Africa, and West Germany. We get mail from behind the Iron Curtain. Some of these people go to the expense of coming to this country to see Richard race. Others beg for magazine and newspaper stories so they can keep up with him, and our members here send these out. We also send out a newsletter regularly.

"We charge five dollars, but that money is spent the day we get it, and after that it's a losing proposition. We have secretaries working sending out packets of pictures, decals, and certificates from the day a person enrolls. I used to run the club myself, but it became too big for me. I was getting twenty-five telephone calls a day on it. So I organized it and we have national, regional, and local leaders.

"Wherever Richard races, the fan club honors him. They bring him birthday cakes and presents and hold dinners for him, and he loves it. We've had four or five hundred people at some affairs. Richard even was best man at the wedding of our Pennsylvania president at Pocono. We bring in Maurice and Dale and try to make these fans more knowledgeable about auto racing.

"Encouraged by Richard, the fans do good works on their own with everything from picking up trash off their city's streets to raising funds with car washes for crippled children. It is heart-warming to see the good he brings out in people. He is a good person himself, a simple person, unspoiled.

"He didn't really like the idea of a souvenir shop at the compound, but so many tours and individual fans come to the place all the time, and they want to leave with something. It was something they wanted, though it also makes a little money for the Pettys.

"Bill Frazier, an ordained minister in the Baptist faith, known as 'the Racing Reverend' and 'Brother Bill' to everyone in racing, runs the shop for Richard and conducts services for drivers at tracks on Sundays. Richard is religious and he and Brother Bill are kind of close.

"I remember one time we were up in a plane and Richard looked out the window and asked me to look down at what was way below and he said to me, 'Bob, look at that and look at us. How small we are, really. And yet we are all big in the eyes of God.'

"I am married. My wife Bobbi and I have sons, Charles, eighteen, and Robbie, seventeen. Charles drives a van because Richard drives a van. Robbie wanted a Colt because Richard drives a Colt. My family feels like part of the Petty family. We are all fanatical fans."

14

JULY

A summer rainstorm poured down on Daytona, where the racers were preparing for the annual Fourth-of-July Firecracker 400. Richard Petty crouched in a corner of his team's truck, opening presents sent him by his fans in honor of his thirty-eighth birthday two days before the race.

There were a pile of presents, including a boxful of trinkets from his most feverish fan, a lady in New York named Elizabeth, who hand-prints long letters to him on all sides and the margins of fancy cards, calling him "King," and "The Lion," and her "Future Bridegroom," describing in detail a forthcoming marriage to him in total disregard of his wife. He has never met the lady.

"Lynda doesn't really want me to, and I don't reckon I do, either," Richard remarks, grinning. "I get a lot of letters like this, but none that really come close to this lady. The gals at the office screen out most of my mail, but Elizabeth writes me on the road. Like the pony express, Elizabeth gets through."

In her gift were a bunch of Band-Aid cans fixed up like firecrackers, a plaster lion, toy houses from a Monopoly set, somewhat smaller than the one she expected Petty to purchase for her after the wedding, and a purple paper crown. Petty placed it on an onlooker's head, and laughed: "Looks like he et the margarine!" He opened presents while he talked to a writer from the latest national magazine to feature him, *Sports Illustrated*.

Asked about the famous jinx associated with that magazine's cover story, Richard remarked, "I don't believe in jinxes. I'll even walk under ladders. Won't climb 'em: that's because I'm afraid of heights. I ain't afraid of racing, only of heights." Asked if it bothered him that the writer went with him wherever he went for the week, Richard smiled and said, "You do it, too, don't you? It's what you writers got to do. It don't bother me. You do what you got to do and I do what I got to do. Lynda at least knows when to close the door."

He crouched at the end of the truck, chewing his cigar, looking through his dark, wraparound sunglasses at the rain, waiting for it to go away so he could get going. Work was not going well with the car. From the day they unloaded it, it would not go faster than 180. They changed the engine, the wedge, the spoiler, the headers, the exhaust pipe, and they still ran 180. Everyone else of consequence was running 185 or 186, but Richard was running 180. "Maurice is getting hard to live with, and Dale ain't no dream," Richard reported, as if he, himself, did not matter.

The skies were clear for qualifying, though the heat was heavy and the air sultry. Donnie Allison ran 186 and Richard Petty ran 180, with David Pearson, Buddy Baker, Darrell Waltrip, Dave Marcis, Benny Parsons, Bobby Allison, and others—even Richard Brooks and Lennie Pond—somewhere in between. A dozen cars separated Petty from the front and he was six miles an hour slower than the fastest car. "We've tried everything. We've even tried changing the radio frequency," he said.

What, then, could they do?

"Just keep pushin'." Richard shrugged. Right then they were pushing out the rear window to change that.

This was one of the traditional tour races he had not won. His victory in the World 600 earlier this 1975 season, had been his first win at the Charlotte Speedway. He had won at Atlanta Raceway before, but his win in the Atlanta 500 had been his first. He had won the Daytona 500 five times; but somehow he had missed the Firecracker 400.

"We've won more races than anyone. One race is almost like another," he said, "You can't win 'em all. But you *can* try." What hurt, he admitted, was that he had finished second four straight years here in this holiday event—second to David Pearson the last three years, last year by a few feet when Pearson slowed drastically to lure Richard around him, then drafted the Petty car and slipped past it at the finish.

"I remember it, I reckon," he remarked. He wasn't going to let it bother him. He said he had other things to think about just then. He was on his way to meet with members of his Florida fan club, who had convened at a service station nearby to conduct a car wash, with the proceeds to go to the family of Richard's late brother-in-law.

"It's not that we've left Randy's family in need, but it's nice that the fans want to do something like this," Petty pointed out.

Walking through and out of the speedway, Richard was surrounded by fans and he was graceful with them, smiling at them, talking to them, signing autographs for them. When he got to the car wash, he just walked up and went to work washing cars. The club members did not seem surprised. They smiled their hellos and went on washing alongside him. After a while he picked up a hose and pretended he was going to squirt them and they jumped out of the way, laughing with him.

The magazine writer wrote later that it was like the scene from *A Death in the Family* when the father went out to sprinkle the lawn with his children. It was full of easy summer affection. He wrote that Richard moved among his fans with an ease that is rarely seen among athletes.

If their problems preparing for the race showed on Maurice and Dale and the rest of the crew, it did not show on Richard. His whole family was with him, and he took Lynda, Kyle, Sharon, Lisa, and even baby Rebecca for a sunset stroll along the beach as the surf broke in near them. Rebecca acted up a bit, so Lynda carried her. The fans kept coming at Richard, who had his hands full with them. Does it ever bother him? "Sometimes," he admitted. "Sometimes they get carried away and go too far. Not most of the time. Most of the time the people are real nice, so it's easy to be nice to them. It bothers Lynda. But not me."

"They just won't leave him alone," she sighs. "We can't go out and relax because the people push in. They mean well, but they don't do right. We can't even walk on the beach without people running up to Richard."

A black man ran up to Richard excitedly. "I've got second sight," he announced. "I'm clairvoyant. If you believe. If you truly believe, you can win the race."

"Ah believe," replied Richard, smiling.

He won the race, though no one is quite sure how. By race time they had changed one engine, three carburetors, and six fuel pumps in the car. As the race unfolded, they still were running 180, but he ran it steadily, without making a mistake, and his pit crew's performance was perfect. As others broke down or fell back, he moved up until he was within reach of the lead. Once it was within reach, he went for it with a steady hand.

There were 70,000 fans packed into that place this Independence Day, and they saw a spectacular race free of serious accidents. A dozen drivers exchanged the lead fifteen times, but some of the hot cars caved in. Former Indianapolis champion Johnny Rutherford failed in the first lap, and Bobby Allison blew early too. Brother Donnie, the fastest qualifier, faded fast.

"The car had more speed than I could handle," confessed Donnie, who finished fifth. He was all over the track. Although he had been appointed president of his sponsoring firm, DiGard, the bosses, the brothers Bill and Jim Gardner, admitted they were thinking of changing drivers and crews. Darrell Waltrip admitted he wanted the ride.

All season long, Donnie had qualified fast and finished slow. "We've had our problems," insisted Donnie, "but we can work them out." A few days later he was out and Waltrip was in.

While Allison was falling back at Daytona, Foyt, Pearson, and Baker were running up front. Dave Marcis had fallen back too, but late in the race he came with a rush that all but blew the leaders out of his way. He unlapped himself and set up a high finish. "I had gearbox problems before I got going," Marcis said.

"He got going so fast he like to run right over us," remarked Petty. "At one point, Baker, Pearson, and me was running in a bunch and he blew by us so close I could hear Buddy bellow from where I was. I can tell you, there were three of us were scared. And if any of us wasn't, we should have been." Joe Biddle of the Daytona *News Journal* later wrote, "Dave Marcis drove like an expectant father trying to get his wife to the hospital before his first was born." Another driver said, "He drove like a guy digging a grave."

As they boomed daringly toward the end of the event, Foyt's engine expired with twenty-four laps left. Pearson pushed far in front with twenty-two laps left, leaving Baker and Petty to fight for second place. Suddenly, Petty had appeared among the leaders. "I just stayed close, drafting quicker cars, and near the end I sneaked up. On our last pit stop, while the others changed right-side tires, we figured we had to do something different, so we changed left-side rubber. It was dirty up high and the right side was sticking. I figured I could use the traction down low. I could never have caught Pearson, but I could handle the corners better than Buddy."

When Pearson's oil line snapped twenty laps from the finish and he coasted to a stop, it was between Buddy and Richard. Richard drafted Buddy until twelve laps were left, then slingshot around him. Instead of waiting, Baker went right back at Petty and passed him. But, as Buddy went into a turn too hard, he got too high and slipped a little. He found himself right behind the slower car of Dick Brooks. As Buddy backed off, Richard took off and opened a large lead. Through the last laps, with the fans screaming, Baker's Coppertone Ford closed in on the STP Dodge but could not catch it. Petty flashed across the finish line two seconds ahead of Baker.

After sixteen attempts, Petty had won this race. Firecrackers popped as he pulled into Victory Lane. "We have waited awhile for this one," he admitted as Maurice and Dale got to him and the crowd closed in around them. He was swallowed up then in the ceremonies and interviews and autographs, as his crew went off to do the dirty work.

"It was one we should never have won," admitted Maurice, "except that we worked our fannies off for it, and Richard took advantage of every opportunity that came along." Dale was laughing like he had fooled someone.

When Richard returned with his $17,000 check, he said, "When you finish a winner like this, you feel you've created something and accomplished something. This is one we didn't buy. We had a slow car, and the boys made the most of it. I drove a smart race. To tell you the truth, if you can keep a secret, when you really come right down to it, I just flat outdrove the lot of 'em." He went away on a wave of wonder, satisfaction showing on his face. He dealt with his happy fans on the way to his wife and kids and home.

Two weeks later Richard was in Nashville for the second of the two night races on the tour. Dale and Wade drove the truck and trailer rigs in and checked the car in. Richard drove down with Barry in the van on Thursday. They left at one in the afternoon on Thursday and got into Nashville at nine that night. They met the others at the motel and went out to eat at the Red Lobster

restaurant. Richard had a fish platter. They went back to the
motel and went to bed.

There was a Ku Klux Klan rally in town that night, and it was
spread all over the Nashville newspaper in the morning.

Qualifying was scheduled for Friday night and the race for Saturday night. The track was not supposed to open until two on Friday afternoon, so Richard was going to sleep in. But when Jim
Donoho of the track asked him to appear on an early-morning
TV talk show, along with Benny Parsons, Richard agreed to it. So
Donoho called him at 5:30 to wake him up and came for him at
six and took him to the studio and they waited until the show
went on at seven.

Richard and Benny did a live interview with the host on camera, then answered telephone calls from viewers for an hour.
Richard said anyone could win, but reckoned he would. Benny
laughed and said Richard could win, but Benny could too.
Donoho told them they did a great job for him. By the time
Richard got back to the motel it was nine and his team was at the
track. He had breakfast and went back to bed.

Bill Donoho has been the promoter at the Nashville Speedway
for more than twenty years. He is chairman of the board. His son
Jim is president and publicist. And Jim's wife, Beverly, is the secre-
tary and custodian at the pass gate. Bill's wife, Mildred, is in charge
of ticket sales. Bill's brother Henry is in charge of the ticket takers.
Henry's wife, Mary, sells tickets. Bill's brother Don directs the
race. Don's son Pat is a flagman. Don's son Rusty cleans up. Bill
and Don's uncle Dewey take tickets. Dewey's wife, Erlene, sells
them. Other relatives do other things.

The family prides itself on it being a tight operation. The
drivers feel it is too tight and consider the $10,000 the promoter
puts toward a total purse of $62,000 too little. A big, gruff guy, a
former assistant police chief, the fifty-nine-year-old patriarch of
the Donoho clan commented, "It is not easy to operate a small
track like this and keep the drivers happy and the fans happy and
come out ahead.

"We only seat 15,000 in the grandstand, we don't let anyone in
the infield, and we let little kids in for free. We only have the two
Grand National races a year, but we run other cars on other weekends. We keep racing alive here. I'm going to build the people

here a one-mile superspeedway as soon as interest rates come down.

"We're not cheap. We're the only small track with an electronic scoreboard. I spent $270,000 to build up the banks because the fans wanted the speed. Then I spent $430,000 to tear them down because the drivers thought it was dangerous. I'm still paying on that $700,000."

Jim Donoho said, "We have a small track in a big town. Tracks like ours have fallen off the Grand National tour, hurting the tour. We help it by offering races every year. We have to hustle to make ends meet. If we had to hire outside help for the top positions, we'd have to quit. If we get a big track, we can make it big in this town. "This is a boom town. Music City, USA, you know. This is the capital of country music. There's more recording here than in New York or Hollywood. The Grand Ol' Opry is here. Opryland is one of the biggest tourist attractions in the world. We have to hustle to keep up in this town."

Wearing his hillbilly hat, a faded sports shirt, jeans, and cowboy boots, Richard Petty reached the track at two, in time to start practice. His crew was working on his car in a gully full of cars beneath a bank at one end of the track.

This was at a fairgrounds where an amusement park flanked the track and a roller coaster ran along the fence outside of one corner. The fence was wooden, plastered with faded signs advertising WNAH All-Gospel Radio and Ellis Funeral Home and other businesses. One sign pointed out that the Nashville Flea Market was conducted at the track the fourth Saturday and Sunday of "ever" month.

The track was a little less than six tenths of a mile around, paved, and slightly banked. Richard said, "NASCAR and Nashville can't decide how far around it is. It depends on whether you measure from the inside or the outside. It used to be dirt. They made a high-bank of it, but it was scary. It became a bowl, like Bristol, which is awful. They cut it back and it's better. This is the only track we run at night. It's the kind of race and race track we used to run. There aren't many like it anymore, so it's sort of fun. The driver really comes into his own at a track like this. It's tough, 420 laps turning in traffic.

"The Donohos are all right, though don't let on to Maurice I said that. Bill is a hard gent. He runs his own show his way and he won't budge an inch. He's an old-style promoter and there's not many like him left. He hires family so he don't have to pay 'em much and I reckon they go home at night after a race and get together in the kitchen and empty their pockets and put all the money on the kitchen table and he divides it up. Jim takes care of the drivers. He does what he can for us and gets what he can out of us.

"I can't kick. The Pettys is a family operation, too." Richard grinned. His cousin had his car ready to roll.

Richard went into a restroom and got into his uniform and took the car out to practice it. The big cars boomed around the little track. It was hot, dry, and dusty. A drought was spoiling crops all over the state, the newspaper reported. Petty brought the car in, reporting, "It's handling loose." He turned it back to Dale and picked up the newspaper and turned to the sports section to read about the race.

Though Darrell Waltrip, the twenty-eight-year-old Tennesseean from Franklin, had won the Music City 420 here in May when Petty's engine failed, Richard, a three-time winner here, was still the favorite for this one. He had won half of the sixteen events so far on the tour and was hot.

A reporter from a local paper, Larry Woody, interviewed him that day and asked if he took this short-track race more lightly than he did the long-track events. Richard said, "The way I figure it, a race is a race. When I race on a big track, one of those superspeedways, I try to win. And when I race on a smaller track, like here, I try to win. Ain't really much difference, I don't reckon."

A visitor observed that it looked like rain. Petty removed a chewed-up cigar from the corner of his mouth, squinted at the sky, and grinned. "Yep," he said. He put his cigar back in his mouth, tired of that conversation.

It did rain, a sudden squall, turning the infield into mud. The drivers huddled under cover, talking. The rain disappeared, but behind it the air was left heavy with moisture. The drivers waited and the mechanics resumed work on the cars while the track dried. Cale came by to visit Petty and they talked, sitting around on tires.

After a while Cale stood and stretched. "Guess I better go to work. See you later," he said.

"Yep," Petty said.

He wore a tiny ring on his left little finger. Engraved on it was the word LOVE. His uniform was unzipped halfway down his chest. He wore a religious medal around his neck and had another in his pocket. On his uniform was a patch which read, "With God, You're Always a Winner." On the dashboard of his car was affixed a plate inscribed with "The Racer's Prayer" and that is the last line. Composed by Brother Bill, it reads in part: "Lord, I pray as I race today . . . Keep me safe along the way . . . Not only me but others, too . . . As they perform the jobs they do. . . ."

"I'm takin' no chances." Richard grinned as he got into his car and drove it onto the track for practice. He went around and around, warming up, picking up speed. Suddenly, coming off the backstretch, he lost control, spun sharply, slowed, braked, and came to a stop without hitting anything. Restarting, he came into the pits.

Dale looked at him sharply. "Too much for you, boy?" he asked.

"Too much for me," Richard smiled.

Dale shrugged and turned to the car to check it.

"Another car cause you trouble?" Richard was asked.

"No other cars."

"Just you?"

"Just me. I just lost it. Went in too far and lost it."

"Worry you any?"

"Worried about wrecking the car, that's all."

"Scare you?"

"Nope."

"Thrill you?"

"Nope."

"Nothing happens?"

"Nothing happens. My heart isn't pounding. My pulse rate probably hasn't even fluttered. They did a deal at Darlington one day where they stuck electronic stuff on some of us and monitored us during a race. They could read our heartbeat and things. They could tell when some drivers got in the car and when they started the race and when they got in traffic.

"They had the deal on Dave Marcis when he got in a wreck and they said just before it happened his heartbeat went out of sight. The way they figured it, there was no reason for the accident, so he apparently got flustered or too hot or too tired and his body went bad. But my heart never missed a beat. I got in trouble at times in the race, but my readings never changed at all at any time. I guess I got that going for me."

Dale decided the car was all right, so he returned it to Richard with a warning to try to keep the darn thing pointed in the right direction. Richard reckoned he'd try to do that little thing and he pulled on his silver helmet and climbed into the blue-and-red car and took it back on the track. Work went on through the muggy afternoon as the day wore along.

It cooled as darkness fell and the lights atop towering poles flickered on to illuminate the old wooden arena. The adjacent amusement park was open for business and lights glowed on the ferris wheel as it turned. The sounds of happy people could be heard drifting across the area. Fans started to drift into the grandstand for the night's program, which would lead off with qualifying for the following night's Grand National race, then conclude with three races for lesser cars.

The Petty team had drawn a late number for their time-trial run. They sat around the open-air "garage area" and waited. Dale fussed inside the car. Some ate hot dogs and drank soda pop. Richard ate nothing, though he had not had a bite to eat since nine that morning. I sensed his stomach was bothering him, and asked him about it, but he refused to admit it. "It's all right," he shrugged.

He walked up the bank through a grassy area littered with crushed soda-pop cups and popcorn containers and sat on a retaining wall just outside the track to watch the early qualifiers. It had cooled down now and it was all right. A young mechanic from another team came up and sat down next to him and asked him about the science of drafting. Richard went into great detail.

"You don't draft too much on a track like this because you're always turning and it can throw the cars out of control. You always have to be careful about drafting in a pack. You can't draft all the time on the superspeedways because the heat builds up in your engine from the exhaust of the other car and you have to break it off before you burn up."

The young fellow thanked Richard and departed. He was wearing a grease-soiled tee shirt and dirty jeans. A lot of the crews were in old clothes, but Petty's team and the other top teams were in

uniforms that had at least been clean when the day began. A lot
of the people around the Petty garage wore red-and-blue jackets
and caps with the STP emblem on them. Other people came up
to ask aides for free STP jackets or caps, which they were prom-
ised.

Down off the bank, Petty started to put on his helmet, then
stopped to take off his sunglasses.

Someone said, "It's night and you're still wearing those sunglasses."

Richard grinned and said, "I went to bed last night and clean
forgot to take 'em off. Lynda wasn't here to remind me," he
added, his grin growing.

They buttoned him into his car and got going. When the announcer called out his name, the fans, half filling the little grandstand, hollered for him. Richard ran high and hard, circling the
oval in a tick or two over twenty-one seconds. His speed of 101.8,
however, was bettered by Cale Yarborough, Darrell Waltrip, and
Benny Parsons. Benny, in the Kings Row Fireplace Chevy, was
the surprise pole-sitter at 103.3.

"It was a little loose," Richard told Dale.

"We'll try to tighten 'er tomorrow," Dale answered.

Richard put his sunglasses on as Wade and Wayne and Barry
began to tie a tarp around the car and to lock up their tools and
other equipment in the truck. Jim Donoho came by to remind
Richard that he and Benny had agreed to tape a TV show that
evening. He offered to take Richard to a private opening of country singing star George Jones' new nightclub later.

"The whole team?" Richard asked.

"Sure," Donoho said.

"I reckon," Richard said.

"We haven't eaten yet," one of the crew commented.

"You can eat there," Donoho said.

"Man does not live by bread alone," Richard remarked.

I commented then when you run with Richard, you do not eat.

"You noticed," Richard said, smiling.

They went back to the motel to wash up and change into civvies. A family of fans were waiting for Richard. They were fans
who always waited for Richard there when he was in Nashville,
and he recognized them and greeted them warmly. They showed
him the latest scrapbooks they had made of his adventures, and

he signed them, and posed with each of them singly and in groups as flashbulbs popped on their Instamatics.

They talked about the Firecracker 400 and the World 600 and the next night's race. They talked and they talked and they talked, and Richard just stood there in the cool evening by the pool and chatted with them. He had been with them an hour when Dale hollered for him to haul his rear out of there and get changed because Donoho was due to pick him up. Richard did, excusing himself excessively, and the fans thanked him.

Richard hurriedly showered and dressed in sports clothes. Donoho, with Benny already in the car, came by and got Richard and they drove through the night to the television studio. The drivers discussed the daring ride of Dave Marcis at Daytona. In the darkened car, Benny's voice was heard to say, "I'm not scared of anybody, but I'm scared of him." And Richard's laughing voice said, "That boy sure put the fear of God in all the atheists."

They got to talking about the television interview, and an earlier interviewer who had asked Benny if he had "a death wish." "Can you believe it?" Benny asked.

"I believe it," Richard replied. "That ol' boy's got blood on his microphone."

They got to the television studio, which was deserted except for technicians and the host, and did the taping, which was to be shown the next day. Richard said the same things he had been saying in interviews for days. He took the short race on the short track as seriously as he did any others. Some of the top drivers did not run the short races because their sponsors did not support a full schedule, but there was a strong field set anyway. Yes, he had been having a good year. Yes, he thought he could win. Yes, he looked forward to the race. "A driver gets to express himself on a track like this," Richard said.

Donoho asked Parsons if he wanted to party, but Benny said he had other business to do, so Donoho dropped him off and took Richard to his motel to pick up the rest of the team. Fans waited for him there and he talked to them until Dale and the rest of the boys dragged him off. They said they were starving. Richard turned to me to ask if I was starving. I said I was. "When Chief gets here, you better latch onto him. You get to eat with him," Richard chuckled. "Maurice never misses a meal."

Dale asked Donoho if the races were on radio. Donoho said

they were and fiddled with the dial until he found the broadcast. Waltrip was winning a sportsman race. Donoho drove through the dark night, saying he was sure he knew where the new nightclub was, but made a couple of wrong turns before finally he curved down a country road and the club, a converted mansion overlooking the Cumberland River, loomed up ahead. A guard stopped the car and asked if they had an invitation. Donoho said they did not, but had been invited. "I'm Jim Donoho of Nashville Speedway," he said.

"I'm sorry, but if you don't have an invitation . . . ," the guard started to say.

"This is Richard Petty," Donoho said, pointing to Petty.

The guard peered in.

"Howdy," Richard said, extending his hand.

The guard shook it and grinned. "Go on in," he said.

A little annoyed, Donoho gunned the car ahead while the others laughed.

The place was plush and packed. Donoho introduced the Pettys to the maitre d', who welcomed them warmly and led them right down front, putting tables and chairs in front of the patrons who had been in front. The show was on. George "Possum" Jones, the owner, was performing. He seemed annoyed until he realized it was Richard, then smiled and nodded in mid song, as he sang:

> *"Step right up, come on in,*
> *If you'd like to take the grand tour. . . ."*

Jones, formerly married to country star Tammy Wynette when they owned a fully outfitted touring bus that was as famous as they were, is a short, dark fellow with an easy style. He had a good grip on his audience and they were listening to him, not talking, as he sang. He finished to a lot of applause. He introduced Richard, who stood up and smiled and received even louder applause.

Commenting that Richard recently had cut a record with other drivers, George asked him if he'd like to sing. Richard laughed and said, "I won't sing you, but I'll race you." Everyone laughed. George said, "Well, I won't race you, so I'll sing." And he sang:

> *"I woke up this morning, aching with pain,*
> *Don't think I can work, but I'll try.*

The car's in the shop, so I thumbed all the way,
These days I barely get by.

I walked home from work, and it rained all day,
My wife left and didn't say why,
She laid all my bills on the desk in the hall,
These days I barely get by

Put my only two dollars on my favorite horse,
He lost by a nose and I cried,
Oh, my boss says come winter, we'll all be laid off,
These days I barely get by,
These days I barely get by,
Gonna' give up, lay down, and die. . . ."

They hollered for more when he finished, so he gave them more. A waitress offered drinks to the Petty party, but they settled for Cokes. Some asked about food, but no one was eating there. Donoho whispered they were saving some for them in the dining room, so they waited, hungry, but hung up on the owner's singing.

He sang his songs, all of them seemingly songs of lost love, and the well-dressed crowd of prominent townspeople and performers and agents hung on his every word. And when he left and the crew started to stir, another performer came on, and started to pick a banjo and tell jokes and sing his song right away, so they settled back down. He was good, but they were groaning with hunger before he finished.

Finally, at eleven—thirteen hours after Richard had eaten last —he was led with Dale and the boys back to the dining room, which was deserted. A waiter was found and he said no meals had been held for them. There was some food left, he said, but it had not been kept hot. They would take anything, they said. So he fetched roast beef, which had gone cold, and some mashed potatoes, also cold, and some rolls, which were hard, and they heated up some coffee. Everyone ate heartily except Richard, who picked at his plate. The Possum man came by to talk for a while. He said he was opening nightclubs on every corner, it seemed like. They said this one was super and wished him well with it.

"You win that race, Richard, y'hear?" Jones said.

"Do my best," Richard said.

Afterwards, he was waylaid in the lobby by well-wishers. Some of the team were taken back into the club by Donoho, who wanted them to see a couple of girls who were coming on. They were beautiful girls and they worked with enthusiasm. Some of the guys liked them and some didn't. Richard got back to his seat late and saw only a couple of songs before the act ended, and the guys started yawning and saying it was time to take off. A couple of lovely ladies came around Richard as he was leaving and played up to him. It would have been easy. But he didn't do it. He left with the rest.

"What a doll," one of the ladies said.

"What a shame," the other pouted.

They went out into the night and got into Donoho's car and he drove them back to their motel. "Did I show you a good time?" he asked.

"Sure did," Dale said.

"Yup," Richard replied.

If there was a tab, Donoho had picked it up.

It was almost one when they retired to their rooms.

They were up early the next morning to eat and go to the track. All except Richard, who slept in. After a while, he came on out without eating. He took the car out to test it. He brought it in and said it was still loose and was sliding. Of course, conditions would be different in the cooler evening, but they decided to try softer springs in hopes the car would stick better. It helped a little, but not a lot. They made other changes: "What say we try this? . . . What say we try that?" It was hot and humid and everyone was bitching about it, but black clouds were moving in. After a while the sky was obscured, and then it began to rain. It came down hard as the drivers and crews huddled in their cars and trucks.

It rained until everyone decided to go back to their motels to wait it out. A caravan of cars drove down muddy roads through the tunnel to the outside world. Back at the motel, the Petty team turned on television and watched and talked and waited.

One by one other members of the crew came in—Kraut and Radar and the rest. Jimmy Martin turned up, and they started to talk about tobacco. Chief arrived and asked how they were. "Wet," Dale said. The rain kept coming and flash-flood warnings were broadcast.

"We'll never race," Maurice said.

"It'll stop," someone said.

"We'll never race," Maurice repeated.

Out of the rain appeared a family loaded with baskets of food. They were welcomed at Richard's room, moved in, and started spreading baked ham, barbecued beef, potato salad, biscuits, iced tea, and cold milk on a table. Everyone helped themselves, filling up on picnic plates and digging in, talking about old times. They acted like Pettys, as if they were family welcoming relatives from Randleman. But they were fans from Murfreesboro who had been making a picnic lunch for the Pettys every time they raced at Nashville for years, usually in the infield on race day, in the motel room now because of the rain.

"Lots of nice people in the world," Richard remarked.

When the food was all gone, the fans left, taking the trash with them, some of the ladies, young and old, kissing Richard and Maurice and Dale and the rest, others shaking hands and wishing them well. Richard asked them if they would stay over if the race was postponed to the next day. They said they wouldn't miss it—no way.

Word came that the race was rescheduled for the following afternoon. Richard got on the phone to get two more rooms for the rest of the crew. The rain stopped in the early evening and there was some grumbling that they could have raced after all, but it would have taken a long time for the track to dry.

Richard stood on the balcony as it grew dark and he tasted the fresh, cool air that follows rain. The same fans came by who had come the night before and held him an hour. He welcomed them warmly and said he was happy they were staying over. They had more scrapbooks with them and wanted more signatures and wanted to take more pictures with him and he gave them whatever they wanted. He just stood and talked to them as others came out of the room and stood awhile and went back in and watched TV. Some of the boys drank beer and Maurice and Dale argued the skills of Sonny Jurgensen and Bill Kilmer, and Richard stood out on the balcony and talked to his fans, who did not seem to run out of things to talk about.

The writer and others excused ourselves in hopes the fans would take the hint, but they hated to leave. Finally, after an hour and a half, they left. Richard stood on the balcony and said he really didn't mind. "They're real nice people. And I really had nothing else to do." He talked about the racing life awhile. "It's ten hours of working and waiting for every hour of racing. You get used to it. You would wear yourself out worrying about it. You have to be able to handle it mentally. That's harder than handling it physically. The race is only the tip of the iceberg. It's only the part that shows."

He looked up at the moon awhile and then went in to call Lynda, who was not coming to the race.

As the motel grew quiet, you could hear a George Jones song coming from a radio in one room:

> *"Oh, the weatherman just said . . . there's gonna' be stormy weather;*
> *I guess he's right . . . I feel it in the air.*
> *He said it'll be some time before it gets any better.*
> *The way I feel I just don't even care.*
> *The forecast on this love of ours don't look much better,*
> *And lately we've been having troubled times. . . ."*

Sunday morning, Richard slept in. Chief got the crew up early. They convened in a cafeteria for breakfast. Chief paid. They piled trays high and dug in. When Chief was finished, he put his knife and fork down, stood up, and said, "Let's go." Everyone put down their knives and forks and followed him out, some of them with food left on their trays. They got to the track at 9:20. A sign at the entrance to the pits said the gate would open at 9:30. They sat and waited in a long line of cars, church music coming out of the truck radios.

After they got inside, they uncovered the car and checked it over. It was cloudy with a breeze blowing, but you could feel the heat beginning to build up. The crew jacked up the car and set to work inside it and under it. Richard showed up about noon and sat on a pit wall in blue slacks and checkered shirt and talked to other drivers and mechanics and other people in the pit area. After a while, he went into the truck and put on his uniform.

The stands were filling up. By the time the call came for the cars to be pulled onto the track and the drivers to go to them, the stands were almost full. The sun was bright now and it was hot. A minister gave the invocation. A recording of the national anthem was played. "Gentlemen, start your engines," announced Bill France. And the engines roared up and the cars moved away, sliding into their starting positions behind the pace car.

The green dropped and the crowd came to its feet as the cars roared into the first turn and through it and around the track. And around and around. Waltrip stole the early lead with Parsons, Yarborough, and Petty right behind him. Cale beat Benny into a corner, and, when Waltrip's transmission gave out on the nineteenth lap, Yarborough roared into the lead.

Petty appeared to Dale to be having handling problems. "He can't get into the corners high," Dale said, concernedly. Cale led into the thirty-fourth lap, pulling farther ahead on each lap until Coo Coo Marlin's transmission stuck and his Chevy went right into the wall, bringing out the first caution period. As the cars ducked into the pits for fuel and tires, Petty's crew swiftly shifted the weight in his car.

Dave Marcis drove in front for a couple of laps, then Walter Ballard for fifteen, before Cale got into the lead again and began to pull away. Round and round they roared in close contact with other cars on this small track in this 420-lap, 250-mile grind. By the halfway point, Cale had lapped his closest rival, Petty. Cale's Holly Farms Chevy was working well. His chief, Junior Johnson, watched him closely each time he came around.

Every time the 43 car came in, Dale directed more shifts of weight. Finally, Richard was seen driving deeper into the corners, picking up the pace, closing in on Cale. "He's coming," Maurice muttered, sweat showing on his face. It was brutally hot now. The crewmen's clothing was wet, stained dark. The drivers roasted in their cars. Several required relief, staggering out of their ovenlike cockpits as other crawled in during brief stops.

At three hundred laps, Petty was pressing Yarborough. Richard ducked in for four tires, figuring he could increase his speed more yet. "Now Cale has to come in or we'll blow right by him," Dale said. Cale's tires were wearing. He was due to stop for four fresh tires in the effort to stay ahead. But, when he came in, he would lose his lead. At that point, Dave Cisco spun on the mainstretch, and Cale spun to miss him. Maurice and Dale jumped in their pit, their eyes wide, counting Cale out, ready for Richard to take over.

But as swiftly as the tide appeared to turn, it turned right back. Cale kept control of his car as the caution signals came out. Under the slowdown Cisco and Cale had caused, Cale was able to get into his pits, get his tires, and get out without losing

Buddy Baker and Richard. NASCAR PHOTO

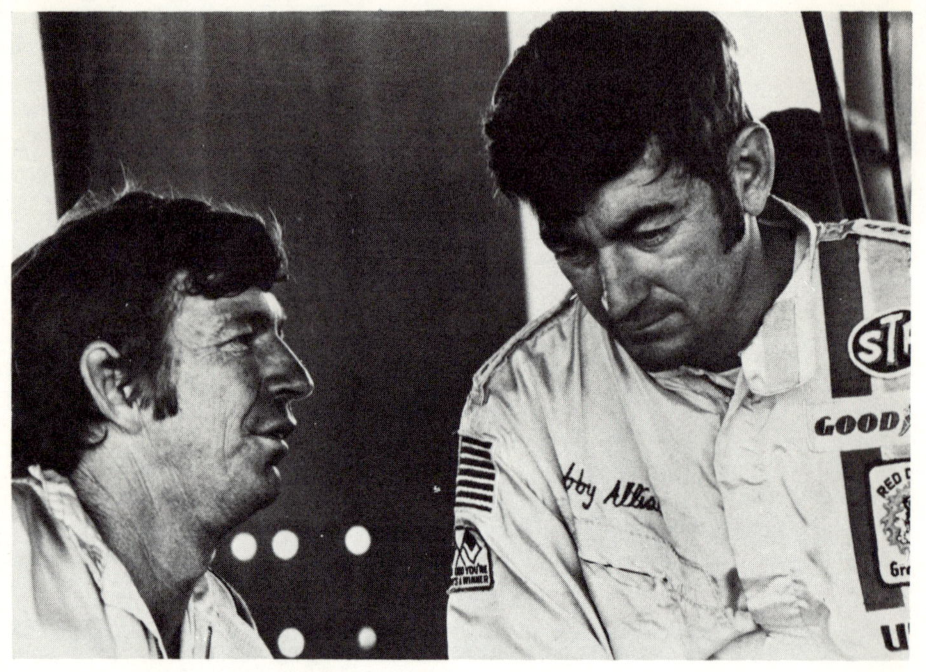

The Allisons, Donny (left) and Bobby. NASCAR PHOTO

Benny Parsons. NASCAR PHOTO

Dave Marcis showers David Pearson with play money representing the pole-position payoff of $10,000 at Charlotte. DOZIER MOBLEY PHOTO

In Victory Lane with Be-Bop Hobel, Miss Winston, at the Atlanta 500, 1975.

Father and son. NASCAR PHOTO

The first- and second-place finishers, Pearson Mercury and Petty Dodge, after crashing conclusion to 1976 Daytona 500. AP WIREPHOTO

Richard Petty.

significant ground to Richard. Yarborough had pitted under the yellow, Petty under the green, and it cost Petty his chance. Maurice muttered an obscenity. The STP crew seemed to sag.

Petty did not give up, but his chance had come and gone. He could not catch Cale. He was a lap back when the checker came out after 2 hours 47 minutes and 16 seconds of grueling racing. As Cale came into Victory Lane to receive the cheers of the crowd, Petty pulled up to his truck and climbed from his car. He came out slowly, wearily.

"I'd have caught him if it hadn't been for the caution. And he caused it," Richard commented.

"A bad break beat us," Dale sighed.

"We're beat, that's all," Maurice grunted as he checked the car.

Richard walked to the restroom, carrying his civvies, so he could shower and change. A few fans had already gotten into the infield and walked with him as he went. He did not sign any autographs. He did not say anything to anyone. He just nodded glumly as his fans sought to console him.

The restroom was little more than a glorified outhouse. It was messy and smelled bad. Men were relieving themselves as King Richard stripped off his damp clothes and stepped ankle deep into water and turned on a shower. His skin was white and wrinkled. The shower was lukewarm but it felt good on his sweaty skin.

He kicked at the water around his feet, smiled, and said, "Nothing but the best for racing stars."

I held his sweaty racer's uniform in one hand and his civvies in the other. Richard dried himself with a couple of rags he had brought with him, knowing there would be no towels. A fan came in to ask for an autograph and Richard asked him to please wait a minute until he got outside. It was hot and it stank in there and he was anxious to get out. He pulled on his undershorts and his slacks and went outside, barechested and with bare feet to finish dressing.

But the fans never gave him a chance. There were about fifty of them peering inside, waiting outside while he showered, and when he came out, they surrounded him, waving pencils and paper and autograph books at him. He started to sign. Wearily he sagged to the ground, sitting with his back to the restroom wall and his knees drawn up, his damp chest and pinched white feet bare, and he signed autographs as the fans talked at him. His feet were white as death.

He had lost, he had not won, but the first fifty fans were followed by another fifty, and another. Word that Petty was trapped in the infield spread until close to two hundred people surrounded him and pressed in on him. A crewman came to hand him an iced cup of Coke over the heads of the crowd. He drank gratefully from it, but when he put it down, the fans pressing in on him kicked it over and it spilled under him. At least two of them stepped on his bare feet. There was no holding them back.

One lady handed him a felt-tip pen and asked him to sign her chest. He did, grinning. Another said his pants looked like the same ones he was wearing the other day. He said, smiling, that they were the only ones he owned. The fans laughed. He sat there for a full hour, so tired the pens and pencils slipped from his fingers twice. But he kept taking the time to sign that elaborate autograph of his, and he talked to the people, and when one young gal offered him a sip of her Coke, he accepted it gratefully and thanked her as if she was sent from heaven.

His crew came for him or he would still be there. Jimmy and a couple of others came and forced their way into the crowd and got him and helped him out through the crush saying he had to go, it was time to go, they were sorry, while the fans asked them to wait a minute, just a minute, they didn't have their autographs yet. The crew got him into the front seat of the van and rolled the windows up and started the engine up as the crowd surrounded the machine and looked like they might turn it over in their anxiety to get at Richard.

He rolled the window down and started to sign autographs as Jimmy moved the van ahead slowly, splitting the fans in front of it. Gradually they drew clear as Richard reached back to hand his last autograph of the day to the fan who was following alongside. As they pulled out on the road, another fan ran beside the van, pounding on the windows, until finally he could not keep up. He came to a stop, receding into the distance, as the wagon pulled away and clear, and turned onto the highway, heading for home.

Maurice and Dale were waiting for them with the big truck and the tow truck along the side of the road, and when the van came along, they pulled out to form a three-car caravan. Richard pulled his shirt and boots on, and leaned back and closed his eyes. "You'da' had him," Jimmy said.

"Yep," Richard said.

"But you didn't."

"Nope," Richard said.

Everyone was silent for a time as they drove through the gathering darkness. After a while, Richard started to return to life. He flipped on the CB radio and called to the truck ahead. "Who's driving, Wade?" he asked.

"Maurice," came Maurice's answer, crackling with static.

"Oh, Lord," Richard said, laughing.

There was quiet talk as the caravan continued on U.S. 40 past Mount Juliet and Lebanon and Cookeville and across the Cumberland Plateau.

"You hungry?" Richard asked.

"Yup," I said.

"We don't stop to eat." Richard smiled.

"I know that by now," I said.

We stopped to eat at a Big Boy Restaurant at ten that night. By then, everyone had to rush to the restroom. After that, everyone was thirsty. Some ordered two Cokes. Richard had two milks. Almost everyone had hamburgers. They ate and talked. No one brooded. They had lost. No one had forgotten. But it was behind them. Another race was ahead of them.

Someone came up and asked if Richard was Richard Petty. Richard said, "Ah think so." He signed his first autographs of the night. No one asked Dale or Maurice or the others for autographs.

Back in the cars, the caravan continued through the night, through Knoxville and Dandridge and Newport and up and through the towering ridge of the Great Smoky Mountains, which stood out cloudy-clear in the moonlight. Someone sang a few words of a song that went with the magnificent mountains, and at that time and in that place it sounded sweeter than it really was.

There was soft, tired talk and a little laughter as the night fell away. The CB radio crackled on and off. The cars of the caravan kidded back and forth a bit. Midnight came and went.

Utterly tired, Richard fell asleep sitting in the front seat. The others grew quiet and they too drifted off. Only the driver and occasionally one of the other passengers were awake as the wagon rolled into North Carolina and through Asheville and Black Mountain and Hickory and Winston-Salem. The passengers stirred as the caravan came into Greensboro. Home was just ahead now.

The trucks and the wagon convened at the dark, deserted compound in the cool of four in the morning. Wearily, everyone unwound from them and went to their own cars. A few had yet a fairly long ride home. The weekend was over.

The crew was given the next day off, but Maurice and Dale and some of the others were there early to start tearing down the chassis and engine. After all, the next race at Pocono was only two weeks away.

15

FANS AND FAMILY

North Carolina is not a small state. In fifty thousand square miles, it has more than five million residents and ranks twelfth in the nation in population. But it has vast uncrowded areas of mountains, forests, and oceanfront. The Great Smoky Mountains, the Blue Ridge Belt, and the Cape Hatteras and Cape Lookout National Seashores lure hundreds of thousands of visitors annually. Driving through the state, you drive through a lot of open and unused land.

It is not a state of big cities. The largest, Charlotte, with fewer than 250,000 residents, is about the size of Dayton or St. Petersburg, and ranks only sixtieth nationally. Greensboro, with fewer than 150,000, barely makes the top hundred. Winston-Salem, with fewer than 135,000, does not make it.

Its growth has been slow, but it has the most cotton mills in the country, the largest tobacco fields, large farms, and some of the most plentiful forests to provide wood. It ranks first in the nation in the production of textiles, household furniture, and bricks, and in both tobacco grown and cigarettes produced. It is second in sweet potato crops, third in peanuts and turkeys, fourth in chickens. There is some mining, and it is first in mica and a few other minerals.

Yet it has the reputation of being a poor place. Certainly it cannot be compared to the rich industrial states. North Carolina has a per capita income of only $4,665 per year. California, New York, and Illinois are among many that surpass $6,000 per capita per year.

In the South, however, South Carolina, Alabama, Louisiana, Mississippi, Tennessee, and Kentucky have lower per capita incomes than North Carolina. So do Arkansas and West Virginia, New Mexico and Utah, Maine and Vermont.

Movies are not made here, nor are television shows shot here. Only occasionally do touring road companies of stage plays or prominent musical stars perform here. There is no big league professional football, basketball, or baseball.

The universities of North Carolina and North Carolina State contend for college basketball titles, but most of the stars come from other states and after a few years go on to other states. None can compare to Richard Petty in popularity.

Stock-car racing is the biggest sport in the state. Junior Johnson and others have represented the state spectacularly, but none so spectacularly as the Pettys in general and Richard Petty in particular.

He is the outstanding sporting star in the South today and the most awesome athletic hero his home state has had. He was born here, reared here, and still lives here. He is Richard Petty from Randleman, North Carolina, wherever he goes, and when he comes home, he is welcomed warmly.

Although the $200,000 to $400,000 in publicized earnings he takes from racing every year make him one of the wealthiest individuals in his part of the world, he is respected for his simple, unspoiled ways.

Most of his fans have not seen or been in his new $250,000 home, which at 290 feet falls just short of being as long as a football field. "If I'da' known, I'da' tacked on ten more feet. It's sort of like being tackled on the five-year line," he says, chuckling.

At the end of the 1967 season, the Pettys celebrated completion of their mechanical compound with a public party. The Randleman Lions Club asked them to have an open house, charge a small admission fee, and contribute the proceeds to needy families in the area. They agreed.

Richard recalls, "We were supposed to start at one in the afternoon, but by that time the people had to park in South Carolina. I sat at a work bench and signed autographs. When the whole affair was over, we'd raised $15,000."

In the summer of 1973, when word went around that another open house was being held, Richard and others desperately called forty or fifty radio stations to announce that it was only an annual convention of the Richard Petty Fan Club. Some three hundred members and three thousand other fans showed up, including North Carolina governor James Holshouser.

When the Governor tried his hand at changing a tire during a practice pit stop, he split his pants. Elizabeth Petty hustled him into her house across the road, repaired the pants with needle and thread, and returned him to his public.

He returned late in 1974 when the Pettys put on another charity open house. Although it is a hard place to locate, tucked away in the countryside, close to 40,000 fans found it and paid a dollar a head to take part in the party. There was an auction of Petty trophies and mementos, including the 1966 Daytona 500 victory cup, and $50,000 was raised in all.

"It was some shindig," Richard remarks. "This time Tennessee, too, was full up with parked cars. The line musta' stretched to the ocean. And some of those people stood in line for two or three hours just to get my autograph. That's why I have to give 'em the fancy one. We had 40,000 people in 50,000 square feet. Everyone held their breath for eight hours. I signed autographs at least that long.

"Even Maurice and Dale and Daddy signed autographs. And the ladies got close to Lynda. And the girls came giggling up to me, all dressed up in their Sunday best. It was surely something."

The event was scheduled for "after church." Richard attends the Mount Lebanon United Methodist Church in Randleman. A small parcel of his property is advertised for sale at two dollars a square inch, with the proceeds to go to church causes. "Own a piece of Petty," the ads say.

"I guess everyone owns a piece of me." Richard remarks. "I'm public property. Our sport is different than others. The fans get in the infield, but they don't get in the dugouts. We drive down the road with 'em, visit with 'em at gas stops, visit with 'em at the motels and in the restaurants. We're all throwed in together.

"I used to feel funny about it. I don't know what makes me so different. I'm good at what I do, but it's no more important than what most people do and a lot less important than what some people do. Jonas Salk and those cats that do important work don't get the attention I do. It's nice to be noticed and appreciated, but I don't deserve the attention I receive. I know my sport is spectacular. I'm used to the attention now. I do the best I can with it.

"One of Daddy's deals was that no matter what you sell in life, you have to sell yourself first in order to sell anything. I place a lot of stock in it and pass it on to my kids. They've been exposed to the best people in the world and the worst, but they have been taught to show the best side of themselves. They say 'sir' and 'ma'am' and 'Thank you' and 'You're welcome.' So do I.

"Some of the fans do overdo it, but I try to take it in stride. The only time I won't stop for them is right after a race. I get out of my car and I got to get somewhere to unwind. I'll turn my back on 'em then, because if I don't, I won't get two minutes to get myself together. But after that, any other time, I'll take the time.

"Lynda doesn't like it. She feels they take advantage of my good nature. I know they do. I'll stay with 'em until I got to go; then they want to go with me. It's hard for us to go out and have a good time because the people won't let us alone.

"There are places we can go and places we can't. We can go to a Randleman High football game and not be bothered much, but I stopped going to hockey games in Greensboro because I never got to see the games. We can go to restaurants around home and not be bothered much, but in some of the big cities it's bad. They watch you eat. Lynda just loves that.

"I figure it's just part of the price you have to pay, but Lynda figures we're entitled to our privacy. So I do a lot more with the fans when I'm alone than when I'm with her.

"Actually, I reach most fans through my interviews. And I owe the publicity to STP. I don't think there's any athlete that's had a better press. But there are writers you can trust and writers you can't. Some you can talk to off the record and some you can't. You learn who's who.

"If a writer takes the trouble to call up and arrange a personal interview in advance, I'll give him one. Those that call up at the last minute, I tell I give interviews at the track. Most of the time I talk to three or four writers at a time.

"Lynda wouldn't like it if I brought writers home all the time. But don't think bad of her because of it. She appreciates our good press. She also appreciates our privacy. I spend so little time home and with the family, she wants to make the most of it. So do I."

Their new house was a typical Petty family affair—designed and built by Lynda's father, Leonard Owens. The single-level, colonial-style, ranch house is a 10,000-square foot residence on four hundred acres of wooded land. There are thirteen oversized rooms and five bathrooms. There are two air-conditioning units and a housewide stereo-speaker system.

There is a five-car garage, although there usually are six or seven cars around. Some of them are company cars. Richard's personal car is a Chrysler Imperial, but he really likes the family van.

When something goes wrong with one of Richard's or Maurice's or Dale's cars, they do not take it to the compound to fix it, they take it to the dealer's repair shop. They constantly complain about their cars, just as you and I do.

Out back will be built a basketball court and a tennis court and maybe a swimming pool. "There aren't many months we can use a pool," Petty points out.

Inside, there is a large paneled den with a fireplace and a basement recreation room with a pool table. There are cases full of Richard's trophies and Lynda's collection of dolls.

Although each member of the family was permitted to pick out the paint and paper color combinations in his or her own room, the dominant color in this large, but low-key old-west and revolutionary-days residence is green. "It's my least favorite color, but it's easiest on the eyes," Lynda comments.

Daughter Lisa is the only one who picked Petty blue. Son Kyle has blue, but it's the blue and orange of his Randleman High sports teams.

In the surrounding piney woods are rolling fields and barns and chicken houses. The Petty property contains black angus cattle and thousands of chickens.

"This is sort of fancy, but Lynda had it coming." Richard apologizes. "We still live simple, even if there's nothing simple about this place. We're not far from our other places. I can throw a rock and darn near hit the trailer I growed up in.

"I'm still a grits-and-gravy guy.

"We have iron gates out front, but they're always open to family and friends. The kids are free to have their friends over whenever they want, of course. It's their house as much as it is mine. To them, I'm their daddy, not the famous race driver."

Richard and Lynda were married in 1959, when he was twenty-two and she was seventeen. Kyle came June 2, 1960; Sharon, June 30, 1961; Lisa, September 20, 1964; and Rebecca, May 14, 1973.

Rebecca was a nice surprise. "We thought we were through," Richard grins.

"I got to think real good thoughts about Lynda. She's the perfect race driver's wife and a a real good mother to our kids. Since a race driver is away so much, he's less of a father to his kids, and his wife has to be more of a mother."

He was asked, "Is it a good marriage in a business that's bad for marriages?"

"Yeh. And I think about that a lot. My life is bein' away a lot, and it could be a glamorous life if I wanted to get involved with a lot of people I come in contact with. There are temptations. I'm only human. But there are risks with those temptations.

"I don't want to take any chances with my marriage. I remember when I was married ten years a man asked me, is an hour's worth of fun worth ten years of my life? I said it wasn't, and I've always remembered that. And for me it might not be fun because I believe in the Bible and the Ten Commandmants. I'm not a religious fanatic, but fooling around would bother me."

"And your wife trusts you?"

"As far as she can throw me. No, she trusts me I think. At least she doesn't say anything about it. We've been married sixteen years now and she's used to my being away a lot. I guess after all this time it's easier to trust me than not trust me. And I've never given her reason not to trust me. Oh, she knows how those gals throw themselves at me. Some of them, it don't make no difference whether she's standing right there or not, they come on strong. I'm polite to them. I kid them. But that's as far as it goes. That's one thing you have to watch. It's the best way I know to break up a family."

"Four of the last five Indianapolis winners have been divorced."

"Yeh, well, they're a little bit more high flyers than we are. Not that some of our boys don't fly high at times, but they mostly come from Christian homes, and their backgrounds are all based on family. I think Buddy's the only one comes from a broken home. Ol' Buck flew high in his day. But Buddy and Bobby and Cale and David and them all have had only one wife. Bobby's got four kids. Cale's got three. David three, I think. Buddy's got a couple of boys. We're family folk.

"I dated right many girls in high school and after, but I never was serious with any until Lynda. I was always away at a race and I'd forget a date and I'd call 'em the next time and they wasn't interested anymore. I did it to Lynda, too, but she maintained her interest. I'd get to working on a car and forget to pick her up until ten or ten-thirty at night, and she'd already have gone to bed. Her mother and daddy didn't like that too much. Neither did she, but she put up with it. She cared enough to put up with me.

"I broke her in right as far as racing goes. I started dating her when I started racing. She started to go to nearby races with us, and she saw what a racer's life was before she married me. She's not a racing fan; she's a Richard Petty fan. If I'm not in a race, she could care less about going. Except that she's good buddies with Buddy's wife and Elmo's wife and some of the others, and she likes to visit with 'em and try to buy the stores out.

"She usually flies in right before a race and leaves with me right after so she won't be away from the kids any more than she has to. We take the kids with us when we can, and they like to go, but I guess as they're growin' up they're getting their own interests. Lots of times they got other things to do. She has to take care of a lot of things that I'm not there to take care of. She takes care of all the details anyway.

"You know, sometimes I'm on a trip and I get a call from Preddy or Dredge and they want me here or there and I got to go. I never know when I'll be home. Sometimes I call and sometimes I don't. I never write. She knows to expect me when she sees me. She asks me, 'What you gonna wear?' She worries about things like that. Sometimes she throws a fit about all the extra travel I do. I tell her, if you want to keep eatin', pack the bags. She packs the bags.

"We lead an unorganized life anyway. People plan things for me, but I don't plan anything for myself. I know I got to be at the track certain times, but beyond that I don't want to know where I'm gonna be and when I'm gonna be there and what I'm gonna do. I get up when I wake up. I sit down when I get tired. I go to sleep when I get sleepy. I eat when I'm hungry. Whatever happens, happens. I take it as it comes. I don't waste it. I live life a day at a time.

"I broke the whole family in that way. We got six people in this house living six different lives. I got my things, Lynda's got her things. Kyle's got his games and stuff. The girls got their things. Schools got schedules, but beyond that we keep our own time. We may eat supper at five, we may eat at nine, we may not eat. There's always something to eat. If we're real hungry, Lynda'll whip something up. But none of this everyone-at-the-table-at-six stuff.

"We don't smother each other. Until I was twenty-two and got married, I lived at home. I never left the house that I didn't tell Mother or Daddy where I was goin' and who I was goin' to be with and when I'd be back. All they ever said to me was, 'Be careful.' It's the same with our kids. We know what's goin' on with them, but we don't tell them what to do or who to do it with. We don't want them to be carbon copies of us; we want them to be themselves.

"We have tried to teach them right from wrong. We have explained to them that they have obligations to us, to one another, to others, and to God; they have to honor these, and if they don't respect their obligations to themselves, they will be dishonoring themselves. If they show us they have to be told again, we will tell them again. But we trust them. Like I tell Lynda, you have to trust. We can't lead our kids' lives for them.

"My kids are not at the center of my world. I am. Lynda and our children surround me, right close to me. Then come my parents and my brother. And my friends. Most people are not part of my private stratosphere. They may touch me for a moment, but then they're gone. Like you. You're writing a book with me. Your world has overlapped my world for the moment. You're making a lap through my life. Then you'll be gone.

"Each of us has our own world, and only so many people can fit into it. You fit in those that you've got room to take care of. You try to fit in too many and you can't do nothing for none of them.

"Dale is my closest friend. I'm with him more than Maurice. Maurice and me are brothers, not friends. If I had trouble I'd go to family first, before I went to friends. I'd probably go to Maurice first, maybe Mother and Daddy. I know there isn't anything they wouldn't do for me or I wouldn't do for them. But I'd go to Dale as quick as to anyone. And I'm probably quicker to confide in Dale than anyone.

"I have a few friends from growing up who have nothing to do with racing. I have a friend, Ronny Hooks, who goes to some races and scores for us. He used to help us in the pits, but he had cancer and they had to cut a leg off. He's the closest friend I have from school days. Lynda has a lot of friends from her school days. She's still on the board of this or that at school. Lynda's buddies drop by a good bit, but we don't socialize a lot. When I come home from the races, I've had it with crowds."

He stood in his backyard, looking over rolling green fields as far as the eye could see. It was twilight, and lovely. He said, "They make jokes about it, but I could stand here a long time just watching the grass grow. When I come home, that's excitement enough for me. When I come home, I want peace, and this place is peaceful. I've bought land near here for the kids. If they want it, fine. If not, fine. But I wanted to buy it before it was gone.

"I want the racing on the one hand and my family life on the other hand. With those two my hands are full.

"I really like my family. Lynda has a real good personality and she gave that to the kids. They have good personalities, they look good, and most important, they're good kids.

"Kyle is a lot like me, lazy. He plays football. He plays basketball. He plays the guitar. He plays around. He likes girls. He hates to work. He's a normal American boy. He's not the greatest ball player in the world, but he doesn't have to be as far as I'm concerned. I just want him to be the best he can be at whatever he does. I go to all his games I can.

"I don't know if he wants to race. He won't tell me. I know he likes to race cars on the back roads, but he ain't got his license yet. Same as me when I was a boy. He likes to drive a motorbike. Me and him used to have a lot of fun doin' it together, but we don't get much time to do it anymore. I'm sorry about that because I really like doing things with him."

"And the girls?" he was asked.

"The girls?"

"What do you do with them?"

"Nothing. Just love 'em."

"You're not together with them much?"

"Well, they're girls, and a guy can't do with them like he can with his son. I mean the sports and all. The girls don't have enough athletic ability to watch a football game. But they're nice girls. Sharon's a real homebody, like Lynda. She sets and sews. She sweeps the floor and cooks meals. She looks after our little girl. She's gonna be a wonderful wife. Lisa's a lively little gal, always going. She's interested in a lot of things outside the house. Rebecca, it's hard to tell yet, she's so young, but maybe she's gonna be a devil. She's always into it. She's got a good hold on all of us.

"We don't get to do a lot together, which is why we go to races together. Sometimes we sightsee, but you don't have time on race weeks. Dale's driving his family back to Nashville to take them through Opryland. He got tickets fixed up, but he didn't want to go race week even though he was already there. We went to southern California one summer and saw Disneyland and Marineland, all those places, and had a good time. We've got a beach house we bought with Ronny Hooks and we both use it, but the Pettys don't seem to get to use it much. It's a couple hundred miles from here, about fifty miles north of Myrtle Beach. Kyle might use it more when he gets his license so he can drive there."

He was asked, "Do you want him to race?"

"It was sort of fun to drive against my daddy and I suppose it would be fun to drive against my son, but I don't know if I'll last five or six more years. I don't dream about dynasties or anything like that. I know he don't want to work, so he may have to race. He won't work on the car. He won't work in the house. He won't work, period.

"But if he wants to drive for Richard Petty, he's gonna have to work for Richard Petty. He's going to have to work on race cars and learn cars before I'll give him one to try. I wouldn't try to tell him how to drive, but I would answer any questions he asked and I'd try to help him all I could. I think he'd be good. He fits. I know he drives a motorbike a lot better than I ever did.

"I guess any daddy would like for his son to follow in his footsteps, but if he never drove, it wouldn't bother me a bit. I doubt that Lynda would want him to, but I doubt that she'd tell him not to. I wouldn't worry about the dangers but she might. I consider it a safe sport. And a clean sport.

"It's funny, but Lynda is scared to death to drive with me. She never was all the time we were going together, no matter how wild I drove. I coulda' turned upside down and I doubt she'd have said a word. But then, 1961, or so, when she was pregnant with Sharon, she was driving to Greensboro in the rain. A cat turned in front of her and she slid into him and just totaled his truck. No one was hurt, but it shook her.

"Now she drives real slow, and when she rides with me she's always saying to watch out for this or that, don't ride so close, blow your horn. She drives me crazy. Here I am, the champion, and my wife is scared to drive with me.

"I'm sure Lynda worries about my races, but she's used to it. The only time she asked me to quit was a bad year we had years ago when Fireball and Jim Pardue got killed in races and Billy Wade got it in a tire test. And Larry Thomas got killed in a highway accident, which is always a risk, driving the roads all tired, all hours. But I wouldn't give it up, and she gave up on asking me to give it up.

"It did hurt her when Randy got killed. Of course that was a freak, but it reminded her of the dangers. The wives wasn't thinking about the dangers while everything was going along peaceful for so long, but Randy's death reminded all of them that racing has danger in it. Lynda was twelve when Randy was born. Her mother and daddy both worked, so she sort of brought him up. She was real close to him.

"He started coming around when he was sixteen or so. He really rooted for me and loved racing. The happiest he was, was when he was around our racing cars. We started him washing cars and gave him jobs in the shop. He was learning how to build racers. We put him in the pits because we had confidence in him. He asked how things worked and wanted to learn. We thought he had a fine future.

"It shook Lynda like it did all the wives. I think she goes to the races because it's easier to see what's happening for yourself than to be home waiting and wondering. She knows what racing means to me. When I killed that boy in the drag racer, I just stopped. After about three weeks of my moping around the house, she said, 'I can't wait for you to start racing again. Until you get happy again, none of us can be happy.'

"I don't think it would work if I was home a lot. We're not used to that way of life where a daddy goes to work at eight in the morning and comes home at six at night. I think the way it is we appreciate each other more. We're glad to see one another and we don't pick on the little faults that pull people apart. The thing I hate is when she's waitin' at the door to say the garbage needs to be taken out and the clock hasn't been fixed yet and we haven't finished movin' the furniture in the den.

"I come home and they're all over me. I come home after they've gone to bed and they're all in bed with me the next morning. But after I've been home a few days, I walk in and they don't even look up and they don't even have a howdy for me. After I start to hear them hollerin' at one another, I'm ready to go on the road again. But they're good kids and I feel good about them."

"Do you worry about them being spoiled, being Richard Petty's children?" the interviewer wondered.

"Some, yeh. I want to be Richard Petty, but Lynda wants to be Lynda, not Mrs. Richard Petty, and the kids want to be themselves, not Richard Petty's kids. That's one of the reasons we've remained in Randleman. Not that we ever even thought of movin' away. But they're sort of accepted here where they growed up, among kids they've known all their lives. Somewhere else, they'd be singled out.

"I went to pick up Kyle at a basketball clinic once and the first thing I knew there were four hundred people around me for autographs. As soon as they realized he was my son, he was something else that he didn't want to be. They've got to learn to live with that, but it ain't easy. If Kyle drives, he's gonna have to live with bein' compared to me, just like I was to my daddy.

"They have a lot more than I had when I was their age and I hope it's not so easy for them they can't cope when it comes time. Daddy worries more than I do. He's got a lot of property and stuff his lawyers want to put in the names of his grandchildren to beat the taxes on inheritance, and he's only done a little of it. He says, what if one of 'em turns out to be a 'doper,' which is what he calls those people. I say me and Maurice turned out all right. He says, yeh, but he raised us. I say, 'Yeh, well we're raisin' ours.' And he says, 'Well, you may not be doin' a good job.'

"All you can do is to be the best husband and father you know how to be. That's all I try to be. That's all my mother and daddy tried to be with me and Maurice. I can't imagine them bein' any better. I think they're proud of me. I hope they are. I think I got a good wife and good kids and I'm proud of 'em. I hope they think good things about me and are proud of me."

Lee Petty

"I don't have anything to say about Richard. He says it all for hisself. I don't even know why you're writing a book with

Richard. You should be writing one with me. I wouldn't want to write one, but I'm the one who knows what racing really is."

Elizabeth Petty

"Racing was different in our day. Times was a lot tougher. Richard has made more money in one day than his daddy made most years. The tracks were bad and the cars were bad and most of the drivers were bad. But Lee and the others, they built something for Richard and those that have followed.

"It was a wild sport and there were some wild people in it. But it's changed, and been changed a long time. They always write about how the bootleggers began it, but that's been written; they don't have to keep riding it.

"The books I read about it are all full of sex and profanity. They could leave that out. It's not a true picture. Maybe there's some of that, but not that much. They're just trying to sell books. I hope this book won't be like that.

"It's a clean sport now we built up.

"There were eight children in my family. My father farmed and saw-milled this country. Depression days, and really was rough. We made do. Lee had ten or eleven kids in his family. One or two of 'em died. Kids died in those days. We didn't have many doctors. Or much medicine. Lee's daddy worked on the roads. We come from working people. But some people were poorer than we were.

"Lee and I were married in 1936. He worked as a salesman and a trucker and we made out. Our house burned down, he built us a home out of a trailer. Later we moved into the house we live in now. My father built it with his own hands. I went into it when I was eight. Richard and Maurice were reared in that house later on, too.

"None of 'em moved far away. This is our home. Why move? What's better? You make your own world.

"I never thought Lee was serious about racing, but he wanted it and he went after it and he got it. It was a side thing at first. Couldn't make money at it. So we raced nights and weekends two or three times a week. All around here. And I went with him. Took the boys with us. They growed into it, too. By the time it began to build up and spread out, they were ready.

"I never worried. I don't know why. I just felt he'd be all right. I never ever once told him to stop. If he was old, it didn't seem so at the time. I mean it was just starting and was the same for everyone, young or old. Now it's different. Now Richard is thirty-eight, but he's been in racing all his life and been driving seventeen, eighteen years, and anyone that is just getting into it is giving a lot of experience away to him.

"It was with drivers like Lee that a man could make a living at this sport after all. I remember that first Daytona 500. We knew he'd won, but we didn't know if they'd give it to him. It took them two or three days and we just had to wait. I know Richard has won much more than his daddy, and I'm proud of him, but there's a lot more to be won now, and don't anyone forget it. Lee was a winner too.

"Now when Lee had his accident, that shook me. I was relieved he was alive when they carried him away, but I knew he was hurt bad when they didn't want me to talk to him in his hospital bed. I talked to him anyway. He said he would be all right, but it was a couple of days before the doctors would say it. They leveled with me. They said he'd make it unless the marrow from his broken bones got in his bloodstream.

"It was an ordeal, but we lived through it. Recovering, he never talked of retiring. I guess he wanted to see if he could drive. Once he saw he could, he didn't have to. He drove I think three races, and then said he didn't think he'd drive anymore. He said it didn't excite him, and maybe it'd be best if he just helped Richard. We didn't have much help then, and it was rough to keep two cars going.

"They carried on while he was recovering. He helped them after he recovered, but they had learned to do for themselves by then. Now, we don't go to the races much anymore. There comes a time you have to let them go out on their own. We gave them a good opportunity, but they made good use of it and we're proud of them.

"Maurice had his physical problems, but I don't believe he ever really wanted to race like Richard did. I think Maurice always looked up to Richard a little. Well, Maurice is good at what he does and Richard is good at what he does. And Dale and all. It's really a team effort, which you never see in the newspapers.

"We put so much of ourselves into this place, I don't guess we ever could get that much back out of it. I never dreamed it would become as big as it has. Maurice really runs it. I help by taking care of the office. Their daddy doesn't do much anymore, but he's there for them if they need him, and they're always asking him this or that. He's happy enough with his golf and all. I'm happy. We don't ask a lot of life. We made a good life for ourselves.

"I wouldn't say I worry about Richard racing. I'm concerned. You're always concerned. But what's gonna happen is gonna happen, and it can happen from here to there, it don't have to be on a race track. He was hurt at Darlington that time, but he came out of it all right.

"He and Lynda have made a nice marriage and they've given us nice grandchildren. And Maurice and Patricia have made a nice marriage and given us more grandchildren. We have nice grandchildren. We've lived to see our family grow and prosper. Our boys are both the same to us. They're not stars to us, just sons."

"Do you care if Kyle becomes a race driver?" she was asked.

"No, I don't care. I don't want him to do it because it's expected of him."

"When Richard was Kyle's age, he was driving wild down the back roads, wasn't he?"

"That's what I've heard, but I didn't know it then."

"Now Kyle's doing the same thing."

"Boys will be boys," she concluded.

Lynda Petty

"I wouldn't care if Kyle didn't become a race driver. I don't feel like I have to keep a dynasty going. He should be free to be what he wants to be without having to live up to something. I would worry about him. I worry about Richard. Not a lot. And I didn't used to at all. I was young and those little old tracks he run didn't seem dangerous at all. But then they got to going fast on the superspeedways.

"When Richard and his dad both wrecked at Daytona in '61, I started to think about how dangerous it was. Kyle was just an infant and I was pregnant with Sharon. At times like that, a woman really worries about something happening to her man and what will happen to her and her young'ns.

"His really bad wreck at Darlington scared me so, I ran so hard

I got to the field hospital before they brought him in. It looked a lot worse than it was. But sometimes something that doesn't look bad can turn out bad. That keeps you on edge.

"I guess wives of racing drivers are different from other wives. They're like maybe policemen's wives or firemen's wives. Or wives of men at war. You know what they're doing is dangerous. When they leave, you can't help wondering. . . . I don't like to talk about it. I don't ever say these things to Richard. The only time I did was one year when several drivers were killed. But he didn't even want to think about it.

"He's happy doing what he's doing, and as long as he's happy, I'm happy. I'd be happy if he retired and was happy doing whatever he did, but if he was miserable, it wouldn't be any good. We all have to do what we have to do. I have to be the wife to a racing driver. We wives have an auxiliary and we meet at races and we talk a little bit about this, but mostly we bottle it up. We share this, though.

"There are times when it's a rough race and Richard's car breaks down and he falls out of it that I'm relieved. Oh, I want him to finish and do well and win if possible, but I got to admit there are times I'm relieved when his race is over and he's safe. And while I hate to admit it, there are times when there's a wreck and I can't see who it is at first and I catch myself hoping it's someone else, anyone else but him. That's awful because I don't want anyone to get hurt. Even his bitterest rival. We may be friends. I wouldn't even want an enemy to get hurt.

"I just don't feel like other women. There are times I can't even go over and talk to my best friend because her husband gets up every morning and goes to work at nine and comes home at five, and what's she got to worry about unless some idiot out on the highway runs into him? My husband goes out on a race track on a Sunday afternoon and runs a car 190 miles an hour. You can't even imagine the feelings going on inside of me. I just pray that God will take care of him.

"It's easier to be there than to be home wondering and worrying. They broadcast those races, but those announcers get so excited they scare me, so half the time I don't listen. I know when the race is on and when it should be over and I turn on the news and as far as I'm concerned no news is good news.

"I get these feelings and sometimes they're right and sometimes they're wrong, but they bother me. I had bad feelings about Talladega and I didn't know why. I couldn't make up my mind whether to go or not. All week I put it off. After Richard got there, he'd call me and ask if I was comin', and I'd say I didn't know. Kyle wanted to go, so finally I told him to go, I wasn't going. I'd made the decision and I should have felt relieved, but I didn't.

"That Sunday was one of the times I didn't even want to listen to the radio, but the girls were and they came to tell me my brother had been hurt. First thing, I called Richard's mother. She came right over and called the hospital and turned to me and told me Randy was dead. I felt terrible, but she told me I'd have to tell our parents. She took me to my mother and daddy's house and I went in and told them. They'd been listening, but they hadn't gotten the final word. It hurt them terrible, of course.

"It's funny, but it was like a load was lifted off me. I knew then why I had stayed home. It was part of God's plan to spare me. I really believe a lot of times when you're having a hard time making a decision, God is trying to tell you something.

"After that the realization sank home. With Richard bringing him home and with the funeral and all, I really felt the loss and really felt for his family. It was such a strange accident, so unnecessary, but I guess a lot of accidents are like that.

"I had never lost anybody really close and it sort of helped when I went out in the world and started to meet and talk to people about it and found almost everyone had lost someone. We all have to learn to live with death and mature and find the strength to go on.

"It made me more aware of the dangers in racing. But I don't blame racing. This was something that could have happened outside of racing. Anyway, Randy just loved racing. He was four or five when I married Richard and Randy just worshiped the ground Richard walked on. We carried him a lot of places and did a lot of things for him and he appreciated it. He was like one of ours and he was as happy as he could be being part of the racing and learning the sport. So there's that. He died doin' what he wanted to do.

"If Richard had some safe job he didn't like and wasn't happy, life wouldn't be worth much to us. The fact is racing is a lot safer sport than most people realize. Our kind of racing. Very few even get hurt. So it's no good reading something into it that isn't there. I know Maurice and Dale and the rest give him the best and safest cars. I know Richard is the best driver and he doesn't take chances. I worry about some of the other drivers gettin' in his way. There are some I hate to see near him. But unless something happens to make me think about it, I really don't think about it a lot.

"I really had no idea my life would be like it is. I grew up in a small town and went to a small school. Just like dozens of my friends, I'd meet a boy and date him and fall in love with him and marry him, and I never dreamed of being anything other than just a wife and mother making a home. I knew Richard's daddy raced and he wanted to, but I never dreamed of it becoming what it has.

"The sport is so big now that if we just stepped into it, it would be hard to adjust, but we sort of growed right along with it.

"I remember how proud we were when he won his first trophies, and now he sets a record every time he wins a race. So much is expected of him now. He not only has his family to support but his brother's family and all the others at the compound. It's a lot of pressure, but he takes it in stride.

"We make a lot of money now and we have built this big home, but inside I don't think we've changed. We've never moved because we're comfortable in this community. We don't have to have big parties or go to fancy restaurants. Making our own ice cream and watching home movies is our idea of a big evening. We wouldn't fit in in another way of life.

"We've never been the sort to spend our winnings between races. We put a lot into the company and we have that to fall back on. Richard and Maurice and all have worked hard to build something up for themselves. Richard didn't do anything by hisself. It's all teamwork, and I'm sure he told you that. I don't think of him being above anyone.

"It is not an easy life. He is away a lot. It was easier when the kids was younger because they kept me busy. But you put 'em to bed and sit around all evening alone, sewing or reading or watching TV, and you get lonely. You go to bed alone and you think, why does life have to be like this? You marry a man and want to have a home and family with him and be with him, but he's not there.

"Here he was five years older than I was and I thought he was going to take care of me and I wouldn't have to worry the rest of my life about anything. Instead, I have most of the responsibility for the kids and the home on my shoulders. He doesn't want to know about bills or anything. He doesn't even know how to write a check. I have one good friend I tell where the insurance policies and the deeds to everything are in case anything happens to me because Richard doesn't want to be bothered.

"Well, I grew up with the kids having to do it all and I'm used to it, but I miss him constantly. You know, when you love someone, you want to share with them. I lay in bed at night and try to remember this thing I saw and that thing Rebecca did so I can tell him, and half the time I forget until he's gone again. But when he's here, we are really close. I think life evens out. Being apart a lot keeps our feelings for each other fresh.

"I was always the one who had to take the kids to the movies or their parties. I decided long ago that they weren't going to be denied anything because he wasn't here. If there was something we wanted to do, we weren't going to wait until he was home. I go to Kyle's games even when Richard can't. I go to the girls' plays. I hate it when parents don't show up for their kids' things.

"I try to figure out what he would do if he was here and I make my decisions accordingly. And I feel real good when he tells me later I done just what he would've done. We've been lucky nothing serious has happened while he was gone. It would take him so long to get back, I don't know if I'd call him, anyway.

"When he's with the kids, he just wants to love 'em, so I've had to discipline them. I overheard one of 'em say they'd rather have their daddy whup 'em than their mama any time. They said mama really whups. But I think they see that shows I care. I'm strict with them because of our circumstances. I don't want them spoiled. And I don't just let them run around the world. I want to know the people my kids are staying overnight with. We don't have as much money as the newspapers make out, but I worry with all the kooks in the world my kids could be in danger.

"They miss him a lot when he leaves, but less than they used to because they're used to it. That's sad, all by itself. I see them growing up and I feel bad that Richard's missed so much of it. But he's home more than some daddies and he gives a lot of love

to 'em when he's here. They get all excited when he comes home.
Our life is a lot of comings and goings.

"I trust him when he's away. I always feel that as long as a man
is made happy and content with what he's got, he won't go looking for something else. And we go with him when we can. We'd
go a lot more if it wasn't for Rebecca. You expect to have your
kids in your twenties and see them growing up and freeing you in
your thirties, but here Becky come along. But we can't complain,
because she's a blessing.

"I've seen wives that wouldn't go to the races, and it's no wonder their husbands run around. If you won't be a part of his life,
he'll have to find someone to take your place. The kids really like
it. They get all excited and root for Richard like crazy. It's nice to
enjoy the wins together and be a consolation in defeat.

"Sometimes it bothers me to be Mrs. Richard Petty and not
Lynda Petty. I'm prouder of him as a person than I am as a race
driver. And when I give my name in a store and they find out who
my husband is and make a fuss over me, it just embarrasses me.
Sometimes I'll be standing in line and someone will tell me to tell
who I am so I won't have to wait, but I won't do it because I
figure I'm not better than the others in line and should wait my
turn.

"One of the reasons I like my work with the Girl Scouts is because to those little girls I'm me, not Richard Petty's wife. I had a
wonderful relationship with one little girl and it tickled me when
I found out she hadn't even known who I was. It's a small town
and all that, but I was just Lynda Petty to her, until she heard I
was Mrs. Richard Petty. She said she was gonna run right home
to tell her mama Richard Petty's wife was her scout leader.

"I think the one thing I worry about is the kids growing up to
be themselves, not Richard Petty's children. That's why I don't
like it when the fans make a fuss over him when we go out as a
family or when we're waiting for him at a race. There's a time and
place for everything. In its place, he gives the fans plenty of his
time, but there are times we're entitled to privacy.

"Most of the fans are nice, but some of 'em are rude and demanding. He's never rude and he gives till it hurts. He just wan-
ders off and forgets me at parties and things like that. I'm an af-
terthought. He knows I'll wait. But some day he will be known as
one of the finest good-will ambassadors the sport has had.

"He sets a great example for kids and I'm proud of that. He is clean-living, hard-working, God-fearing, sportsmanlike. I wrote a poem about that. It's up on my refrigerator. Let me read part of it: 'To an athlete. . . . There are little eyes upon you and they're watching night and day . . . There are little ears that quickly take in every word you say . . . There are little hands all eager to do anything like you do . . . And a little boy who's dreaming of the day he'll be like you. . . .'"

Kyle Petty

"Is it hard being Richard Petty's son? I've never known anything else. I get a lot of attention on his account. Sometimes I like it and sometimes I don't. It makes it easier for me to meet people, but I don't know that it gets me any girls. Sometimes it gets to be too much. Usually I go to a camp or something and the first day everyone wants to ask me questions about my dad, but after that they just take me for myself, so that's all right.

"I went to a convention thing where we wore name tags and people started to make so much of who I was that I exchanged tags with another fellow. He enjoyed getting attention like he'd never had before and I enjoyed being left alone. But it's not bad most of the time. I mean I've grown up in this small town here where people has known me all my life and they don't make a lot out of who my father is and they just accept me for what I am.

"I'm proud of him. I really like him. Him and Mom are all right. Mom does a lot for us. And Daddy would do anything for us. Oh, he made me buy my own car. He said he had to buy his first car so I had to buy mine. He said he wants me to learn to respect money. He's somewhere about halfway between not wanting to spoil me and wanting to give to me. All parents are like that, I guess.

"I miss him when he's away, but I'll tell you, a lot of fathers are home all the time and they don't give their kids all their time, but when Daddy's home he gives us a lot of time. And I go to a lot of his races and I've spent a lot of summers on the road with him. Not as much lately because I've been going to clinics and camps. I like to play all sports. I don't know how good I can be at 'em, but I like to play 'em."

"Do you want to be a race driver?" he was asked.

"Yes, sir."

"Just like that?"

"Yes, sir."

"Your daddy said you haven't said that to him."

"No, sir. But I want to try it. If I don't like it or I'm not good at it, I won't go on with it, but I want to try it."

"Do you think you'll be good at it?"

"I don't know. I'm just in driver training in school now. I've driven motorbikes and cars over the back roads. I like to go fast. I would like to be a winner. I don't feel any fear."

"Do you want to drive because your daddy is a driver? A lot more racer's sons go into racing than the sons of other athletes go into their sports."

"I guess because racing is a year-round sport and we grow up with it. I guess a baseball player lives differently half the year. I guess I wouldn't have thought of it if Daddy wasn't a racer, but he is. I've grown up with it, and I like it.

"I don't see any glamour in it. I just see an exciting sport. I see the dangers in it, but I don't worry about that. I don't worry about Daddy. I like to see him race. Our racing is the safest sort of racing.

"No, sir, I don't think it would bother him if I didn't drive. He told me one time he'd help me with whatever I wanted to do, and I mean whatever, anything, as much as he could. But I think he'll like it if I try racing. I know it will be a tough act to follow."

"Does that bother you?" he was asked.

"No, sir. I don't care what people try to put on me. I'll just do my best."

"Will it bother you to be bothered by the press and the public?"

"It wouldn't bother me. I like people. I could handle it."

"You sound like you look forward to it."

"I might change my mind, but, yes, sir, I do!"

Sharon Petty

"If people don't like me, they just don't like me, and I can live with that, but if they don't like me because I'm Richard Petty's daughter and they think I think I'm better than they are, I don't like that. And I don't like it when they think I should like them just so they can go around saying they're friends with Richard Petty's daughter. I wish people would just judge me on myself.

"But I wouldn't want to be anybody's else's daughter. He's a good daddy. He doesn't lose his temper. If I do something wrong, he just tells me not to do it again. Mom hasn't got as much patience and it doesn't take as much to make her mad."

The interviewer wondered, "Have you ever thought about it the way she does, that she's the one who has to be strict because she's with you all the time while he might tend to spoil you when he's home?"

"No, sir. I guess I haven't."

"Do you miss him when he's away?"

"I miss him, but I'm used to it. In the summertime we go with him a bunch. I like going. I keep up with his races. I'm excited when he wins. I'm mad when he loses. I like watching the races. It embarrasses me when strangers talk to me, but I kind of like it."

"Would you race if you could?"

"Yes, sir, I would."

"You really would? Women are racing these days."

"Well, then, I just might. I think it would be fun. Kyle is teaching me to drive. Daddy tried, but he called me a hopeless case. I get along real well with Kyle. Better than with Lisa sometimes. If Kyle raced, I'd really root for him."

"What about the crowds and the fans?"

"Well, sir, sometimes I wish they wouldn't butt into our lives. But Daddy says that's the way it works so I have to accept it."

"Does he spoil you?"

"No, sir. He thinks he does, but I don't think so."

"Are you happy here?"

"Yes, sir. I like my life. And I like it here. I wouldn't want to move where there was no room. Daddy owns a bunch of land he says he's going to give us. I think we all want to stay here," she said.

Lisa Petty

"I like it here. I like to do different things. I like to play basketball. No, sir, I don't think I'd like to drive a race car like Daddy.

And if Kyle did, I'd be afraid for him. I'm afraid for Daddy, but he's done it so long and does it so good I reckon he'll be all right.

"I don't like school. I don't like people making fun of me when Daddy loses. They don't say anything when he wins, but they have a lot to say when he loses. But I like my friends. I have friends who don't care that Daddy is a driver. They're my friends.

"I used to miss him when he went. I still like to be with him. I love to travel and meet new people. I like it when he's home. I'm proud of him. I'm proud of my mom, too. I feel like we've got a good family and it doesn't matter that much that my daddy is a race driver and famous. He doesn't make that much of it. He's just Daddy."

16

AUGUST AND SEPTEMBER

It took Richard Petty 551 races to win his first million dollars. In 120 more races he had moved within $6,207 of his second million. A first or second in the eighteenth race of the 1975 season, the Purolator 500 at Pocono, Pennsylvania, would do it.

"I would like to do it with a win. I would rather it be at one of our southern tracks, but I will take it wherever I can get it." he said with a grin.

When it was pointed out that Purolater, the sponsor of the race and of his strongest rival, David Pearson, was his sponsor's keenest competitor, Richard's grin grew and he said, "If their money is good, I'll take it."

Purolator was gracious enough to turn over its infield tent to STP for a meeting of the northeastern Richard Petty Fan Club prior to the race. Admission was charged, but Purolator refused to accept rent. All proceeds went to Randy Owens' family.

Some 50,000 fans turned out for the race in its scenic mountainous setting on a hot, humid day that wilted everyone. A radio disc jockey fried an egg on the track. "Today's special, roast race driver," Richard remarked.

The race was as hot as the day. Six drivers swapped the lead forty-five times in a high-speed dash around this low-bank tri-oval with three straights and three corners. "It was built for the Indy cars and we run better on big banks, but it's a nice track to run on," Petty pointed out.

Midway in the race, rain brought out the red flags. The cars were stopped and it was ninety minutes before they were started again. Richard said, "You just gotta wait. A lot of the drivers get edgy, but it don't bother me none. When it's time to race, I race. When it's time to stop, I stop.

"I do think a rain delay hurts us more than it does most. Most set up to run fast. We set up to handle good. During a delay, the others can change their cars to handle better. Any advantage we have from smart strategy or sharp pit stops is washed out."

Glen Wood, crew chief on Pearson's Purolator 21, admitted later that during the delay he made changes that helped his car handle better.

"In the late stages he could just flat outrun me," Petty commented afterwards.

Buddy Baker and Benny Parsons pressed Petty and Pearson until close to the finish, then dropped back. Pearson passed Petty with fourteen laps of the two-hundred-lap event left, and pulled away as the two roared around the 2½-mile course.

However, with ten laps left, Pearson's car started to blow black smoke out of its rear end. Lap by lap, the smoke increased. Petty had to drop back a bit because he could not see as he got close to Pearson's smoking car.

Usually, cars that are smoking heavily—and presumably throwing oil—are black-flagged off the race course to be repaired or retired, but not cars that are leading late. Dale Inman rushed from the Petty pit to protest to the chief steward, but he was advised that the track did not seem to be getting slippery and so Pearson would be permitted to continue for the time being. Angrily, Inman moved to Pearson's pit to confront Leonard Wood, but Leonard did not want to talk about it.

Maurice cursed over Richard's radio, but there wasn't anything they could do except hope Pearson's engine was about to blow. It did not. Smoke filled his cockpit and made him sick, but David drove on determinedly. With two laps left, the track was growing slippery and the official did point a black flag at Pearson. But the rules allow a driver four laps to respond to this signal. There was no way Li'l David was going to come in short of the finish.

"They waited just long enough, until it was too late. They just didn't want to take a Purolator race away from a Purolator car," Dale complained as Pearson passed under the checkered flag five seconds in front of Richard. Dale and Maurice moved to the officials to protest. Richard joined them as soon as he parked his STP car. It was in vain. They left, furious.

In Victory Lane, Pearson shrugged and said, "Richard wouldn't have stopped either. In fact, it's happened to him and he hasn't."

Glen Wood grinned and added, "We had a little oil leaking on a radiator pipe. It's not the big black bunch of smoke you got to worry about. It's the little white puffs, when you blow engines. We lasted, so we won."

The Petty team calmed down a few days later. Maurice admitted, "I wouldn't have wanted them to stop us, either." Richard observed, "I think maybe the Pocono people had Purolator on their mind. They sure didn't want to take the race away from the cats that put up the cash and give it to their rival from STP. But Purolator didn't run the race itself; the officials did. They let us have our party at their place. They're nice people. If we can't win, why not them?"

While Pearson picked up $15,000, Petty took $10,000 home with him, which moved him over the magic two-million-dollar figure. "It's just a number, but it's a nice number," he said. "I'd rather have made it with a win, but I'll settle for second this time.

"Money is a measure of how well you're doing in this sport, but we've been able to pay our bills and live good a long time. Money no longer motivates me. It's something I need to do well, but it's not a goal in itself.

"My only goal is to do better today than I did yesterday. And better next year than I did this year. I'm not running against rivals, I'm running against Richard Petty. If I lose a race by five seconds, I want to run six seconds better next time. If I win by one lap one time, I want to win by two laps the next time.

"You can't always win, but you can try. All I want to be is better than I am."

Tiny Lund died at Talladega. It happened on the eighth lap of the Talladega 500 on the third Sunday in August. The remainder of the drivers had to drive 180 more of the 2.6-mile laps to finish the fatal race after that. Buddy Baker beat Richard Petty over the last hundred miles to win $23,390 and a victory trophy.

The race was delayed one week by rain, so maybe it would have developed differently if it had gone off as scheduled, but, of course, no one can know that.

Six cars crashed. Lund's car ran into the rear end of another as they came out of a corner and the two cars spun up into the wall. As Lund's Dodge came down off the wall, Terry Link's Pontiac plowed into it at the driver's door. Other cars were caught up in it and careened around the track before coming to a halt in a tangle of twisted metal.

Link's car caught fire. While the track rescue team waited for traffic to permit them to get to him, two fans vaulted a fence and rushed to him. As they started to cut him free from his car, a guard tried to stop them and started to hit them with his night stick, ordering them away.

They warded off his blows and continued to pull Link free, saying they wanted to save him. It was not until driver Walter Ballard got there to get the guard away that the pair were able to lift Link from the wreckage. He was not breathing, but one of them administered mouth-to-mouth resuscitation, and he recovered.

They accompanied him to the field hospital, where they were treated for burns of their hands, and the driver was treated for cuts and bruises on his face.

The six-four, 250-pound Lund was carried from his cockpit unconscious and expired ten minutes later in the field hospital from massive head injuries. The 60,000 fans at the track were informed of the driver's death by a loudspeaker announcement midway in the race.

When Richard drove past the wreck, he recognized Tiny's car and radioed Dale, "I don't believe Tiny is going to get out of that one." Dale did not say anything. Later in the race, Richard radioed Dale to ask about Tiny. Dale only said, "It's pretty bad." Richard didn't reply. He comments, "That's all he had to say. I knew what it was."

Richard says, "I didn't even want to go to Talladega. Because of Randy and all. It's the biggest and fastest track we run, though I don't look at it as a dangerous track. It's better than it was when they built it and they only had one other death there. It's just another track really.

"I try not to get too close to the other drivers because I don't want it to get to me if anything happens. I don't stay at the same motels as most of them, and things like that. But I was kind of close to Tiny. He had driven for us. In fact, when he had to drive in a sportsman race, he asked me to test this car for him Saturday and I did.

"I put it out of my mind. I had a race to run."

It was a rough race. Half the starting field of fifty cars crashed or caved in. But at the finish it was just the Petty 43 and the Baker 15. Pearson's engine had expired with a hundred miles, and no one else was close. Baker burst by Petty with fifteen laps left and held him off to the wire, though Richard drafted him, swung alongside him, and was within three feet of him at the finish. "I hated to get beat, but if Buddy's up there at the finish he's hard to overtake. He used up the track and I just couldn't catch up."

He had Lynda and the kids at the race. Tired as he was, he drove them home. It seemed a long ride. They did not talk about Tiny, but they thought about him. Tiny was forty-three. He had a wife, Wanda, and a son, Chris. He had been successful on the lesser Grand American tour but mostly unsuccessful on the Grand National circuit, though he won the Daytona 500 in 1963. He won less than $200,000 in his entire racing career. An ardent fisherman, he made a living by operating a fishing camp near Cross, South Carolina.

The funeral was held on Tuesday in Monck's Corner, near the lakes he fished. Richard and Lynda drove four hours there and four hours back. "It took all day, but it had to be done," Richard said. "Out of respect. And, since Lynda'd just gone through something like this with Randy, she felt she might have something to offer Wanda. I'll tell you, they wrote that Tiny was unsuccessful. I guess he was as a big-time racer. But it depends on how you measure success. He was doing what he liked in life, so, as I see it, he was successful."

The very day of the funeral, Mark Donohue crashed and died following brain surgery in a practice run for the Austrian Grand Prix in Zweltweg. Ironically, the former Indianapolis 500 winner and Grand National competitor had been at Talladega only ten days earlier, setting a closed-course speed record of better than 220 miles per hour in a Porsche.

"These things seem to run in packs, like killer dogs," commented Petty.

Some drop to the side of the road, but the racing goes on. The survivors were at Brooklyn, Michigan, the following week for the Champion Spark Plug 400. After two straight runner-up finishes, the Petty team seemed driven even more than usual, but it was a difficult event.

About 135 miles into the race, Coo Coo Marlin's Chevy blew

an engine, careened out of control off a concrete wall, and bounced off other cars like a crazily spinning billiard ball.

No one was seriously hurt, but the race had to be halted for forty minutes while repairs were made to a damaged guard rail. Then at about 135 miles, a rainstorm struck with almost hurricane intensity. The cars again had to be parked, this time for 2¼ hours.

Foyt dominated more than half the race before the engine in his Chevy came apart. Bobby Allison became the primary pacesetter until Petty pulled past him and away with one hundred miles left. Pearson and Yarborough came up to challenge Bobby in the late stages, but Petty began to build a big lead.

With just ten of the two-mile laps left, Marcis clipped Yarborough as Cale tried to lap him. Later, Cale complained, "Marcis won't move over even when he's being lapped. He turned into me. He did it deliberately." Cale's mechanic, Herb Nab, added, "Marcis is crazy." Marcis said, "Whatever they say I am, they are." His mechanic, Harry Hyde, said, "Cale hit David twice, so David decided to even it up."

The tangle brought out the yellow slowdown signals, and the trailers were able to pull up to Petty and bunch behind him.

"I had a half lap on the others. That cost me my lead. I cussed, I got to admit," Petty recalled later.

The green flew with five laps left and the 47,000 fans came to their feet and stayed there as Petty and Pearson pulled away from the pack and dueled daringly through the last ten miles. Pearson passed Petty to take the lead on lap 197. Petty repassed Pearson to take the lead back on lap 198. Pearson pushed in front on lap 199. But Petty pushed back in front on lap 200, the last one and the one that counted.

Petty set up Pearson with precision. On the next to last turn, Petty started to pass Pearson on the inside, Pearson swung low to shut him off, and Petty backed off. Then on the last turn, Petty started to go to the outside and as Pearson moved up to block him, Petty suddenly cut to the inside and pulled alongside Pearson. They were racing deep into the corner and eased off for a split second. Pearson slid a little, and Petty surged into the lead. Pearson came right back down at him through the stretch, as the fans screamed at them, but he could not catch him.

"Our cars was even," Richard remarked later. "He was quicker through the straights, but I took the turns better. I had to take him in a turn. I faked a pass to the inside on the third turn, hoping he'd think I'd take the high road on the fourth turn. I made like I was going to go high and he went for it. He got a little out of shape and that was it. I bluffed him and beat him. Next time he might outsmart me. You play high-stakes poker with cars for cards out there."

Petty picked up a pot worth $15,000 to put him over the $200,000 mark in earnings for the fourth time in five seasons. "We went home in style. Our hamburgers had all the trimmings on 'em."

The Southern 500 at Darlington on Labor Day, the first Monday of September, was something else. Richard was sick with the flu. There are worse things, but few that make you feel worse. He had a fever and chills, his bones ached, he couldn't keep food in his stomach, and he stopped eating.

Somehow, he qualified fourth fastest, then flew home to rest on Saturday. He returned to Darlington on Sunday but stayed in bed in his motel room. Monday morning he went to the race track but went to the shower room and lay down on a bench until it was time to get into his uniform.

He did not to to the driver's meeting before the race, nor to pick up a $10,000 check from a Winston official at the ceremonial prerace presentation of the award he had won for having led the second straight of the three legs of the seasonal drivers' race.

"I have never felt physically as bad before a race," he confessed before climbing into his car. Wasn't it, then, dangerous to drive? "Maybe," he admitted. But later he said, "Sometimes you drive better under those circumstances. You concentrate harder. I figured I couldn't finish, so I figured, dadgum, I'm gonna go like blazes as long as I last."

He did. He led six times for 146 laps, and had lapped all except Bobby Allison, David Pearson, and Dave Marcis to build a big lead before he started to tire midway in the 367-lap classic over the torturous 1.3-mile speedway. He tried hard to lap those three before he had to turn his car over to a relief driver, but he began to fade badly.

Adding to his discomfort was the fact that it was a dreadful day, hot and humid, as the annual Darlington demolition derby unfolded.

Darrell Waltrip's engine exploded on the seventy-fifth lap. Buddy Baker's engine blew up on the 163rd lap. Parsons was overcome by heat and he turned his car over to Waltrip at 166 laps. David Pearson put his car into the wall on the 184th lap and decided he could not steer it any longer. He retired from this classic contest he had never won. The engine in the Marcis car began to overheat at 210 laps and it had to be parked.

Maurice and Dale did not try to discourage Richard from driving. When he decided he'd gone as far as he could go, they encouraged him to go a little farther. Black clouds had blown overhead. "It's gonna rain, Richard. Hang onto the lead," Dale hollered over the radio. Richard refused. "If anything happens in front of me, I won't have the strength to turn the car out of the way," he said.

He came in, sick at his stomach and ready to throw up. Maurice had brought Marcis into the Petty pit. He was a Dodge driver and fit Richard's car. As Richard was helped from his car, Marcis moved into it. That was at lap 230 and they lost a lap making the change. While Richard was being revived with oxygen, Marcis was spinning the Petty car on the track to avoid an accident, losing another lap. And at 269 laps, the rain came, interrupting the race.

Eighty minutes later, they were ready to resume. Richard was ready to resume. He looked pale as death and was weak, but he no longer was sick at his stomach. He wanted to go again. Maurice and Dale buckled him back into the big car and he went back onto the track as the green flag sent the cars back into competition. But he was two laps back.

Allison and Yarborough now led. But at 289 laps, Bruce Jacobi's car ran into James Hylton's car from behind, and Waltrip wrecked Parsons' car trying to avoid their spinning machines. Petty brushed the wall as he got by but suffered only some bent metal on the side of his car. He was able to close in on the leaders during the caution period, then dart around them on the restart to pull within one lap of Allison and Yarborough.

Hylton muttered, "Jacobi ran out of brains if he ever had any. He just ran right into me."

When Cale's engine expired at 298 laps, Allison was left in the lead, with one lap on Petty. The third-place car was ten laps back. As Ken Squier reported over the nationwide network carrying the radio broadcast, Richard put the hammer down. He went at Allison, caught, and passed him. But that only put him in the same lap with the leader and left him more than a mile down.

Only another slowdown period would permit him to catch up. It never came. After 367 laps and 500 miles, Allison put his Roger Penske–prepared American Motors Company Matador across the finish line a half mile ahead of Petty's STP car.

Petty said, "That was the longest day of driving of my life. I was so sick, second place looks all right this time. But I got to give it to Bobby. I took it to him at the end and he just outdrove me."

Allison said, "That's the greatest compliment I've ever had. As sick as he apparently was, he gave one of the guttiest exhibitions I've ever seen."

There was, then, this bond between these bitter rivals: they were racers.

Allison accepted a little more than $22,000 for his first victory since April, while Petty settled for a little less than $15,000 for his long day's journey. Asked about the choice of Marcis, of all people, as his relief driver, Richard smiled and said, "He was available. And he did all right. The accident wasn't his fault. I'd probably have wrecked the racer."

He went home to rest. He had a busy week ahead of him. It turned out to be a hectic two weeks.

The Petty team traveled to the Virginia State Fairgrounds for the Capital City 500 in Richmond, qualified for the event, but sat around Sunday while it was rained out and rescheduled for October.

Returning home, they readied their race for the Delaware 500 at Dover the following Sunday. However, Richard also had a date at Brooklyn, Michigan, for the first leg of the annual International Race of Champions, an exhibition event in which top drivers from various circuits compete in sports cars prepared by a "house team" of mechanics.

The schedule was extremely tight and Michigan promoter Penske provided helicopters for Petty, Pearson, Parsons, and

Allison—NASCAR's representatives in the IROC. Petty flew into Michigan to qualify for the IROC event on Thursday, but it was washed out by rain. The NASCAR quartet went to Jackson, Michigan, and flew to Wilmington, Delaware, from where they drove to Dover. Friday they practiced their regular cars on the Dover mile.

They were permitted to qualify first Saturday morning. Then they were rushed by helicopter from the track to the airport in Wilmington, jetted to Jackson, and helicoptered to the track in suburban Brooklyn. They arrived, were allowed a few practice laps, then thrust into their race.

When it was over, the helicopter returned them to Jackson, the jet took them back to Wilmington, another helicopter returned them to Dover by Saturday night, and they were ready to race on Sunday.

"Yeh, it was sorta' tirin'," Richard admitted. "The worst of it was the anxiety of getting where we was supposed to be when we was supposed to be there. But it was better than last year when we drove between the tracks and the airports and didn't have a helicopter. This time, they had the timing down good."

He did not do well in the IROC race, as he has not done well in prior runnings. Why, then, does he do it?

"Well, it's sort of fun. You get to meet Grand Prix drivers and all. But it's not my sort of race. I rely on my team too much to expect to do well with a strange team. I rely on a handling car that's fit to my style, while these are supposed to be all the same. But they're not all the same. No matter how much you try, there will be differences from car to car.

"The race doesn't mean much to me. Maybe it does to some of the others, but not to me."

Pearson nosed out Allison to win the hundred-mile event, which was run in conjunction with a two-hundred-mile Indy car race. Foyt, Parsons, Emerson Fittipaldi, and Petty followed. Petty tangled with Mario Andretti on the last lap: "We went into the corner together and neither of us would back off, so we came together. He happened to get the worst of it because his back end broke loose and he spun off the track, while I got a little sideways but was able to straighten out and keep going.

"It's too short a race for me," he grinned. "If we go four hundred or five hundred more miles, those cats wouldn't still be so racy and my 'bad health' would come into it and I'd beat 'em."

He needed all five hundred miles to win at Dover in one of the most remarkable races of his career. He completely dominated the event after Pearson's engine failed, and led Lennie Pond and Cale Yarborough by two laps and the rest by four or more after 348 of the 500 one-mile laps. However, when Elmo Langley's engine exploded, a broken flywheel flew off, was sucked into Petty's car, and cracked a tie rod, crippling his steering.

Richard radioed Dale and a crew member was rushed to the truck for a replacement. As Petty pulled into the pits, the team pulled his car apart and hurried repairs. But by the time they got him back on the track, the yellow period had ended, the green had come back out, he had lost eight laps, and fallen six laps behind Pond and Yarborough with 170 miles left.

From eighth place, Petty flew through the field. He knocked off one car after another, lap after lap. Pond's engine expired and he retired. Cale's engine went sour and he slowed drastically. Benny Parsons led, then Richard Brooks, but Petty was coming. He'd spotted them only four laps and he kept lapping them until, with eight laps left, Petty passed them to take the lead. He was widening it at the wire with the fans shouting for his spectacular comeback.

"We was flat flying," Richard reported. "It was one of those days when we were so much better than everyone else, we should have won by six or eight laps. Because of circumstances we had to use up that advantage just catching up, and we won by less than a lap, but we won. My crew gave me the chance to catch up with their work in the pits. I put it to them on the track. We never gave up. This is my track, anyway."

One of his tracks, anyway. It was his fifth victory in a dozen events in Delaware, where he had completed 5,500 of a possible 5,550 laps for an astonishing 99 per cent durability mark. His $15,000 first-place prize pushed his earnings at this six-year-old track to $85,000.

It did not come without controversy. Petty gained ground late in the race when Buddy Arrington's car stopped twice on the track. The second time, the officials brought out the slowdown flag, permitting Petty to close in on the leaders.

Arrington used to drive the Petty second truck and had just purchased it. "Maybe he needed to have it marked paid for," protested Brooks later. Others complained, too. Cale said, "I'll bet everything I own Richard didn't know about it, but I'll bet Buddy did it for Richard, just the same."

Arrington denied the accusations. "I was overheating and my brakes locked. I spun twice. I was in and out of the pits. I shoulda' quit, but I wanted to keep trying. It's not the first time a car had to stop and a yellow had to come out late in a race. I've been racing ten years and I wouldn't pull any dirty tricks on any-one. I like the Pettys, but I don't owe them any favors, and they don't need any."

Richard said, "I don't know what happened. I took advantage of a situation that turned up, but I'd have won without it."

Dale simply smiled and said something about bread cast upon the waters.

Reporters were more concerned with a story that had broken in the Charlotte *Observer* that Petty and Pearson were ready to re-tire. Both denied it emphatically and the report was removed from the newspaper after the first edition.

Richard says, "It's an example of how you got to watch who you're talking to. We were layin' around a room in Richmond with a reporter and he asked us when we were going to retire. I said when my sponsor left me.

"David said I was sicker than I ever let on and probably wouldn't make it to the next season. I said Doctor David and I probably would wind up retirin' at the same time without saying a word to one another.

"We was just makin' conversation. Didn't mean nothin'.

"Then this story comes out that we were ready to retire. I couldn't believe it."

Reporters rushed to STP chairman John Jay Hooker, who said, "As far as I know, Richard plans to remain in racing. And as long as we remain in racing, we hope Richard will remain with us."

Reporters surrounded Richard after the race at Dover and he asked them, "Did it look like I was ready to retire? I plan to race next year, and the year after that, and the year after that. I think I've got ten good years left in me.

"It's just getting to be fun. I don't seem to have slowed down any, do I? I didn't look sick out there, did I? Hey, you boys know you can't believe everything you read. You just report that poor Petty, sick old man that he is, limped to another win here today."

It was the tenth victory of the season for Petty. No one else had more than three. He got his eleventh in the next race, the Wilkes 400 on the five-eighths-mile oval in North Wilkesboro, North Carolina. This set a "short-season" record. It was his thirteenth victory at this track where no one else had won more than two. With thirteen victories at Richmond and fourteen at Martinsville, he had won enough races, forty, at these small tracks to rank among the top ten winners in Grand National history if he had never even won elsewhere.

It did not come easily, as so few have. Petty and Yarborough dueled almost the entire 250-mile distance. Cale led with sixty miles left, but pulled out of the pits from his last stop with a power-wrench hose attached to a compression tank still hanging on his car. The tank pulled free as he took to the track, but he had to be black-flagged off to remove the hose.

Cale caught Richard with twenty laps left, but Petty passed him and won the sprint to the wire. Cale brushed a rail in his desperate drive near the end and finished two seconds short. He settled for close to $4,000, while Petty took in twice that much.

It was, at it turned out, the end of maybe the most impressive series of races in NASCAR records. In eleven straight races between May 25 and September 21 Richard Petty finished first six times and second five times and won almost $150,000. The Petty team car ran for 4,700 racing miles without a failure. All but two of the races were 500 miles or more, and those two were 250 miles or more. When Petty won ten straight races in 1967, only one was a 500-miler, only two were 250-milers and the rest ranged all the way down to 62½ miles. His winnings then were $130,000.

"Credit the crew," commented Richard.

"You're darn right," remarked Maurice.

"I agree," grinned Dale.

Richard led only one lap and lasted only 243 of the 500 laps in the 265-mile Old Dominion 500 in Martinsville, Virginia, on the final Sunday of September. He bottomed out when he ran over a curb and broke his gearbox. This sidelined him as Dave Marcis drove the K&K Insurance Dodge to the first victory of his 225-race Grand National career, by a few seconds over Benny Parsons.

The race paid a record short-track total of $75,000 with $14,250 going to the winner. Petty was almost embarrassed to pick up his twenty-second-place prize of $860. "The crew let me down," he said later, laughing. Dale didn't find it funny. The fact is everyone was grumbling a little all the way home.

17

OCTOBER AND NOVEMBER

"It will hurt bad when I have to retire from racing." Richard Petty said, perched on a pit wall in his uniform, his eyes hidden behind his sunglasses. "I am thirty-eight years old and I get sick sometimes just like anyone else. I have my problems, but I would be crazy to drive race cars if I was in bad health. I do not have bad health. I have a good life. I like the racing life and want to go on as long as I can.

"That stuff about cutting off your uniform before you'll stop applies more to race drivers than other athletes. Most ball players have to quit when someone tells them they can't make the team anymore. A driver can always get a ride and go on. A lot of good drivers drop down to bad rides and go on. I wouldn't want to do that, but I wouldn't want to quit, either.

"I'm just like the cats that like to write books or paint pictures or build buildings. The difference is they can do what they do until they're a hundred. An athlete loses his ability to compete before he's fifty. I like to drive race cars and I might do it until I'm fifty if I hold my health. Some race drivers have to die before they're done.

"My head hurts sometimes, sometimes my back hurts, once in a while my legs ache, and every so often my stomach hurts, but so far as I know there's nothing wrong with me."

There did not appear to be at Charlotte, where the National 500 was staged on the first Sunday in October. Almost all the top competitors took turns in the lead through the rough race over the 1½-mile speedway. All but fifteen of the forty-two starters broke down. Allison, Waltrip, Marcis, and Foyt fell out along the way.

Pearson started first and Petty started ninth, but when it came down to the last laps, it came down to these two, as it so often has. From time to time another car is brought up into it, and this time it was Buddy Baker's Ford. But Buddy was battling a broken sway bar and couldn't quite keep up.

With fifty of the 334 laps left, Cale Yarborough's Chevy spun wildly out of contention. He got out and came down into the garage area and said, "Ol' Blue's headed home. It's going to be a good finish, but I think I know who is going to get there first. Ol' Blue has her ears to the wind and is on her way."

With almost 70,000 fans urging their heroes home, the final forty miles, following the final yellow, were furious. As the green flew, Petty accelerated, but Ol' Blue, as Cale calls the car, hesitated, allowing Pearson and Baker to burst by. Petty pulled up and they raced three abreast along the narrow ribbon of concrete for a while. Riding inside, Petty went high into a turn, forcing his foes to back off and fall back.

They hung close through the last laps. Pearson had problems passing Baker. When he finally got by Buddy, he went after Richard. But he could not pass Petty. Petty put his foot to the floorboard and held it there through the last lap. He flashed through the finish fifteen feet in front of Pearson, and David came across fifteen feet in front of Baker. Richard had his twelfth win in twenty-five races of the 1975 season and had pulled to within one of Pearson in lifetime superspeedway wins, thirty-two to thirty-three.

Pearson had picked up a special $10,000 pole-winner's prize to go with his $22,945 runner-up prize, so he actually took home more of promoter Richard Howard's money than Petty's $27,970 first-place payoff. But after the mountainous Howard, "the fabulous fat man," as the Charlotte chief was called, had handed Petty his check, Richard shrugged: "You run for the pole, or you run for Victory Circle. I run to win. The rest is gravy and I'm not gonna be seduced by it. A pole prize like this is a con game they play with the people. They try to make them think the race before the race is as important as the race. I won't play a part in it."

In the Capital City 500 at Richmond, where Richard had won nine of the prior ten races, he not only did not win, he finished last for the first time in ten years. His engine failed after only thirty-four laps and he was the first car out of the race, which had been postponed by rain a month earlier. It was won by Darrell Waltrip, with Lennie Pond second to match the highest finish in his career.

"I should be content, but it's not like finishing second to Petty," Pond groused.

It was reported that a valve spring had snapped, but later Richard revealed privately that a new type piston had broken. There were rumors that the Petty team, with the seasonal title clinched, was experimenting with new equipment. Richard confessed, "We want to win next year as much as this year. If we're going to try something new, this wouldn't be a bad time."

Just starting the race not only earned Richard $700 to put him close to $300,000 for the year, but provided him with thirty-four points to clinch his sixth driving title. As the 14,000 fans filed out of the fairgrounds arena, the last-place finisher and his team drove away without complaint. King Richard reported, "They had to hunt far down in the field to find me to fit the crown on me."

Cale commented, "That son-of-a-gun is playing games with us."

The rumors persisted at the American 500 in Rockingham, where Cale came through with his third triumph of the campaign in Junior Johnson's Holly Farms Chevy. Richard finished thirty-fifth among the thirty-eight starters.

Richard denied the rumors this time. "A rocker arm broke this time," he said. "It coulda' happened any time and it happened early, but it hadn't happened all season. Bad luck beginning to catch up with us, I guess. We sort of wanted to win this one."

The day before the race, the Richard Petty Fan Club convened at the Randleman community grounds, were fed a picnic lunch, and taken on a tour of the compound. Rain had put Friday's scheduled qualifying for the race off until Saturday, and Richard had to rush home from Rockingham to take a part in the party. Most of the six hundred fans were waiting for him, he shook six hundred hands, signed six hundred autographs, and had to ice his sore right hand afterwards.

Governor James Holshouser declared Sunday "Richard Petty Day" in North Carolina, so Richard announced he was declaring Saturday "Governor Holshouser Day." His fans laughed, but no one was laughing when he failed fast the following afternoon.

"Sort of spoiled the party," grumbled Richard as his team packed up and departed.

The last weekend in October Richard returned to Riverside to run the second and third legs of the International Race of Champions. He did not do well. He had tire trouble in the races both days, put his car into a wall the second day, finished sixth and ninth and failed to qualify for the final race at Daytona in February.

"I just had all kinds of trouble," Richard observed. "On Saturday, one tire went flat on me, then another one blowed and I spun out in turn nine, where I always leave the track. On Sunday I blew another one, got it replaced, then ran over some debris on the track and cut still another one, and that threw me right into the wall."

"Was it a bad wreck?" he was asked.

"Well, it wasn't good. It was over real quick, but I coulda' done without it. I totaled the car, but didn't total me. I skinned my arms and bruised my shoulder. That was in turn nine, too. I might run Riverside again if they let me skip turn nine.

"I like bein' with the different guys. But it's funny. We automatically segregate ourselves. I swear I can tell 'em apart from a distance. I can see one bunch and know those are my crowd, and another bunch and know they're Indy guys, and another and know they're the sporty car set just by the way they walk and carry themselves."

"You could tell by the way they talk, too," I said.

"Yeh, the northern cats talk funny," he said, grinning.

"You failed to make the finals for the third straight year."

"Yeh, but it don't bother me. It would bother me if the other cats come to my circuit and beat me."

He was sore for a week. He was still sore the following weekend at Bristol, but back in his own backyard he beat the best of his bunch. As he had at Charlotte, where he had not won before, he completed a sweep of the season's two races at Bristol, where he had won only once before.

He fell two laps back with a flat tire, but after Yarborough's engine came apart, Petty came on to win by more than a lap over Lennie Pond. It was, as it always is, a hard race in this brutal bowl, and several drivers required relief before the race ended, but Richard endured to win this Volunteer 500 and $5,500.

Afterwards, exhausted, Richard said, "We made some changes to try to help the handling, but we hurt 'er instead, and it just plumb wore me out. But everyone has a hard time here. It's just a hard place. I lost it two or three times, but I was lucky no one was near me each time, and I was able to straighten her out and get pointed in the right direction again. I brushed the wall a couple times, too. And banged a couple cars, too. Put marks on both sides of my car."

He was just tired, a winner who looked like a loser. He laughed a little and said, "Dale told me on the radio when I took the checker there was just a hundred more laps to go. I told him I was bringing it in anyway, and he could drive the last hundred." He stopped laughing and the smile faded, as if it was too much effort.

Kyle drove him home. This was one of the four or five races Lynda passed up during the year because she does not like the race track, but Kyle came to see the race and was there to chauffeur the old man through the long ride home.

The road ran on, endlessly it seemed, though now the end was in sight. The next week they were in Atlanta for the Dixie 500, the next-to-last race of the long season. Petty qualified at close to 160 mph on Friday. He took only one of the two trial laps he was allowed, and while it was only fourth-fastest, he settled for that. "It was as fast as I've run here. No need to run faster," he shrugged.

That night he and Barry drove to Gainesville, Georgia, to see a high-school football game. A friend of Kyle's, the son of a friend of Richard's, was playing. Kyle had given his friend a half-dozen Richard Petty tee-shirts, and he and his teammates had worn them before their first game of the season. Winning it, they asked for and were given tee shirts for the entire team, which wore them before every game. Now, they had won ten in a row with not only the players but the cheerleaders and many of the fans wearing the "lucky shirts." They won this one, too. "It looked like a Richard Petty for President rally," Richard observed with a smile.

Special prizes were posted for the leader of Sunday's 228th lap, which was the ten-thousandth in Grand National history. Although he insists he does not give in to such gimmicks, Richard led that lap, which was exactly one hundred laps from the finish of the event, and won $17,000 worth of gifts, including a motorboat and truck and trailer rig. Asked if he would swear on his youngest that he did not go for it, Richard laughed and said, "I don't reckon I would, but it was about the time we do go for the lead, and it just worked out that way. I would not have risked winning the race in an attempt to win that race within a race."

He did take the lead long before that lap, which paid more than the winner's purse of $15,550, but gave it back to Buddy Baker a few laps later. In fact Richard was more than a mile ahead and seemed well on his way to winning until an accident involving two tail-enders slowed the pace and permitted Baker and Dave Marcis to move in right behind him. Through the last hundred miles the three swapped the lead. Baker was leading when a sudden downpour required an hour's delay with only thirty-five miles left.

Baker figured he had won, because he did not figure officials would restart the race at that point. However, after the rain eased, they readied a restart. Baker walked over to where Richard was sitting in his new boat and asked, "If there's no water on this track, how come Richard's in his boat?" They restarted the race with Richard in his car instead of his boat.

David Pearson was a lap behind. He lost the lap earlier when a tire went flat on him and his Wood Brothers pit crew changed the wrong wheel, then had to bring him right back in to change the right one. Now, he offered Baker the sort of opportunity to defeat Petty which Richard had given Benny Parsons in his Daytona defeat of Pearson. David hooked up with Buddy in a high-speed draft which left Petty and Marcis scrambling to keep up. Richard brushed the wall a couple of times in a desperate drive to maintain the pace, and not only lost the race but lost second place to Marcis. Leading the final fifty laps, Baker won going away. But Petty's third-place finish clinched the third and last leg of the Winston series, worth another $10,000.

Later, Richard reported, "The rain changed the track. It washed the grime off it and made it sticky and we lost the handling advantage we had. We didn't handle well at all at the end and I had all I could do to keep it on the track, much less beat Buddy. Bud Moore built him a new Ford and it may be just what Buddy needed. Marcis couldn't catch him, but he may be the most improved driver on the tour. Dave's no kid. He's near as old as I am. But he hasn't been driving the big time near as long. He's had bad cars and did bad with 'em. But now he's getting better cars and he's getting experience driving full, long races at speed, and he's steadying down. That yellow licked us. We had it locked till then."

Richard drove to Talladega on Monday to participate in an annual Alabama program honoring mentally handicapped and others with learning problems who are receiving driver education. There were seven hundred youngsters there, and they were taken on a tour of the track, shown movies, given a lecture on safety and given a chance to meet and get autographs from driving heroes.

Richard drove home, got there about midnight, then left early the next morning to fly to Fort Lauderdale to discuss the team's 1976 contract with STP officials. That night he flew cross-country to Los Angeles to put in two days of promotion for the final races of the season, the Los Angeles Times 500 at Ontario, California, the following week. He wanted to pass on this one because he had a date with Kyle in Washington on Friday, but Bill Dredge talked him into it.

Bright and early Wednesday morning, Richard was making the rounds. Wednesday afternoon he appeared at the monthly luncheon of the Orange County Sports Writers and Broadcasters at former baseball star Don Drysdale's Dugout restaurant in Santa Ana. Another honored guest was ex-con Mickey Cohen, onetime southern California gang lord, who had been a boxing bigwig and who was promoting a book on his life.

Richard was introduced to him, but seemed embarrassed when he found out who Cohen was. He noticed that the mobster used a napkin so his hands did not touch his silverware or a microphone that was handed him. Observed the racer, "I guess he don't want to leave no fingerprints."

As Cohen was interviewed and answered questions, he spoke with gutter good humor of mob murders and such. Almost all enjoyed it, laughing a lot, apparently so pleased to be in the company of such a celebrity they could forgive him his sins. Clearly Richard did not enjoy it. He hung his head. Asked quietly about it, he admitted, "Where I come from, the way we was raised, we don't honor such men." But the only reference Richard made to

Mickey's bloody tales was to say, when it was his turn to speak, "I thought mine was supposed to be the dangerous sport."

He made a hit wherever he went. Asked on a radio interview where Randleman was, Richard said it was right by Level Cross. "That just blowed his mind," Richard laughed later. He gave interview after interview, day after day, until his stint was finished. "The same questions asked a little different. The same answers given a little different," Richard reported.

His son had come home one day and asked his father for a favor: "I want to see the White House." Richard said, "Hey, I'm from Randleman. I can't take over Washington for you." But he arranged a VIP tour for Kyle and his school friends, though the President would not be there, and flew there Thursday night.

"Kyle and the kids got into the hotel that night. There was sixty of them, fifty kids and some school people and coaches and parents. We went to the zoo, the Smithsonian Institute, and the Washington Monument on Friday and on to the White House on Saturday. The President wasn't home. Everyone was out of town. Sunday, we drove to Baltimore to see a Colts game. I'd gotten us tickets. We got back home about one Monday morning. I stayed home a couple days then."

"Doesn't Lynda get tired of this?"

"You better believe it. She says I've got time for everybody but her. She says I live on the road and visit home. She says I say yes to everyone else and no to her."

The race car was trucked out Monday, so it was waiting when Richard and Lynda arrived in Ontario on Wednesday. Lynda stayed at the motel with some of the other wives while Richard went to the track. A fat lady waved from behind the fence near the garage as Richard went in. He told Maurice some lady wanted to see him, "mebbe" his wife. Maurice looked up from his engine, saw the lady, and waved back at her. "Hi, honey," he called, then returned to his engine. Everyone laughed, but Richard went to sign an autograph for her.

A half hour after the track opened for practice, something broke in the Petty car's engine. Maurice muttered and went with Dale to the truck. Rather than try to repair the engine, they replaced it. They hoisted the broken engine out of the car and into the truck and hoisted a new one out of the truck and into the car. They worked hard for two hours, sweating and swearing, in the stuffy garage while Richard sat in the sunshine of late November in southern California and chatted with visitors.

The afternoon was fading when Richard got back on the track and ran at better than 151 miles per hour, unofficially surpassing the track record for stock cars. "I figured I owed a fast run to the fellas for all the hard work they put in," he commented. They were pleased when they buttoned the car down for the night.

Richard took Lynda out to eat that night. Where did they go? He said, "Dadgum it, I can't remember the name, but it's a real nice place. Had us steaks. You go down here about three miles and just turn left. We been there before. I don't know the names of the places we eat in each town, but I know how to get to 'em."

On Friday, warm winds were blowing dust and sand around this beautiful but financially troubled track, and the drivers waited for the dust to settle before taking to the track. Richard sat in the sun with the San Gabriel Mountains, shrouded in smog, behind him, talked and chewed his cigar, and waited. When it was time, he took out his car, but it did not handle well and he was not happy with it.

Maurice and Dale set to changing it. They shifted the weight around. Richard took it out and came in complaining. They changed the sway bars. He took it out and came back complaining again. They altered the tilt of the spoiler. He took it out again. They went on working.

"We tried power steering once for a while and it worked and was easier, but it didn't have the feel so I told 'em to forget it," Richard said. "We tried power brakes, but the response was too sharp, so we forgot them, too. We just got a basic car and just got to work hard to work it."

They got it as good as they could before time trials started. They pushed it into line, but they had drawn a late number and had to wait two hours for their turn. An official came along checking off the cars on a list he had. He asked Richard his name and Richard looked at him as if he was crazy, then saw the smile on the man's face, smiled and said, "Jus' go by the number." The official laughed and checked off 43.

They waited, kidding around with visitors. Dale kept grabbing at his teammates or coming up behind them and pounding them on the back or grabbing them in bear hugs. "He's a very physical person," Richard observed with a smile. Dale heard him and asked if he wanted some of the same. Richard smiled and said, "No way. Remember, I'm your bread and butter. You don't want to break me." Dale shrugged and turned on Wayne.

After a while, Richard sat down on the ground with his back to the pit wall and grew quiet. The bill of his STP cap shaded his face. Once he went into this retreat, no one bothered him.

The wind had blown up again by the time he went out. His run of 151.5 proved to be only sixth fastest of the day, behind Pearson, Baker, Marcis, Allison, and Foyt. Two miles per hour faster than Petty, Pearson became the favorite, but Baker pointed out, "Placing on the pole is about as significant as throwing a tin can off the back side of the grandstand."

This seemed a turnabout for the big guy. He said, "I used to think leading wire-to-wire was the ultimate accomplishment, but now I see that winning is all that counts. I've enrolled in the Richard Petty School of Race Tactics and I've adopted the strategy of the master. I'll extend myself and my car only as much as necessary."

Richard was asked, "Who's the driver to beat?"

"Whoever finishes second," he answered.

On Sunday, race day, he stood alongside Baker along garage row and they talked about their wives rather than racing. Richard said when he got back to the motel Saturday he couldn't get the door to his room open because Lynda had so many purchases packed into the place.

Wistful with wonder, he observed, "She bought all kinds of stuff, the same junk she coulda' bought back in Greensboro for half the price." She said, 'Yeh, but it wouldn't be from southern California.'"

Baker nodded his head knowingly. "When they go out shopping, there isn't a store that's safe. Coleen spent so much money I have to win to break even on the trip."

They laughed about it, relaxed before the race.

After the cars were pushed onto the track, Dale sat on the pit wall, keeping his car company. I said to him, "It's been a good year."

Dale said, "I guess."

"Maybe your best?"

Dale said, "Mebbe. We won more other years, but not in money. And there's a lot less races and they're harder to win now.

And because our car didn't outclass the field the way it did some years in the past, we had to outperform them.

"But," he said, sighing and looking down at his empty hands, "this wasn't a good year because we lost Randy this year. Nothing we could have done would have made up for that. It's like a black cloud that has followed us since it happened, shutting out the sun. We don't talk about it and we try not to think about it, but it's there."

When Richard came up, he was asked about what Dale had said. Richard sat down on the wall and looked off at the mountains and said, "Yes, sir, that's right. Oh, God, yes. I would trade every race we won, every one we ever won, to get him back. But you can't do that, can you?"

"What can you do?"

A smile illuminated his face. "Keep truckin'," he said.

Baker led most of the way, but Petty led as late as the four-hundred-mile mark. After Baker got by, Petty was pressing him until a valve came apart in his engine, sidelining him with only eighty miles left.

It was Baker who received the cheers of the crowd of 55,000 fans as he crossed the finish line in his Norris Industries Ford seventeen seconds in front of David Pearson's Mercury. The $32,300 check was the largest he'd ever won and he enjoyed the hoopla surrounding his fourth victory of the campaign. "It's been our best season in a long time," he said.

Softly, Petty said, "For us it would be a bad year."

Someone asked, "What's Buddy have?"

Petty said, "He'd have had second place if we hadn't cut two tires and had trouble replacing them in the pits and then had the engine give out."

"Could you have caught up?"

"No sweat," he said, sweating and sipping a Coke.

Dredge came to take him to the press box and Richard made the rounds of the writers and broadcasters and visited the sponsors' suites. Wherever he went, he praised Baker's drive.

Richard had raced more than 20,000 miles and completed 9,082 of 10,628 laps. The Petty team had completed twenty-four of the thirty races. No one else had finished more than eighteen. The Pettys led twenty-six races. No one else led more than twenty. The Pettys had finished in the first five twenty-one times. No one else had more than sixteen times. Richard had finished first thirteen times, second five times, third three times. No one else had won more than Baker's four. Pearson, Allison, and Yarborough had won three each. Richard never lost more than three races in a row. Cale and Allison each lost twelve in a row and Pearson lost the last twelve.

NASCAR paid out $3.5 million in prizes during the year. Petty's final purse of almost $5,000 pushed his race earnings, including sponsors' posted prizes, to $378,865, a new NASCAR record. This included $21,000 from Winston, $14,000 from Goodyear, $5,000 from Champion, and $1,000 from Bell. With a $50,000 bonus from STP and other bonuses from others, his income from the tour surpassed $400,000. Pearson earned just under $180,000, Baker $170,000, Marcis $150,000, Parsons $140,000, Yarborough $140,000, Hylton $100,000 and Waltrip $100,000.

Marcis and Parsons won only one race each, while Hylton did not win any, but because they ran all the races, and placed in the top ten in half or more of them, they accumulated enough points to fill out the first four in the driver's standings. But Petty was far in front at the finish. Pearson finished fourteenth, Baker fifteenth.

Richard now had six national titles. No one else had more than three. He had won 177 of 681 races. Pearson was second with 87, less than half as many. And Lee Petty still stood third with 54. Well down the list were Allison with 46, Yarborough with 31, and Baker with 12.

Richard still trailed Pearson in superspeedway wins, thirty-two to thirty-three, but led him in five-hundred-mile victories twenty-eight to seventeen, and they were the top two in this in the history of car racing. The Petty team still trailed the Wood Brothers in superspeedway wins, forty to forty-six. Pete Hamilton pitched in three, Buddy Baker two, Lee Petty, Jim Paschal, and Marvin Panch one each to Richard's thirty-two on the Petty list.

In four seasons and 119 races since moving under STP sponsorship, the Petty team had captured thirty-seven races worth almost a million dollars.

STP's big Bill Dredge had his arm around Richard's shoulder, holding onto him as though he were gold, as he walked him back through the tunnel and the fans to the garage where Maurice and Dale and the rest of the crew were loading up the red-and-blue 43 for the long ride home.

From there, fans following, Richard went to the parking area, where Lynda waited patiently in their rental car, reading a historical romance in paperback, *The Wolf and the Dove.* "It passes the time," she said with a smile, as Richard climbed into the driver's seat, still signing autographs.

NASCAR led all racing circuits with 1,286,000 fans at its thirty Grand National events. It seemed like every one wanted the Petty autograph at least once.

I reached in and shook Richard's hand. "Well, you won thirteen."

"Yeh, but we lost seventeen," Richard said.

18

THE NEW YEAR

December may be the last month of the old year for most, but it is the first month of the new year for the southern stock-car crowd. There are about eight weeks between the last race of one season and the first race of the next season, and they are spent preparing for the coming campaign. There are, of course, weekends at home and holidays spent with the family and vacations squeezed in, but basically it is a busy time for the racers.

What should have been a period of pleasure for Richard Petty as 1975 moved into 1976 turned out to be a month or so of misery. He had not felt well throughout the 1975 season, although he would not say anything to anyone about it, and when he felt worse at Christmastime, he continued to keep it to himself for fear of spoiling his family's celebration. His stomach hurt horribly and he feared ulcers.

News that he had been voted by the motorsports press the national driver of the year came as a Christmas present, but he was hurting throughout the holiday period. The racers' road runs on, however, and the third week in January Richard and the rest returned to Riverside for the opening event of his nineteenth campaign, the Wintson Western 500.

He showed up with a bushy beard, grown to take part in a bicentennial celebration planned for April at home. Worried about Richard's image, Bill Dredge pleaded with him to shave, but Richard refused. "I'm a big boy now," he grinned.

Five minutes before the completion of practice prior to the time trials on Friday, the STP car's engine blew up in a burst of smoke. This was the second time in the last two races in California that the Pettys had blown an engine, and they had to exchange it with the spare they pulled off the truck.

Maurice was muttering to himself. "I can't tell you why the engines have begun to break. If I could, I'd fix 'em so they wouldn't break. I just build 'em bad," he snapped, shoving his greasy hands into the guts of the power plant as he tried to get it installed in time to qualify. Dale worked with him. It was hard, dirty work. Their hands not only got dirty, they got scraped and cut. They slaved for six hours while Richard sat in the winter sun outside. "As you can see," he said, "they have the easy job on this team."

The engine was not ready in time to run that day. They had to put off their run until the next day, when Richard would have to start behind the others, no matter how fast he qualified. His speed of 109.6 on Saturday was ninth fastest in the field, but put him twenty-seventh in the starting field. Then he went to town to lecture to a University of California at Riverside class on "The World of Auto Racing." Professor Petty drew diagrams on a blackboard and discussed the science of his sport for an hour, receiving a standing ovation at the finish. Then his students lined up for autographs.

The appeal of auto racing was never more evident than when almost 55,000 fans turned out at the dusty arena on Super Bowl Sunday, during which pro football's championship game was televised.

Petty battled Pearson and Allison for the lead until he limped into the pits after 190 miles with a broken valve train. Parking his car, he walked away from it to shower and change.

In the shower room, he stripped off his sweaty and soiled uniform and boots and sat on a bench, looking weary and wilted. "Ah hope this is not gonna be one of those years," he sighed. He lit a cigar and puffed on it, gathering the strength to shower. Finally he got up and took his shower. He was drying himself when a crew member came in to tell him they'd fixed the engine and to ask if he wanted to resume running.

"If we can run, we'll run," Richard said, without hesitation. By then he was bound to be many laps back, but he swiftly pulled on his soggy uniform and boots and ran to the garage, where his car waited for him. He climbed into the car and backed out so fast he knocked over a pile of tires. Running right over one of the tires, he raced through the garage area, down pit road, and back onto the track and into the race.

A few laps later, he was finished. Maurice and Dale had done the job with adhesive tape. It had not held.

"We tried," Dale said, shrugging. "Who won the football game?"

Told Pittsburgh had, he reported he had won a bet which required Barry to walk back to North Carolina. Dale decided he would not hold Barry to it.

Slowly Richard returned to the shower, stripped, and stepped back into the water. "I'm gonna' be the cleanest man in town," he sighed.

Pearson won the race, his first ever at Riverside.

Returning home, Richard turned himself over to a doctor, who promptly put him into a hospital. Recalling it later, Richard grinned and said, "I just went to the doctor without telling Lynda where I was going, then called her from the hospital to tell her where I was. She was upset, but not surprised, because she'd been after me awhile to get checked over. I think she thought I'd die before I'd do anything. They acted like I was dying. They put me in bed, stuck tubes in me, and wouldn't let me eat for almost two weeks. It was terrible."

He admits, "My stomach got so bad I had to see a doctor about it. I couldn't sleep, couldn't eat, couldn't even go to the bathroom. I was suffering from headaches and stomach cramps. I kind of knew I had ulcers, but I didn't want to know. An easygoing guy like me getting ulcers, it's awful! Maybe I feel more than I admit. I hold things in rather than let them out. But it was more than that. I had a tube all clogged up. Man, I was a mess."

He was treated in the hospital for twelve days, during which he lost twenty pounds while he was fed intravenously. Daytona drew near and there was some discussion of the wisdom of Richard racing there. Lynda said, "He'll race. He won't take care of hisself, but he'll race. He don't care if he's dying, if there's a race to run the dang fool will be there."

Richard said, "I'm going to Daytona and I'm going to drive."

He did, still bearded. Weak, but determined, he drove a brilliant race.

After more than three hours of grueling, daring racing, Petty and Pearson found themselves battling for a big one once again—

one Richard has won five times and Pearson never had won. As they neared the finish, Petty passed Pearson rather than drafting him. Pearson picked up Petty in a draft. Pearson said later that as they entered the last lap he put his foot to the floorboard and never let up after that. He pulled up tight to Petty as they drove at 200 miles per hour through the 3,000-foot backstretch.

Coming off the third turn, Pearson executed the slingshot skillfully, and pulled in front as they neared the end of the short chute. As Richard moved up against the wall in what writer Deke Houlgate called "his familiar frightening line," Pearson moved ahead of him to block him.

Circling the fourth corner, Petty cut sharply to his left and pulled below and alongside Pearson. As they came out of the corner, they came together and crashed into a tangle. Both bashed the concrete barrier and came into the homestretch skidding and spinning wildly as the fans stood and screamed.

Later, Richard revealed, "He was faster, but wasn't handling as well. He got to loafing on the lead to keep his tires cool. I decided I couldn't outsprint him, so I might as well pass him to make him run hard and heat up his tires. I did and I tried to get away from him, but he kept contact. He did heat his tires, however. That's why he slid when I passed him.

"When he passed me coming off the third corner, I decided to shoot the works and try to pass him coming off the fourth. When I went high, he didn't expect me to go low. But instead of sliding into the wall, he slid into me.

"But it was my fault. There wasn't room to make the move I made. I took a chance and was lucky to get out of it without hurting us. When I started spinning, I thought I might spin right across the finish line to win, but I wasn't that lucky."

The two came together five hundred feet from the finish line. Both slid down into the infield grass, but Pearson, thinking fast under heart-stopping conditions, held his clutch to keep his engine running, while Richard did not. Richard's car died less than fifty feet from the finish.

Pointed the wrong way, Pearson was one hundred feet away. "Has he crossed the line yet?" he hollered to his crew through the radio. "No, no," Glen Wood said. "Get going." David got going.

Turning and driving back onto the track, right into the midst of lapped cars, Pearson limped at 20 miles per hour to the checkered flag, passing Petty, who was being pushed.

It was the most spectacular finish in the history of this classic contest, this one Richard Petty lost, surpassing even the one Lee Petty won.

"Richard tapped me as he went past and that started it, but he was only trying to win," Pearson said as he embraced the coveted trophy he had sought so long.

"If I had spun out of Victory Lane here for the second straight year, I'd be mad, but now I'm not mad at anyone."

"Why should he be mad? He won," drawled Richard sadly.

As they were pushed away, the two bent racers both looked like losers.

It turned out to be that sort of year for Richard Petty.

He lost by six feet to Marcis in the Richmond 400.

He won the Carolina 500 at Rockingham, leading 362, including the last 220, of the 492 laps, but he had to snake through an eight-car crash near the end, in which Bobby Allison's car barrel-rolled ten times, bringing Bobby severe but not serious back, chest, and eye injuries. A little later in the season, Bobby, busy on one of his four-race weekends, crashed at the Minnesota Speedway, again suffering severe but not serious injuries, and he was back behind the wheel of a racing car in about a week.

At Bristol the Sunday following the Rockingham race, competing in the Southeastern 500, Petty spun out, slid sideways across the track, was rammed hard at the driver's door by Cecil Gordon's car, then was bashed in the back end by Rich Childress's car.

Lynda was there, though she often is not at this track both she and Richard dislike, and she let out a gasp and did not breathe until Richard hopped unhurt from the wreckage of his racer. "I was relieved," she said later with a sigh.

Smiling, Richard said, "It totalled the car but not me. It drove the insides, with me buttoned into it, out the other side, but it just shook me up a little. It was the kind of accident that could be bad but wasn't."

He said he was feeling fine. "I have to give a medical report to the news guys at every track, but I'm not the first guy who ever got ulcers. I'm gaining back most of the weight I lost, but mostly I just have to watch my diet. I have to eat, but I have to eat the right things.

"It's helped me. I feel better than I have in years. Those headaches that used to last for weeks go away in hours. The only thing wrong with me right now is we're not winning."

NASCAR's latest rules change, which took effect in March, worried the Petty team. It reduced the size of the carburetors permitted on the racers. Because of the engine setups of the various cars, it provided a power advantage to the Pearson Mercury and Yarborough Chevrolet over the Petty Dodge, according to Maurice.

"Our crew will be hard-put to make up the difference," Maurice said with disgust.

The crew had altered. Beginning a new business, Radar had been forced to leave the traveling team. Billy Biscoe took his place as a regular on the tour.

Jerry continued to travel despite a separation from his wife. "I'm trying to get it back together," he admitted. "I try not to think about it at the races. I owe the Pettys my concentration at the track. We're at a disadvantage right now and are working our rear ends off without good results."

After Petty's crew won the annual Union 76 Pit Crew Race in February at the North Carolina Motor Speedway, Maurice was asked whether the crew made any special preparations. "Yeh, we've been practicing for twenty years," Maurice said with a grin.

But practice did not make perfect.

The Petty engine failed in the Atlanta 500 as Richard finished twenty-eighth. It failed again in the Rebel 500 at Darlington and he finished twenty-third.

The latter was another of Darlington's annual "demolition derbies." When Jerry Sisco's car caught fire and he crashed down the mainstretch into the pit wall, Barry and Dale ran from the Petty pits, hurdled the barrier, were the first to get to the car, reached into the fiery wreck, and, with the help of others, pulled the dazed driver to safety.

"I would want someone else to do as much for Richard," observed Dale, shrugging it off.

"You see something like that, you just react," Barry said.

In April, Barry married Randy's widow, Jan. "I guess it surprised a lot of people, but it didn't surprise all the people on this team," observed Barry, smiling.

Pearson won both at Atlanta and Darlington. It appeared to be

Pearson's year, but Cale was coming on too. Meanwhile, Petty was struggling.

"It does not appear to be a Petty year, but we will just keep pushing," Richard remarked. Maurice was muttering to himself, and Dale was subdued.

Richard was second, but half a lap behind Cale in both the Gwynn Staley 400 at North Wilkesboro and the Music City 420 at Nashville. Richard finished fourth in the Martinsville 500, two laps back of winner Waltrip.

After the April affair in celebration of the bicentennial in North Carolina, Richard shaved off his beard, but it didn't change his luck. However, he was clean-shaven when he and Lynda were invited by President and Mrs. Ford at the request of King Hussein of Jordan to a reception in honor of the visiting dignitary. Richard had met the king when Andy Granatelli brought him to Daytona a few years before.

"I talked about that visit with the king," Richard reported. "I remember when they left, Andy banged the king on the back and asked, 'Howdja' like it, King?' The king told me he had liked it real well, but he didn't offer me any oil. Kissinger and a lot of other political people were there. The way that cat Kissinger talks, I could hardly understand him."

So King met King.

"Muhammad Ali and Bill Shoemaker were there, too, like Mutt and Jeff. We met the President. This was right after I did some stuff for him in the North Carolina primary, but he lost. He said, 'You're gonna have to work harder for me.' I said, 'Yeh, and you're gonna have to work harder for me.' We just talked politics, not racing. My racing isn't a fit topic for talk these days."

Still, when he and Lynda returned to the outside world, they were set upon by autograph-seekers. "You must not get race reports," Richard remarked. This champion who broke bread with kings and presidents continued to treat "commoners" with comparable courtesy.

The road ran on.

The first Sunday in May, Richard finished fourth in the Winston 500 at Talladega, two laps behind winner Baker. In mid-month, he finished sixth in the Mason-Dixon 500 at Dover, eight laps back of Benny Parsons, the winner. Richard's engine lost a cylinder in the Delaware event. He made his pit stops in his garage rather than the pits. Repairs kept him running, but far behind.

Richard sighed and said, "I don't know what it is. We're outpowered, but we prepare properly and should be competitive. One thing or another runs bad or breaks. Little things. Things you can't anticipate."

Added Dale, "All the things that went right all last year are going wrong this season."

They drove the fanciest truck in town into Charlotte for the World 600 at the end of May. Wanting a trailer rig big enough to house their entire car and hold all their gear and equipment, unable to find the one they wanted, they built one themselves at a cost of about $100,000. The fifty-two-foot rig was splendidly designed, with wood paneling inside provided by Lynda's dad.

Everyone visited it and came away with awe, but after the Petty's rolled their car down the ramp at the back of the truck and into action, Richard settled for second place, six seconds short of Pearson in the grueling long-distance classic. Li'l David, riding high, grinned and remarked, "It takes more than a truck to beat us on the track."

Janet Guthrie, one of the pioneers among women race drivers, made her debut in NASCAR competition by finishing fifteenth at Charlotte, twenty-one laps back of the winner. At one point she permitted Petty to pass Pearson when she dropped down so sharply she almost drove David off the track.

"We were expecting the worst, so we were ready for it when it came," Petty commented. "We gave her room this time. But now she's a good ol' boy and the next time we'll run right up her tail."

He sat in the truck in Riverside in mid-June sipping from a can of milklike nutrient recommended by his doctor. "It's better than beer," he said, laughing. "It's healthier. And I've become a health nut, whether I wanted to or not."

Growing serious, he admitted that his stomach was not yet entirely right and he confided that he would need surgery in the off season. "Nothing serious, I don't think," he said. "I've got a tube that's clogged that they have to clean out.

"I'm not looking forward to it," he confessed.

Had it affected his driving?

"Maybe, but I don't think so. I'm driving as hard as ever, I'm just not getting to the finish as fast as usual. We just can't get a car right and keep it right. And I don't know what I can do about it except stay home."

"You can do that as soon as we find a better driver," Dale said.

"We're lookin'," Maurice said.

Richard drove hard in the Tuborg 400 race at Riverside, an experimental race that was run at 400 kilometers instead of miles and actually covered a little less than 250 miles. But ignition troubles forced him into several long pit stops. Trying to make up lost ground, he spun and stalled in turn nine. Restarted, he finished the race, but settled for ninth place. Meanwhile, Pearson proceeded on a trouble-free course to the triumph at record speeds.

The following week in the Motor State 400 in Michigan, Pearson, Petty, Cale, and Bobby Allison hooked up in a four-car contest for the lead over the last laps. At the conclusion, Pearson was first, Petty fourth. That's the way it was going this year. At Daytona for the Fourth of July Firecracker 400, Petty spent five minutes in the pits while Dale and Maurice replaced a dead battery, then the car retired with a broken valve. Cale topped David, while Richard settled for twenty-second place. "It was some way to celebrate my thirty-ninth birthday," he said. Still, his fans had a cake for him.

Parsons won the Nashville 420 by fifteen seconds over Petty, who passed Waltrip in the final laps to take second place. At this point, the Pettys had not won in five months and had lost fourteen races in a row, their longest stretch without a victory since they hit the top.

Richard remarked, "We are so used to winning, we can't stand losing like this. Now we know how the other fellows feel. But we haven't given up. We're taking everything we can get. We've placed pretty good in a lot of races and piled up points. We're making some money. We still have a shot at the points and dollar titles. We could use a win badly, however."

They got it at Pocono in the Purolator 500 the first Sunday in August. It was the 179th of Richard's career and his second of the season. Pearson appeared headed for his seventh of the season until he cut a tire on some debris on the track going into turn one with five laps left. As Pearson swerved and slowed, Petty sped past and never relinquished the lead after that. The $20,000 first-place prize pushed Petty into the lead in seasonal earnings with almost $190,000 and put him within a few points of Parsons and Yarborough in the push for the driving title.

As his relieved crew celebrated, Richard said, "We were a little lucky, but we were overdue, too. I cut a tire earlier that cost me some ground I had to make up later. Anyway, the win was a long time coming. A long time coming. Seemed like an eternity."

He admitted they had benefited from another rules change on the carburetor that took effect with this race and put them back to about where they had been the year before, but pointed out yet another rules change was on its way which would benefit the small-track cars such as Cale's. "We'll have so many carburetors to try out every race, we won't have time to race," Richard remarked. "As it is, we don't have time to keep up with the new rules they keep throwing at us."

He confessed he was running a four-year-old chassis though existing rules limited chassis to three years, but said they had made metal changes to conform to the rules. He admitted more recent Dodges were so wide and big that they were considering racing another kind of car the following year. Shortly thereafter, NASCAR announced new rules which would permit four-year-old cars to compete in 1977.

Junior Johnson called France Junior "an idiot" and charged, "The last two rules changes have been to benefit one team, the Pettys." Maurice snapped, "I don't see that we've been getting any breaks."

In the Talladega 500, the Petty car, which led late, suffered engine failure twenty laps from the finish, fell out of the race, and finished twentieth. Marcis captured the event by thirty seconds over Buddy Baker, who had just become NASCAR's newest winner of a million dollars in prizes, joining Petty, Pearson, Yarborough, and Bobby Allison.

After Waltrip finished thirty-seventh in the field of forty, his sponsor fired team manager Mario Rossi and his two engine-builders. "It's tough to keep most of these teams together when you don't win," remarked Richard.

In the Champion Spark Plug 400 in Michigan, Pearson, Yarborough, and Petty finished in that order in a dramatic skirmish. "I could stay close to them, but I couldn't catch them at the end," Richard said. However, with his third-place points and his winnings of almost $10,000, he clinched the middle leg of the Winston Cup driving race, worth another $10,000 to him, and passed the $200,000 mark in seasonal earnings. Surprisingly, he remained in the running for another driving title.

In the worst of years, he continued to push for any position he could get and was consistently placing high though seldom winning.

In the Volunteer 500 at Bristol, Petty was second, though two laps in back of Cale, who led in search of his first driving crown. In the Southern 500 at Darlington, Petty was second, about a half lap back of Pearson, despite brushing the wall twice and hitting it once, leaving his car damaged badly and out of balance the last laps. Democratic presidential candidate Jimmy Carter of Georgia and Republican vice-presidential candidate Robert Dole of Kansas paraded around the track prior to the prestigious event and watched the early laps.

"Maybe I should run for president," Petty said.

"You're already king," Dale said drily.

"Not no more, I don't think," remarked Richard.

Apparently STP still thought so. Following the usual bargaining, the company announced on Labor Day weekend it had signed the Petty team to represent it in NASCAR competition for another year. A press release prepared by Jeff Cushing, now the company's racing publicist in place of the semiretired Dredge, quoted board chairman Craig Nalen as saying, "We're proud to have the Pettys on our team again in 1977."

Remarked Richard, "Seems like we've lost everything but our sponsor. Their loyalty means a lot to us."

In the Capital City 500 in Richmond, Richard was third, behind Bobby Allison and Yarborough. It was a rough race in which Cale claimed he was bumped by Bobby and Richard and admitted he later tapped Petty to get even. "That's racing," he drawled.

In the Delaware 500 at Dover, Yarborough went by Pearson in seasonal victories with his eighth, coming from two laps back with fifty laps left to pass Petty with twenty laps to go, going on to win.

"When you've got your car running the way Cale has now and the way David did earlier, the rest of us are running for crumbs," sighed Richard.

However, it was the fifth straight time and seventh time in the last eight races he had finished in the first three. "Consistency counts," commented the king as he struggled to retain his throne.

"We're going a long time between wins, but we're not breaking down every race right now," Richard remarked hopefully.

The crew was working hard. There were changes on the crew. Billy Biscoe stopped traveling so he could stay home to work on his own car. Two youngsters, transplanted New Yorkers who had settled in the South, had joined the gypsies—Steve Hmiel, who had a wife, Cristi, and was from Albany, and Mike Pfister, who was single and from Watertown. Steve was working in fabrication and carrying tires in the pits, while Mike was working in the body shop and catching gas.

Wayne became the main gas man, while Barry turned to jacking the cars for tire changes.

Jerry was back together with his wife, Barry had married in April, and now Wayne married his girl friend, Judy Chaney, just before the Old Dominion 500 in Martinsville.

The 500-lapper became a 340-lapper, reduced by rain, but the $100,000 in prizes was the most ever offered for a short-track event. A big turnout of 32,000 fans saw Cale come through again to pick up the $22,000 first-place purse. The Pettys had tire troubles, made three more stops than the leaders, and Richard finished fourth.

Cale captured his fourth consecutive race, the Wilkes 400, at North Wilkesboro the first Sunday in October. The 250-miler was his fifth win in the last six starts and ninth of the season. It would be his last, but it put him well ahead of Petty in the points race. Herb Nab was doing an excellent job on the engine of the Junior Johnson Holly Farms Chevy and it led the last 291 laps of this one, with Parsons second and Petty third.

After three days of torrential rain, the National 500 at Charlotte was staged before a record crowd of 74,500 fans and surprisingly was won by Donnie Allison. It was his first Grand National victory since 1971 and the first ever for one of Hoss Ellingson's cars, although Hoss was one of the better-known veterans on the tour. Foyt had just quit the team with the complaint that its Chevy Monte Carlos weren't worth running, and Donnie ran one right into Victory Circle.

It was one of those races. All the top teams had troubles. Cale led so many laps and made so much lap money he actually made more money finishing second than Donnie did finishing first, but Yarborough was slowed when his low gears gave out and he had to settle for second in the end. Petty was leading early, when a torsion-bar bolt pulled out of his car's front suspension and he lost nine laps in the pits making repairs. But he returned to the race and finished eighth.

At the wish of his sponsor, Richard had reluctantly returned to the International Race of Champions in September with another of those commuting chores between Delaware and Michigan. Camaros crashed all over Cambridge Junction. Jody Scheckter knocked Gordon Johncock into Richard after he had led a lap for the first time in this series. Buddy Baker took the lead two laps from the finish and won this hundred-miler when three remaining contenders wrecked on the last lap.

Now, in October, they had twin seventy-fives on consecutive afternoons on the road course in Riverside. Bobby Unser started on the pole and won wire-to-wire on Saturday for his record fourth victory in the series, with Pearson and Petty finishing second and third. They inverted the finish for the start on the second day, Sunday, and Bobby battled his way through the pack but could get no higher than fourth by the finish. Richard had his problems and finished ninth. Meanwhile, Cale won his first of the series. It just seemed to be his season.

It looked like another lost month for the Pettys when Kyle, who was quarterbacking his high-school team and passing surprisingly well, was hit in a game, hurt a leg, and was lost for the season. Consequently he turned his attention to basketball, which he liked better anyway.

However, on the fourth Sunday of the month, Richard ended his latest losing streak in Grand National events at nine when he won the National 500 at Charlotte. Pearson took the pole and led thirty laps, but faded. Cale did not lead a lap for the first time in any race since February, Bobby Allison had all sorts of troubles, as he had been having all season. Brother Donnie could not come back with a big effort. Marcis and Baker bombed out.

Petty's real rival this Sunday turned out to be Lennie Pond. Petty and Pond swapped the lead back and forth eight times, leading ten, twenty, thirty laps at a time, for the last two hundred laps of the 412-lap event. Richard pulled away over the last seventy laps to win by one lap, with Waltrip another two laps back.

It was Petty's third victory of the year, all at five hundred miles, and his second at Rockingham. It was the 180th of his career and rewarded him with a $20,000 first-place purse. It put him back in the running in money won for the year and points.

The Pettys paused to celebrate briefly. "It was the best we've run all year," remarked Richard, "but we've lost so much we're not going to make much of one win."

It did brighten up the third annual open house at the Petty place. The party pulled in more than 15,000 fans although it rained all the night before and the day was cloudy and cold. The fans paid a dollar a head, purchased souvenirs, and wound up contributing $20,000 to charity. Richard signed autographs from 9:00 A.M. to 6:00 P.M. and several times suffered from cramps in his hand.

Among guests again was North Carolina Governor Holshouser, a regular at these affairs, as well as South Carolina Senator Strom Thurmond. Also on hand was President Ford's brother Dick, later killed in a car crash. Richard campaigned for Ford a little when he had the opportunity, while Cale campaigned for former Georgia governor Carter as well as for himself and did so as a Democrat, switching parties to please his candidate.

Later, after Cale's candidate won the presidential election from Petty's preference, Richard remarked, "It looks like this is just Cale's year to win. This just ain't my year and I may have jinxed my man." Cale also won his own re-election as a county commissioner.

The Pettys lost again at Atlanta in the Dixie 500 the first Sunday in November. Their car lost oil pressure and they were finished before the midway mark in the event. Dave Marcis drove like a demon to win this one by two car lengths from Pearson in a furious finish.

Pearson's second-place purse put his earnings out of reach of Richard. Donnie Allison beat out Yarborough for fourth, but that finish was enough for Cale to wrap up the points title. All he had to do was start the finale, the Los Angeles Times 500 at Ontario, to pick up enough points to take the title.

So, the Pettys were bound to be at most second-best as they came to the conclusion of the long tour in 1976. They didn't like that and they admitted privately that the rumors that they might switch to a Chevy or Ford for 1977 were real.

"I'm almost sure we won't, but we thought about it awhile," Maurice confided. "We figured out a Ford might work for us, but we're still stocked with Chrysler parts. If Chrysler will rework a part or two for us, we figure we'll be okay. The thing that settled it was those rules changes that could make us competitive again. The other teams think the changes were for us, but they were for racing. They've changed for other teams other times. You can't have only one or two kinds of cars running these races and keep the crowds interested."

Chief sighed and added, "All we ask is to be allowed an engine chassis that can be competitive, and we'll take care of the rest. I don't want to take anything away from Cale's crew, or David's, for that matter.

"Cale ran all the races, won the short ones, and was competitive in the long ones. His crew worked their fannies off to keep him competitive, and I know what it took and admire their work. Cale drove good. He had the title coming to him. He waited a long time for it.

"David ran the long races and won them. They did it, so they deserve it."

Dale said, "I guess if we couldn't win another title, we'd just as soon Cale could."

"I'll go along with that," Richard said. "Cale had a title coming to him, the kind of career he's had. Still, I wish it had been us.

"I can't complain about the crew. With all the problems we had, we still had a shot at the points title with a race or two to go, and we're up in top money won. Now we got just this last one to go. I want to win it, but I want to get it over with so I can go on to the next season. It's funny, but 1976 has been as bad as 1975 was good."

Richard led the Times 500 early, but broke a spring, which led to a blown valve, and he was finished after 127 of the two hundred laps. Cale's clutch caved in on him while he was contending for first at 168 laps and he had to drop out. Pearson came off the pole to lead most of the laps and win the race easily, with Lennie Pond second. Pearson earned $27,715, while Pond picked up the top payoff of his career, just under $12,000.

It was Pearson's tenth victory of the season to nine for Cale, three each for Petty and Marcis, two for Parsons, and one each for Waltrip and Donnie Allison. Bobby Allison won none and quit the Roger Penske Mercury team in disgust. At Penske's request he had passed up the extra races he usually ran, and it hadn't paid off.

All of Pearson's victories came on long tracks and he now led Petty in superspeedway wins, 43–39, but he still trailed in career wins by an imposing 96–180. All but one of Yarborough's victories came on short tracks, though twenty-two of his forty career wins had come on long tracks.

In the six years since the Grand National tour became the Winston Cup competition, the three drivers Petty, Pearson, and Yarborough had established their domination by winning three of every four races run.

This year Cale captured his first points title in eighteen years on the tour (though he had competed extensively in only twelve)—concluding with 4,644 points, to 4,449 for Richard. He has been second twice.

Pearson finished ninth in points, but he ran only twenty-two races. All eight drivers ahead of him ran all thirty races. In seventeen years he has been first three times, never second.

Petty has been first six times, and now was second for the fifth time in nineteen years.

Petty's career earnings were boosted above $2.5 million. He was first in money won in 1976 with $308,074. Cale earned $307,591, and Pearson picked up about $275,000. "Even in a bad year we beat the boys to the bank," observed Dale.

Eight second-place finishes boosted the take, but did not satisfy Maurice. "We take what we can get, but we run to win," he commented.

"We made money, we didn't go broke, and we're still in business," observed Richard. "By our standards, it was a bad year, but 1977 is another year."

It would be his milestone twentieth in competition.

"Things keep changing. The competition stays tough. We'll have to be better next year than we were this year. We've bounced back before and we will again," he remarked as he changed into civvies.

He gathered up his gear to go get Lynda and go home. He was headed for the hospital and a checkup to determine if he might need treatment on his ulcers. "They can do what they want, but they can't cut," he commented, laughing a little. "I feel fine and I'm determined to drive for a few years yet."

For King Richard, the road runs on. "Every road has its rough places and its smooth spots. It goes on, so we do too."

Undiscouraged by defeats?

"You just keep pushin'," he said.